Justice Rosalie Silberman Abella

A Life of Firsts

Justice Rosalie Silberman Abella

A Life of Firsts

Edited by Vanessa A. MacDonnell,
Stephen Bindman, and Gerald Chan

UNIVERSITY OF TORONTO PRESS
Toronto Buffalo London

Irwin Law
An imprint of University of Toronto Press
Toronto Buffalo London
utppublishing.com
Printed in Canada

ISBN 978-1-55221-671-2 (paper) ISBN 978-1-55221-672-9 (PDF)
ISBN 978-1-4875-6915-0 (EPUB) ISBN 978-1-4875-1720-5 (OA)

Cataloguing in Publication available from Library and Archives Canada

Cover design: John Beadle
Cover image: Portrait of Rosalie Silberman Abella by Charles Pachter

We wish to acknowledge the land on which the University of Toronto Press operates. This land is the traditional territory of the Wendat, the Anishnaabeg, the Haudenosaunee, the Métis, and the Mississaugas of the Credit First Nation.

University of Toronto Press acknowledges the financial support of the Government of Canada, the Canada Council for the Arts, and the Ontario Arts Council, an agency of the Government of Ontario, for its publishing activities.

Canada Council for the Arts Conseil des Arts du Canada

ONTARIO ARTS COUNCIL
CONSEIL DES ARTS DE L'ONTARIO
an Ontario government agency
un organisme du gouvernement de l'Ontario

Funded by the Government of Canada Financé par le gouvernement du Canada Canada

FSC www.fsc.org MIX Paper | Supporting responsible forestry FSC® C103567

Contents

Acknowledgments ix

Introduction: Justice Abella and Feminist Judicial Methods 1
VANESSA A. MACDONNELL

Part 1: Early Years, Career, and Influences

1 Justice Abella's Overture: Rosalie Abella's Early Life and Career 23
ERIC ADAMS

2 Les suites du Rapport Abella au regard de l'élaboration du concept de discrimination systémique en contexte d'emploi 41
CHARLES TREMBLAY POTVIN

3 Assessing Justice Abella's Contributions to the Law of Systemic Discrimination in Canada 57
JOËLLE PASTORA SALA

4 A Courageous "Love": Three Acts on the Abella Legacy in Administrative Law 71
LORNE SOSSIN

5 Justice Abella: Confronting the Authenticity-Professionalism Paradox 87
ROSALIE JUKIER

6 Engaging Abella: Humanity, Imagination, and the Legal Profession 103
MARY LISTON

Part 2: Justice Abella's Jurisprudence — Empirical Analysis and Constitutional Law

7 Abella by the Numbers 131
STEPHEN BINDMAN AND KEENAN MACNEAL

8 Her Fundamentals: Justice Abella and Section 2(b) of the *Charter* 147
JAMIE CAMERON

9 Reaching to See Through Another's Eyes: Justice Abella's Religious Freedom Jurisprudence 171
HOWARD KISLOWICZ

10 Equality and Equity: An Essay in Honour of Justice Rosalie Abella 185
MARTHA MINOW

11 The Pursuit of Reconciliation: Justice Abella's Contribution to Drawing Back the Curtain on Canada's (Hi)storied Relationship with Indigenous Peoples 203
AIMÉE CRAFT

Part 3: Justice Abella's Jurisprudence — Labour and Employment Law

12 Dignity at Work in Justice Abella's Jurisprudence: Recognizing Worker Vulnerability and Power Imbalance 217
COLLEEN BAUMAN

13 Speaking Rationality to Power 235
BRIAN LANGILLE

Part 4: Justice Abella's Jurisprudence — International Law, Immigration and Refugee Law, and Children's Rights

14 Justice Abella's Global Impact 259
HAROLD HONGJU KOH

15 Understanding *Nevsun* Through an Equality Lens 269
YOUSUF AFTAB AND ELINOAM ABRAMOV

16 Reflections on Justice Abella's Legacy in Immigration and Refugee Law 283
JAMIE CHAI YUN LIEW

17 Les droits (de la personne) de l'enfant : regard sur les notions de vulnérabilité et d'égalité dans la jurisprudence de la juge Abella 299
MONA PARÉ

Part 5: The Future of Justice Abella's Jurisprudence

18 Dot-com Justice: The Progressive Bent in Justice Abella's Technology Jurisprudence 317
ANDREW BERNSTEIN AND AMANDA WOLCZANSKI

19 Justice Abella: Staunch Defender of Privacy in the Digital Age 335
GERALD CHAN AND YADESHA SATHEASWARAN

20 Pushing the Boundaries of International Law in Canada: The Legacy of Justice Rosalie Abella 349
SARA GHEBREMUSSE

21 Equality and the Judicial Role: Lessons from Singing in a Choir 361
ROSEMARY CAIRNS-WAY

Part 6: Speeches

22 Remarks 377
ALBIE SACHS

23 Writing Around the Rosie 383
BERNIE M. FARBER

24 Rosie the Law Reformer: Viewing Public Policy Through Rosie-Coloured Glasses 389
DAVID LEPOFSKY

25 To Honour the Gatekeeper: A Beacon of Human Rights and Freedom 403
DORIT BEINISCH AND GONEN ILAN

Index 415

Acknowledgments

This volume is literally a labour of love — a long labour of love.

These essays were first presented at a two-day symposium in Ottawa in May 2022 entitled *The Honourable Rosalie Silberman Abella: A Life of Firsts* — or AbellaFest, as some preferred to call it.

Despite the uncertainties of COVID-19 and the on-and-off requirements of masking, more than 180 people attended in person and another 80 online to honour Justice Abella (Rosie, as many call her affectionately).

The event was sponsored by the uOttawa Public Law Centre, the Canadian Institute for the Administration of Justice (CIAJ), the Human Rights Research and Education Centre, and the Advocates' Society.

An advisory committee composed of Miriam Ingber, Mona Paré, John Packer, Rosemary Cairns Way, Carissima Mathen, Colleen Bauman, Vanessa Gruben, Adam Dodek, Karen Eltis, James M. Johnson, Errol Mendes, Ewa Krajewska, Allan Rock, and Justice Colleen Suche provided helpful guidance throughout.

But the conference would not have been possible without the organizational prowess of the CIAJ — particularly executive director Christine O'Doherty and then project manager Robin Duffie — and the Public Law Centre's Airianna Murdoch-Fyke.

We are grateful to our conference partners Stockwoods LLP, Supreme Advocacy LLP, Henein Hutchison Robitaille LLP, Lenczner Slaght LLP, and the Royal Society of Canada.

The event began with a reception at the National Gallery of Canada featuring a tour of specially selected works to reflect Justice Abella's journey in different ways. Thank you to the Gallery's then director Alexandra Suda for her support and to Colleen Bauman and Rosemary Cairns-Way for their vivid commentaries.

The first day of the conference examined Justice Abella's life before the Supreme Court of Canada — the non-legal influences (art, Judaism); her work as a family court judge, law reformer, and commission of inquiry head; and her importance as a role model for women in the legal profession.

The Royal Society of Canada presented the inaugural winners of the Justice Rosalie Silberman Abella Prize, which will be presented annually to a graduating law student from each law school in Canada who is most likely to positively influence equity and social justice in Canada or globally upon graduation. Thank you to executive director Darren Gilmour and his team for making this possible.

The lunchtime speaker was the former Minister of Justice who appointed Justice Abella to the top court, the Honourable Irwin Cotler.

Special video greetings were sent by US Supreme Court Justice Sonia Sotomayor, noted Canadian author Margaret Atwood, and a group of Osgoode Hall law students.

The second day examined her jurisprudence in various areas — labour law, administrative law, human rights and international law, constitutional law — and considered how her opinions might resonate in the future.

In between, a wonderful gala dinner was attended by many of Justice Abella's friends from far and wide. Guy Pratte of Borden Ladner Gervais LLP was the brilliant MC, and a highlight that left no eye dry was a musical tribute from Gershwin's *Porgy and Bess* performed by Evan Pyne of the Royal Conservatory of Music, accompanied by his mother, Ellen Annor-Adjei.

We were thrilled that several of Justice Abella's Supreme Court colleagues — past, present, and future — took part as speakers: the Honourable Louise Charron, the Honourable Andromache Karakatsanis, and the Honourable Sheilah Martin.

The then Minister of Justice and Attorney General of Canada David Lametti also attended.

Sadly, Justice Abella attended the dinner in person but watched the rest of the conference from the Toronto hospital room where her beloved husband, Irving, "Itchy" to all, was gravely ill.

Journalist and author Paul Wells ended the conference with a humorous and eye-opening fireside chat with Justice Abella.

We are grateful to all our authors who persevered throughout the several years it took for this volume to come out and who met our ridiculously tight deadlines despite the myriad other demands on their lives. Thanks to the Public Law Centre's research assistants Mathieu

Tovar-Poitras and Mélanie Davidson for keeping track of the chapter comings and goings.

Our peer reviewers, again on short notice, provided universally helpful and relevant suggestions and recommendations for improvements of the contributors' drafts.

We are also grateful to renowned Canadian artist and Rosie's friend Charles Pachter for the beautiful cover design.

Thank you to our original publisher, Irwin Law — and especially Jeffrey Miller, Lesley Steeve, and Danna Petersen-Deeprose — for their work on the collection, and to University of Toronto Press, which picked up the publishing ball after acquiring Irwin's assets in 2024. At University of Toronto Press, we thank Ashley Bernicky, Janice Evans, Josephine Mo, and Sandra Shaw.

And so here we are.

Sadly, Irving Abella passed away a few months after the event.

With this volume, we remember Itchy and the special place he had and continues to have in all our hearts, but especially in Justice Abella's.

Vanessa A. MacDonnell
Stephen Bindman
Gerald Chan

Introduction: Justice Abella and Feminist Judicial Methods

VANESSA A. MACDONNELL*

A. Introduction

When a justice of the Supreme Court of Canada retires, it is an opportunity to reflect on their judicial legacy: on the contributions they have made to the law and to the Court as an institution. Although multi-member courts engage in collective decision-making, it is also true that in our system, individual judges matter.[1] Who a judge is affects their approach to law and their ability to persuade colleagues of their positions. And while it was once considered taboo to acknowledge that judges' personal characteristics and commitments shape their decision-making, the work of legal realists and, later, critical legal studies scholars, feminists, and critical race theorists has gone a long way toward dispelling the myth that judges can — or should — separate themselves from who they are in the process of judging.[2] Once the fiction of complete judicial objectivity is set aside, it is possible to have more nuanced conversations about how judges can bring the wisdom of their experiences to bear in deciding cases, while also treating the parties fairly and dispassionately.[3]

---

* Associate Professor, uOttawa Public Law Centre & Co-Director, uOttawa Public Law Centre. I am grateful to Mathieu Tovar-Poitras for research assistance and to Jena McGill, Sylvia Rich, Sam Singer, Eric Adams, Stephen Bindman, Laurence Ricard, Carissima Mathen, Constance Backhouse, participants in the Queen's Feminist Legal Studies lecture series seminar, and the peer reviewer for useful comments and suggestions. In this volume, the authors refer both to Justice Abella and to "Rosie," depending on their relationship with her.

1 I am grateful to Baptiste Bonnet for a conversation on this topic.

2 See Eric Adams, Chapter 1 in this volume.

3 Bertha Wilson, "Will Women Judges Really Make a Difference?" (1990) 28:3 *Osgoode Hall Law Journal* 507; Ruth Sullivan, "The Era of Concealed Underlying Premises Is

For Justice Rosalie Silberman Abella, whose life and jurisprudence are the subject of this volume, it is clear that the personal and the professional are intertwined. In compiling this collection, we quickly realized that it would be insufficient to consider the impact of her Supreme Court jurisprudence alone, or even the sum of her professional accomplishments in isolation from her larger life story.[4] It is only when the personal and the professional are considered together that a true account of her legacy emerges.

Justice Abella was born in 1946 in a displaced persons camp in Germany, arriving in Canada four years later with her parents.[5] She has often remarked that her decision to study law was influenced by her family's experiences of injustice. Her father completed law school in Poland amid a climate of antisemitism.[6] His career plans were interrupted by the horrors of World War II, and he was later prevented from practicing law in Canada because he was not a citizen.[7] Rosalie Abella, still a small child, resolved to become a lawyer.[8] She would go on to complete her undergraduate and law degrees at the University of Toronto, where her commitment to social justice was already apparent.[9]

As a young advocate, Abella dedicated herself to the legal concerns of women. Eric Adams writes in his chapter that:

> First, she joined Women's Place, an institution providing general support and advice to women on legal matters, which eventually evolved into one of the first women's shelters in Canada. By 1974, Abella served on the executive of the National Action Committee on the Status of Women and was working for the Toronto firm, JV Kelly Law.[10]

Over: L'Heureux-Dubé J's Contribution to Statutory Interpretation" in Elizabeth A. Sheehy, ed, *Adding Feminism to Law: The Contributions of Justice Claire L'Heureux-Dubé* (Toronto: Irwin Law, 2004) 49. See also Mary Liston, Chapter 6 in this volume.

4 I am grateful to Stephen Bindman for noting this at a very early stage in our conference planning.

5 Supreme Court of Canada, "Biography – The Honorable Rosalie Silberman Abella", (1 January 2001, modified 01 July 2021), online: www.scc-csc.ca/judges-juges/bio-eng.aspx?id=rosalie-silberman-abella. See also Bernie Farber, Chapter 23 in this volume.

6 "How Justice Rosalie Abella Made Yale Law Grads Cry on the Happiest Day of their Lives" *CBC Radio: The Sunday Magazine* (27 May 2016), online: www.cbc.ca/radio/sunday/the-angry-populism-of-68-sadik-khan-on-urban-revolution-margot-bentley-justice-abella-goes-to-yale-1.3600952/how-justice-rosalie-abella-made-yale-law-grads-cry-on-the-happiest-day-of-their-lives-1.3601155.

7 *Ibid.*

8 *Ibid.*

9 Adams, Chapter 1 in this volume.

10 *Ibid.*

Her talents were gaining the attention of others in the profession, and "[h]er reputation in both the feminist movement and Toronto's legal community was rapidly ascending."[11]

After just four years practicing law, Abella was appointed to the Ontario Family Court. By then she was expecting her second child, and role models were hard to come by. "I didn't know any other mothers who were lawyers, so it was a risk," she has explained.[12] Along with her husband, historian Irving Abella, she would raise two children while pursuing a career that would take her to the Ontario Court of Appeal and the Supreme Court of Canada, the first Jewish woman and first refugee to be appointed to Canada's top court.[13] She did so on her own terms, combining passion with rigour and defying the gendered expectations of the profession.[14] Along the way, she authored the landmark 1983 Ontario *Study on Access to Legal Services by the Disabled* and led the 1984 federal Royal Commission on Equality in Employment.[15] She also left the bench to chair the Ontario Labour Relations Board and the Ontario Law Reform Commission and to serve as a member of the Ontario Human Rights Commission and the Ontario Public Service Labour Relations Tribunal.[16]

As a justice of the Supreme Court, Abella participated in over 900 cases, writing opinions in 205 of them.[17] She developed a particular reputation for her decisions in the areas of equality law, administrative law, labour law, and international human rights, though, as Stephen Bindman and Keenan Macneal demonstrate in their chapter, she also contributed significantly to the Court's criminal law and private law jurisprudence.[18] In her 2020 decision in *Fraser*,[19] she consolidated a fractured body of equality jurisprudence into a bold re-statement of what is required to make out a violation of section 15 of the *Canadian Charter of*

11 *Ibid.*

12 "Outgoing Supreme Court Justice Rosalie Abella on Family and Learning to Be a Judge" *CBC Radio: The Current* (22 June 2021), online: www.cbc.ca/radio/thecurrent/the-current-for-june-22-2021-1.6075053/outgoing-supreme-court-justice-rosalie-abella-on-family-and-learning-to-be-a-judge-1.6075237.

13 See Farber, Chapter 23 in this volume; Jamie Chai Yun Liew, chapter 16 in this volume.

14 Rosalie Jukier, Chapter 5 in this volume.

15 See chapters by Jöelle Pastora Sala, Chapter 3 in this volume; Charles Tremblay Potvin, Chapter 2 in this volume; and Martha Minow, Chapter 10 in this volume.

16 See David Lepofsky, Chapter 24 in this volume.

17 Stephen Bindman & Keenan MacNeal, Chapter 7 in this volume.

18 *Ibid.* See also Gerald Chan & Yadesha Satheaswaran, Chapter 19 this volume.

19 *Fraser v Canada (Attorney General)*, 2020 SCC 28 [*Fraser*]. But see *R v Sharma*, 2022 SCC 39.

Rights and Freedoms.[20] She played a defining role in a series of important freedom of association cases and authored the majority decision in *Saskatchewan Federation of Labour* (2015), which recognized a constitutional right to strike under section 2(d) of the *Charter*.[21] She developed a framework for evaluating whether administrative decision-makers had properly integrated *Charter* considerations into their decisions in *Doré v Barreau du Québec* (2012)[22] and held that Canadian companies that commit human rights violations abroad can be pursued in Canadian courts for breaches of customary international law in the path-breaking *Nevsun* decision (2020).[23] In *R v DB* (2008), she struck down amendments to the *Youth Criminal Justice Act* that did not sufficiently account for young people's "heightened vulnerability, [decreased] maturity and . . . reduced capacity for moral judgment."[24] And in *Bruker v Markovitz* (2007), she affirmed a woman's right to access divorce, delicately balancing freedom of religion and the right to equality in a case in which provisions of the *Quebec Civil Code* requiring a man to grant a Jewish divorce as part of civil divorce proceedings were challenged on religious freedom grounds.[25]

B. The Collection

This volume is the product of a remarkable two-day conference held in Ottawa in 2022 to mark Justice Abella's retirement from the Supreme Court of Canada. Like her judgments, the essays in this collection are alive with music, literature, theatre, art, and pop culture, reflecting Justice Abella's embrace of and passion for the arts.[26] The collection is also dotted with personal reflections and anecdotes. Rosalie Jukier recalls

20 Part I of the *Constitution Act, 1982*, being Schedule B to the *Canada Act 1982* (UK), 1982, c 11 [*Charter*]. See also Minow, Chapter 10 in this volume; Dorit Beinisch & Gonen Ilan, Chapter 25 in this volume.

21 *Saskatchewan Federation of Labour v Saskatchewan*, 2015 SCC 4 [*Saskatchewan Federation of Labour*]. See also Colleen Bauman, Chapter 12 in this volume.

22 *Doré v Barreau du Québec*, 2012 SCC 12 [*Doré*]; *Loyola High School v Quebec (Attorney General)*, 2015 SCC 12; *Law Society of British Columbia v Trinity Western University*, 2018 SCC 32. See also Lorne Sossin, Chapter 4 in this volume.

23 *Nevsun Resources Ltd v Araya*, 2020 SCC 5. See also Sara Ghebremusse, Chapter 20 in this volume; Yousuf Aftab & Elinoam Abramov, Chapter 15 in this volume; Harold Hongju Koh, Chapter 14 in this volume.

24 2008 SCC 25 at para 41. See also Mona Paré, Chapter 17 in this volume.

25 2007 SCC 54. See also Howard Kislowicz, Chapter 9 in this volume.

26 See Rosemary Cairns-Way, Chapter 21 in this volume; Adams, Chapter 1 in this volume; Jukier, Chapter 5 in this volume.

meeting Justice Abella at the beginning of her career and being dazzled by the self-possessed young judge:

> I had never encountered a professional woman, let alone such a brilliant and accomplished professional woman, who unabashedly revealed her inner life, her true colours, her warm and personal side, her authentic self, which, in addition to being warm, is also humorous, charismatic, and engaging.[27]

Albie Sachs, former Justice of the Constitutional Court of South Africa, was left with a similar impression upon meeting Justices Abella and Claire L'Heureux-Dubé at a conference in the late 1990s: "The impact that they had on me came not only from their unforgettable style and manner, [but also from] their irreverential challenge to stultifying and overbearing formalism and egotism."[28]

The link between the personal and the professional is a central theme of this volume.[29] It is also a topic about which Justice Abella has spoken frequently. "We are all shaped by what we come from," she has said. "I've never felt anything but a seamless relationship with who I was, so I am unabashedly committed to the values that increase justice for people."[30] This chapter introduces the collection by considering how Justice Abella's embrace of the personal contributed to her judicial method. As Sachs' comments suggest, Justice Abella's warmth and engaging style are more than just appealing character traits; they also informed her distinctive approach to judging.[31] Indeed, some of the most well-recognized elements of Justice Abella's judicial method — on people and their experiences, and being attuned to power differentials and vulnerability — reflect the feminist maxim that "the personal is political."[32] Although she sometimes encountered opposition in insist-

27 *Ibid.*

28 Albie Sachs, Chapter 22 in this volume.

29 See also Jukier, Chapter 5 in this volume; Adams, Chapter 1 in this volume; Cairns-Way, Chapter 21 in this volume; Liew, Chapter 16 in this volume; Farber, Chapter 23 in this volume.

30 I am grateful to Christine O'Doherty for pointing out this quote to me, which comes from an interview with Justice Rosalie Abella that is transcribed on *Creative Canada 150*, online: https://web.archive.org/web/20211026085540/http://creativecanada150.com/justice/rosalie-silberman-abella/.

31 See Jukier, Chapter 5 in this volume.

32 I am grateful to Jena McGill for this point. Diana Majury, "Introducing the Women's Court of Canada" (2006) 18:1 *Canadian Journal of Women and the Law* 1 at 5. See also Peter C. Oliver, "'A Constitution Similar in Principle to that of the United Kingdom': The Preamble, Constitutional Principles, and a Sustainable Jurisprudence" (2019) 65:2 *McGill Law Journal* 207.

ing that lived experience should be placed front and centre in the legal analysis, there is much to be learned from her commitment to applying the common law method in ways that see and serve all people.[33]

The themes that tie the collection together are therefore primarily methodological. They include attention to lived experience and context, including that of the judge; awareness of power dynamics and vulnerability; and prioritizing local sites of decision-making. Of course, separating these elements out and treating them as distinct tends to deconstruct what is ultimately an integrated approach. But there is nevertheless value in cataloging these aspects of her method, which together comprise a distinctive — and I argue, feminist — approach to judging.

In suggesting that aspects of Justice Abella's judicial approach are consistent with feminist methods, I do not intend to imply that a single factor or approach determined how she decided cases during her seventeen years on the Supreme Court. Indeed, an interesting question that arises when we analyze her jurisprudence is whether the bottom-up, people-centered approach that appears in some of her cases is in tension with her commitment to universal human rights.[34] However, the weaker claim remains significant in terms of what it suggests about the universe of "legitimate" approaches to judging.

Second, I do not argue that feminist judging is one dimensional, or that Justice Abella's decisions always lived up to the many and varied aspirations of contemporary Canadian feminism.[35] Rather, my point is that Justice Abella is one of the first, if not the first, self-proclaimed feminists to be appointed to the Supreme Court of Canada, and her judicial approach reflects the feminist commitments in which she was steeped in her early career.[36] This differs from the dominant approach to judicial decision-making and is therefore worthy of study.

---

33 Beinisch & Ilan, Chapter 25 in this volume. For more general meditations on women judges and feminist approaches to judging, see Constance Backhouse, "Justice Bertha Wilson and the Politics of Feminism" (2008) 41 *Supreme Court Law Review* (2d) 33.

34 See generally Herbert Wells, "The Caribbean Court of Justice and International Human Rights Laws and Norms: Universalism, Cultural Relativism and Transformation" (2022) (doctoral dissertation; copy on file with author).

35 See, for example, Kristin Kalsem, "Feminist Judging: Theories and Practices" in Deborah Brake, Martha Chamallas & Verna Williams, eds, *The Oxford Handbook of Feminism and Law in the United States* (New York: Oxford University Press, 2021); Rosemary Hunter, "More than Just a Different Face? Judicial Diversity and Decision-making" (2015) 68:1 *Current Legal Problems* 119.

36 Adams, Chapter 1 in this volume. See also Constance Backhouse, "The Chilly Climate for Women Judges: Reflections on the Backlash from the Ewanchuk Case" (2003) 15:1 *Canadian Journal of Women and the Law* 167 at 188. But see Beverley Baines,

While feminist methods appear in Justice Abella's caselaw, they are never explicitly labelled as such, and must therefore be surfaced through close reading and analysis.[37] When we do so, however, we can begin to develop an account of the vision of judging they offer up and evaluate them properly, both on their own terms and in comparison with other approaches. Justice Abella's story is therefore an important one, and also only one, part of a longer horizon of developments that offer new perspectives on judging in a modern society.[38]

C. Justice Abella's Jurisprudence

1. Taking Lived Experience and Context Seriously

One of the distinctive elements of Justice Abella's judicial approach was her willingness to acknowledge that lived experience — both her own and that of the litigants — mattered to the task of judging.[39] Feminist legal scholars have long emphasized the importance of lived experience and context. In this realm of adjudication, they require the judge to examine the litigants' concrete experiences of the law, the wider social matrix within which the legal dispute is embedded, and the legal scheme as a whole.[40] Embrace of a contextual approach is more widespread today than it was in the early decades of Justice Abella's career. However, the perceived relevance of lived experience and other forms of context remains a question of degree for most judges, and feminist scholars continue to interrogate the ways that common law reasoning and statutory interpretation are shaped by the "concealed premises" of the majority.[41]

"Must Feminist Judges Self-identify as Feminists?" in Ulrike Schultz & Gisela Shaw, eds, *Gender and Judging* (London: Hart Publishing, 2013) 379; and Backhouse, "Justice Bertha Wilson and the Politics of Feminism," above note 33 at 34.

37 On surfacing, see Patricia Williams, *The Alchemy of Race and Rights* (Cambridge: Harvard University Press, 1992). See also Baines, above note 36.

38 I note that the path toward more equal and just approaches is not always linear, with regression being not only possible but a usual feature of social development.

39 Adams, Chapter 1 in this volume; Liew, chapter 16 in this volume; Beinisch & Ilan, Chapter 25 in this volume.

40 Sullivan, above note 3 at 52.

41 *Ibid* at 49. Justice L'Heureux-Dubé sat on the Supreme Court between 1987 and 2002. See Supreme Court of Canada, "Biography – The Honorable Claire L'Heureux-Dubé" (modified 04 September 2008), online: www.scc-csc.ca/judges-juges/bio-eng.aspx?id=claire-lheureux-dube. See Mari Matsuda, "Looking to the Bottom: Critical Legal Studies and Reparations" (1987) 22 *Harvard Civil Rights-Civil Liberties Law*

Justice Abella's decision in *Kanthasamy v Canada (Citizenship and Immigration)*[42] shows how attention to lived experience can shape outcomes. Jeyakannan Kanthasamy was a Tamil teenager who came to Canada after an encounter with Sri Lankan military and law enforcement personnel. He applied unsuccessfully for refugee status. He then sought admission to Canada on humanitarian and compassionate grounds, but that claim was also denied. The decision was upheld as reasonable by the Federal Court and Federal Court of Appeal.

At the Supreme Court, Justice Abella, writing for the majority, held that the Federal Court had erred in affirming the decision to deny him admission. In assessing whether an individual is admissible to Canada on humanitarian and compassionate grounds, Justice Abella explained, immigration officers should adopt an approach grounded in the equitable and compassionate purposes of the legislative scheme.[43] She noted that two conflicting strands had developed in the caselaw. One, influenced by internal departmental guidelines, required the applicant to demonstrate "unusual and undeserved or disproportionate hardship"[44] to be admitted to Canada. The other adopted a more flexible and contextual approach to weighing the factors for and against admission. Justice Abella concluded that the latter approach was more consistent with the scheme's purposes.

Justice Abella's decision was particularly critical of the way the immigration officer "atomize[d]"[45] the ways in which Kanthasamy was vulnerable rather than treating him, subjectively, as the sum of his experiences:

> [The decision maker] failed to give sufficiently serious consideration to his youth, his mental health and the evidence that he would suffer discrimination if he were returned to Sri Lanka. Instead, she took a segmented approach, assessed each factor to see whether it represented hardship that was "unusual and undeserved or disproportionate", then appeared to discount each from her final conclusion because it failed to satisfy that threshold. Her literal obedience to those adjectives, which do not appear anywhere

---

Review 323; Katharine T. Bartlett, "Feminist Legal Methods" (1990) 103:4 *Harvard Law Review* 829; and Robin West, "Jurisprudence and Gender" (1988) 55 *University of Chicago Law Review* 1.

42 *Kanthasamy v Canada (Citizenship and Immigration)*, 2015 SCC 61.

43 *Ibid* at para 33.

44 *Ibid* at para 26 [internal quotation marks omitted].

45 On objectification, see Dorothy E. Smith & Alison I. Griffith, *Simply Institutional Ethnography: Creating a Sociology for People* (Toronto: University of Toronto Press, 2022).

> in s. 25(1), rather than looking at his circumstances as a whole, led her to see each of them as a distinct legal test, rather than as words designed to help reify the equitable purpose of the provision. This had the effect of improperly restricting her discretion and rendering her decision unreasonable.[46]

Another example of Justice Abella's engagement with factual context can be found in her majority decision in *Fraser*. In that case, members of the RCMP who had participated in a job-share program and were therefore ineligible for the pension for full-time members challenged their exclusion under section 15 of the *Charter*. Although the job-share program was not restricted to women, participants in the program were overwhelmingly women and mothers. They argued that the pension discriminated on the basis of sex and other grounds. Writing for the majority, Justice Abella gave effect to the sex discrimination claim. However, she declined to consider other grounds of disadvantage or, as in *Kanthasamy*, to consider how intersecting forms of vulnerability might have compounded the disadvantage the claimants faced, a fact that some scholars have criticized.[47]

Justice Abella explained that in making out a claim of indirect discrimination, "[t]wo types of evidence will be especially helpful."[48] The first is "evidence about the physical, social, cultural or other barriers which provide 'the full context of the claimant group's situation.'"[49] "The second is evidence about the outcomes that the impugned law or policy (or a substantially similar one) has produced in practice."[50] In applying the law to the situation faced by members of the RCMP who had job shared, Justice Abella cited statistical evidence that women face particular challenges in attempting to meet both their professional and care obligations, and that this sometimes led them to take on part-time employment for a period of their careers.[51] She also cited government reports that found that women's tendency to work part-time heightened their vulnerability as employees, with many being forced into precarious job situations.[52]

---

46 At para 45.

47 Jonnette Watson Hamilton, "*Cautious Optimism: Fraser v Canada (Attorney General)*" (2021) 30:2 *Constitutional Forum* 1.

48 *Fraser*, above note 19 at para 56.

49 *Ibid* at paras 55–56, citing *Withler v Canada (Attorney General)*, 2011 SCC 12 at para 43.

50 *Ibid* at para 58.

51 *Fraser*, above note 19 at para 98.

52 *Ibid* at paras 99–102.

Justice Abella's sensitivity to factual context was sometimes paired with an emphasis on developing the full legal context of a case. This tended to involve examining the statute or regulation as a whole and/or consulting a wide range of legal sources.[53] In *Quebec Inc*, decided in 2020, Justice Abella registered her disapproval of the majority's decision to curtail the use of foreign and international law sources in *Charter* interpretation.[54] The question in *Quebec Inc.* was whether the section 12 *Charter* guarantee against cruel and unusual punishment was available to corporations. The Court was unanimous in concluding that it was not. However, the Court split on the question of how foreign and international law should inform *Charter* interpretation.[55] Justices Rowe and Brown, writing for the majority, stated that foreign and international law is only relevant to the process of *Charter* interpretation in the sense of "supporting" or "confirming" interpretations arrived at through the purposive approach.[56] They also envisaged a more circumscribed role for non-binding international law, explaining that some rationale would need to be offered before resorting to such sources as part of the interpretative exercise.[57]

Justice Abella, concurring in the result, defended a broader approach, in which both foreign and non-binding international law could be considered in interpreting the *Charter* without resorting to the framework imposed by the majority. She described her approach as a "search" for full legal context, explaining that:

> Narrowing our approach by putting unnecessary barriers in the way of access to international and comparative sources gratuitously threatens to undermine Canada's leading voice internationally in constitutional adjudication, a role based on its willingness to go wide and deep in the global search for the best intellectual resources it can find.[58]

Other examples of contextual reasoning emerge from the contributions to this book. For instance, Jamie Cameron's chapter demonstrates that factual context contributed in critical ways to Justice Abella's

53 See Elizabeth Sheehy, "Introduction" in Sheehy, above note 52; Sullivan, above note 3.

54 *Quebec (Attorney General) v 9147-0732 Québec inc*, 2020 SCC 32.

55 Justice Kasirer, concurring, expressed no opinion on this issue.

56 *Quebec (Attorney General) v 9147-0732 Québec inc*, above note 54 at para 28.

57 *Ibid* at 38.

58 *Ibid* at para 106 [references omitted].

approach to the *Charter*'s freedom of expression guarantee.[59] Justice Abella's protection of freedom of expression was robust in cases where the freedom of expression claim was connected to the realization of democratic objectives, such as full citizen participation in elections in the *City of Toronto* case.[60] However, Cameron writes that her approach was different where the case concerned a clash between expressive rights and the dignity interests of another, such as in the *Ward* case, where a stand-up comedian made disparaging jokes about a child with special needs. In that context, she demonstrated a greater willingness to balance freedom of expression against the human rights of others, with the balance often favouring the latter.[61]

2. Power and Vulnerability

Another distinctive feature of Justice Abella's judicial method was the way it was attuned to power, hierarchy, and vulnerability. Indeed, this was a feature of virtually all her major decisions. As the authors in this collection show, however, these concepts emerged as particularly salient in her decisions in the realm of labour and equality law.

In her chapter, Colleen Bauman explains that the defining themes of Justice Abella's labour law jurisprudence are "enhancing dignity at work" and "recognizing the vulnerability of workers and the imbalance of power between employers and employees."[62] The importance of the latter theme can be seen in *Saskatchewan Federation of Labour*, where the Court was asked to reconsider its earlier conclusion that the *Charter*'s freedom of association guarantee did not include a right to strike. Building on the Court's nascent jurisprudence on the right to bargain collectively, Justice Abella held for the majority that the right to strike was also protected by freedom of association. As Bauman notes, the concepts of power and vulnerability played an important role in the judgment.[63] In her review of the history of industrial action in Canada, Justice Abella highlighted the power dynamics inherent in labour relations, explaining that it is only by coming together and pursuing common purposes that workers can counter the power of the employer: "Striking . . . promotes equality in the bargaining process. . . . This Court

59 Jamie Cameron, Chapter 8 in this volume.

60 *Toronto (City) v Ontario (Attorney General)*, 2021 SCC 34.

61 *Ward v Quebec (Commission des droits de la personne et des droits de la jeunesse)*, 2021 SCC 43, dissenting.

62 Bauman, Chapter 12 in this volume.

63 *Ibid.*

has long recognized the deep inequalities that structure the relationship between employers and employees, and the vulnerability of employees in this context."[64] She rejected the dissenting judges' argument that "true workplace justice looks at the interests of all implicated parties,"[65] concluding that this view wrongly implied equal agency on the part of employers and employees.

Power and vulnerability also played an important role in the *Fraser* decision. These considerations framed her discussion of both the procedural and substantive demands of section 15 in indirect discrimination cases. For instance, she explained that although claimants must provide sufficient evidence of group disadvantage to allow a court to adjudicate the claim, they did not need to prove (a) that the entire group experienced the disadvantage, (b) that "the protected characteristic 'caused' the disproportionate impact," or (c) that "the law itself was responsible for creating the background social or physical barriers which made a particular rule . . . disadvantageous for the claimant group,"[66] thus recognizing that already vulnerable equality claimants should not have unreasonable evidentiary demands imposed upon them.[67] Substantively, she explained that the test for indirect discrimination seeks to root out forms of discrimination that may be invisible on their face, but which structurally disadvantage groups in practice. And she rejected a framing of section 15 that would have denied claims on the basis of a "problematic" conception of choice, one that failed to account for the ways that individuals' agency was constrained by their circumstances.[68]

3. *Local Justice*

A final component of Justice Abella's judicial method involved reasoning from the ground up, whether the context was the fight for workplace justice, the circumstances of the child refugee, the lived realities of individuals experiencing indirect discrimination, or the local justice supplied by the administrative state. Where a judge reasons *from* is important because it tends to prioritize different aspects of legal reasoning. When a decision-maker begins with an abstract legal rule, concepts and principles

64 *Saskatchewan Federation of Labour*, above note 21 at para 55.

65 *Saskatchewan Federation of Labour*, above note 21 at para 125, dissent cited in para 56.

66 *Ibid* at paras 70–72.

67 *Ibid.*

68 *Fraser*, above note 19, citing Margot Young, "Blissed Out: Section 15 at Twenty" (2006) 33 *Supreme Court Law Review* 45 (2d) at 55–56.

are given priority. Legitimacy results from a perception of fidelity to text or rule.[69] When one begins with how individuals experience the law, by contrast, individuals' subjective experience of law is given priority. To be legitimate, the vision of law that emerges from the interpretative process must speak in some way to that lived reality. Reasoning from the ground up also has institutional implications. When a judge is committed to this form of reasoning, they usually take the position that the first instance decision-maker has some advantage over decision-makers operating at a greater distance from the parties and their experiences.

This approach to decision-making is visible in a number of Justice Abella's opinions. However, it is especially pronounced in the administrative law context. As Justice Lorne Sossin explains in his contribution to this volume, Justice Abella knew intuitively that the dynamics of an administrative decision are usually most visible at the local level.[70] In *Doré v Barreau du Québec*, decided in 2012, the Court was asked to decide how administrative decision-makers should approach decisions that implicate constitutional rights. In an opinion penned by Justice Abella, the majority concluded that administrative decision-makers are required to balance the statutory objectives with the "*Charter* values" engaged.[71] If the decision was subsequently challenged on *Charter* grounds, the court should adopt an administrative law approach on judicial review rather than assessing the constitutionality of the administrative decision using the traditional two-step *Charter* analysis.[72] The former requires the court to determine the reasonableness of the decision by asking whether, "given the nature of the decision and the statutory and factual contexts, the decision reflects a proportionate balancing of the *Charter* protections at play."[73] In Justice Abella's view, this approach to rights protection was better tailored to the administrative law context than a formal *Charter* analysis.

Doré has proven a controversial decision. Particular criticism has been levelled at the fact that it abandons the language of rights in favour

69 On legitimacy, see Nathalie Des Rosiers, "Être le miroir de son époque : la primauté du droit, la critique égalitaire, et la contribution de Madame la juge L'Heureux-Dubé" in Sheehy, above note 52; Wilson, above note 3; Claire L'Heureux-Dube, "Outsiders on the Bench: The Continuing Struggle for Equality" (2001) 16:1 *Wisconsin Women's Law Journal* 15–30; and Rosalie Silberman Abella, "Women in the Legal Profession" (1990) 48:4 *Advocate* (Vancouver Bar Association) 507.

70 Sossin, Chapter 4 in this volume.

71 *Doré*, above note 22.

72 *Ibid* at para 56.

73 *Ibid* at para 57.

of a less structured analysis grounded in "values."[74] In justifying her approach, Justice Abella demonstrated a high degree of sensitivity to the form of local justice that administrative decision-makers provide.[75] Her analysis recognized that facts are as much a part of decision-making as law, and that administrative decision-makers are not, and should not be regarded as, inferior to courts.[76] Rather, as Mary Liston explains in her contribution, they are to be understood as part of the larger rule of law project.[77] The vision that emerges from Justice Abella's reasons is an approach that recognizes the expertise of administrative decision-makers and thus "the distinct advantage that administrative bodies have in applying the *Charter* to a specific set of facts and in the context of their enabling legislation."[78]

4. *Analysis/Conclusion*

Justice Abella's decisions contain many examples of feminist judicial reasoning. If we consider these examples together, we see that they represent a distinctive approach to judicial reasoning. When a judge reasons from the bottom up, and is attuned to lived experience, context, power, and vulnerability, facts and law sometimes show up differently than they would otherwise. Taking these methods seriously does not mean that formal legal rules cease to have significance, or that more traditional approaches should be abandoned. Indeed, when one examines Justice Abella's decisions, it is clear that she is not solely concerned with the vision that emerges from below. At the same time, her use of feminist legal methods meant that she was forced to confront the potential inequities that become visible when one attends to feminist concerns. These inequities can either be addressed or exacerbated by the way judges interpret and apply the law. The integration of feminist

74 See, for example, Matthew Horner, "*Charter* Values: The Uncanny Valley of Canadian Constitutionalism" (2014), 67 *Supreme Court Law Review* (2d) 361 at 361–62. I am also grateful to Mark Walters for this point.

75 *Multani v Commission scolaire Marguerite-Bourgeoys*, 2006 SCC 6; *Doré*, above note 22. On local justice, see Margaret Doyle & Nick O'Brien, *Reimagining Administrative Justice: Human Rights in Small Places* (Palgrave Pivot, 2020).

76 On hierarchy, see Mary Liston, "Governments in Miniature: The Rule of Law in the Administrative State" in Colleen M. Flood & Lorne Sossin, eds, *Administrative Law in Context*, 3d ed (Toronto: Emond, 2018) 139; Kate Glover Berger, "The Constitution of the Administrative State" (2018) 86 *Supreme Court Law Review* (2d) 161.

77 Liston, above note 76; Berger, above note 76. See also Sossin, Chapter 4 in this volume, citing *Vavilov* at para 241, Abella and Karakatsanis JJ.

78 *Doré*, above note 22 at para 48.

methods into judicial decision-making therefore makes a more inclusive and effective form of judicial reasoning possible.

In my view, the feminist legal methods Justice Abella employed are more than capable of standing on their own two feet. They are informed by, and linked to, a distinct epistemology, which is that knowledge is socially constructed.[79] They do not permit open-ended reasoning, but rather require that courts identify relevant facts, interpret legal sources, and apply law to facts, much as the traditional common law method does.[80] They are not, however, the dominant judicial approach, and some of these methods have occasionally been criticized by those who would prefer to see traditional methods adhered to.[81]

It is here, again, that Justice Abella's story, her force of personality, and her singular determination are relevant. One of the claims that tends to accompany resistance to feminist legal methods is that they lack legitimacy and undermine the rule of law because of their positionality. As Justice Abella herself has noted, however, the reverse is actually true.[82] False claims of neutrality undermine the legitimacy of our legal order. Judges can demonstrate their commitment to the rule of law and access to justice by making their positionality explicit and seeking to understand the positionality of others.[83] In its transparency and concern for the other, the legal system is rendered more, not less, legitimate.[84]

D. The Chapters

The chapters in this collection weave together a story about an extraordinary life and career. The collection opens with a series of essays on Justice Abella's early years and influences. Eric Adams writes about Justice Abella's youth, her "close-knit family life," her love of books and music, and her parents' frankness about the Holocaust.[85] He also describes her university education and her experiences as one of a very small number of women lawyers in private practice in the early 1970s. Picking

79 Smith & Griffith, above note 45.

80 Mary Jane Mossman, "Feminism and Legal Method: The Difference It Makes" (1987) 3 *Wisconsin Women's Law Journal* 147, Hunter, above note 35 at 1291.

81 See, for example, Leonid Sirota, "The Rule of Law All the Way Up" (2019) 92 *Supreme Court Law Review* (2d) 79.

82 Abella, above note 69; Liston, this volume; Elizabeth Sheehy, "Introduction" in Sheehy, above note 52 at 15; See Sullivan, above note 3; Des Rosiers, above note 69.

83 See Des Rosiers, *ibid* and Sullivan, above note 3.

84 Liston, Chapter 6 in this volume.

85 Adams, Chapter 1 in this volume.

up where Adams leaves off, Rosalie Jukier discusses the "authenticity-professionalism paradox" that confronted so many women lawyers during this period. This paradox continues to place limits on the range of identities that lawyers of all genders are able to assume as legal professionals. By refusing to be constrained by the profession's stated and unstated demands, Jukier argues, Justice Abella made the profession a more welcoming one for others.[86] In twin essays, Joëlle Pastora Sala and Charles Tremblay Potvin reflect on the far-reaching impact of Justice Abella's Royal Commission Report, which not only shaped early interpretations of section 15 of the *Charter* but remains relevant today as a roadmap for achieving substantive equality in Canada.[87] Justice Lorne Sossin returns to her days as Chair of the Ontario Labour Relations Board and finds the seeds of her later judicial views on administrative law. This section concludes with an essay by Mary Liston on how Justice Abella's affinity for the humanities influenced her approach to judging. Building on the law and literature scholarship, she explains that the creative arts open up a space in which the judge is able to toggle between empathy and dispassion, both of which are necessary for good decision-making.[88]

Part Two turns to an in-depth examination of Justice Abella's Supreme Court jurisprudence, beginning with an empirical analysis of her case-law by Stephen Bindman and Keenan Macneal. This chapter helps situate Justice Abella on the Court by identifying how often she was in the majority versus in dissent, tracking her judicial allies, and highlighting other salient features of her jurisprudence. The chapters then move to a discussion of Justice Abella's decisions in the realm of constitutional law. Jamie Cameron explains that while Justice Abella is not always associated with the freedom of expression and freedom of the press jurisprudence, "with the exception of Justice Beverley McLachlin, she has written more opinions [on these subjects] than any other member of the Court." Her approach in the cases, Cameron explains, "is unapologetically Abellian."[89] Howard Kislowicz examines Justice Abella's freedom of religion jurisprudence and finds a body of cases characterized by two features: respect for difference and self-awareness, which he describes as essential for cross-cultural communication. Martha Minow argues that Justice Abella's decades-long leadership on equality issues has

86 Jukier, Chapter 5 in this volume.
87 Tremblay Potvin, Chapter 2 in this volume.
88 Liston, Chapter 6 in this volume.
89 Cameron, Chapter 8 this volume.

helped advance the transnational conversation on substantive equality. And in her chapter, Aimée Craft turns her attention to the ways Justice Abella's jurisprudence "contributed to re-storying parts of Canadian Aboriginal Law in ways that better reflect the long-standing relationships of Indigenous people with the Crown, the fiduciary obligations aligned with the honour of the Crown, and the current imperative of reconciliation."[90]

Part Three delves into Justice Abella's labour and employment jurisprudence. Colleen Bauman suggests that the two key principles that animate Justice Abella's decisions in this area are "enhancing dignity at work" and "recognizing the vulnerability of workers and the imbalance of power between employers and employees."[91] These principles, which Bauman locates in domestic and international labour rights law, came together in *Saskatchewan Federation of Labour* to support recognizing a constitutional right to strike, despite earlier Supreme Court precedent holding that there was no such right. In his contribution, Brian Langille returns to first principles, reminding us that one of the central functions of law is to "speak rationality to power." This means that law, by its very nature, prohibits the arbitrary exercise of public power. And yet, Langille explains, courts have occasionally upheld labour legislation that authorizes arbitrary action. He questions whether there is room in Justice Abella's vision of section 15 of the *Charter* for a constitutional requirement of legislative non-arbitrariness.

Part Four of the collection examines Justice Abella's contributions to international law, immigration and refugee law, and children's rights. Harold Koh opens this part by explaining that Abella's "global perspective has placed [her] at the heart of two central jurisprudential debates: First, what is the proper role of domestic courts in interpreting international law? And second, what is the proper role of international law in the evolution of Canadian public law?"[92] "[O]n both issues," Koh concludes, "Rosie has emerged not just as a national, but as a worldwide, judicial leader."[93] Next, Yousuf Aftab and Elinoam Abramov take a deep look at the *Nevsun* case. They draw mixed conclusions about Justice Abella's majority decision. On the one hand, they argue that aspects of its reasoning are at odds with prevailing principles of corporate liability for wrongdoing. On the other hand,

90 Aimée Craft, Chapter 11 in this volume.

91 Bauman, Chapter 12 in this volume.

92 Koh, Chapter 14 in this volume.

93 *Ibid.*

they suggest that Justice Abella's unorthodox approach may push international law in new directions. Jamie Liew analyzes Justice Abella's major immigration and refugee law decisions and identifies *Kanthasamy*, in which she endorsed a more generous test for admission to Canada on humanitarian and compassionate grounds, as a high point in the jurisprudence.[94] Mona Paré's contribution emphasizes the uncertain status of children's rights under domestic law and argues that Justice Abella's jurisprudence helped further embed these rights in Canadian law.

Part Five takes up the future of Justice Abella's jurisprudence. Andrew Bernstein and Amanda Wolczanski examine her technology decisions in the domains of copyright, defamation, contract, and civil procedure. They argue that while her practice has been to work with, rather than against, technology, she has "retained a progressive's suspicion of influential private institutions, including the powerful companies that [have come] to dominate the digital landscape."[95] Gerald Chan and Yadesha Satheaswaran engage in a close reading of Justice Abella's jurisprudence on section 8 of the *Charter*, which protects individuals from unreasonable search and seizure. They conclude that in her decisions, she "consistently and vigilantly stood guard to ensure that technological advances do not erode privacy."[96] Sara Ghebremusse considers Justice Abella's international human rights legacy. She argues that Abella's willingness to "push the boundaries of the interpretation and application of international human rights law" will have impacts both for the continued vitality of international law in domestic courts and for the overall development of international law.[97] Finally, Professor and classically trained singer Rosemary Cairns-Way offers a lyrical reflection on Justice Abella's vision of equality, drawing parallels between choral singing and substantive equality.

The volume ends with a series of tributes given at the conference. Former Justice of the Constitutional Court of South Africa Albie Sachs describes the "tsunami effect" of Justice Abella's jurisprudence on human rights worldwide. Bernie Farber reflects on what it meant for a woman like Justice Abella — the child of Holocaust survivors — to have reached Canada's highest court. He also considers the values

94 Liew, chapter 16 in this volume.

95 Andrew Bernstein & Amanda Wolczanski, Chapter 18 in this volume.

96 Chan & Satheaswaran, Chapter 19 in this volume.

97 Ghebremusse, Chapter 20 in this volume.

she brought to the Court as a judge who strongly identified as Jewish. David Lepofsky analyzes Abella's tenure as Chair of the Ontario Law Reform Commission and concludes that this experience equipped her to deal with the many policy issues that inform legal analysis. And Dorit Beinisch, former President of the Supreme Court of Israel, and Gonen Ilan discuss Justice Abella's impact on Israeli jurisprudence across a range of subjects, emphasizing her "humanitarian approach" and her commitment to judicial independence and democracy.

E. Conclusion

Just as only time will tell what the long-term impact of Justice Abella's jurisprudence will be, it will also be some time before the impact of her distinctive approach to judging is apparent. One thing is clear, however: Justice Abella contributed substantially to making an approach to judging possible that was less accepted before she rose to Canada's highest court. By adopting this approach, she not only increased justice for people, she also pioneered a new vision of judging.

PART 1

Early Years, Career, and Influences

1 Justice Abella's Overture: Rosalie Abella's Early Life and Career

ERIC ADAMS*

A. The Overture

Musicals often begin with an overture to introduce the audience to the musical motifs and dramatic notes of the story to come. As you settle into your seat, you hear snippets of the sonic arcs of upcoming triumphs and traces of the minor keys of future tragedies. The astute listener will be aware that the entire show is being musically presented in miniature before the curtain rises. The musical's overture is its formal beginning, but it is also provides an outline of the action to come.[1] Of course, familiar notes and melodies only become so in retrospect, just as the connected happenings of a life — its patterns, themes, and trajectories — can only be connected when looking back. The overture must be composed after the end, even though it is played before the beginning.

This chapter is an overture of sorts to Justice Rosalie Silberman Abella's judicial career at the Supreme Court of Canada. In the same way that the overture is not the score, this is not a full biography but rather focuses on important aspects of her pre-Supreme Court of Canada life and career. As Philip Girard explains it, judicial biography explores "the particular judge's patterns of thought, and how the events of his or her life contributed to the formation of those patterns."[2] I intend to highlight the notes

---

* Professor of Law, University of Alberta, Faculty of Law. My thanks to Alexis Newman for excellent research assistance, to Noah Weisberg for helpful comments, and to the organizers of the conference *A Life of Firsts*, where this material was first presented.

1 On the role of the overture in musicals, see Scott McMillin, *The Musical as Drama: A Study of the Principles and Conventions Behind Musical Shows from Kern to Sondheim* (Princeton: Princeton University Press, 2006) at 128.

2 Philip Girard, "Judging Lives: Judicial Biography from Hale to Holmes" (2003) 7 *Australian Journal of Legal History* 87 at 89.

that mattered in Justice Abella's biography and professional life before the curtain opened on her most famous long-running performance at the Supreme Court of Canada. The biographical overture to the judicial career of a Justice of the Supreme Court will have a difficult time outshining the big numbers that follow and is seldom more famous. But there are pleasures and insights to be found in the subtle and condensed signals of the future plot, as well as lessons about what matters when professional identities first take shape, when choices coalesce with values and the happenstance of fortune to create the makings of a career.

Justice Abella's personal and professional values, identities, and passions, indeed her judicial persona and philosophy, have been shaped by the experiences of her life.[3] Those values, identities, and passions — the content and expression of which marked so much of her judicial career at the Supreme Court — were particularly shaped and expressed in the earliest years of her professional life. Judicial biography that extends beyond the years of appellate adjudication for which a judge is usually best known remains a worthwhile pursuit for those seeking a deeper understanding of the workings of judges and their jurisprudence. And so, as Maria tells us in the *Sound of Music*, "let's start at the very beginning, a very good place to start."

B. Act I: "I Am Shaped by Who I Am"

One does not need to delve deeply into the archives to find the outlines of Rosalie Abella's remarkable early life.[4] As she has candidly and poignantly described in many speeches and interviews, she was born on 1 July 1 1946 in a displaced person's camp in Stuttgart, Germany, the daughter of Jewish refugees and survivors of the Holocaust,

---

3 "I think the older you get the more you realize how much your childhood has shaped you," Justice Abella says. "And I don't think there's any doubt . . . that my parents' experiences and my growing up and who they were as people shaped me in ways conscious and unconscious." Terry Davidson, "Supreme Court Justice Rosalie Abella: The Exit Interview" (28 June 2021) *The Lawyer's Daily*, online, available at https://www.law360.ca/ca/articles/1755262/supreme-court-justice-rosalie-silberman-abella-the-exit-interview.

4 The details of Rosalie Abella's early life and family history are taken from multiple sources, especially: Rosalie Silberman Abella and Matthew Diller, "A Conversation with the Honorable Rosalie Silberman Abella and Dean Matthew Diller" (2018) 87:3 *Fordham Law Review* 843; Nurse, above note 4; Sean Fine, "Doing Justice to His Dream" *Globe and Mail* (30 July 2016) F1; Sean Fine, "How Rosalie Abella's Personal History Shaped her Legal Legacy" *Globe and Mail* (26 June 2021); Jennifer Yang, "Fanny Silberman, 92, Loved Heroically" *Toronto Star* (18 February 2010).

Jacob and Fanny Silberman. Rosalie's Polish-born parents had suffered, like so many millions, the unfathomable horrors of Nazi atrocities, including the murder of their parents, siblings, and two-year-old son Julius. Jacob and Fanny (Krongold) married in 1939, at the outset of Germany's invasion of Poland, but spent most of the war separated in labour and concentration camps. Reunited in one of the many displaced persons camps scattered across Germany after the war, Fanny and Jacob attempted to rebuild their lives.[5] In the camp in Stuttgart, Jacob relied on his pre-war law degree to work for US officials in providing rudimentary legal services to the camp's occupants.[6] As the camps began to wind down in the late 1940s, Jacob and Fanny sought to begin life anew. Loosening slightly its antisemitic closed-door immigration policy of the 1930s, the Government of Canada had belatedly begun to accept the immigration of some Jewish refugees from Europe beginning in 1947, so long as employment could be prearranged for the adult men.[7] Over the next five years, approximately 34,000 Jews immigrated to Canada, including 11,000 Jewish refugees.[8] Rosalie Silberman was one of them.

After Jacob secured a designation from the Canadian government enabling him to work in clothing manufacturing, the Silberman family travelled by train from Stuttgart to the German port city of Bremerhaven. From there they boarded the SS General Stuart Heintzelman, a

5 On the Jewish experience of displacement following the end of the war, see Angelika Königseder and Juliane Wetzel, *Waiting for Hope: Jewish Displaced Persons in Post-World War II Germany*, translated by John A. Broadwin (Evanston, Ill: Northwestern University Press, 2001).

6 The position would have encountered controversy since the US military was particularly concerned that a parallel unauthorized legal system had sprung up among the displaced persons "contrary to the strict military government law." See Rivka Brot, "Conflicting Jurisdictions: The Struggle of the Jews in the Displaced Persons Camps for Legal Autonomy" (2017) 31:3 *Studies on the Holocaust* 171 at 184.

7 See Irving Abella and Harold Troper, *None Is Too Many: Canada and the Jews of Europe, 1933–1948* (Toronto: University of Toronto Press, 2012). Capturing the incoherence of the transition in immigration policy, in 1948, Hugh Keenleyside, the Deputy Minister of Mines and Resources, explained that "[a]bove all, of course, we are governed by the Prime Minister's statement that immigration is to be non-discriminatory, but at the same time is not to be used as an instrument to effect any major change in the racial, religious or social constitution of Canada." Quoted in Julie Frances Gilmour, *"The Kind of People Canada Wants": Canada and the Displaced Persons, 1943–1953* (PhD Dissertation, Department of History, University of Toronto, 2009) at 106.

8 Steven Schwinghamer and Jan Raska, *Pier 21: A History* (Ottawa: University of Ottawa Press, 2020) at 122 and 130.

former US troop ship bound for Canada.[9] "The life of a [displaced person] seeking to emigrate," Julie Frances Gilmour explains, "included a seemingly endless round of registration, administrative checks, medical checks and identification verification."[10] Overcoming those bureaucratic hurdles, the Silberman family, consisting of Jacob, Fanny, Rosalie, and her younger sister, Toni, arrived in Halifax, Nova Scotia with their handful of possessions on 30 May 1950. After passing through a further round of administrative and medical checks at Pier 21, the family was given train tickets to their final destination: Union Station in Toronto. The family first settled, like so many Jewish immigrants before and alongside them, in Toronto's bustling Kensington Market neighbourhood. After a short stint working in a factory as arranged, Jacob took up a position selling insurance for the Continental Life Insurance Company, while Fanny assisted with the paperwork from home. Moving into a house near St. Clair Avenue, the family transitioned from the depths of wartime horror and deprivation into middle class life in Canada.

Rosalie Silberman's childhood was marked by the rituals of piano practice and homework, a voracious appetite for reading satisfied by weekly trips to the local library, and the regular ups and downs of her close-knit family life — a family led by the example set by loving and hardworking parents.[11] Motivated by the high expectations and support of her parents, Rosalie excelled in music and academics alike. She graduated from the Royal Conservatory of Music and Bathurst Heights Secondary School with considerable distinction. Looking back, Justice Abella links her burgeoning passion for the law to the impact of Victor Hugo's *Les Misérables*. "Reading Les Mis," she has said, "was the moment when being a lawyer wasn't something I wanted to do because my parents thought it was a good thing. It turned into something I wanted to do so that people would be protected from those kind of injustices."[12]

---

9 "That was my tag," Justice Abella said looking over a photograph of the voyage. "It was so we wouldn't get lost. We were packed in like baggage." Quoted Nurse, above note 4.

10 Gilmour, above note 7 at 140.

11 Nurse, above note 4.

12 *Ibid*. "[N]ovels have always been a magical way to learn the additional lessons our lives are too limited to teach us," Abella writes. "Literature helps us know. It is a constant tutor in human experience." Rosalie Silberman Abella, "Law, Literature, and Identity: Seeking Equality" (2000) 63 *Saskatchewan Law Review* 1 at 2.

If it was a novel that cemented her plan to become a lawyer, the foundations of her interest in law had been previously laid by family experience. Among the few discordant notes Justice Abella has relayed of her otherwise happy childhood is the family memory of an early injustice: the denial of her father's ability to become a lawyer by joining the Law Society of Upper Canada. Jacob's intention on arriving in Canada had been to take up the legal career he had not been allowed to pursue in Poland and had worked to revive in the displaced persons camp in Germany.[13] It was not to be. The Law Society of Upper Canada, like other law societies in Canada at the time, required members of the Bar to be Canadian citizens. As a recent immigrant, looking at years of residency before he could hope to qualify, Jacob abandoned hopes of a legal career. It was a blatant discrimination that ended one legal career but sparked another. Justice Abella locates her childhood's inchoate desire to be a lawyer to her father's story of abandoned hopes and the arbitrariness of state prejudice.

Of course, the injustices endured by her parents went much deeper than the professional discrimination Jacob experienced in Canada. "In our house," Abella recalled, "there was no silence about the past. The stories [of her family's experience of the Holocaust] were told and retold in response to my endless questioning. . . . I was transfixed by the stories and transformed by the optimism of the parents who told them. You cannot be born in the shadow of the Holocaust to two Jews who survived it without an exaggerated commitment to the pursuit of justice."[14] Speaking of her past, she has said, "We're all shaped by what we've come from. Some people embrace what they've come from. Some people spend a fair bit of energy trying to distance themselves. I never felt anything but a seamless relationship with who I was. My religion, my gender, my origins, the holocaust that my parents had survived . . . I am not at all embarrassed about the fact that I am shaped by who I am."[15]

That last observation — "I am shaped by who I am" — is a beautifully simple and insightful tautology about the formation of identities: the feedback loop of making meaning out of who we are, and who we want to be, in the world. Her family history — the enormity of its

13 Sean Fine, "Doing Justice to His Dream," above note 4.

14 Rosalie Silberman Abella, "Nothing Expected and Everything Hoped For," *Globe and Mail* (28 June 1996) A15.

15 CTV Television, "Interview with Justice Rosalie Abella" (23 May 2021), *Question Period — CTV Television* (ProQuest), online: https://www.proquest.com/docview/2531417164/677612C86964CF0PQ/1?accountid=14474&sourcetype=Newspapers.

tragedies and the strength of its resilience during and after the war — not only provided the impetus for Rosalie's decision about a career in law, but also clarified what mattered to her about the law and its ideals. For Abella, human rights and the consequences of their denial would always remain at the forefront of her conception of justice.

C. Act II: "Agricultural Marketing Boards, Not Everyone's Favourite Subject in Law School"

In the fall of 1963, Rosalie Silberman, with her driven work ethic, love of literature, passion for music, and attentiveness to issues of injustice, began pursuing a Bachelor of Arts degree at University College at the University of Toronto. In characteristic fashion, she has a good story to tell about it. "When I was in first year university, everyone told me to take philosophy," Abella recounts. "In the very first class, [the professor] asked: 'If a tree falls in the middle of a forest and no one hears it, does it make noise?' I turned to my best friend Sharon and said: 'I'm outta here. Who cares?!'"[16] She did not have to look far for things she did care about. Rosalie began her studies at the University of Toronto during an exciting moment of engaged students and rising campus activism, and she was quickly caught up in the wave of growing student concern with issues of rights and justice, war and peace.[17] As the University of Toronto grew with new buildings, rising enrolment, more generous public funding, and expanding ambitions, the campus pulsed with student politics, often involving figures who would go on to have influential political careers: Bob Rae and Michael Ignatieff, among them. "Unlike the apolitical 'silent generation' of students of the 1950s, students in the 1960s were, on the whole, vocal, active, and involved," Martin Friedland writes in his history of the University of Toronto.[18] Rosalie Silberman fit right in.

In the spring of her second undergraduate year, Rosalie joined a group of students and faculty members planning a "teach-in" addressing

16 Rosalie Silberman Abella, "Our Civil Justice System Needs to Be Brought into the 21st Century" (24 April 2020) *Globe and Mail*.

17 David S. Churchill, "SUPA, Selma, and Stevenson: The Politics of Solidarity in mid-1960s Toronto" (2010) 44:2 *Journal of Canadian Studies* 32; Frances Early, "Canadian Women and the International Arena in the Sixties: The Voice of Women / La Voix des femmes and the Opposition to the Vietnam War" in Dimitry Anastakis, *The Sixties: Passion, Politics, and Style* (Montreal & Kingston: McGill-Queen's University Press, 2008) 25; Bryan D Palmer, *Canada's 1960s: The Ironies of Identity in a Rebellious Era* (Toronto: University of Toronto Press, 2009).

18 Martin L. Friedland, *The University of Toronto: A History*, 2nd ed (Toronto: University of Toronto Press, 2013) at 525.

revolutionary politics, Latin America, and the Vietnam War. The University of Toronto's International Teach-In took place at Varsity Arena in October 1965. Thousands of students attended to listen to more than a dozen speakers — intellectuals, professors, and activists.[19] The event captured the internationalist turn student politics had taken across North America. "The year 1965 marked a crucial transformation and expansion of the student movement in Toronto," a scholar of the period explains, heralding a decisive turn towards the "global context" of student concerns.[20] Student activists at the University of Toronto, like others across Canadian campuses, "match[ed] their own political aspirations with those of the US New Left . . . particip[ating] in a larger transaction of political ideals, strategies, protest tactics, and sites for involvement and organizing."[21] Still, a certain degree of distinctive Canadianess remained. The escalating Vietnam conflict sparked spontaneous demonstrations, sit-ins, and teach-ins on US campuses, some of which would end in violence. At the University of Toronto, a committee of students, including Rosalie, worked with faculty members to organize the officially-sanctioned event with the aim of providing "a 'balanced' tone . . . one that would allow all sides of the conflict to voice their opinions."[22] Drawn to the people involved, and the pressing nature of the issues to be explored, Rosalie jumped into assisting with the event.[23] It is tempting to trace the influence of at least some of Justice Abella's internationalist outlook to such moments in her undergraduate career, but, in addition, the International Teach-In impacted the course of Rosalie's life in a much more intimate way. It was at an organizational meeting for the Teach-In that she met her future life partner, Irving Abella.

If her undergraduate degree exposed her into the vivid student politics of the period, she arrived at the University of Toronto Faculty of Law in the fall of 1967 to discover a more staid corner of campus. At the

19 The original, idealistic, some might say naïve plan for the event was to contrast opposing views of various political figures representing the various governments involved in the Vietnam conflict. Diplomatic and other hurdles prevented participation from most of the invited political figures. "I look back on the Teach-In with mixed feelings," one of its faculty organizers confessed. "It was a unique success as a venture in public education concerning international affairs, but it was not a first step towards peace in Vietnam." Donald Evans, "The Diplomacy of a Teach-In" in Charles Hanly, ed, *Revolution and Response: Selections from the Toronto International Teach-In* (Toronto: McClelland and Stewart, 1966) 133 at 140.

20 Churchill, above note 17 at 35.

21 *Ibid* at 34.

22 *Ibid* at 57.

23 Nurse, above note 4.

Faculty of Law, Rosalie Abella (she would marry Irving in December 1968, just before first-term exams) began her legal education during an anxious period in the law school's illustrious history. Martin Friedland, who joined the Faculty in 1965, describes the late 1960s at the Faculty of Law as marked by research stagnancy, student complaints, and financial crisis.[24] There had been a recent changing of the guard at the Faculty with the departure of Bora Laskin for the Ontario Court of Appeal in 1965, and the death of the indomitable figure, Cecil "Caesar" Wright in 1967.[25] Outstanding legal scholars remained, of course, including Dean Ronald St. John Macdonald, along with James Milner, Angela Swan, and Albert Abel; an influx of new faculty, among them R.C.B. Risk, Martin Friedland, Frank Iacobucci, and Stephen Waddams, would also soon leave their scholarly imprint on the place. All the same, Friedland goes so far as to describe a "crisis atmosphere" at the law school, noting a 1969 memo sent by the University's President expressing "great[] concern about the Faculty of Law" and offering the bleak assessment that it "was falling behind in all of the basic areas that determine academic quality."[26] It would, however, be a mistake to single out the University of Toronto in this period. Canadian legal education in the late 1960s shared a largely mandatory curriculum, doctrinal courses, and modest scholarly ambition.[27] Students at the University of Toronto Faculty of Law, even perceptive ones like Rosalie Abella, were unlikely to have known of the depth of institutional drift and concern among the administration and faculty members, but it is notable that her law school years figure so little in the many interviews she has given about her past.

Despite the accelerating cultural and political change across Canadian campuses in the late 1960s, legal education persisted much as it had been for the previous two decades. Male professors taught groups of overwhelmingly white male students mandatory courses according to the case method of instruction. Canadian law school remained rigorous and challenging in the usual ways, and the material could always be elevated in the hands of a gifted law teacher, but it was also true that Canadian

24 Martin L. Friedland, *My Life in Crime and Other Academic Adventures* (Toronto: University of Toronto Press, 2007) at 194–95.

25 On Laskin's influential academic career see Philip Girard, *Bora Laskin: Bringing Law to Life* (Toronto: University of Toronto Press, 2005). On Wright, see C. Ian Kyer and Jerome E. Bickenbach, *The Fiercest Debate: Cecil A. Wright, the Benchers, and Legal Education in Ontario, 1923–1957* (Toronto: The Osgoode Society for Canadian Legal History, 1987).

26 Friedland, above note 24 at 196.

27 See Eric M. Adams, "Bruce Ziff's Legal History" 61:1 *Alberta Law Review*.

legal education in the 1960s had yet to make significant inroads into situating law in larger context or thinking of the evaluation of students in ways other than final exams worth 100 percent of the grade. Rosalie Abella entered first year law in a class of 150 or so students — almost all of them men. She would be one of eight women to graduate in 1970. With few exceptions, it was men teaching at the front of her classes, too. When Abella began law school, the Faculty of Law had one female professor, Diana Priestley, the Law Librarian.[28] Hired in 1965, Priestley had been scheduled to teach the first-year class Introduction to Legal Research in Rosalie's first year, but she left the University of Toronto for a position at Osgoode Hall Law School in frustration at the financial constraints on the library budget. There were no other female faculty members during Abella's time at the Faculty of Law. The 1970s, and its "revolution in numbers" of women entering law school, would change Canadian legal education, but not during Rosalie's time in law school.[29] For Abella's generation, women remained both anomaly and afterthought in legal education — still too few available women's washrooms in the building, still banned from places like Hart House, the men-only facility on the University of Toronto's campus, and still rare enough in classrooms that they faced difficulty challenging the prevailing masculine culture.[30]

The legal education Abella received was closer in style, content, and student body to the decade preceding it than the one that would follow. The modest expansion of course offerings for upper-year students into critical and experiential perspectives and the loosening of some of the compulsory upper-year courses were still a few years away.[31] At

28 Ann Rae & Balfour Halevy, "Diana Mary Priestly: An Appreciation" in (1998) 90 *Law Library Journal* 123 at 123–24. Professor Priestly had received her law degree from the University of British Columbia in 1950 and after finding the doors closed to her in the Department of External Affairs because of her gender, she elected to pursue a graduate degree in library studies.

29 Constance Backhouse, "'A Revolution in Numbers': Ontario Feminist Lawyers in the Formative Years 1970s to the 1990s" in Constance Backhouse & W. Wesley Pue, eds, *The Promise and Perils of Law: Lawyers in Canadian History* (Toronto: Irwin Law, 2009) 265.

30 Woman University of Toronto law students were distinguished in the course calendar with a slightly lower fee schedule, since women were not charged the small fee associated with Hart House. Annual tuition totaled $558 for men and $533 for women, less than 20% of law school tuition at the University of Toronto today taking inflation into account. University of Toronto Faculty of Law, *Calendar 1967–68* at 28.

31 On the curricular developments of the 1970s, see Rod Macdonald, "Legal Education on the Threshold of the 1980's: Whatever Happened to the Great Ideas of the 60's?" (1979–80) 44:1 *Saskatchewan Law Review* 39. Abella's required first-year curriculum included courses in Agency, Civil Procedure, Contracts, Criminal Law, Property,

the University of Toronto Faculty of Law during Abella's time there, as at other Canadian law schools, law students focused on reading and discerning legal meaning from hundreds of appellate-level court judgments. The dominant legal philosophy viewed law as a relatively autonomous enterprise driven by judicial decision-making nuanced by a "mix of pragmatic and realist" ideas about the nature of legal reasoning.[32] Abella would have been at least partially exposed to some of the emerging, still inchoate, ideas of legal pluralism and those of the legal process school, especially when she took Contracts with Professors James Milner or Dick Risk. In his excavation of the intellectual currents at the Faculty of Law during this period, David Sandomierski highlights the tentative steps a handful of professors were making to steer students away from an exclusive focus on courts in understanding how law worked in its broader social context. But he also identifies the ways such efforts stalled, failed to take institutional hold, and did not amount to much.[33]

Constitutional Law, a subject Justice Abella would come to be associated with during her time on the Supreme Court, does not seem to have rated highly in her memories of law school. She admits to looking to the United States Supreme Court and the jurisprudence of the Warren Court with envy. "[W]hat did we learn from our 700-page casebook [in Constitutional Law]?" she once remarked to a US audience. "Who was in charge of egg marketing boards — the federal or the provincial government."[34] More succinctly, in one of the media interviews marking her retirement from the Supreme Court, she quipped that her education in Constitutional Law focused on "[agricultural] marketing boards, not

---

and Torts. Her second year required courses in Civil Procedure, Commercial Law, Constitutional Law, Evidence, Family Law, and Real Estate Transactions. Third year law required courses in Administrative Law and Wills and Trusts. In 1969, the Law Society and Ontario law schools agreed to some loosening of the mandatory curriculum. See W.R. Lederman, "Canadian Legal Education in the Second Half of the Twentieth Century" (1971) 21 *University of Toronto Law Journal* 141 at 156.

32 See David Sandomierski, "Catalytic Agents? Lon Fuller, James Milner, and the Lawyer as Social Architect, 1950–1969" (2021) 71 *University of Toronto Law Journal* 91 at 122.

33 David Sandomierski, "Decentering Adjudication at the University of Toronto Faculty of Law" in Ian Pilarczyk, Angela Fernandez & Brian Young eds, *Law, Life, and the Teaching of Legal History: Essays in Honour of G. Blaine Baker* (Montreal-Kingston: McGill-Queen's University Press, 2022) 415.

34 Abella and Diller, above note 4 at 847. The casebook in question was Bora Laskin, *Canadian Constitutional Law: Cases, Text and Notes on Distribution of Legislative Power*, 3d ed (Toronto: Carswell, 1969). The casebook, before appendixes, is 1028 pages.

everyone's favourite subject in law school."[35] The course description for Constitutional Law, which Abella would have taken in second year, with its almost comedic repetition of different ways to describe the legal issues of federalism, confirms the relatively narrow approach to the subject Abella would have encountered.[36] Yet there were also larger dynamics at play heralding a significant change in Canadian constitutional law, politics, and culture that would have also been apparent as Rosalie proceeded through law school. The Confederation of Tomorrow Conference in November 1967 reinvigorated constitutional discussions among the premiers and helped lead towards patriation of the Constitution in 1982. The Royal Commission on the Status of Women beginning in 1967 galvanized the women's movement. Trudeaumania and its grip on 1968 seemed to momentarily capture the energy of youth culture. Meanwhile, the Supreme Court of Canada's decision in *R v Drybones* in November 1969 appeared to give life to the *Canadian Bill of Rights*. Together, such moments suggested the tectonic movements of constitutional change and the dawn of a new culture of rights.[37]

In her upper years of law school, Abella gained exposure to topics that matched her intellectual interests: Family Law, Labour Law, Administrative Law, and Dean Macdonald's seminar on Human Rights and Fundamental Freedoms. If her Constitutional Law course had been dominated by a focus on federalism, she encountered in Dean Macdonald's seminar the burgeoning statutory human rights movement, the jurisprudence of the *Canadian Bill of Rights*, and the Supreme Court's famous "implied bill of rights" cases from the 1950s.[38] Immersed in the

---

35 CTV Television, "Interview with Justice Rosalie Abella," above note 15.

36 Taught by Professors Albert Abel and Colin McNairn, the calendar described Constitutional Law as "A course in Canadian federalism; Crown and legislature in the Canadian federation; constitutional amendment; delegation; distribution of legislative power between Parliament and provincial legislatures; problems of federal-provincial relations arising out of distribution of legislative power; federal-provincial financial arrangements; constitutional guarantees." University of Toronto, Faculty of Law, *Calendar 1968–69* at 18. During Abella's time in law school, Abel would publish his highly influential article on the division of powers: Albert S. Abel, "The Neglected Logic of 91 and 92" (1969) 19 *University of Toronto Law Journal* 487.

37 See Paul Litt, *Trudeaumania* (Vancouver: UBC Press, 2016). On *Drybones* and its contributions to shifts in Canadian constitutional culture see Eric M. Adams, "Judicial Agency and Anxiety Under the *Canadian Bill of Rights:* A Constitutional History of *R. v. Drybones*" (2018) 39 *National Journal of Constitutional Law* 63.

38 University of Toronto, Faculty of Law, *Calendar 1968–69*. See generally Eric M. Adams, "Building a Law of Human Rights: *Roncarelli v Duplessis* in Canadian Constitutional Culture" (2010) 55 *McGill Law Journal* 437.

legal topics that would come to define her judicial career, family tragedy struck. In her third year, Abella's father Jacob was diagnosed with cancer. He died just before her graduation in the spring of 1970 — a ceremony she could not bear to attend without his presence.[39] In her grief, she had also abandoned the search for an articling position, a search that had not been going well in the first place. "I don't know whether it was about being Jewish or a woman, but it was tough to get an articling job," Abella recalls. "I hope you understand," one firm told her, "we're just not hiring women."[40] In 1970, women were still expected to understand, accept, and navigate an array of arbitrary barriers, sexist policies and attitudes, and blatant discrimination facing them in the legal marketplace.[41] For Abella, the arduous path through to the next stage of her legal career involved an intervention from the Dean, whom she had no doubt impressed during her studies. Dean Macdonald arranged an interview for Abella at the Toronto firm, Risk, Cavan, Garfield, and Gardner, likely assisted by the connection between Professor Dick Risk and his father, John, the senior partner at the firm. Abella got the job, and her legal career began.[42]

D. Act III: "What Came First, the Words or the Music?" "The Phone Call."

Rosalie Abella's extraordinary legal career began in the most ordinary of ways — articling at a mid-sized firm in Toronto focusing on commercial work, real estate, and a smattering of litigation. John Risk founded the firm in the 1950s and by the early 1970s it had grown to a handful of partners, one or two associates, and, occasionally, an articling student. The firm had no woman lawyers, save Abella. One of the partners, Howard Garfield, was Jewish; so-called "mixed" law firms of Jews and Gentiles were becoming more common in Toronto. Assisting on files, meeting clients, and searching land titles at Risk, Cavan, Garfield, and Gardner, Abella enjoyed a typical articling experience of

39 Abella, "Nothing Expected and Everything Hoped For," above note 14.

40 Quoted in "Women in Law Through the Decades: 1960s" University of Toronto Faculty of Law: online: www.law.utoronto.ca/about/brief-history/women-in-law-through-decades/1960s.

41 Cameron Harvey, "Women in Law in Canada" (1970) 4 *The Manitoba Law Journal* 9; Linda Silver Dranoff, "Women as Lawyers in Toronto" (1972) 10:1 *Osgoode Hall Law Journal* 177.

42 "Women in Law Through the Decades: 1960s" above note 40. Email correspondence with Stephen Risk, a lawyer at the firm during Abella's articles (28 March 2022).

being mentored by good lawyers and doing routine legal work. Nonetheless, Abella's interests quickly had her on the move. As one of only twenty women out of nearly 500 new lawyers called to the Bar of the Law Society of Upper Canada in 1972, Abella undertook to make representation of women an important aspect of her practice. First, she joined Women's Place, an institution providing general support and advice to women on legal matters, which eventually evolved into one of the first women's shelters in Canada.[43] By 1974, Abella served on the executive of the National Action Committee on the Status of Women and was working for the Toronto firm, JV Kelly Law, focusing on family law, an area undergoing rapid development in the wake of the passage of the federal *Divorce Act* in 1968.[44] Her reputation in both the feminist movement and Toronto's legal community was rapidly ascending. In the fall of 1973, Abella was one of a dozen Toronto lawyers selected to produce videos explaining legal subjects to the general public. She was frequently approached by the media for her commentary on family law issues, especially systemic inequalities faced by women in the legal system, even at this early stage of her career.[45] Her reputation for legal acumen and eloquence in equal measure led to appointments as a Commissioner on the Ontario Human Rights Commission and on the Ontario Place Service Labour Relations Tribunal.[46] But her success still came with the consciousness of being an anomaly in a male-dominated profession. "I never saw another woman in a courtroom," Abella recalls of her early career. "I did not know any lawyers who were mothers."[47] Abella was part of a generation of woman lawyers pushing into places in the profession they had not previously been welcomed.

In the summer of 1976, Abella's successful career as a lawyer ended almost as abruptly as it had taken off. Conscious of the lack of diversity on Ontario's provincial courts, Ontario Attorney General Roy McMurtry asked the chief judge of Ontario's Family Court to reach out to Abella to

---

43 "Legal Advice Varies on Whether Women Can Use Own Name" *Globe and Mail* (2 October 1973) 12; Constance Backhouse, above note 29 at 289.

44 Dorothy Lipovenko, "Contracts Between Couples Untested in Courts" *Globe and Mail* (21 February 1974) W4.

45 Zena Cherry, "Of Tapes and Law" *Globe and Mail* (31 October 1973) 12; Ann Farrell, "Family court: Battleground for Hired Guns" *Toronto Star* (25 October 1975); "Men Are Fragile . . . Tied to Epididymis" *Globe and Mail* (12 July 1975) 7; "Six Women Talk about Men" *Globe and Mail* (11 July 1975) 7. Given the nature of her practice, Abella shows up only fleetingly as counsel in reported decisions: *Ungar v Ungar*, [1975] OJ No 1141.

46 "Time Is Only Limit" *Globe and Mail* (25 October 1976) 5.

47 Abella and Diller, above note 4 at 854.

see if she would be willing to accept appointment to the bench.[48] While some friends advised her to wait for a more prestigious judicial position, Abella jumped at the opportunity.[49] Just thirty years old and eight months pregnant when she took up the appointment in August 1976, Abella became the first female Jewish judge in Canadian history. Media coverage of Judge Abella was positive, noting the "stir of excitement in legal and court circles" caused by her selection.[50] Still, it remained an era when it was appropriate for articles to describe Abella as a "lady judge" and make note of the fact she did not cook.[51] With a more positive spin, the *Toronto Star* described her as "a symbol of what a woman can be in the 1970s."[52] Alongside her judicial work, Abella remained deeply engaged in other projects, including work at the Ontario Human Rights Commission and as a member of the Premier's Advisory Committee on Confederation. It was her judicial work as a Family Court judge, however, that Abella describes as the most challenging of her career.

"More than any other area of law, family law has a pervasive influence on the way society functions," Judge Abella wrote of her time as a judge on the Family Court.[53] While grappling with heart-wrenching decisions about the care of children in custody disputes, Abella recognized the need "to see law from the experiences of the people who were before me, not top-down."[54] "I never found, after seven years of doing it, that it was easy," she has said. "I always felt I had a particular responsibility . . . to try to bring the reality of their lives — the reality of the law — into some form of synchronization that made their lives less awful."[55] In Family Court, Judge Abella built important elements of her judicial philosophy in the crucible of experience: an ethic and a practice of what it meant to truly listen to evidence, and how to decide cases and write judgments with sensitivity to context and regard for the weight of the responsibility judges held in shaping the outcomes of people's lives.

---

48 Roy McMurtry, *Memoirs and Reflections* (Toronto: University of Toronto Press, 2013) at 185–86.

49 Abella and Diller, above note 4 at 855.

50 Helen Worthington, "Bench Welcomes Judge Abella and Baby" *Toronto Star* (20 July 1976) E2. Margaret Mironowicz, "Once a Family Court Lawyer, Judge Sees Both Sides Now" *Globe and Mail* (25 October 1976) 5.

51 "Time Is Only Limit," above note 46.

52 Anne Carey, "B'nai B'rith Honors Woman Judge" *Toronto Star* (19 November 1977) G2.

53 Rosalie Silberman Abella, "Family Law in Ontario: Changing Assumptions" (1981) 13 *Ottawa Law Review* 1 at 1.

54 Abella and Diller, above note 4 at 856.

55 Davidson, above note 3.

Other chapters in this volume delve in greater detail into Rosalie Abella's particular contributions to law and extra-judicial work in the decades that followed her time on the Family Court bench. But even in overview, the list of positions Justice Abella took on after leaving Family Court — Royal Commissioner on the Commission on Equality in Employment (1983–84), Chair of the Labour Relations Board (1984–89), Chair of the Ontario Law Reform Commission (1989–92) — is impressive in its scope and diversity, idiosyncratic in its trajectory, and novel in its career arc. One can see in these various positions evidence of the subjects that would later come to define her judicial career and jurisprudence — discrimination, especially systemic discrimination and equality rights, family law, labour law, and a belief in legal reform. But there is more to it than that. Her early legal career was a crash course in the experience of legal pluralism — a steady training in how the law was made, how it functioned, and how it worked (and often did not work) in the everyday happenings of marriages and families, workplaces and union halls, government bureaucracies and agencies. In her government work in law and policy, Abella saw that the textures of law — its norms, values, and experiences — were products of human interaction as much as commands of the state. Lawyering and judging had taught her one way of seeing law, but working outside the courtroom opened her eyes to others. The imprint and impact of that diversity of experiences remained. As she would write near the end of her career, "I see both the Courts and administrative decision-makers as equally responsible for, and capable of, interpreting the applying law within their separate and assigned legal spheres."[56]

In 1982, she began the first of several contributions to law reform that lay at the intersection of rights, discrimination, and systemic inequalities. First, she chaired and authored the *Ontario Study on Access to Legal Services by the Disabled*, a report prescient and clear-eyed in its assessment of the systemic barriers facing persons with disabilities.[57] After completing that work, Abella agreed to serve as sole commissioner of the federal Royal Commission on Equality in Employment. Appointed in the last days of Pierre Trudeau's Liberal government, Abella continued the work, but did not have high hopes for its reception after the

56 Rosalie Silberman Abella, "Canadian Administrative Law: The Case for Judicial Humility" (2020) 75:1 *Industrial Relations* at 169.

57 Ontario, *Report of the Study into Access to Legal Services by the Disabled* (Toronto: Queen's Printer, 1983). On the report's recommendations regarding legal education, see M. David Lepofsky, "Disabled Persons and Canadian Law Schools: The Right to the Equal Benefit of the Law School" (1991) 36 *McGill Law Journal* 636.

election of a new Conservative government led by Brian Mulroney in 1984. The project was audacious in its ambitions. As Carol Agócs writes, "[i]t was a complex mandate, on a shoestring budget, and in a tight time frame."[58] The mandate was to study the opportunities for employment for women, Indigenous peoples, racialized minorities, and persons with disabilities in a number of Crown corporations.[59] Given the Royal Commission's limited budget, Abella decided to function as her "own research director" and commissioned twenty-nine research reports addressing the issues before her. Perhaps more importantly, she focused on the successful and unsuccessful examples of Canadian and US jurisprudence grappling with questions of inequality. She also set off across Canada, setting up seventeen sessions to gather first-person accounts on workplace policies and procedures and the discriminatory practices surrounding them, as well as to meet with representatives of the Crown corporations and federal unions. The sessions, and the different experiences they conveyed, made a deep impact. "My opinions changed," Abella recounts, "and I learned how to listen in a different way."[60] The resulting *Report of the Commission on Equality in Employment*, released in 1984, would stand as perhaps her most influential intervention in Canadian law.

In her report, Abella provided a template for the definition of equality and discrimination as it would evolve in Canadian human rights and constitutional law alike. "Discrimination," she wrote, "means practices or attitudes that have, whether by design or impact, the effect of limiting an individual's or group's right to the opportunities generally available because of attributed rather than actual characteristics."[61] It was not intention that mattered, but rather the operation of systems in denying full and equal participation to many individuals on the basis of their identities. "Sometimes equality means treating people the same, despite their differences," Abella reasoned, and "sometimes it means treating them as equals by accommodating their differences."[62] Finding the existing legal language inadequate to the task of capturing

58 Carol Agócs, "The Making of the Abella Report: Reflections on the Thirtieth Anniversary of the Report of the Royal Commission on Equality in Employment" in Carol Agócs ed, *Employment Equity in Canada: The Legacy of the Abella Report* (Toronto: University of Toronto Press, 2014) 13 at 16.

59 Rosalie Silberman Abella, *Report of the Commission on Equality in Employment* (Ottawa: Governent of Canada, 1984) at i.

60 Agócs, above note 58 at 19.

61 *Report of the Commission on Equality in Employment*, above note 59 at 2.

62 *Ibid* at 3.

the nuance of this richer version of equality, Abella coined the phrase "employment equity." Despite negative reaction from some quarters on the report's release, Flora MacDonald, the Minister of Employment and Immigration in the Conservative government, surprised Abella by announcing that Canada would enact employment equity legislation on the basis of the report.[63] However, it was the Supreme Court of Canada's adoption of Abella's approach to equality under the *Canadian Charter of Rights and Freedoms* in *Andrews v Law Society of British Columbia* that struck her most deeply.[64] "The Supreme Court of Canada used my words and my definition of equality to strike down what had kept my father out of the practice of law," she noted. "Life is quite amazing, isn't it?"[65]

A fuller biographical account than this would be needed to do full justice to Rosalie Silberman Abella's work in labour relations, her law reform initiatives, and her frequent forays into government work through the 1980s and 90s. Nonetheless, the range of experiences Justice Abella accrued among diverse branches of the legal system is striking. What ties this otherwise unorthodox judicial career path together? Certainly a certain restlessness of spirit, a desire to be challenged, and the high opinion of her held by those making the offers all account for something. Perhaps the simplest explanation, and her own, is that she was compelled to just keep saying yes. She is fond of drawing on the aphorism of the songwriter Sammy Cahn in explaining her atypical career trajectory. When Cahn was asked, "what came first, the words or the music?" he replied, "The phone call." Abella received a number of them. And, more often than not, saying yes to those calls led her on a distinctive path that helped to forge her singular judicial temperament and philosophy.

E. Finale

Rosalie Abella's remarkable life took her from being a refugee born to Holocaust survivors in a displaced persons camp to having a seat on the Supreme Court of Canada. It is perhaps fitting that such a journey did not involve an ordinary legal career. When appointed to the Ontario Court of Appeal in 1992, she was already a national figure, although now one with vocal critics of her views on feminism and advocacy for

63 *Employment Equity Act*, SC 1986, c 31.

64 *Andrews v Law Society of British Columbia*, [1989] 1 SCR 143.

65 Abella and Diller, above note 4 at 856.

a robust judicial role in pursuing just outcomes.[66] Tempering her views in light of such critics was always unlikely. Perhaps the final unifying theme of her legal career was simply the constellation of life experiences, values, and legal philosophies that combined to form the professional identity of Rosalie Abella — an identity with the protection and promotion of human rights at its core. "I never wanted to be anybody else," she says. "I never tried to be like anybody. I couldn't. I was a Jewish woman in a white, male, mostly Christian professional environment, which was very welcoming, very accommodating. But I never tried to be one of them."[67] More to the point, Justice Abella has sometimes quoted one of author Philip Roth's characters: "I can't stop being me, that's all there is to it."[68]

In September 2019, Justice Abella gave the orientation speech to the first-year students at the University of Alberta Faculty of Law. Justice Abella has always known and appreciated the impact of a story: the particular magic words can weave when put together with the cadence and music of a voice. Justice Abella did not, as I had assumed she would, come to talk to the students about being a judge. She spoke instead about being a lawyer, about the good that law and lawyers can do in this world. In doing so, she told her story. It was the story of a life. And in that story she wove her life and her vision of law into a single powerful thread. Many in the audience began to cry. Justice Abella cried. For many of us, perhaps for all of us, Justice Abella's early legal career would have been more than enough accomplishment, of difference-making in the law. How lucky for Canada that it was the overture, and that the show was about to begin.

66 "A Judicial Balance" *Toronto Star* (24 March 1992) A18; Gerald Caplan, "Women's Battle for Justice Still Rages On" *Toronto Star* (24 May 1992) B3; David Vienneau, "Women Await PM's Choice for High Court" *Toronto Star* (19 July 1992) A2.

67 Interview with Justice Rosalie Abella, CBC Radio, *The Current* (22 June 2021): www.cbc.ca/radio/thecurrent/the-current-for-june-22-2021-1.6075053/tuesday-june-22-2021-full-transcript-1.6076213.

68 Philip Roth, "Defender of the Faith" in *Goodbye Columbus and Five Short Stories* (New York: Vintage Books, 1993), quoted in Rosalie Silberman Abella, "Law, Literature, and Identity," above note 12.

2 Les suites du Rapport Abella au regard de l'élaboration du concept de discrimination systémique en contexte d'emploi

CHARLES TREMBLAY POTVIN*

Les propos qui sont tenus à l'égard de l'égalité donnent souvent lieu à des réactions très vives. On prend fréquemment position sans réfléchir suffisamment, quel que soit le point de vue, et malgré tout on s'entête dans ses opinions, si bien qu'il devient pratiquement impossible d'avoir une discussion constructive. A la longue, les paroles elles-mêmes l'emportent sur le débat et engendrent une espèce de résistance excluant le bon sens. Dans pareils cas, il peut être utile de modifier le vocabulaire de manière à rendre le débat plus raisonnable. Il faut opposer des principes et non des émotions.

Rosalie Silberman Abella, 1984

A. Introduction : la « méthode Abella »

Un hommage à la foisonnante carrière de la juge Rosalie Silberman Abella ne saurait faire l'économie de son passage à titre de commissaire unique à la Commission royale d'enquête sur l'égalité en matière d'emploi. Le « Rapport Abella »[1], tel qu'il fut baptisé, a fait couler beaucoup d'encre depuis sa publication en 1984. Le moins qu'on puisse dire est qu'il n'a pas été accueilli dans l'indifférence. Durement critiqué au moment de sa sortie, tant par les représentants du monde des affaires

---

* Charles Tremblay Potvin est professeur à la Faculté de droit de l'Université Laval et cochercheur au Centre de recherche interuniversitaire sur la mondialisation et le travail (CRIMT). Une partie de la recherche à l'origine du présent texte a été financée par la Fondation du Barreau du Québec. L'auteur tient à remercier le doctorant Marc Zongo pour son aide précieuse dans le repérage des sources et l'analyse des documents, tout en spécifiant que les propos contenus dans le présent texte n'engagent que lui.

1 Rosalie Silberman Abella, *Rapport de la Commission sur l'égalité en matière d'emploi*, Approvisionnements et services Canada, Ottawa, 1984, 426 p.

que des groupes minoritaires[2], il aura néanmoins une influence phénoménale sur la législation, la jurisprudence et la doctrine au cours des années suivantes. Le présent texte porte sur la réception du Rapport Abella par la jurisprudence de la Cour suprême du Canada en centrant l'analyse sur le domaine de l'emploi.

L'influence du Rapport Abella sur le droit du travail a déjà fait l'objet de plusieurs analyses et commentaires[3]. Le départ de la juge Abella à titre de membre de la plus haute Cour canadienne impose toutefois une mise à jour afin d'y inclure les plus récentes décisions dont elle a elle-même rédigé les motifs et qui constitueront en quelque sorte son dernier lègue, du moins à ce prestigieux titre. Nous aborderons cette question sous l'angle du concept de « discrimination systémique », un terme qui, sans être défini précisément par la juge Abella, revient à plusieurs reprises dans le Rapport. C'est sans doute par lui que l'influence du Rapport Abella sur la jurisprudence aura été la plus marquante[4]. Or force est de constater que près de quarante ans après la Commission royale sur l'égalité en matière d'emploi, ce terme continue de susciter des débats, parfois acrimonieux, et en particulier dans la province de Québec d'où provient le soussigné.

Pour mener à bien cette analyse, il convient certainement de nous inspirer de la méthode suivie par la juge Abella elle-même dans le cadre de ses travaux à titre de commissaire, en insistant sur l'importance de discuter sur la base des principes plutôt que de se perdre dans les querelles de langage[5]. Nous commencerons donc par exposer brièvement cette méthode, laquelle a servi de modèle quant à la manière d'appréhender le phénomène de la discrimination systémique en contexte d'emploi et qui a en quelque sorte tracé la voie à suivre pour permettre sa transposition sur le plan juridique.

Cette méthode peut se résumer en quatre grandes étapes : 1) définir les concepts au cœur de la problématique ; 2) interroger et écouter les

---

2 Rosalie Silberman Abella, *Reflections on the Abella Report : 25 Years Later*, Koskie Minsky University Lecture in Labour Law, University of Western Ontario, London, 30 October 2009.

3 Notamment en 2014, à l'occasion du trentième anniversaire du Rapport : Mary Cornish, Fay Faraday et Jan Borowy, « Securing Employment Equity by Enforcing Human Rights Laws », dans Carol Agócs (dir.), *Employment Equity in Canada : The Legacy of the Abella Report*, Toronto, University of Toronto Press, 2014.

4 Sur le lègue de la juge Abella en cette matière au-delà du domaine du travail et de l'emploi, voir le texte du présent ouvrage de Joëlle Pastora Sala, « Assessing Justice Abella's Contributions to the Law of Systemic Discrimination in Canada ».

5 Comme le rappelle justement de manière éloquente la citation placée en exergue du présent texte, tirée du Rapport Abella, préc., note 1, partie I, p. 7.

membres et les représentants des groupes concernés par la discrimination en contexte d'emploi — en l'occurrence les femmes, les autochtones, les minorités visibles et les personnes en situation de handicap — mais aussi les dirigeants d'entreprise et les syndicats ; 3) identifier les écarts statistiques entre les groupes visés et le groupe majoritaire et documenter les perceptions à l'égard de ces groupes et les pratiques d'emploi qui les affectent directement ou indirectement ; 4) déterminer les mesures à prendre pour remédier à la situation.

Il convient de s'intéresser d'abord à la définition des concepts, car c'est de cet effort définitionnel que découleront logiquement les étapes subséquentes du travail de la Commission. Dans le premier chapitre de son Rapport, la juge Abella s'attarde à définir ce qu'est l'« égalité en matière d'emploi », qu'elle définit *a minima* de manière négative comme étant l'« absence de discrimination dommageable[6] ». La « discrimination » est quant à elle définie de manière large comme étant toute forme d'obstacle à l'emploi, que ce soit au niveau de l'embauche, des possibilités de promotion ou de l'exécution du travail lui-même, et qu'un tel obstacle ait été posé dans l'intention ou non de discriminer, mais qui revêt un caractère « arbitraire », c'est-à-dire qu'il n'est pas véritablement lié aux exigences réelles du poste. Dès lors, la réalisation de l'égalité en matière d'emploi passe par l'abolition de ces obstacles arbitraires, quels qu'ils soient. Or selon la juge Abella, l'approche strictement négative, laquelle consiste simplement à interdire la discrimination en établissant un processus de plaintes à traiter au cas par cas, ne suffit pas pour parvenir à l'égalité réelle. La suppression de la discrimination nécessite donc une approche proactive. Ce sont les mesures et les programmes adoptés au Canada dans le cadre d'une telle approche proactive visant à résorber la discrimination au travail que la juge Abella baptisera « équité en matière d'emploi[7] », une expression qui a laissé sa marque dans le droit canadien[8].

Cette définition du concept d'égalité en emploi, tracée ici à grands traits et sur laquelle nous reviendrons dans les sections suivantes, dicte la marche à suivre pour attaquer le problème de la discrimination : il s'agit d'identifier les obstacles arbitraires qui se dressent dans l'accès à l'emploi de ceux et celles qui en sont victimes. Pour ce faire, il faut s'en remettre à certains « indicateurs sociaux », c'est-à-dire les écarts

---

6 *Id.*, p. 1.

7 *Id.*, p. 7.

8 Comme le rappelle le titre de la principale loi adoptée pour mettre en œuvre le Rapport Abella : *Loi sur l'*équité en matière d'*emploi*, LC 1995, c 44.

statistiques observés faisant état de la sous-représentation ou la sur-représentation des membres des groupes-cibles dans plusieurs secteurs d'emploi. Ce sont précisément ces indicateurs sociaux qui amènent la juge Abella à introduire la notion de discrimination systémique dans l'analyse, car c'est la *persistance de ces disparités statistiques* malgré l'interdiction de la discrimination directe ou intentionnelle qui indique la nécessité d'adopter une perspective systémique sur le problème de la discrimination. Voilà pourquoi la juge Abella insiste sur l'importance de diriger notre attention vers les *conséquences* des systèmes et des pratiques que nous avons adoptés, parfois même à notre insu, et qui causent préjudice aux membres de certains groupes[9].

Cependant, comme nous l'avons déjà évoqué, la juge Abella ne s'attarde pas à définir précisément la notion de discrimination systémique, utilisée à plusieurs reprises dans le Rapport, de sorte qu'elle semble parfois se confondre avec d'autres concepts qui occupent une place importante dans son analyse. Tout d'abord, on peut avoir tendance à assimiler la discrimination systémique aux « indicateurs sociaux » eux-mêmes, c'est-à-dire aux écarts statistiques qui indiquent que certains groupes peuvent être considérés comme défavorisés sur le marché de l'emploi de manière persistante[10]. Ensuite, comme nous le verrons, l'étude de la jurisprudence montre qu'on tend à confondre le concept de discrimination systémique avec la notion de discrimination « indirecte ou par suite d'un effet préjudiciable », laquelle invite justement à s'attarder aux conséquences d'une pratique ou d'une norme plutôt qu'à l'intention de discriminer.

La thèse qui sera développée dans le présent texte est que le concept de discrimination systémique doit être distingué de ces deux autres notions, car la richesse de ce concept ne se laisse pas épuiser par le seul constat empirique des écarts statistiques entre les groupes, pas plus qu'il ne doit se confondre entièrement avec la discrimination indirecte. Pour le démontrer, nous reviendrons d'abord sur l'état de la jurisprudence en cette matière au commencement des travaux de la commission, afin d'analyser ensuite son influence subséquente sur la jurisprudence

9 Rapport Abella, préc., note 1, p. 9–10.

10 Pour un exemple d'une telle confusion, voir *id.*, p. 16 : « Une telle enquête, dans le contexte de l'emploi, chercherait probablement à prouver que les membres d'un groupe particulier connaissent un taux de chômage plus élevé, perçoivent des salaires plus bas et ont tendance à être confinés a des emplois jouissant d'une moins grande considération sociale. C'est ce qu'on a appelé les "indicateurs sociaux" de la discrimination en matière d'emploi. On peut également les qualifier de discrimination systémique. » [Références omises].

canadienne. Nous terminerons par quelques remarques d'ordres terminologique et pratique inspirées du Rapport, en lien avec l'état actuel du débat sur le droit à l'égalité.

B. L'état de la jurisprudence avant les travaux de la Commission

Rappelons que le mandat de la Commission royale d'enquête sur l'égalité en matière d'emploi a été établi par décret en juin 1983 par le gouvernement libéral de Pierre-Elliott Trudeau. La *Charte canadienne des droits et libertés*[11] avait été adoptée un an plus tôt, mais son article 15 relatif au droit à l'égalité n'allait entrer en vigueur qu'en 1985. Il n'existait donc aucune jurisprudence sur cette disposition au début des travaux. À l'occasion du trentième anniversaire de la Commission, la juge Abella dira que cette absence de jurisprudence a en réalité facilité son travail, puisqu'elle avait alors toute liberté pour élaborer une définition de l'égalité qui permettrait de rassembler le résultat de ses lectures et l'ensemble des voies entendues à travers le Canada durant ses travaux[12].

Il existait certes à l'époque une certaine jurisprudence sur la notion d'égalité au Canada, celle-ci provenant surtout des instances inférieures ou s'appuyait, pour ce qui est de la jurisprudence de la Cour suprême du Canada, sur la *Déclaration canadienne des droits*. Celle-ci protège le droit de tout individu à « l'égalité devant la loi[13] », formulation qui laisse peu de doute sur son caractère purement formel. La Cour suprême adoptera en effet une interprétation formaliste de cette disposition[14], consistant simplement au droit à l'égalité de traitement dans l'application des lois du Canada. Or par sa seule formulation, l'article 15 de la *Charte canadienne* entendait clairement rompre avec cette conception strictement formelle de l'égalité[15].

11 Partie I de la *Loi constitutionnelle de 1982*, annexe B de la *Loi de 1982 sur la Canada*, 1982, c. 11 (R.-U.).

12 Rosalie Silberman Abella, « Foreword », dans C. Agócs (dir.), préc., note 3, p. vii.

13 Déclaration canadienne des droits, SC 1960, c 44, al. 1*b*).

14 Voir *Procureur général du Canada c. Lavell*, [1974] RCS 1349 ; *Bliss c. Le Procureur. Général du Canada*, [1979] 1 RCS 183.

15 Le libellé de l'article 15 de la *Charte canadienne*, préc., note 11, garantit en effet non seulement le droit à l'égalité *devant* la loi (« equality before *the law* »), mais aussi *en vertu* de la loi (« *under the law* »), ainsi qu'au droit à la même *protection* et au même *bénéfice* de la loi, sans discrimination. Voir notamment à ce sujet : Beverley McLachlin, « Equality: The Most Difficult Right », (2001) 14 *Supreme Court Law Review* 17.

Pour définir le droit à l'égalité, la juge Abella décide donc de se tourner vers la jurisprudence américaine en se référant au célèbre arrêt rendu par la Cour suprême des États-Unis dans l'affaire *Griggs v. Duke Power Co.*[16]. Cette affaire constitue un cas emblématique de ce qu'on appellera la discrimination indirecte ou par effet préjudiciable. Il s'agissait en l'occurrence d'une exigence d'emploi qui, sans avoir été adoptée dans l'intention de discriminer, avait néanmoins pour effet d'exclure les candidats afro-américains de manière disproportionnée de certains postes. Selon la Cour suprême des États-Unis, si l'employeur n'arrive pas à faire la preuve que l'obstacle n'est pas arbitraire, alors il est illégal et doit être supprimé. La partie plaignante n'a donc pas à faire la preuve d'une intention de discriminer. Dès qu'une norme ou une pratique d'emploi a un effet disproportionné sur les membres d'un groupe protégé par le droit à l'égalité, il revient alors à l'employeur de faire la preuve que cette norme ou cette pratique est justifiée par les exigences du poste. On passe ainsi d'une perspective orientée vers la recherche d'un coupable à celle, retenue par la juge Abella, de l'abolition des « obstacles arbitraires » à l'emploi.

L'affaire *Griggs* permet ainsi de comprendre la conception du droit à l'égalité retenue par la juge Abella, mais aussi d'écarter la première confusion que nous avons évoquée et qui consisterait à réduire la discrimination systémique, au sens légal du terme, au seul constat des écarts statistiques entre les groupes. C'est qu'une exigence d'emploi aux effets *a priori* discriminatoires ne sera jugée illégale que si elle s'avère, après analyse, arbitraire. Autrement dit, pour reprendre les mots de la juge Abella, les écarts statistiques sont des « indicateurs », des « indices », qui doivent nous pousser à « examiner la situation de plus près pour déterminer si cette grave incidence résulte effectivement de pratiques injustes et nécessite l'adoption de mesures correctives, ou si elle découle d'une situation non discriminatoire.[17]» Nous pourrions même ajouter[18] que plus l'écart observé dans la représentation d'un groupe est important et persistant, plus forte sera la « présomption » que cet écart découle de pratiques discriminatoires

---

16 401 U.S. 424 (1971). Rapport Abella, préc., note 1, p. 9–10. Voir aussi à ce sujet David J. Garrow, « Toward a Definitive History of *Griggs v. Duke Power Co.* », (2014) 67-1 *Vand. L. Rev.* 197.

17 Rapport Abella, préc., note 1, p. 2–3.

18 Avec Muriel Garon, « Pour une approche intégrée de la discrimination systémique : convergences et contributions des sciences sociales et du droit », (1986) 17-1 *R.D.U.S.* 194, 220.

de nature systémique, donc potentiellement subtiles et difficiles à décelées, et par conséquent, plus impérieux sera le besoin d'examiner la situation de près.

Il découle de ce qui précède que le concept de discrimination systémique ne renvoie pas à l'écart statistique lui-même, mais bien à la *cause* de cet écart. La discrimination systémique, c'est ce qui peut expliquer la persistance du déficit de représentation d'un groupe, malgré l'interdiction formelle de discriminer les membres de ce groupe. C'est d'ailleurs ici que se trouve la raison pour laquelle la juge Abella a décidé de rejeter les politiques de quotas dans ses recommandations. Cette orientation a été critiquée par les représentants des groupes-cibles, mais force est d'admettre qu'elle découle logiquement de la définition de la discrimination qui ressort du Rapport, car c'est en réduisant le phénomène de la discrimination systémique à l'existence même des disparités statistiques qu'une politique de quotas aurait pu se justifier. Voilà pourquoi la juge Abella optera plutôt pour des programmes d'équité qui oblige les employeurs à revoir leurs pratiques d'emploi pour s'assurer que celles-ci ne sont pas discriminatoires. Cela dit, elle n'écarte pas complètement la possibilité de recourir à des quotas, ceux-ci pouvant selon elle se justifier en certaines circonstances[19]. On peut penser, par exemple, au cas d'un employeur récalcitrant qui refuserait de mettre en œuvre certaines mesures correctives.

Cela nous amène à la deuxième confusion que nous avons évoquée précédemment. Si le concept de discrimination systémique réfère aux causes des disparités statistiques et que ces causes incluent notamment tout obstacle arbitraire à l'emploi, alors qu'est-ce qui le distingue de celui de discrimination indirecte ? Pour le dire autrement, la discrimination systémique n'est-elle rien d'autre que la somme des effets d'exclusion de la discrimination directe et indirecte[20] ? L'analyse de la jurisprudence de la Cour suprême du Canada subséquente au Rapport Abella permet d'apporter une réponse à cette question.

---

19 Rapport Abella, préc., note 1, partie II, p. 235.

20 Faisant ainsi écho à la définition élaborée par le Tribunal des droits de la personne du Québec, puis reprise par la Cour d'appel, dans l'affaire *Gaz Métro* : *Commission des droits de la personne et des droits de la jeunesse (Beaudoin et autres) c. Gaz Métropolitain inc.*, 2008 QCTDP 24, par. 36 ; *Gaz Métropolitain inc. c. Commission des droits de la personne et des droits de la jeunesse*, 2011 QCCA 1201, par. 47.

C. L'influence du Rapport Abella sur la jurisprudence canadienne

Le concept de discrimination systémique n'est pas défini expressément dans le Rapport Abella, mais on peut l'extraire à partir d'une lecture d'ensemble et une attention portée à la méthode suivie par la commissaire. C'est précisément ce qui ressort de l'affaire *Action travail des femmes* qui a donné lieu à une décision de la Cour suprême du Canada en 1987[21].

La première chose qu'on constate à la lecture de cette décision, c'est que la preuve déposée et analysée par la Cour a toutes les caractéristiques de la méthode suivie par la juge Abella dans le cadre des travaux de la Commission. Rappelons que cette affaire portait sur une allégation de discrimination systémique envers les femmes au sein de la Compagnie des chemins de fer nationaux du Canada (CN). Les éléments de preuve à l'appui de cette allégation comprennent notamment des statistiques faisant état d'une nette sous-représentation des femmes dans l'entreprise. Des rapports détaillés et les témoignages provenant de plusieurs intervenants, dont celui des femmes concernées, fait aussi état de plusieurs pratiques d'emploi directement ou indirectement discriminatoires en vigueur dans l'entreprise, mais il y a plus. On constate la présence de nombreux stéréotypes négatifs à l'égard des femmes tant du côté des dirigeants de l'entreprise que des collègues masculins en général. En d'autres mots, la preuve démontre l'existence d'une culture hostile à l'endroit des femmes, laquelle a aussi un effet psychologique sur les femmes elles-mêmes qui ressentent cette hostilité et qui craignent constamment de subir ses effets négatifs.

Sur la base de cette preuve, tant le tribunal de première instance que la Cour suprême ont reconnu la présence de discrimination systémique au CN. La Cour se réfère alors directement au Rapport Abella, qu'elle voit comme étant « une étude exhaustive de la "discrimination systémique" au Canada[22] » et duquel on peut extraire la définition de ce concept, bien que la juge Abella n'en ait pas donné une définition précise, écrit le juge en chef Dickson au nom d'une Cour unanime. C'est toutefois lorsque vient le temps de statuer sur la réparation appropriée dans un tel contexte que la Cour nous semble mettre le doit sur ce qui caractérise véritablement le concept de discrimination systémique par rapport aux notions de discrimination directe et indirecte.

21 *CN c. Canada (Commission canadienne des droits de la personne)*, [1987] 1 RCS 1114.
22 *Id.*, 1138.

La Cour suprême conclut que pour « combattre la discrimination systémique, il est essentiel de créer un climat dans lequel tant les pratiques que les attitudes négatives peuvent être contestées et découragées[23] ». Par conséquent, elle confirme le pouvoir du Tribunal canadien des droits de la personne d'émettre, dans de telles circonstances, des ordonnances de type systémique, lesquelles comprennent en l'occurrence l'obligation pour le CN de respecter un quota d'embauche jusqu'à l'atteinte d'un seuil de femmes jugé acceptable. Ces mesures sont justifiées, nous dit la Cour, et c'est précisément là que se situe à notre avis l'élément central du concept, afin de « rompre le *cercle vicieux* de la discrimination[24] ». La Cour renvoie ici à l'idée centrale de la perspective systémique dans les sciences en général et les sciences sociales en particulier, soit l'idée de *récursivité,* ou *boucles récursives,* c'est-à-dire l'idée que le système produit des effets qui se retournent pour alimenter ses propres causes[25]. Les ordonnances de nature systémique remplissent alors une fonction réparatrice, parce qu'elles permettent aux femmes d'accéder aux postes qui leur ont été refusés, mais aussi une fonction préventive, parce qu'une plus grande proportion de femmes devrait contribuer à modifier la culture de l'entreprise dans l'avenir et à briser ainsi ce phénomène de causalité circulaire.

On constate ainsi que le concept de discrimination systémique ajoute quelque chose aux notions plus restreintes de discrimination directe et indirecte. Cet élément additionnel apparaît nettement dans le cas du CN, car la preuve va au-delà de l'addition des éléments de discrimination directe ou indirecte pris isolément, par exemple un cas de harcèlement sexuel envers une employée ou une pratique d'embauche ayant un effet d'exclusion disproportionné à l'égard des femmes. Par-delà ces éléments qui font indéniablement partie du tableau, nous constatons l'existence d'une « culture institutionnelle d'exclusion »[26] prenant la forme d'un « cercle vicieux » : parce que les femmes sont minoritaires ou ont été historiquement exclues de l'entreprise, elles sont mal perçues par les dirigeants et les collègues masculins, mais parce qu'elles sont ainsi perçues, elles rencontrent davantage d'obstacles lorsque vient le

---

23 *Id.*, 1139, référant aux pages 9 et 10 du Rapport Abella, préc., note 1.

24 *Id.*, 1143 (nos italiques).

25 Voir à ce sujet Charles Tremblay Potvin et Ugo Gilbert Tremblay, « Juridicité, normativité et scientificité du concept de discrimination systémique », (2023) 52-2 *Revue de droit de l'Université de Sherbrooke* 311.

26 Pour paraphraser l'expression développée ultérieurement par le Tribunal des droits de la personne du Québec : *Commission des droits de la personne et des droits de la jeunesse (Beaudoin et autres) c. Gaz* Métropolitain inc., préc., note 20.

temps de prendre la place qui leur revient, et finalement, ces difficultés elles-mêmes contribuent à alimenter la perception négative des autres membres de l'entreprise à leur endroit.

Ce concept de discrimination systémique élaboré à partir du Rapport Abella aura une postérité notable dans la jurisprudence de la Cour suprême du Canada. Il est cité à nouveau dans l'important arrêt *Andrews*[27] deux ans plus tard et la Cour se référera directement ou plus accessoirement au Rapport Abella à plusieurs reprises dans les années subséquentes[28]. Cela dit, dans ces décisions, le concept de discrimination systémique est utilisé en appui à l'argumentaire des juges dans des cas relevant plutôt de la discrimination directe ou indirecte. Les cas où on a établi l'existence de la discrimination systémique au sein d'une organisation, comme dans l'affaire *Action travail des femmes*, demeurent plutôt rares dans la jurisprudence[29], ce qui fera dire à certains que les espoirs suscités par cette décision n'ont pas été satisfaits[30]. Autrement dit, les juges font plus souvent référence à la discrimination systémique à des fins argumentatives que pour justifier l'émission d'ordonnances de nature systémique[31].

---

27 *Andrews c. Law Society of British Columbia*, [1989] 1 RCS 143.

28 Voir notamment *Forget c. Québec (Procureur général)*, [1988] 2 RCS 90 ; *Janzen c. Platy Enterprises Ltd.*, [1989] 1 R.C.S. 1252 ; *Brooks c. Canada Safeway Ltd.*, [1989] 1 R.C.S. 1219 ; *Syndicat des employés de production du Québec et de l'Acadie c. Canada (Commission canadienne des droits de la personne)*, [1989] 2 RCS 879 (j. L'Heureux-Dubé, dissidente) ; *Mckinney c. Université de Guelph*, [1990] 3 RCS 229 (j. Le Dain, dissident) ; *Symes c. Canada*, [1993] 4 RCS 695 ; *Egan c. Canada*, [1995] 2 RCS 513 (j. McLachlin, dissidente) ; *Québec (Commission des droits de la personne et des droits de la jeunesse) c. Montréal (Ville); Québec (Commission des droits de la personne et des droits de la jeunesse) c. Boisbriand (Ville)*, 2000 CSC 27, [2000] 1 RCS 665 ; *Terre-Neuve (Conseil du Trésor) c. N.A.P.E.*, 2004 CSC 66, [2004] 3 RCS 381.

29 Voir par exemple *Alliance de la capitale nationale sur les relations inter-raciales c. Canada (Ministère de la santé et du bien-être social)*, 1997 CanLII 1433 (TCDP) ; *Perera c. Canada*, 1998 CanLII 9051 (CAF), [1998] 3 CF 381 ; ainsi que l'affaire *Gaz Métro*, préc., note 20. Voir aussi Béatrice Vizkelety, « Les développements jurisprudentiels relatifs à l'"égalité réelle" en emploi : maintenant aux employeurs d'agir », dans Service de la formation continue du Barreau du Québec, vol. 405, *Le Tribunal des droits de la personne : 25 ans d'expérience en matière d'égalité*, Montréal, Éditions Yvon Blais, 2015, p. 43, aux pages 68–73 ; ainsi que le texte de J. Pastora Sala, préc., note 4.

30 Dianne Pothier, « Adjudicating Systemic Equality Issues: The Unfulfilled Promise of Action Travail des Femmes » (2014) 18 *Canadian Labour and Employment Law Journal* 177.

31 Dans un jugement signé par la juge Abella elle-même, la Cour suprême a statué que l'émission de ce type d'ordonnances nécessite une preuve spécifique de discrimination systémique, laquelle n'est pas forcément évidente à produire : *Moore c. Colombie-Britannique (Éducation)*, 2012 CSC 61, [2012] 3 RCS 360. En l'absence d'une telle preuve, le tribunal doit donc en rester aux réparations ordinairement

Un bon exemple de cet usage argumentatif du concept de discrimination systémique se trouve dans la décision rendue par la Cour suprême dans le cadre de l'affaire *Meiorin* en 1999[32]. Il s'agit typiquement d'un cas de discrimination indirecte ou par suite d'un effet préjudiciable, soit une norme d'embauche ayant des effets d'exclusion disproportionnés envers les femmes sans être justifiée par les exigences du poste. La Cour a statué que dans un tel cas où l'employeur n'a pas été en mesure de faire la preuve de la justification de la norme, celle-ci doit être abolie. Il ne suffit pas d'imposer à l'employeur une obligation d'accommodement raisonnable tout en laissant la norme discriminatoire en place. Une telle approche, nous dit la Cour, permet de mieux lutter contre le phénomène de la discrimination systémique, mais la réparation susceptible d'être obtenue en présence d'une telle discrimination indirecte se limite à l'abolition de la norme discriminatoire, sans s'étendre à l'obligation d'adopter un programme d'équité en emploi ou des quotas d'embauche par exemple[33]. Évidemment, l'abolition d'une norme discriminatoire aura tout de même des effets systémiques, justement pour les raisons évoquées par la Cour dans *Meiorin*, mais cette décision confirme que les concepts de discrimination directe, indirecte et systémique, bien qu'étant inexorablement liés, demeurent des concepts distincts. Pour le dire autrement, le fait d'abolir une norme a des effets au-delà du cas d'espèce et permet ainsi de lutter contre la discrimination systémique, mais il s'agit néanmoins d'une mesure *réactive*, laquelle n'équivaut pas à l'obligation d'adopter des mesures *proactives* comme une politique antidiscriminatoire ou un programme d'équité en emploi.

En 2004, la juge Abella a été nommée à la Cour suprême du Canada, lui permettant ainsi d'occuper une place de premier plan dans l'évolution du droit à l'égalité au Canada. Rédigeant un jugement unanime avec la juge en chef McLachlin dans l'arrêt *Kapp* en 2008[34], elle adopte une interprétation large du paragraphe 15(2) de la *Charte canadienne*, favorisant ainsi l'adoption de programmes de lutte contre les inégalités par le législateur et les gouvernements. Cette décision avalise l'importance des mesures proactives de lutte contre la discrimination, allant ainsi

---

accordées en matière de droit à l'égalité : la cessation de la discrimination, l'abolition de la norme discriminatoire, le versement de dommages-intérêts, etc. Voir le texte de J. Pastora Sala, préc., note 4, pour une critique de cet arrêt.

32 *Colombie-Britannique (Public Service Employee Relations Commission) c. BCGSEU*, [1999] 3 RCS 3.

33 Voir *Moore c. Colombie-Britannique (Éducation)*, préc., note 31.

34 *R. c. Kapp*, [2008] 2 RCS 483.

dans la droite ligne des conclusions du Rapport. En 2013, dans l'affaire *Québec c. A*, la juge Abella marqua plutôt sa dissidence dans des motifs s'inscrivant directement dans la suite des réflexions amorcées dans son Rapport[35], même si le sujet se rapportait plutôt aux droits des conjoints de fait au Québec. Trois décisions récentes lui ont toutefois permis de revenir sur la question plus spécifique du droit à l'égalité en contexte d'emploi.

Dans les deux premières décisions, rendues en 2018[36], la Cour suprême s'est penchée sur la constitutionnalité de la *Loi sur l'équité salariale* du Québec qui énonce expressément, à son article premier, qu'elle a pour objet « de corriger les écarts salariaux dus à la discrimination systémique fondée sur le sexe[37] ». Cette loi fait ainsi directement écho au Rapport Abella qui contient une importante section sur les manières de corriger ces écarts dans la rémunération[38]. Néanmoins, écrivant au nom de la majorité, la juge Abella conclura que certains aspects de ce programme sont contraires au droit à l'égalité parce qu'ils ont pour effet de perpétuer le désavantage salarial subi par les femmes[39].

La dernière décision, rendue dans l'affaire *Fraser* en 2020[40], présente pour sa part un cas particulier de discrimination indirecte. La GRC a adopté un programme de partage de poste permettant le travail à temps partiel afin de faciliter la conciliation des obligations professionnelles et familiales, notamment à la faveur des femmes en retour d'un congé de maternité. Ce programme ne permettait toutefois pas le rachat des périodes de service à temps plein ouvrant droit à la pension de retraite, contrairement à la norme établie au sein de la GRC dans d'autres contextes. Cet élément du programme a été jugé contraire au droit à l'égalité par la majorité de la Cour, s'exprimant sous la plume de la juge Abella, à cause de ses effets préjudiciables disproportionnés à l'endroit des femmes.

Ainsi, dans ces deux cas, même si le programme avait pour objet ou pour effet de s'attaquer à la discrimination systémique à l'endroit

---

35 *Québec (Procureur général) c. A*, 2013 CSC 5, [2013] 1 RCS 61, par. 283 et suiv., voir notamment les par. 328 et 332 : « Les actes de l'État qui ont pour effet d'élargir, au lieu de rétrécir, l'écart entre le groupe historiquement défavorisé et le reste de la société sont discriminatoires. »

36 *Québec (Procureure générale) c. Alliance du personnel professionnel et technique de la santé et des services sociaux*, 2018 CSC 17, [2018] 1 RCS 464 ; *Centrale des syndicats du Québec c. Québec (Procureure générale)*, 2018 CSC 18, [2018] 1 RCS 522.

37 *Loi sur l'*équité salariale, LRQ c E-12.001, art. 1.

38 Rapport Abella, préc., note 1, partie II, p. 257 et suiv.

39 Position qui rappelle justement la dissidence de la juge Abella dans l'affaire *Québec c. A., supra*, note 35.

40 *Fraser c. Canada (Procureur général)*, 2020 CSC 28.

des femmes, une mesure particulière a été jugée inconstitutionnelle au motif qu'elle avait pour effet de perpétuer, plutôt que d'éliminer, l'écart constaté et le désavantage historique auquel on voulait remédier. La méthode adoptée par la Cour, en particulier dans l'arrêt *Fraser*, rappelle celle qui a été suivie par la juge Abella dans son Rapport. La Cour affirme notamment que la discrimination par suite d'un effet préjudiciable peut être démontrée tant par des éléments de preuve qui se rapportent à la situation du groupe auquel appartiennent les demandeurs que par des preuves statistiques faisant état des effets de la mesure contestée à l'égard de ce groupe. La preuve que les effets d'une norme ou d'une mesure consistent en une exclusion ou une différenciation persistante et désavantageuse à l'égard du groupe de demandeurs permet de conclure à l'existence d'une discrimination illicite, à moins que le défendeur puisse démontrer que la mesure n'est pas arbitraire. Il ne revient pas au demandeur de faire la preuve du caractère non arbitraire de la mesure. En statuant de la sorte, la Cour suprême du Canada continue de suivre l'approche adoptée par la Cour suprême des États-Unis dans l'affaire *Griggs v. Duke Power Co.*

La « méthode Abella » s'avère ainsi l'un des principaux lègues du rapport de la Commission sur l'égalité en matière d'emploi, qui nous invite à adopter une approche intégrée de la discrimination, tenant compte à la fois des caractéristiques et de l'expérience des groupes concernés que des normes et des pratiques d'emploi, des perceptions, ainsi que du contexte social général dans lequel elles s'inscrivent. Cette approche intégrée ne doit toutefois pas faire oublier l'apport du concept de discrimination systémique qui ne se laisse pas saisir par les seules notions de discrimination directe et indirecte. Cet apport additionnel de l'approche systémique permet d'appréhender la nature récursive du phénomène, laquelle est susceptible d'expliquer la persistance des inégalités malgré l'interdiction formelle de discriminer.

D. Conclusion : quelques considérations d'ordres terminologique et pratique

Il ne fait aucun doute que le Rapport Abella a laissé une marque profonde et durable en droit canadien. S'agissant de souligner cette influence exceptionnelle, il convient toutefois de conclure cet hommage sur une note prospective, car au-delà des précédents établis sous le signe du travail de la juge Abella qui continueront de fournir un éclairage à l'évolution future du droit, le Rapport lui-même n'a certainement pas épuisé son potentiel de luminosité. C'est du moins ce que peut illustrer le cas du Québec, où les débats font rage entre les porte-étendards de la lutte contre la discrimination et ceux qui refusent de reconnaître l'existence du « racisme systémique », incluant le gouvernement du Québec qui n'est pas le seul à faire preuve d'une telle réticence, tout en s'engageant à lutter contre le racisme et la discrimination.

Comme le mentionnait déjà la juge Abella en 1984, la lutte contre la discrimination a connu un tournant majeur lorsqu'elle a cessé de prendre la forme d'une recherche de « coupables ». À l'interdiction de la discrimination intentionnelle s'est ainsi substituée la volonté d'abolir tous les obstacles arbitraires dans l'accès à l'emploi des groupes minoritaires, que ces obstacles aient été adoptés ou non avec l'intention de discriminer. La discrimination se résume donc simplement au fait d'exclure indument certains groupes, sans égard à la culpabilité morale de l'auteur de la discrimination. Cependant, dans le langage courant, le terme de « racisme » continue de porter une lourde connotation de culpabilité morale, et ce, malgré les tentatives d'en élargir la signification[41]. C'est là sans doute que se trouve l'explication des réticences devant l'idée d'un racisme qui serait de nature systémique. En ce sens, si le terme de « racisme systémique » ne semble pas ajouter quoique ce soit au concept de « discrimination raciale systémique » sur le plan normatif, on peut toujours distinguer les termes de « racisme » et de « discrimination » sur le plan sémantique.

La juge Abella a rencontré le même genre de problème durant les travaux de la Commission à l'égard du terme « action positive », largement répandu aux États-Unis. Elle a finalement décidé de rejeter ce terme pour lui préférer celui d'« équité en matière d'emploi »[42]. Or les raisons qui ont motivé ce choix paraissent encore d'une criante actualité aujourd'hui, du moins au Québec, et c'est tout le sens de la citation que nous avons placé en exergue du présent texte. La juge Abella constate d'abord que le terme « action positive » renvoie parfois à l'idée de quotas dont elle n'a pas recommandé l'implantation au Canada, ce qui peut donc expliquer son choix au premier chef, mais elle constate également que même lorsque ce terme renvoie exactement au même concept que celui d'équité en emploi, elle rencontre des réticences chez plusieurs personnes qui s'effacent naturellement si elle y substitue un terme plus neutre ou moins péjorativement connoté. Plutôt que d'insister sur les questions de vocabulaire, elle choisit alors de centrer son argumentation sur la question des principes. Nous ne pourrons sans doute jamais

41 Voir par exemple Robin DiAngelo, *White Fragility : Why It's So Hard for White People to Talk About Racism*, Beacon Press, Boston, 2018.

42 Rapport Abella, préc., note 1, p. 6–8.

établir avec précision l'impact qu'a pu avoir ce choix pragmatique sur l'influence exceptionnelle de son travail, mais il est permis de penser que cet impact a été majeur. C'est là à tout le moins un élément important de la « méthode Abella » qui mériterait à notre avis de faire l'objet d'une sérieuse réflexion chez tous ceux qui sont engagés dans la lutte contre la discrimination.

3 Assessing Justice Abella's Contributions to the Law of Systemic Discrimination in Canada

JOËLLE PASTORA SALA

A. Introduction

Systemic discrimination is often relied upon in human rights and equality law, but its definition and application produce confusion. Only two Canadian human rights Acts explicitly define "systemic discrimination."[1] In most cases, the systemic discrimination analysis relies on inconsistent jurisprudence.

As a human rights practitioner, I have observed the ways a lack of consistency relating to systemic discrimination can be weaponized by government respondents against complainants and how it is used by decision makers to avoid addressing systemic elements of complaints or to avoid ordering systemic remedies. These inconsistencies cause confusion for litigants and practitioners alike. This paper proposes a framework for approaching systemic discrimination, drawing on Justice Rosalie Silberman Abella's work.

In Part I, I describe Justice Abella's influence on the law of systemic discrimination, including her *Report of the Commission on Equality in Employment* (the Abella Report), her decision in *Moore v British Columbia (Education)* on the systemic discrimination analysis, and her decision *Fraser v Canada (Attorney General)*.[2] The Abella Report is the starting point for discussions in Canadian law about systemic discrimination. The *Moore* decision continues to influence discrimination cases as it outlines the current *prima facie* test for discrimination. And the influences of both the Abella Report and *Moore* are seen in the *Fraser* decision.

1 *The Human Rights Code*, CCSM, c H175, s 9(3); *Human Rights Act*, RSY 2002, c 116, s 12.

2 Rosalie Silberman Abella, *Report of the Commission on Equality in Employment*, Supply and Services Canada, Ottawa, 1984 [Abella Report]; *Moore v British Columbia (Education)*, 2012 SCC 61 [*Moore*]; *Fraser v Canada (Attorney General)*, 2020 SCC 28 [*Fraser*].

In Part II, I examine *MacLean v Nova Scotia*[3] as a case study in which the Nova Scotia Human Rights Commission Board of Inquiry relied on problematic elements of *Moore* to avoid ordering systemic remedies.

In Part III, I use *Caring Society v Canada*[4] to highlight three guiding principles for systemic discrimination cases. First, neither an express allegation nor a finding of systemic discrimination should be required for systemic remedies to be ordered. Second, the focus of the analysis should always be the source of discrimination and its impact on a protected group. Third, decision-makers should not be required to hear from numerous victims to order systemic remedies. *Caring Society* is a clear example that takes the "good" and leaves the "bad" from Justice Abella's influence on systemic discrimination.

Drawing on Justice Abella's contributions, I conclude by defining systemic discrimination as occurring when policies, practices, and attitudes create barriers to inclusion for members of a protected class. When the discrimination is systemic in nature, systemic remedies are necessary to prevent the same type of discrimination from reoccurring.

B. Part I: Justice Abella's Contribution to the Law of Systemic Discrimination

Today, the starting point for cases involving systemic discrimination is the Abella Report.[5] The report was prepared at a time when women were entering the workforce at a higher rate.[6] Its mandate was to "inquire into the . . . means of promoting employment opportunities, eliminating systemic discrimination and assisting all individuals to compete for employment opportunities on an equal basis."[7] The Abella Report focused on substantive equality within the context of employment and considered what it meant to be discriminated against.[8] Justice Abella introduced "systemic discrimination" as:

3 *MacLean v Nova Scotia (Attorney General)*, (4 March 2019), 1414-0, Nova Scotia Human Rights Commission Board of Inquiry [*Maclean*].

4 *First Nations Child and Family Caring Society et al v Attorney General of Canada (for the Minister of Indian and Northern Affairs Canada)*, 2016 CHRT 2 [*Caring Society*].

5 See, for example, *Fraser*, above note 2; *CN v Canada (Canadian Human Rights Commission)* [1987] 1 SCR 1114, 40 DLR (4th) 193 [*CN*]; *Quebec (Attorney General) v Alliance du personnel professionnel et technique de la sante et des services sociaux*, 2018 SCC 17 [*Alliance*]; see also cases at note 11.

6 Abella Report, above note 2 at i.

7 *Ibid* at ii. See i–iv for full terms of reference.

8 *Ibid* at 2–5.

> practices or attitudes that have, whether by design or impact, the effect of limiting an individual's or a group's right to the opportunities generally available because of attributed rather than actual characteristics . . . It is not a question of whether this discrimination is motivated by an intentional desire to obstruct someone's potential . . . If the barrier is affecting certain groups in a disproportionately negative way, it is a signal that the practices that lead to this adverse impact may be discriminatory. This is why it is important to look at the results of a system.[9]

This description of systemic discrimination includes three essential elements, which remain instructive today.[10]

First, there should be no distinction between the analysis of an *individual* and a *systemic* discrimination claim. The focus must always be on the *source and results* of the discrimination. In making this assertion, Justice Abella cautioned against creating different legal tests or evidentiary burdens for *individual* and *systemic* discrimination. Second, an intention to discriminate is not necessary for a finding of discrimination.[11] And third, systemic *remedies* are essential to abolish discriminatory practices, attitudes, and systems.[12]

Justice Abella's articulation of systemic discrimination was later adopted by the Supreme Court of Canada in 1987 in the *CN* decision — an employment discrimination case.[13] Relying on the Abella Report, the Court focused on the Canadian National Railway's operations and procedures, which created barriers to inclusion for women in the workforce.[14] The Court found that these employment policies and practices reinforced negative attitudes and stereotypes about the ability of women to do their work.[15] The Court upheld the creation of an employment equity program to ameliorate the circumstances of female CN employees.[16]

Importantly, the *CN* decision addressed the role of systemic remedies by stating that "in attempting to combat systemic discrimination, it is essential to look to the past patterns of discrimination to prevent the

9 *Ibid* at 2.
10 *CN*, above note 5 at 1138–39.
11 Abella Report, above note 2 at 8; *CN*, above note 5 at 1137–38.
12 Gwen Brodsky et al, "The Authority of Human Rights Tribunals to Grant Systemic Remedies" (2017) 6:1 *Canadian Journal of Human Rights* at 13 [Brodsky et al], citing *CN*, above note 5 at 1145.
13 *CN*, above note 5 at 1139–40.
14 *Ibid* at 1138–39.
15 *Ibid*.
16 *Ibid* at 1145.

same type of discrimination in the future."[17] Put simply, remedies must attack the root causes of discrimination. Failing to do so risks perpetuating discrimination.

The *Moore v British Columbia (Education)* decision was Justice Abella's first contribution as a justice of the Supreme Court to the law of systemic discrimination.[18] The case originated as a human rights complaint by Frederick Moore against the School District and the British Columbia Ministry of Education alleging that his son Jeffrey had been discriminated against in the provision of education services based on his disability.[19] Notwithstanding Justice Abella's previous clarity on systemic discrimination, the *Moore* decision sends mixed messages and continues to be weaponized by respondents to justify discrimination.

On the one hand, *Moore* is known for establishing the current *prima facie* discrimination test.[20] In establishing this test, Justice Abella writing for the majority confirmed the Supreme Court's 1999 decision in *Meiorin*, which rejected different remedial approaches for direct versus adverse impact (or indirect) discrimination.[21] Within this context, she warned against approaching the discrimination analysis in a binary way:

> [t]he inquiry is into whether there is discrimination, period. The question in every case is the same: does the practice result in the claimant suffering arbitrary — or unjustified — barriers on the basis of his or her membership in a protected group. Where it does, discrimination will be established.[22]

On the other hand, *Moore* has been described as a "missed opportunity."[23] It espoused unduly restrictive views on the overall application and

17 *Ibid*.

18 *Moore*, above note 2.

19 *Ibid* at paras 1–2.

20 *Ibid* at para 33. The two-stage approach to the discrimination analysis dates back to the 1980s (see *Ontario Human Rights Commission v Etobicoke*, [1982] 1 SCR 202), but since *Moore*, cases have relied upon it as the current *prima facie* test. See, for example, *Stewart v Elk Valley Coal Corp*, 2017 SCC 30; *Bangloy v Canada (Attorney General)*, 2021 FCA 245; *Davidson v Canada (Attorney General)*, 2021 FCA 226.

21 *Moore*, above note 2 at para 61; *British Columbia (Public Service Employee Relations Commission) v BCGEU*, [1999] 3 SCR 3, 176 DLR (4th) [*Meiorin*]. *Meiorin* defines adverse effect discrimination as "where the facially neutral standard discriminates in effect" (at para 19).

22 *Meiorin*, above note 21 at para 60.

23 Brodsky et al, above note 12 at 35.

remedial approach to systemic discrimination. The overall impacts of *Moore* are not consistent with Justice Abella's own direction and warnings about systemic discrimination.

The Court determined that Jeffrey's original complaint was not systemic in nature and so systemic remedies were not appropriate.[24] The Court relied on the concept that a "remedy must flow from the claim" to arrive at this conclusion.[25] In practice, the analysis ignored that Jeffrey was an illustrative example of someone failed by the education system;[26] that at the root of the discrimination were the government and school board policies and practices; and that systemic remedies were required to prevent future discrimination.[27] As stated by Dianne Pothier, "the complaint pertained to the inadequacies of the public school system for any and all students like Jeffrey . . . what more would have been needed to lay the foundation for systemic remedies?"[28]

Moore has since been used by respondents as an invitation to narrow human rights complaints from systemic to individual claims.[29] It has also been relied on by respondents to argue that human rights complaints must be treated as pleadings — that is, if a specific program or service is not listed in a complaint, it is not within its scope.[30] This is contrary to caselaw confirming that complaints do not need to particularize every adverse impact or remedy sought.[31]

---

24 *Moore*, above note 2 at para 57.

25 *Ibid* at para 64.

26 Dianne Pothier, "Adjudicating Systemic Equality Issues: The Unfulfilled Promise of Action Travail des Femmes" (2014) 18 *Canadian Labour and Employment Law Journal* 177 at 199.

27 *Moore*, above note 2 at paras 37–40.

28 Pothier, above note 26 at 199.

29 While unsuccessful, see, for example, *Desmarais v Correctional Service of Canada*, 2014 CHRT 5 at paras 33–36, 42, 43, 82, 93 & 94; *Richards v Correctional Service of Canada*, 2020 CHRT 27 at paras 48–49.

30 *Sumner-Pruden v Government of Manitoba*, Manitoba Human Rights Adjudication Panel (17 August 2020) at para 26, online: www.manitobahumanrights.ca/decisions/pdf/2020/decisionsumnerpruden.pdf.

31 See, for example, *Pollock v Winnipeg Condominium Corp No 30*, Manitoba Human Rights Board of Adjudication (12 October 2011) at 66, online: www.manitobahumanrights.ca/v1/decisions/pubs/2011/2011-mhrbad-no-1-pollock-et-al-v-wpg-condo-corp-30.pdf; *Damianakos v University of Manitoba*, (10 March 2015), Manitoba Human Rights Adjudication Panel at paras 32 –35, online: www.manitobahumanrights.ca/v1/decisions/pubs/2015/2015-mbhr-1-damianakos-v-the-university-of-manitoba.pdf.

In the wake of *Moore*, academics have raised concerns that access to systemic remedies, even in the face of discrimination, may be constrained.[32]

The *Moore* decision stands in stark contrast to Justice Abella's later decision in *Fraser v Canada (Attorney General)*.[33] In *Fraser*, Justice Abella found that a job-sharing arrangement that created pension reductions for three women who retired from the RCMP violated section 15(1) of the *Charter* as it had disproportionate negative impacts on women.[34] *Fraser* is perhaps most instructive as it expands on previous jurisprudence[35] by clarifying the section 15 analysis, particularly what is meant by "disproportionate impact."[36] Of direct relevance to systemic discrimination, Justice Abella again reminds us to prioritize the *actual impacts* of the law and "persistent systemic disadvantage [that limits] opportunities available [to claimant groups]."[37] The systemic nature of the discrimination in *Fraser* was highlighted and systemic remedies were ordered.[38]

C. Part II: Existing Misunderstandings About Systemic Discrimination

The case *Disability Rights Coalition v Nova Scotia (Attorney General)* at the Nova Scotia Court of Appeal offers a cautionary tale. It provides a concrete example of how *Moore*'s legacy lives on within governments' responses to allegations of discrimination. In my role as counsel to

32 Joanna Birenbaum & Kelly Galagher-Mackay, "From Equal Access to Individual Exit: The Invisibility of Systemic Discrimination in *Moore*," (2013) 10 *Journal of Law and Equality* 93 at 107–8; Shelagh Day, "*Moore*: The Bad News" (2013) 14:1 *Human Rights Digest* 9 at 9; Gwen Brodsky, "*Moore v British Columbia*: Supreme Court of Canada Keeps the Duty to Accommodate Strong" (2013) 10 *Journal of Law and Equality* 85 at 85; Mona Paré, "Refining the Test for Discrimination in the Context of Special Education: *Moore v British Columbia*," (2013) 10 *Journal of Law and Equality* 71 at 79.

33 *Fraser*, above note 2.

34 *Ibid* at para 5.

35 See, for example, *Kahkewistahaw First Nation v Taypotat*, 2015 SCC 30 at paras 21, 24, 26, and 34.

36 *Fraser*, above note 2 at paras 55–56 and 63.

37 *Ibid* at paras 42 and 116.

38 *Ibid* at para 138. *Fraser* has been criticized, however, for its interchangeable use of the terms "systemic discrimination" and "adverse effects discrimination." *Ibid* at paras 29 and 36. In Chapter 2 of this volume, Charles Tremblay Potvin describes the differences between the two. While systemic discrimination includes both direct and adverse effects (indirect) discrimination, adverse effects discrimination is always systemic. See Colleen Sheppard, "Institutional Inequality and the Dynamics of Courage" (2013) 31 *Windsor Yearbook of Access to Justice* 103 at 105.

the Council of Canadians with Disabilities (the CCD) and Inclusion Canada,[39] I witnessed how *Moore* encourages individualized approaches while the root causes of discrimination remain unaddressed.

The case originated in human rights complaints filed by individuals and the Disability Rights Coalition (the DRC).[40] The complaints alleged that persons with disabilities receiving social assistance were denied the supports necessary to live in community. Consequently, they were institutionalized regardless of their actual mental health and medical needs. Changes by Nova Scotia in the 1990s led to a moratorium on small option homes and increased the backlog of persons waiting for community living options with appropriate supports.[41] As a result, persons with disabilities were confined in institutions against medical advice, including in locked facilities with very little control over their lives and limited access to community.[42] Some were also exposed to physical, sexual, and emotional abuse while institutionalized.[43]

The Board of Inquiry of Nova Scotia (the Board) recognized that the individual claimants were not alone in their experience.[44] It found evidence relating to the adverse effects suffered by persons with disabilities in institutions due to the policies, practices, and attitudes of the province.[45] The Board determined that Nova Scotia had *prima facie* discriminated against the individuals by needlessly institutionalizing them. Yet, despite the evidence and its own findings of facts, it determined that there was no *prima facie* case of systemic discrimination.[46]

So, what happened? The CCD and Inclusion Canada intervention focused on the systemic discrimination analysis. First, they argued that the Board mistakenly bifurcated the analysis between individual and systemic discrimination. In doing so, it applied a higher evidentiary burden to the DRC's systemic discrimination complaint. This is contrary to Justice Abella's guidance to avoid approaching discrimination in a binary way.[47] At the same time, the Board's approach was unsurprising, given the confusion caused by *Moore* regarding systemic discrimination.[48] The CCD and Inclusion Canada argued that the Board

39 *Disability Rights Coalition v Nova Scotia (Attorney General)*, 2021 NSCA 70 [*Disability Rights Coalition*].

40 *MacLean*, above note 3 at paras 273 and 342–43.

41 *Ibid* at paras 134, 177, and 208.

42 *Ibid* at para 177.

43 *Ibid* at paras 71–77 and 355–357.

44 *Ibid* at paras 413–414.

45 *Ibid* at para 413.

46 *Ibid* at para 331.

47 *Meiorin*, above note 21 at para 60.

48 *Moore*, above note 2 at paras 56–57.

should have looked at the source of discrimination (the policies, practices, and attitudes of the government) and the results (the unnecessary institutionalization of persons with disabilities). As such, the Board should have ordered systemic remedies.

Second, the CCD and Inclusion Canada argued that the Board adopted an erroneous legal threshold by requiring each member of the class to individually prove a denial of "meaningful access" to the service. The Board relied on *Moore,* which addressed whether Jeffrey had been denied "meaningful access" to education.[49] It cited *Moore* for the proposition that "the only difference [between a systemic and individual discrimination claim] is quantitative, that is, the number of people disadvantaged by the practice."[50] In other words, it adopted a definition of systemic discrimination that focused on statistical disparities.[51]

Based on *Moore,* the Board determined that a *prima facie* case of discrimination is found when there is a denial of "meaningful access" to services.[52] The Board's consideration of "meaningful access" was confusing at best. It held that to prove discrimination (i.e., no meaningful access to the services), "[a]dverse effects on each individual will have to be assessed."[53] This approach effectively required class members to challenge systemic barriers on a person-by-person basis. It created additional legal hurdles and made systemic discrimination extraordinarily difficult, if not impossible, to prove.

Third, the CCD and Inclusion Canada argued that the Board incorrectly focused on intent. The Board became sidetracked by the "good people" working in the system who had "devoted their lives to supporting" people with disabilities.[54] This was the wrong approach. The correct analysis would have examined whether the system (and its policies and practices) was a contributing factor, if not the direct cause, of the denial of the community living supports for persons with disabilities eligible for social assistance. As stated in the Abella Report, the discrimination analysis is not a search for "guilty parties."[55]

The Court of Appeal of Nova Scotia corrected the Board's flawed analysis. It concluded that the Board erred in its analysis of systemic

49 *Maclean,* above note 3 at para 32.

50 *Moore,* above note 2 at para 58.

51 In Chapter 2 of this volume, Charles Tremblay Potvin discusses this concept.

52 *Moore,* above note 2 at para 36; *Maclean,* above note 3 at para 3.

53 *Ibid* at para 460.

54 *Ibid* at paras 413 and 284.

55 Abella Report, above note 2 at 8–11.

discrimination and that the DRC had established a *prima facie* case of systemic discrimination.[56] While the Court's decision did not explicitly address each of the CCD and Inclusion Canada's arguments, the decision was responsive to the intervenor's concerns. For instance, the Court found that the Board had erred in stipulating that the systemic claim required evidence that all potential members of the group suffered a disadvantage or burden.[57] Consistent with the CCD and Inclusion Canada's arguments that the Board had applied an erroneous legal threshold to the systemic claim, the Court noted that "[t]he practical result of [the Board's] approach is that no meaningful systemic remedies could ever be awarded."[58]

Maclean is a recent example of *Moore*'s legacy. It is a reminder that the application of systemic discrimination law has real consequences, including on the lives of the most vulnerable in society. In the DRC complaint, access to justice was delayed and denied to hundreds of persons with disabilities in Nova Scotia who remained institutionalized. Sadly, two of the three complainants passed away before the decision of the Court of Appeal was rendered and their dream to live in community realized.

D. Part III — Guiding Principles for Systemic Discrimination Cases

Justice Abella's foremost work in systemic discrimination law is given practical effect in the analysis and remedial orders in *Caring Society v Canada*.[59] The decision draws on the strengths of Justice Abella's contributions to systemic discrimination while not importing its problematic elements.

The Caring Society decisions send a clear message that the source and impact of discrimination must be the focus of the analysis and that when the root causes are systemic in nature, systemic remedies are required. The series of decisions flowing from the original complaints represent the most sweeping systemic remedies ordered by a decision maker in Canadian history.

In 2007, the Assembly of First Nations (AFN) and the First Nations Child and Family Caring Society (Caring Society) filed human rights complaints against Canada alleging discrimination of First Nations children on reserve and in the Yukon in the provision of child welfare

56 *Disability Rights Coalition*, above note 42 at para 311.
57 *Ibid* at para 210.
58 *Ibid*.
59 *Caring Society*, above note 4.

services.[60] One of the key issues at stake in *Caring Society* was the application of the Jordan Principle, a child-first principle that calls for needed services and supports to be provided to First Nations children without denials, delays, or disruptions.[61] The complainants argued that the government was applying the principle too narrowly, resulting in serious gaps in justice for First Nations children.

Three guiding principles relating to systemic discrimination can be drawn from the Caring Society decisions. First, neither an express allegation nor a finding of systemic discrimination is required for systemic remedies to be ordered. It is telling that the complaint leading to the largest systemic discrimination case in Canadian history does not expressly allege systemic discrimination, nor does it explicitly include a finding of "systemic" discrimination. This was assumed, even by the respondent, because the complainants claimed that the cause of the discrimination was Canada's child welfare funding formulas, as well as its policies and practices. The complaint was sustained, including with evidence of the impacts of Canada's allocation of inadequate funding for First Nations children and family services, the narrow application of Jordan's Principle, and the resulting harm to children.[62]

Based on the Canadian Human Rights Tribunal's findings, wide-ranging systemic remedies were ordered as they were necessary to

60 Chief Lawrence Joseph and Cindy Blackstock on behalf of the Assembly of First Nations and the First Nations Child and Family Caring Society of Canada, "Human Rights Complaint against the Government of Canada" *First Nations Child and Family Caring Society* (23 February 2007), online: fncaringsociety.com/sites/default/files/Caring%20Society_AFN%20HR%20complaint%202007.pdf.

61 The principle was developed following the death of Jordan River Anderson, a citizen of Norway House Cree Nation, who was born in Winnipeg with complex disabilities that required significant medical interventions and ongoing medical care. After two years in hospital, Jordan's medical team determined he could go home as long as he could access the proper medical care. Jurisdictional disputes between Manitoba and Canada over responsibility for costs associated with Jordan's care ensued. Jordan passed away at the age of five, having spent his entire life in hospital while governments argued over who should pay for his necessary supports. See the Jordan's Principle Working Group "Without Denial, Delay, or Disruption: Ensuring First Nation Children's Access to Equitable Services through Jordan's Principle" *Assembly of First Nations* (2015), online: www.mcgill.ca/crcf/files/crcf/jordans_principle-report.pdf; *Caring Society*, above note 4 at paras 351–52; Vandna Sinha et al, "The Implementation of Jordan's Principle in Manitoba: Final Report" *Assembly of Manitoba Chiefs* (2022) at 8, online (pdf): manitobachiefs.com/wp-content/uploads/22-01-28-The-Implementation-of-Jordans-Principle-in-Manitoba-Final-Report.pdf.

62 *Caring Society*, above note 4 at paras 121–254 and 350.

"prevent the recurrence of" and "eliminate discrimination."[63] These included an order that Canada cease the discriminatory practices and take measures to redress and prevent them.[64] Canada was also ordered to cease applying its narrow definition of Jordan's Principle and to take measures for its full implementation.[65] Lastly, the Panel retained jurisdiction of the matter and subsequently made several orders, including compensation orders for First Nations children and families who suffered the discrimination.[66] In retaining jurisdiction over the matter, the Tribunal sent a strong message about the jurisdiction of tribunals and, to borrow language from Justice Abella, their role in "remedy[ing] inequity."[67]

Proving a sufficient *pattern* of systemic discrimination has been one of the biggest challenges to obtaining systemic remedies in Canada since at least the *Moore* decision.[68] Following that decision, the "viability of systemic remedies" has been put in question.[69] In finding that Canada's practices were discriminatory and ordering wide sweeping systemic remedies in *Caring Society*, the Tribunal sent a clear message about the necessity and importance of systemic remedies. It refused to ignore the inherently harmful practices and policies of Canada, which had disproportionally negative impacts on First Nations children. It provided clear direction about the "balance between the institutional capacity and competence of human rights adjudication and the enforcement of Tribunal orders."[70] In doing so, it heeded the advice of Justice Abella that "systemic discrimination requires systemic remedies,"[71] that "equal-

63 *Ibid* at para 468. See also *Robichaud v Canada (Treasury Board)*, [1987] 2 SCR 84 at para 13, 40 DLR (4th) 577.

64 *Caring Society*, above note 4 at paras 474–75.

65 *Ibid* at para 481.

66 *First Nations Child & Family Caring Society of Canada et al v Attorney General of Canada (representing the Minister of Indigenous and Northern Affairs Canada*, 2019 CHRT 39 at paras 245–57; *First Nations Child & Family Caring Society of Canada et al v Attorney General of Canada (representing the Minister of Indigenous and Northern Affairs Canada*, 2021 CHRT 12 at para 42.

67 Abella Report, above note 2 at 6.

68 Ronald Craig, *Systemic Discrimination in Employment and the Promotion of Ethnic Equality* (Boston: Martinus Nijhoff, 2007) at 131; Jean-Simon Schoenholz, "Opening the Doors of Justice: Group Litigation and Claims of Systemic Discrimination" (2017) 48:2 *Ottawa Law Review* 691 at 702. Also see generally: Andre Pinto, "Report of the Ontario Human Rights Review 2012" *Ontario Ministry of the Attorney General* (2012), online: academicwomenforjustice.org/downloads/OHR-APinto.pdf.

69 Pothier, above note 26 at 208.

70 *Ibid* at 196–97.

71 Abella Report, above note 2 at 9.

ity demands enforcement,"[72] and that failing to rectify discrimination "guarantee[s] its survival."[73] A note of caution, however: practitioners and complainants may want to identify when their complaints are systemic in nature given the confusion flowing from *Moore*.

The second guiding principle that can be drawn from *Caring Society* is that the focus of the analysis should always be the root causes of the discrimination and the disproportionate results on a group.[74] If the discrimination is grounded in discriminatory policies, practices, or procedures and there are disproportionate impacts on a group, systemic remedies are required. In *Caring Society*, the Panel determined that it was Canada's "design, management and control of the . . . Program, along with the corresponding funding formulas and the other . . . agreements that have resulted in the denials of services and created various adverse impacts for many First Nations children and families on reserves."[75]

The focus by the Panel on the root causes and the results of the system on First Nations children and families on reserve reinforces the systemic discrimination discussion in the Abella Report and subsequent decisions that cite Justice Abella.[76] It is consistent with Justice Abella's repeated reminder that proof of discriminatory "intent" is not required.[77]

The third guiding principle is that decision-makers should not be required to hear from numerous victims to make a finding of discrimination and to order systemic remedies. Justice Abella's influence on this principle cannot be denied. Based on the Abella Report, it ought not matter whether the complaint is brought by an individual or a group.[78] Within the context of Jordan's Principle and distinct from *Moore*,[79] the Tribunal did not require several First Nations children affected by similar jurisdictional issues to testify. Despite Canada's arguments that Jordan's Principle ought only to apply to First Nations children with complex medical needs and multiple disabilities,[80] the Tribunal focused on the causes of the denial of services without requiring evidence from other affected First Nations children.

72 *Ibid* at 10.

73 *Ibid* at 6.

74 *Caring Society*, above note 4 at para 398.

75 *Ibid* at para 458.

76 Abella Report, above note 2 at 2; *CN*, above note 5 at 1138, 1139, and 1141–42.

77 Abella Report, above note 2 at 2; *Fraser*, above note 2 at para 69; *Alliance*, above note 5 at para 35; *Centrale des syndicates du Québec v Quebec (Attorney General)*, 2018 SCC 18 at para 35.

78 Abella Report, above note 2 at 8.

79 *Moore*, above note 2 at paras 64–69.

80 *Caring Society*, above note 4 at paras 359 and 380.

The Tribunal's commitment to grappling with the source of the discrimination led to creative remedies that benefited all First Nations children in Canada. It cleared a path for the implementation of systemic remedies with transformative agreements-in-principle on child and family services reform and compensation for the long-standing underfunding of the service. *Caring Society* offers an example of how Justice Abella's guidance on systemic discrimination can be applied to combat inequities.

E. Conclusion

Based on Justice Abella's contributions, I propose defining systemic discrimination as occurring when policies, practices, and attitudes create barriers to inclusion for members of a protected class. When the discrimination is systemic in nature, systemic remedies are necessary to prevent the same type of discrimination from reoccurring.

While prevention remains critical in advocating for equality,[81] tribunals and courts will continue to be called upon to look at systemic cases. We cannot ignore this reality. Failing to meaningfully apply the systemic discrimination analysis has real consequences on the lives of members of equity-deserving groups.[82] It can deny them the necessary remedies to which they are entitled, delay access to justice, and fail to address the root causes of discrimination.

Justice Abella's contributions to the law of systemic discrimination have been mixed. To borrow Fay Faraday's language, she has brought us several steps forward but one major step back.[83] Justice Abella has led the charge in identifying the essential elements of systemic discrimination and emphasizing the need for systemic remedies. And yet, the *Moore* decision provides fodder to governments keen to deny discrimination and fight against systemic remedies.[84]

Looking past the troubling aspects of *Moore*, the essential understandings of systemic discrimination can all be drawn from Justice

81 Colleen Sheppard "Of Forest Fires and Systemic Discrimination: A Review of British Columbia (Public Service Employee Relations Commission v BCGSEU" (2001) 46 *McGill Law Journal* 533–99 at 559.

82 See, for example, *R v Kokopenace*, 2015 SCC 28.

83 Fay Faraday, "One Step Forward, Two Steps Back? Substantive Equality, Systemic Discrimination and Pay Equity at the Supreme Court of Canada" (2020), 94 *Supreme Court Law Review* 301.

84 Mary Eberts & Kim Stanton, "The Disappearance of the Four Equality Rights and Systemic Discrimination from Canadian Equality Jurisprudence" (2018) 38:1 *National Journal of Constitutional Law* 89 at 91.

Abella. The preponderance of her contributions is underpinned by a recognition that the discrimination analysis must focus on the source and results of the harm.[85]

Together, the *Caring Society* decisions illustrate how focusing on the source and results of discrimination can lead to systemic change. The decision is a hopeful harbinger for Justice Abella's legacy in remedying inequity.

85 Christine Tsang, "Uncovering Systemic Discrimination: Allowing Individual Challenges to a 'Pattern or Practice'" (2013) 32:1 *Yale Law and Policy Review* 319 at 321 and 330.

4 A Courageous "Love": Three Acts on the Abella Legacy in Administrative Law

LORNE SOSSIN*

Rather than dive deeply into the jurisprudence, what I would like to try to do is explain how I learned to understand administrative law, and, by understanding it, came to appreciate and then love it. So what follows, in brief, is the story of a rare creature in the legal universe: someone who has been a judge *and* on a tribunal.

Rosalie Silberman Abella, "Canadian Administrative Law: The Case for Judicial Humility"[1]

The rule of law is not the rule of courts. A pluralist conception of the rule of law recognizes that courts are not the exclusive guardians of law, and that others in the justice arena have shared responsibility for its development, including administrative decision-makers.

Canada (Minister of Citizenship and Immigration) v Vavilov[2]

A. Introduction

In this chapter, I highlight Justice Rosalie Silberman Abella's courageous love for administrative law as a product of her experience with administrative justice.[3] Justice Abella has described her attachment to the field in extra-judicial writings and speeches over the years. She identifies her own experience as a tribunal member (in tandem with

* I am grateful to Jesse Abell, then a law clerk at the Court of Appeal for Ontario, for her exceptional research assistance. I also benefitted from the panel discussion at the "A Life of Firsts" conference on 13 May 2022 with Julie Baril, Geneviève Cartier, Joëlle Pastora Sala, and Paul Daly.

1 Rosalie Silberman Abella, "Canadian Administrative Law: The Case for Judicial Humility" (2020) 75:1 *Industrial Relations Law Journal* 168 at 170 [emphasis in original].

2 2019 SCC 65, per Abella and Karakatsanis JJ (concurring) at para 241 [*Vavilov*].

3 Administrative law and administrative justice capture two different dynamics. Administrative law is the collection of statutory and common law rules which

her judicial perspective) as the key source of this passion. Arguably, no justice of the Supreme Court of Canada has brought as much passion and depth of experience to the field of administrative law (at least not since former Chief Justice Bora Laskin). In this brief contribution, I seek to elaborate on why.

In her article, "Canadian Administrative Law: The Case for Judicial Humility," Justice Abella wrote that as a result of her tenure as Chair of the Ontario Labour Relations Board, "I became not only an advocate for my tribunal and others, I felt relentlessly protective of their uniqueness, of their specialized wisdom, and especially of their right to be called an institutional justice sibling with the courts."[4]

Her belief in, and defence of, the specialized expertise of administrative decision-makers is reflected most poignantly in her early extrajudicial writings on administrative law and administrative justice, and I will draw on those in this analysis. In my view, her passion and experience shed important light on her judicial philosophy, as well as her signature administrative law judgments, including *Doré v Barreau du Québec*,[5] *Newfoundland and Labrador Nurses' Union v Newfoundland and Labrador (Treasury Board)*,[6] *Wilson v Atomic Energy of Canada Ltd*,[7] and *Canada (Minister of Citizenship and Immigration) v Vavilov*,[8] among others, which are discussed in more detail by other contributors to this collection.

Justice Abella's judicial philosophy can be summarized around the following principles: first, public decision-makers are responsible for safeguarding important rights and in this sense play a parallel (rather than subordinate) role in relation to the judiciary; second, public decision-makers merit respect and deference from judges; and third,

---

govern the conduct of administrative decision-making (the duty of fairness, the requirements that decisions be reasonable, and so forth), while administrative justice includes broader aspects of administrative decision-making, including the experience of parties before tribunals, the mechanisms of appointment, training, and governance of tribunal members, and the relationship between the tribunal sector with other democratic and bureaucratic institutions, See, for a broader discussion, Lorne Sossin, "The Ambivalence of Administrative Justice in Canada: Does Canada Need a Fourth Branch?" in *The Sacred Fire: The Legacy of Antonio Lamer (Chief Justice of Canada)*, Adam Dodek and Daniel Jutras (eds) (Toronto: LexisNexis Canada, 2009).

4 Abella, "Canadian Administrative Law: The Case for Judicial Humility," above note 1 at 172.

5 2012 SCC 12, [2012] 1 SCR 395.

6 2011 SCC 62, [2011] 3 SCR 708 [*Newfoundland and Labrador Nurses' Union*].

7 2016 SCC 29, [2016] 1 SCR 770.

8 2019 SCC 65. Justices Abella and Karakatsanis wrote concurring reasons.

recognizing the importance of deference to the expertise and specialized statutory mandate of public decision-makers promotes democratic institutions, the rule of law, and public confidence in the justice system.

While so many of Justice Abella's cultural and intellectual loves emerged from these early experiences,[9] and were deepened and enriched by her professional life as lawyer and judge, her relationship with administrative justice came later, almost as a surprise, as she found herself a stranger in a strange land — a judge appointed to a tribunal. She found herself captivated by the most unlikely (many might say unlovable) subject — administrative law. For this reason, I see her love of administrative law as distinct from her other well-known passions and commitments — an acquired and unexpected love, in other words, as opposed to her abiding and deeply rooted commitment to fields such as human rights and equality.

Justice Abella has been celebrated for her many loves. Her love of literature, Broadway theatre, and jazz, for example, are apparent to anyone who has ever walked into her office or heard her speeches. In a lively lecture on legal professionalism, for instance, she observed:

> The public is our audience, the people for whom we perform the justice play. They do not direct us, but they are very interested in what is going on. If they stop clapping, we are in deep trouble. We have to figure out if it is because of the script, the props, the cast, or all of them. We know we will always have an audience, because the play is called the Rule of Law, and the public's attendance is mandatory. Since we give the public no choice about whether or not they are subject to the rule of law, we have to care about whether they like the performance. They may not always be right, but they always have a right to be heard.[10]

Taking my cue from her commitment to the theatrical narrative, I organize this analysis into three Acts: In the first Act, I explore her

---

9 As discussed elsewhere in this volume, Rosie's values were forged early in her life, products of her family's journey as Holocaust survivors from the Displaced Persons Camp where she was born to the blend of old world and new world culture in the Toronto household where she was raised. She and her family had experienced discrimination first-hand, and as members of the Jewish community, they could see the gap between the ideals of equality and the realities of post-war Canadian society.

10 Justice Rosalie Silberman Abella, "Professionalism Revisited" Opening address delivered at the Benchers' Retreat of the Law Society of Upper Canada, Hockley Valley, Ontario (14 October 1999), online: www.ontariocourts.ca/coa/about-the-court/archives/the-law-society-of-upper-canada-professionalism-revisited/.

perspective on the sibling relationship between courts and tribunals; in the second Act, I examine her consideration of the particular expertise and valued perspective those in the administrative justice realm bring to the disputes that come before them. Finally, in Act III, I consider the future of her vision of administrative law.

B. Act I: Courts and Tribunals

While virtually all those who have experience both with courts and tribunals begin as tribunal adjudicators and then become judges, Rosalie Silberman Abella is a rare case of the reverse. Appointed to the Ontario Family Court at just twenty-nine years old in 1976, her experience with tribunals came later, most notably as Chair of the Ontario Labour Relations Board (1984–89). In her writings and speeches, she has often returned to the significance of her time on the Labour Board. The experience of working with people who spent their professional lives "wrestling with law to blend the statutory mandate with common sense and good labour relations" left her, in a word, "smitten."[11]

In "Courts, Boards and Labour: Reconciling Competing Cultures," Justice Abella, then the Chair of the Labour Board, spoke of her fascination with the Board. She observed that her role as Chair introduced her not only to the realm of labour relations, but also to an institutional framework that was distinct from the court system. She explained:

> I was no stranger to dispute resolution or hostile adversaries, but I approached them through a formalistic model of decision-making, with strict rules of procedure, accepted notions of reviewability by a higher court, and clear evidentiary guidelines. What I faced when I joined the Labour Board was a very differently constituted legal environment called an administrative tribunal. . . . *Over time, I bec[a]me intensely institutionally patriotic, and became totally preoccupied with how the Board works, who it works with, and its proper role in the legal system.* What emerges is a fascinating collage of conflicting cultures — government, courts and tribunals.[12]

11 Abella, "Canadian Administrative Law: The Case for Judicial Humility," above note 1 at 171.

12 Rosalie Silberman Abella, "Courts, Boards and Labour: Reconciling Competing Cultures" Larry Sefton Memorial Lecture at the University of Toronto Woodsworth College (8 March 1988), online: https://cirhr.library.utoronto.ca/sites/default/public/sefton_lectures/SeftonLecture06th_1987-88_Abella.pdf at 1–2 [emphasis added].

She goes on to write of how her intellectual engagement and institutional affections for administrative law and administrative justice intertwine. She has come to view the culture of tribunals as distinct from that of the courts, as she has come to know the people involved in shaping that culture, and the people that culture, in turn, has shaped.

For Justice Abella, the distinctiveness of administrative justice also reveals a tension — between formality, which she equates with fairness, and informality, which she equates with access. One can see this tension in her emphasis on procedural fairness alongside efficient processes.

While Chair of the Labour Board, she stated in a 1988 lecture that the Board must strive to ensure that all parties feel "that the process is fair — that they had an opportunity to make their case, and to hear and attempt to meet the case against them." She observed, "To those who harken wistfully to days of greater informality, one can only observe that one person's informality may be another person's denial of due process." Nonetheless, she noted the Board's obligation to ensure efficiency alongside due process:

> But in our quest for a process less rigorous than the courts and more apposite to the informality expected of tribunals, we cannot disregard the central fact that as a quasi-judicial adjudicative body, we are obliged by law to provide for the determination of rights as quickly as possible, as expertly as possible, as wisely as possible, but also as fairly as possible.[13]

While I might quibble about whether informality always means less fairness or that formal due process always means more, it is clear that Justice Abella is here reacting to the bygone culture of a lack of transparency and the absence of consistently applied procedures in some corners of administrative justice.

Subsequently, in "Canadian Administrative Tribunals: Towards Judicialization or Dejudicialization?" she put the distinction between courts and tribunals as such:

> Our processes may not be identical to the courts, but our objectives may not be either. We are *both* legal creatures, but we are siblings, not twins, of the courts. We have a separate and unique character in pursuit of a common cause — just decision-making. If our uniqueness offends, so be it.[14]

13 Abella, "Courts, Boards and Labour: Reconciling Competing Cultures," above note 12 at 13 and 16.

14 Rosalie Silberman Abella, "Canadian Administrative Tribunals: Towards Judicialization or Dejudicialization?" (1989) 2 *Canadian Journal of Administrative Law and Practice* 1 at 7 [emphasis in original].

In this passage, Justice Abella rejected the Diceyan precept that only courts are charged with safeguarding "just decision-making." Elsewhere in the same article, she elaborates on this point, observing that while administrative tribunals are obliged to provide a fair hearing, the integrity of administrative decision-making cannot be evaluated against the standard of court processes. She explains:

Our integrity rests on a unique concept of process, one that is expeditious and can best serve the integrated needs of law, policy, and the delineation of rights. It is for each tribunal to assess. What works for the Labour Board, for example, may not be appropriate for the Freedom of Information Commission. But it is not a question of moving towards or retreating from judicialization. It is a question of remaining true to our own character, without ignoring the basic values of the court's process, but without ignoring our own, either.[15]

This theme of mutuality between courts and tribunals finds expression both in Justice Abella's writings and in many of the leading Supreme Court of Canada administrative law judgments she participated in.

In "Thinking about Administrative Law in Canada: From Doctrine to Principle,"[16] Justice Abella, then a Justice of the Supreme Court, and Teagan Markin, her law clerk for the 2017–18 term, charted the development and the current state of administrative law and judicial review in the United Kingdom, New Zealand, Australia, the United States, and Canada. They discussed the evolving standard of review analysis in Canadian jurisprudence, and the state of the law following *Dunsmuir v New Brunswick*, 2008 SCC 9, [2008] 1 SCR 190 (the chapter was written just prior to the release of *Canada (Minister of Citizenship and Immigration) v Vavilov*, 2019 SCC 65[17]). They advocated for the relationship of mutual respect between courts and administrative decision-makers, stating, "This paper seeks to make the case for a mutually respectful relationship between the courts and administrative decision-makers, one which gives administrative decision-makers the authority — and legitimacy — to implement their own mandates."[18] Justice Abella and Markin asserted

15 Abella, "Canadian Administrative Tribunals: Towards Judicialization or Dejudicialization?" above note 14 at 9.

16 Rosalie Silberman Abella & Teagan Markin, "Thinking about Administrative Law in Canada: From Doctrine to Principle" in Simon Mount and Max Harris, eds, *The Promise of Law: Essays marking the retirement of Dame Sian Elias as Chief Justice of New Zealand* (Wellington, NZ: LexisNexis, 2020) 271.

17 *Ibid* at 304, n 234.

18 Abella & Markin, "Thinking about Administrative Law in Canada: From Doctrine to Principle," above note 16 at 272.

that both courts and administrative decision-makers "have the authority to consider and apply the law; neither is subservient to the other."[19]

In "Canadian Administrative Law: The Case for Judicial Humility,"[20] published in 2020, near the end of her judicial career, Justice Abella pursued this theme in greater focus. She asserted that courts and administrative decision-makers are equally responsible for, and capable of, interpreting the law in their own spheres. She stated:

> *I see both the Courts and administrative decision-makers as equally responsible for, and capable of, interpreting the applying law within their separate, assigned legal spheres.* In other words, the rule of law *and* respect for the right of administrative decision-makers to decide questions of law are not binary concepts, they are parallel legal universes.[21]

There is something intentionally provocative in depicting courts and tribunals as coordinate branches of the justice system, rather than as standing in a hierarchical relationship with "inferior" administrative decision-makers supervised by "superior" courts.

Justice Abella's vision of courts and tribunals as siblings is not so much intended as a slight to courts as it is a validation of administrative justice. The thread of co-equal courts and tribunals thus requires a prior thread, recognizing and affirming a distinct and equally valued sphere of administrative justice. It is to this second thread I now turn.

C. Act II: Administrative Justice

Justice Abella's sentiments for administrative law cannot, and should not, be disentangled from her lived experience with administrative justice. Her view that courts and tribunals are coordinated branches of the justice system, in my view, rests both on a particular vision of Canada's public law architecture *and* on a particular experience with both institutional settings.

One can see this dynamic on display, for example, in her forceful views on the value tribunals add to the justice system and in her insistence that they therefore deserve respect from the judiciary. For example, in "The Independence of Administrative Tribunals,"[22] Justice Abella wrote

19 *Ibid* at 272.

20 Abella, "Canadian Administrative Law: The Case for Judicial Humility," above note 1.

21 *Ibid* at 169 [emphasis added].

22 Rosalie Silberman Abella, "The Independence of Administrative Tribunals" (1992) 26 *Law Society's Gazette* 113.

about the "perfectly normal" impulse on the part of judges to substitute their decisions for those of tribunals and the corrosive impact of this impulse:

> The problem lies in the courts' unwillingness to appreciate that tribunals have been established to deal with specialized issues, many of which do not lend themselves to the usual cerebral exercises judges invoke in assessing contract breaches, negligence claims, or criminal liability.

She asserted that governments chose to delegate decision-making responsibility for particular matters to tribunals because of a recognition that a more generalized judicial forum was not appropriate for those matters:

> And having given tribunals the sole responsibility for decision-making over that area precisely because they can better identify, administer, and adjudicate a particular policy issue, it violates both the territoriality and credibility of the tribunal if the courts feel little reluctance to impose their own sensibilities and conclusions on the tribunal. Until the intervention is replaced by respect for, and understanding of the unique perch tribunals occupy in the legal system, tribunals are rendered anaemic in their capacity to be the final arbiters in their own areas, areas that require both speed and integrity in decision-making.[23]

In this sense, the often (perhaps too often) debated question of the standard of review stands as a proxy for asserting the legitimacy and value of administrative decision-makers. It is for this reason that Justice Abella emphasizes and reiterates so often that the framework of judicial review rests on a premise of the court's "respect" for tribunals.[24]

The standard of review debate, as is well known by students of administrative law, revolves around the degree of deference which courts should pay administrative decision-makers when their decisions are

23 *Ibid* at 119–20.

24 See, for example, *Newfoundland and Labrador Nurses' Union*, above note 6 at para 15. In this decision, Justice Abella relies on Professor David Dyzenhaus' formulation of deference as "respect" in David Dyzenhaus, "The Politics of Deference: Judicial Review and Democracy" in Michael Taggart, ed, *The Province of Administrative Law* (Oxford, England: Hart Publishing, 1997) 279 at 286, which the majority of the Supreme Court adopted in *Dunsmuir v New Brunswick*, 2008 SCC 9, [2008] 1 SCR 190 at para 48.

judicially reviewed.[25] The Supreme Court's decision in *Canada (Minister of Citizenship and Immigration) v Vavilov*[26] was advertised as an opportunity to reset (and perhaps revamp) the Court's approach to the standard of review. The Court took the highly unusual step of telegraphing publicly that it viewed an upcoming trilogy of appeals (with *Vavilov* as the lead appeal) as an opportunity to reconsider the standard of review, and as a result, the appeals featured no less than twenty-seven interveners and two *amici curiae* appointed by the Court.

The majority decision, authored jointly by Chief Justice Wagner and Justices Moldaver, Gascon, Côté, Brown, Rowe, and Martin, reaffirmed several existing principles underlying the standard of review, including a presumption of deference (requiring the application of a reasonableness standard of review), with some well-accepted exceptions such as decisions involving constitutional interpretation and decisions involving the competing jurisdiction of more than one tribunal. The majority also, however, established a broad distinction between judicial reviews, which attract deference, and statutory appeals from administrative decisions, which do not. That such appeals would be reviewed without deference to the administrative decision-maker (requiring the application of a correctness standard of review) represented a sharp departure from a generation of Supreme Court caselaw and meant that a new swath of administrative justice would be subject to the possibility of greater intervention by the courts. While the majority made a number of other notable tweaks to the judicial review framework in *Vavilov*, it is this shift that arguably altered the relationship between courts and tribunals.

Objecting to this shift, Justices Abella and Karakatsanis wrote a spirited set of concurring reasons in *Vavilov*.[27] As they stated at the outset of their concurrence, a deferential standard of review represented the doctrinal mechanism through which respect for administrative justice could (and should) be expressed and reinforced by courts. Justices Abella and Karakatsanis point to *CUPE, Local 963 v New Brunswick Liquor Corporation*[28] as the turning point after which the Supreme Court embarked on a course to recognize "the unique and valuable role of administrative

25 See Paul Daly, *A Theory of Deference in Administrative Law: Basis, Application and Scope* (Cambridge: Cambridge University Press, 2012).

26 2019 SCC 65.

27 *Vavilov*, above note 2 at paras 198–43. It is likely no coincidence that Justice Abella's *Vavilov* concurrence co-author, Justice Karakatsanis, also had experience as the Chair of an administrative tribunal (the Liquor Licence Board of Ontario (1988–95)).

28 [1979] 2 SCR 227 [*CUPE*].

decision-makers within the Canadian legal order."[29] Breaking away from the court-centric theories of years past, judges were encouraged to show deference when specialized administrative decision-makers provided reasonable answers to legal questions within their mandates. According to Justices Abella and Karakatsanis, subsequent decisions of this Court sought to operationalize deference and explain its relationship to core democratic principles.

While the majority judgment in *Vavilov* shifted to a less deferential standard in the case of statutory appeals, Justices Abella and Karakatsanis argued strongly against veering towards more judicial intervention in administrative justice, or as they put it, taking the standard of review "back to the formalistic judge-centred approach this Court has spent decades dismantling."[30]

Justice Abella's full-throated endorsement of a distinctive sphere of administrative justice was — and is — an invaluable gesture of support and respect for the thousands of administrative adjudicators, in wildly disparate statutory and institutional contexts, who serve the public interest through their decisions, dispute resolution, discretion, and problem-solving. Justice Abella also points beyond the statutory mandate of tribunals to another distinguishing feature of administrative justice — expertise.[31]

For Justice Abella, courts are inherently generalist (presumably even the specialized family court she was first appointed to) while tribunals are specialists. This view, entrenched through her years at the Labour Relations Board, was no doubt also affected by the Supreme Court's adoption of an expertise-based lens through which to view the standard of judicial review (in cases such as *National Corn Growers Assn. v Canada (Import Tribunal)*,[32] *United Brotherhood of Carpenters and Joiners of America, Local 579 v Bradco Construction Ltd.*,[33] and *Canada (Director of Investigation and Research) v Southam Inc*[34]).

As former Justice Frank Iacobucci, one of the architects of this approach to administrative law, explained, the new institutional

29 *Vavilov*, above note 2 at para 198, per Abella and Karakatsanis JJ (concurring).

30 *Ibid* at para 199, per Abella and Karakatsanis JJ (concurring).

31 For an excellent review of the role of expertise in Canadian administrative law before and after *Vavilov*, see Audrey Macklin, "Seven Out of Nine Legal Experts Agree: Expertise No Longer Matters (in the Same Way) After Vavilov!" (2021) *Supreme Court Law Review: Osgoode's Annual Constitutional Cases Conference* 100.

32 [1990] 2 SCR 1324 at 1336–37, per Wilson J (concurring).

33 [1993] 2 SCR 316 at 335.

34 [1997] 1 SCR 748 at para 50.

relationship between the courts and administrative actors was premised on an understanding of the role of expertise in the modern administrative state, which acknowledged that judges are not always in the best position to interpret the law.[35] In their concurrence in *Vavilov*, Justices Abella and Karakatsanis take issue with the majority's reasons precisely because for the majority, deference no longer rests on the foundation of expertise: "Although the majority's approach extolls respect for the legislature's 'institutional design choices', it accords no weight to the institutional advantages of specialization and expertise that administrative decision-makers possess in resolving questions of law. In so doing, the majority disregards the historically accepted reason *why* the legislature intended to delegate authority to an administrative actor."[36]

Expertise has a broader meaning in administrative justice than just referring to an individual's background or training, such as an employer or employee representative in the specialized sphere of labour, or the expert economist on the Competition Tribunal. Expertise may also refer to institutional competence developed as a result of an administrative decision-maker's specialized jurisdiction. For example, a member of the Landlord and Tenant Board or the Immigration and Refugee Board of Canada may not have degrees in the subject or deep background in those fields. Nonetheless, expertise may capture a tribunal adjudicator's daily exposure to, and encounters with, a particular field. These decision-makers may be — and often are — drawn from diverse educational and professional backgrounds, which often do not include any legal training. But their familiarity with the governing statutory framework, and their repeated engagement with particular issues every day, give rise to a different kind of expertise, and one which ought to be no less valued.

Justice Abella's respect for the role such decision-makers can play in the justice system, in my view, also animates one of her more controversial jurisprudential legacies — *Charter* values. In *Doré v Barreau du Québec*, writing for a unanimous Court, Justice Abella affirmed that all administrative decision-makers must adhere to *Charter* values in the exercise of their statutory discretion. She referred to this approach as "a richer conception of administrative law, under which discretion

35 See Justice Frank Iacobucci, "Articulating a Rational Standard of Review Doctrine: A Tribute to John Willis" (2002) 27:2 *Queen's Law Journal* 859 at 866, cited in *Vavilov*, above note 2 at para 213, per Abella and Karakatsanis JJ (concurring).

36 *Ibid* at para 236, per Abella and Karakatsanis JJ (concurring) [emphasis in original].

is exercised 'in light of constitutional guarantees and the values they reflect.'"[37] Justice Abella elaborated on this approach, in which recourse to a section 1 *Oakes* analysis is unnecessary in order to protect *Charter* values. Rather, administrative decision-makers must *always* consider fundamental values. Justice Abella linked this approach to recognizing "the legitimacy that this Court has given to administrative decision-making in cases such as *Dunsmuir* and *Conway*."[38] Such cases established that administrative decision-makers are required to consider *Charter* values within their scope of expertise. For Justice Abella, integrating *Charter* values into the administrative approach reflected an institutional dialogue about the appropriate use and control of discretion, rather than the more traditional administrative law "command-and-control relationship."[39]

One sees again in *Doré* the themes of mutual recognition between courts and administrative decision-makers and the distinct expertise that distinguishes administrative justice. Justice Abella pushed the envelope further, reasoning that just as administrative decision-makers bring specialized expertise in the interpretation and application of their statutory authority, so they do in the interpretation and application of *Charter* values. Accordingly, administrative decision-makers are entitled to deference in balancing *Charter* values with statutory objectives on a reasonableness standard of review.

This aspect of the *Charter* values framework was a bridge too far for some,[40] but entirely consistent with Justice Abella's expansive vision of administrative justice. For her, there is every reason to think diverse administrative decision-makers, in light of their specialized expertise, would have important and meaningful insights about *Charter* values.

---

37 *Doré v Barreau du Québec*, 2012 SCC 12, [2012] 1 SCR 395 at para 35, citing *Multani v Commission scolaire Marguerite-Bourgeoys*, 2006 SCC 6, [2006] 1 SCR 256 at para 152, per LeBel J.

38 *Doré v Barreau du Québec*, above note 37.

39 *Ibid*.

40 See, for example, Chief Justice McLachlin's concurring reasons in *Law Society of British Columbia v Trinity Western University*, 2018 SCC 32, [2018] 2 SCR 293 at paras 116–19. See also Carmelle Dieleman, "Accommodating Rights in Administrative Law: A Critique of the *Doré/Loyola* Framework" (2021) 34:2 *Canadian Journal of Administrative Law and Practice* 197; and Audrey Macklin, "*Charter* Right or *Charter*-Lite?: Administrative Discretion and the *Charter*" (2014) 67 *Supreme Court Law Review* (2d) 561. For further critique, also see *Gehl v Canada (Attorney General)*, 2017 ONCA 319, 2017 CarswellOnt 5673 (Ont CA) at para 79.

D. Act 3: The Future of Administrative Law and the Meaning of Love?

This third Act of Rosie Abella's drama has yet to be written. What will courts, tribunals, academics, policy-makers, and those affected by administrative decisions do with her legacy? Will history be kind to her vision, or will it be yet another twist in the long and winding road of Canadian administrative law jurisprudence?[41]

Rather than focus on doctrine, I have chosen to focus this brief analysis on love.

One reason is that this collection is intended to shed light on Justice Abella's distinctive approach and commitments, and in my view, there is no better way to explore this than by focusing on her passion for administrative law because of her experience with administrative justice. To explain her engagement with administrative law, she deploys some of her most beloved metaphors and distinctive style. Consider this passage from "Canadian Administrative Law: The Case for Judicial Humility":

> If I can borrow a metaphor from the arts, just as it took a while for people to come to appreciate that jazz, a deeply distinct form of music, was nonetheless "music" albeit differently textured, so it has taken a while for the legal world to appreciate that administrative decision-making, although a deeply distinct form of dispute resolution, is still law albeit differently textured. And that, in turn, leads to understanding that *both* are entitled to respect, that law is not only the domain of judges, and that courts are not the only legal apothecaries that dispense justice.[42]

The other explanation for my focus on Rosie's love of administrative law and administrative justice is that her writing and thinking about the topic resonate with why I find these fields so compelling (and, indeed, how her engagement with the field in the tribunal, judicial, and academic communities has deepened my own). Like her, I have had the chance to work as a tribunal adjudicator and as a judge (though unlike

---

41 It appears the Court's repeated attempts since *CUPE*, above note 28, to bring stability and coherence to the judicial review framework have been short-lived, and according at least to some measures, resulting in little change: see Andrew Green, "How Important are the Groundbreaking Cases in Administrative Law?" *SSRN* (19 May 2022), online : https://ssrn.com/abstract=4114959 or http://dx.doi.org/10.2139/ssrn.4114959.

42 Abella, "Canadian Administrative Law: The Case for Judicial Humility," above note 1 at 169.

her, I did so in that order), and the opportunity to see firsthand the dedication, skill, and professionalism of tribunal adjudicators.

However, there is another side to this coin of exposure to administrative justice. The dizzying number of tribunals at all levels of government, all with their own rules and cultures, and the inconsistencies of training, capacity, resources, and transparency, combine to make administrative justice, as a coherent branch of the justice system, as much an aspiration as a reality. While administrative justice delivers more access to more justice to more people than courts could ever hope to reach, the limitations of administrative justice must be acknowledged and addressed as well.

I have also had time to reflect on the field as an academic. Through that lens, I have seen administrative law evolve and adapt to a changing world. My academic work has challenged me to think about how administrative law will engage with AI and digital decision-making, how administrative law may contribute to, and be shaped by, Indigenous dispute resolution practices, and how administrative law will interact with the growing complexity of public-private partnerships in many areas of economic and social life, among other pressing questions. In these and other areas poised to define the future of administrative law, the distinctiveness and value of administrative justice will be more apparent than ever, as will the challenges that remain in navigating the relationship between courts and public decision-makers.

Whatever the fate of the judicial review framework set out in *Vavilov*, I believe history will be kind to Justice Abella's conviction that courts and tribunals play equally vital roles in the justice system. And wherever the shifting winds of Supreme Court jurisprudence take these concepts, it is clear her vision coalesced from what she has lived. As she put it: "So back to where I started — I am very proud to be a judge and I am very proud to have been on a tribunal. My respect for both is limitless and so is my gratitude for what each has taught me."[43]

As with Justice Abella, I cannot disentangle my approach to administrative law from my exposure to the people, issues, and challenges involved with administrative justice. These dynamics are what make the field so compelling. My passion for administrative law and administrative justice has to do with its near-infinite variation and relevance, its commitment to accountability, and its attention to how people actually experience state authority.

---

43 *Ibid* at 174.

At the end of the day, love is not simply about affection, but about care. Justice Abella's love for administrative law is a reflection of her care for the difficult puzzles administrative law gives rise to — like how to ensure fairness at the same time as advancing accessibility or effectiveness and how to instill an enduring rule of law culture within the daily exercise of public authority, among others.

This love is also bound together with the potential of administrative justice to solve problems and improve the lives of people and communities affected by public decision-making. Here is hoping that the Abella legacy, and her love for administrative law and administrative justice, will continue to inspire new generations of afficionados. I have a feeling that the third Act of this drama, the one in which future generations take over the script, will be the most compelling of all.

5 Justice Abella: Confronting the Authenticity-Professionalism Paradox

ROSALIE JUKIER*

A. Introduction

I first met Justice Rosalie Silberman Abella in the fall of 1988, when I was a junior professor in the Faculty of Law at McGill University and she was starting out as a Boulton Visiting Professor, a position she held from 1988 to 1992. The Dean at the time, Roderick A. Macdonald, someone who would go on to be of great influence to both me and Justice Abella, was giving her a tour of the Faculty when they bumped into me. The Dean introduced us, and when he said my name was Rosalie Jukier, she asked, without missing a beat, "Oh, are you a Rosie too?" Here I was, a young academic being introduced to this powerhouse of a woman judge and all I could do, in my starstruck and flustered state, was mutter uncomfortably, "Uh, no." The Dean then suggested that I continue the tour of the Faculty. I proceeded to take Justice Abella to what we call our Common Room, a spectacular space sometimes featured in movies,[1] in what was the main entertaining room of the Ross Mansion and now

---

* Professor and Sir William C. Macdonald Chair, Faculty of Law, McGill University. I wish to thank McGill law graduate Garima Karia for her invaluable research and editorial assistance, generously funded by the Roberto and Michelina Buffone Research Assistantship Support Fund. This chapter is based not only on my own presentation at the "Life of Firsts" conference in honour of Justice Rosalie Abella, but also on the contributions of my co-panelists in the session, "Justice Abella and Women in the Legal Profession," which took place on 12 May 2022, moderated by Toronto lawyer Deborah Palter. These panelists include Supreme Court Justice Andromache Karakatsanis, Manitoba Court of Appeal Justice Freda Steel, and leading practising jurists Linda Rothstein, Shantona Chaudhury, and Sana Halwani. I am grateful for their permission to include their perspectives.

1 Notably, the room was featured as the Harvard Law Dean's office in the movie *On the Basis of Sex*, a film about Justice Ruth Bader Ginsberg, often dubbed Justice

the McGill Faculty of Law's home. Her immediate reaction was that it would be great space for her son Zachary's Bar Mitzvah! Remember, at the time of this reaction, I had known her for all of five minutes.

I had never encountered a professional woman, let alone such a brilliant and accomplished professional woman, who unabashedly revealed her inner life, her true colours, her warm and personal side, her authentic self, which, in addition to being warm, is also humorous, charismatic, and engaging. Indeed, Justice Abella's career and legacy demonstrate that passion can sit easily with rigour.[2]

This paper focuses on the authenticity-professionalism paradox, which suggests that a person cannot be professional, and respected as professional, while at the same time being one's authentic self.[3] Justice Abella was recently interviewed by Steve Paikin on *The Agenda*, together with Barry Avrich, who produced the documentary on her life, *Without Precedent: The Supreme Life of Rosalie Abella*.[4] In that interview, Paikin asked Abella, "What made you think you could have a career in that profession (the judiciary) and be 'Broadway'"?[5] Justice Abella responded: "I honestly never thought about how I was supposed to behave now that I was a judge . . . there was no little voice inside me saying, 'So it's time not to wear bling or lose the colours.'"[6] But her most telling statement was, "You can't not be who you are no matter what you do, I just don't believe it."[7]

The authenticity-professionalism paradox has hit women particularly hard, because when women began entering the legal profession

---

Abella's "sister-in-law." See Rosalie Silberman Abella, "A farewell to Ruth Bader Ginsburg, from a Sister in Law" *The Globe and Mail* (25 September 2020), online: www.theglobeandmail.com/opinion/article-a-farewell-to-ruth-bader-ginsburg-from-a-sister-in-law/.

2 This is how Justice Karakatsanis characterized Justice Abella on the panel.

3 Susan McPherson, "How Much of Your 'Authentic Self' Should You Really Bring to Work?" *Harvard Business Review* (12 February 2021), online: https://hbr.org/2021/02/how-much-of-your-authentic-self-should-you-really-bring-to-work; Kimberley Young Milani, "Authenticity in the Workplace" *Ivey Business School* (18 November 2020), online: www.ivey.uwo.ca/leadership/for-leaders/leadership-blogs/2020/11/authenticity-in-the-workplace/.

4 The Agenda, "Rosalie Abella and Barry Avrich: Documenting a Supreme Life" *TVO Today* (May 2023), online: *YouTube* www.youtube.com/watch?v=_XJ5Tog9M60.

5 *Ibid* at 00h: 12m: 31s. Steve Paikin uses the term "Broadway" to refer to Justice Abella's colourful sense of style and personality, as well as her outspokenness. Justice Abella also happens to love Broadway musicals and so the metaphor of "Broadway" to describe her nature is quite apt.

6 *Ibid* at 00h: 13m :04s.

7 *Ibid* at 00h: 13m :35s.

in the 1970s and 1980s, they felt that they had to fit a mould, wear a uniform of sorts,[8] and leave their families and personal lives completely segregated from the workplace. Justice Abella confronted this paradox head on and resolved it by demonstrating that it is indeed possible to be the most professional, intellectually rigorous powerhouse of a jurist while, at the same time, remaining authentic to herself.

Indeed, throughout her career, Justice Abella's unique personal and intellectual style championed women in the legal profession in a myriad of ways. This paper will examine her impact on: 1) the value of a woman's point of view and participation in the law; 2) overcoming tangible and intangible challenges for women in the legal profession; and 3) confronting (and resolving) the authenticity-professionalism paradox.[9]

Throughout the paper, I will return to one particular Supreme Court of Canada decision rendered by Justice Abella, *Bruker v Marcovitz*,[10] to illustrate and inform each of these themes. The *Bruker* case concerned the conundrum of a Jewish woman whose husband refused to give her a religious divorce (a *get*); of course, Justice Abella herself is also a Jewish woman. Justice Abella brilliantly balanced her objectivity and impartiality as a judge with her own knowledge of the unfairness of the *get* to women and wove that balance into a masterful judgment using the objective tools of Quebec's private law of contracts, all the while couching the judgment in the discourse of equality. This balancing act was especially important given the unilateral impact of the *get* on women (the woman remains "chained" to the marriage if the husband refuses to grant her the *get*). As Justice Abella herself acknowledges, her judgment melds together "the public interest in protecting equality rights,

8 Details about this "uniform," as described by Linda Rothstein, are recounted later in this paper.

9 The division of this chapter into these topics mirrors the three-part division of the panel discussion at the conference itself, expertly led by the moderator, Deborah Palter: Deborah Palter, Andromache Karakatsanis, Sana Halwani, Freda Steel, Rosalie Jukier, Linda Rothstein, & Shantona Chaudhury, "Justice Abella and Women in the Legal Profession" panel, *The Honourable Rosalie Silberman Abella: A Life of Firsts* (Conference, Ottawa, 12 May 2022) ["Justice Abella and Women in the Legal Profession" panel].

10 2007 SCC 54 [*Bruker*]. See also Rosalie Jukier and Shauna Van Praagh, "Civil Law and Religion in the Supreme Court of Canada: What Should We Get Out of *Bruker v Marcovitz*?" (2008) 43 *Supreme Court Law Review* (2d) 381; Richard Moon, "*Bruker v. Marcovitz*: Divorce and the Marriage of Law and Religion" (2008) 42 *Supreme Court Law Review* (2d) 42; Norma Baumel Joseph, "Civil Jurisdiction and Religious Accord: *Bruker v. Marcovitz* in the Supreme Court of Canada" (2011) 40:3 *Studies in Religion* 1.

the dignity of Jewish women in their independent ability to divorce and remarry, as well as the public benefit in enforcing valid and binding contractual obligations."[11]

B. Part 1. The Value of a Woman's Point of View and Participation in the Law

Justice Abella's four and a half decades on the bench demonstrate that a woman's point of view undoubtedly influences legal discourse as well as the deliberative process of judgment-writing.[12] As Justice Andromache Karakatsanis remarked on the panel at the conference in honour of Justice Abella, decisions of women judges necessarily reflect a woman's perspective, which cannot be divorced from lived experience.[13] A clear example of this can be found in the Supreme Court of Canada's *Symes* decision,[14] where the appellant, a female lawyer, attempted to deduct the wages she paid to her nanny as a business expense in her personal income tax returns. Characterizing these outlays as "personal expenses" rather than proper "business expenses," the majority of the

11 *Ibid* at para 92.

12 However, as several scholars point out, there is not one singular women's perspective or point of view. See, for example, Trina Grillo, "Anti-Essentialism and Intersectionality: Tools to Dismantle the Master's House" (1995) 10 *Berkeley Women's Law Journal* 16 at 19; Deborah L. Rhode, "The 'Woman's Point of View'" (1988) 31:1/2 *Journal of Legal Education* 39.

13 Andromache Karakatsanis, speech, "Justice Abella and Women in the Legal Profession" panel, above note 9. This paper does not mean to assert that only women's perspectives are influenced by lived experience; this is true of all genders. The difference is the acknowledgment of the impact of lived experience by feminist scholars. See, for example, Katharine T. Bartlett, "Feminist Legal Methods," (1990) 103 *Harvard Law Review* 829. Moreover, Justice Abella is not the only woman judge to reflect her lived experience in her judgments. A notable example is that of Justice Corinne Sparks in her acquittal of a Black youth in *R v S (RD)*. As a Black judge living in Nova Scotia, she took judicial notice of the racialized tendency of white police officers to overreact when dealing with Black youths charged with an offence. The Supreme Court ultimately held her remarks not to be evidence of bias: see [1997] 3 SCR 484, 151 DLR (4th) 193. See also Justice McLachlin's dissenting judgment in *Rodriguez v British Columbia (Attorney General)*, [1993] 3 SCR 519, 107 DLR (4th) 342 and the Supreme Court's decision in *Carter v Canada (Attorney General)*, 2015 SCC 5, which established the constitutional right to assisted dying. Justice McLachlin openly discusses her experience living with a terminally ill spouse in her autobiography: see Beverley McLachlin, *Truth be Told: My Journey Through Life and the Law* (Toronto: Simon & Schuster Canada, 2019) at 242–44.

14 *Symes v Canada*, [1993] 4 SCR 695, 110 DLR (4th) 470. Note that Justice Abella was not, at this time, a justice of the Supreme Court of Canada.

Supreme Court disallowed the deduction of the cost of childcare. In a 7–2 decision, it is telling that the two dissenting judges were both women. Justice Claire L'Heureux-Dubé and Justice Beverley McLachlin were the only two women on the Court at that time. They seemed to be the only ones who understood that a woman's ability even to participate in the workforce may be completely contingent on her ability to acquire childcare.[15]

While Justice Abella was not yet a justice on the Supreme Court when this particular decision was rendered, her decisions always reflected her perspectives as a woman. As Justice Karakatsanis pointed out, it is difficult to read an Abella decision without remarking how attuned she is to the many forms of inequality, including gender inequality.[16] There is no doubt that her groundbreaking work on employment equity, a term she coined when serving as the sole commissioner of the 1984 Royal Commission on Equality in Employment, has continued to influence the tone and tenor of her decisions.[17] As Professor Adelle Blackett stated on another panel at the conference, not only was Abella's report on employment equity "trailblazing," it also "taught us how to listen deeply to equity-deserving groups."[18] The "narrative" nature of Justice Abella's judgment writing reflected this quality and demonstrated her desire to make her decisions as accessible as possible; she always drafted her decisions very clearly for the parties, in language they could readily understand.[19] As Professor Mary Liston remarked on another

---

15 *Ibid* at 792 and 798–800.

16 See, for example, Justice Abella's judgments in *Alberta v Hutterian Brethren of Wilson Colony*, 2009 SCC 37; *R v NS*, 2012 SCC 72; *Federation of Labour v Saskatchewan*, 2015 SCC 4 and, most notably, *Fraser v Canada (Attorney General)*, 2020 SCC 28.

17 Rosalie Silberman Abella, *Equality in Employment: A Royal Commission Report* (Ottawa: Commission on Equality in Employment, 1984), online: https://publications.gc.ca/site/eng/471737/publication.html; Carol Agócs, *Employment Equity in Canada: The Legacy of the Abella Report* (Toronto: University of Toronto Press, 2014). In her remarks during the conference, Justice Dorit Beinisch, Ninth President of the Supreme Court of Israel, made mention of the great international impact of Justice Abella's work on employment equity: Dori Beinisch, speech, "International Impact" panel, *The Honourable Rosalie Silberman Abella: A Life of Firsts* (Conference, Ottawa, 12 May 2022).

18 Adelle Blackett, speech, "Early Career" panel, *The Honourable Rosalie Silberman Abella: A Life of Firsts* (Conference, Ottawa, 12 May 2022).

19 See, for example, *Toronto (City) v Ontario (Attorney-General)*, 2021 SCC 34 at para 86. Justice Abella began her dissenting opinion with the following line: "Elections are to democracy what breathing is to life, and fair elections are what breathe life into healthy democracies."

panel of the conference,[20] there is sincerity in an Abella judgment; it is clear where she is coming from, which therefore gives "trustworthiness to her judicial voice." The panelists concurred in emphasizing that Justice Abella's entire judicial process always reflected an understanding that her role as a judge was not about her, but about the parties and the greater Canadian public.

Justice Abella's impact cannot be fully understood with a focus solely on the substantive aspects of the decisions she rendered. Her overall judicial style must also be examined. Justice Freda Steel commented that her impact — like that of many women judges — goes beyond her written decisions, and that she actually helped to shape Canadian judicial culture. This impact of women judges is echoed by Justice Bertha Wilson in her 1990 article, "Will Women Judges Really Make a Difference?" where she wrote that women judges change the deliberative process at the appellate level and influence it to be more collaborative.[21] Wilson writes: "women judges, through their differing perspectives on life, can bring a new humanity to bear on the decision-making process . . . perhaps they will succeed in infusing the law with an understanding of what it means to be fully human."[22]

Justice Karakatsanis picked up on this theme in recounting how Justice Abella valued collaboration and teamwork on the Supreme Court. She spoke about how Justice Abella set the tone for collaboration as she insisted that deliberations at the Court be more of a discussion that proceeded by issue, rather than by rank of the judge. They became more of a conversational exchange. As a result, Justice Abella changed the way Supreme Court justices deliberated. Interestingly, Justice Sonia Sotomayor of the US Supreme Court recently attributed this same quality to another leading woman judge, Justice Sandra Day O'Connor, stating, "there is a sense of collegiality, a sense of cooperativeness, that women tend to insist upon."[23]

20 Mary Liston, speech, "Influences" panel, *The Honourable Rosalie Silberman Abella: A Life of Firsts* (Conference, Ottawa, 12 May 2022). Professor Liston's speech has been adapted as another chapter in this volume; see Chapter 6, "Engaging Abella: Humanity, Imagination, and the Legal Profession."

21 Bertha Wilson, "Will Women Judges Really Make a Difference?" (1990) 28:3 *Osgoode Hall Law Journal* 507. See also Ruth B. Cowan, "Do Women on South Africa's Courts Make a Difference?" in Ulrike Schultz and Gisela Shaw, eds, *Gender and Judging* (London: Hart Publishing, 2013).

22 *Ibid* at 522.

23 Adam Liptak, "Sotomayor Says Supreme Court Can 'Regain the Public's Confidence'" *New York Times* (16 June 2022), online: www.nytimes.com/2022/06/16/us/sonia-sotomayor-supreme-court.html.

Justice Abella also showed us that a rich and meaningful legal career should, as Shantona Chaudhury put it, be about "professional fulfillment rather than professional success."[24] Justice Abella epitomized this in the way she participated in, and contributed to, decisions even when she did not author the judgment[25] and the way she demonstrated that even respectful differences of opinion, as expressed in dissenting opinions, should not diminish the collegiality of the Court. As David Rankin and Mahmud Jamal (as he then was) write in their article "Dissents and Concurrences: Seven Debates in Charter Jurisprudence," "Abella J.'s dissent employs non-confrontational, outcome-directed language that does not risk 'jeopardizing collegiality or public respect for and confidence in the judiciary'."[26]

The *Bruker* decision serves as an illustration of many of these themes and it teaches us valuable lessons that have important ramifications as the Canadian bench becomes more diverse. Many might question the choice to have Justice Abella, a Jewish woman, pen this decision for the majority of the Court, citing reasons related to judicial impartiality, one of the hallmarks of our judicial system. Would it be possible for a Jewish woman to really be impartial in this case? But Justice Abella ably demonstrated that one can be a Jewish woman, thereby profiting from a deeper understanding of the situation at hand, and still maintain impartiality. This reality is clearly summed up in Justice Abella's statement in the *Yukon Francophone School Board* case of 2015, a leading case on judicial impartiality, where she wrote that there is "a crucial difference between an open mind and an empty one . . . A judge's identity and experiences are an important part of who he or she is, and neither neutrality nor impartiality is inherently compromised by them."[27] She could be impartial and have an *open* mind even though she was a Jewish woman herself, and her mind was not *empty* regarding the issues, values, and consequences at play.

---

24 Shantona Chaudhury, "Justice Abella and Women in the Legal Profession" panel, above note 9.

25 Karakatsanis, above note 13.

26 W. David Rankin & Mahmud Jamal, "Dissents and Concurrences: Seven Debates in Charter Jurisprudence" (2013) 63 *Supreme Court Law Review* 89 at 99.

27 *Yukon Francophone School Board, Education Area #23 v Yukon (Attorney General)*, 2015 SCC 25 at paras 33-34. This echoes what Justice Abella has previously written, namely, "Every decisionmaker who walks into a courtroom to hear a case is armed not only with the relevant legal texts, but with a set of values, experiences and assumptions that are thoroughly embedded." Rosalie Abella, "The Dynamic Nature of Equality" in Sheilah L Martin & Kathleen E Mahoney, eds, *Equality and Judicial Neutrality* (Toronto: Carswell, 1987) 3 at 8–9.

The takeaways from *Bruker* have important implications for a diverse Canadian bench. In 2006, a complaint was made to the Canadian Judicial Council about Justice Roy McMurtry's participation in the Ontario Court of Appeal case dealing with the constitutionality of the same-sex marriage bill in Canada.[28] The complaint was made on the basis that he had a daughter in a same-sex relationship and therefore, it was alleged, he could not be impartial. This is ridiculous, of course, because that would mean other judges with children in heterosexual relationships would also technically be unable to be impartial in cases involving heterosexual relationships! But more seriously, Justice Abella's authenticity, combined with her professionalism and intellectual rigour, teaches us that judges who are members of minority groups (or have family members who belong to minority groups) need not automatically recuse themselves when a case concerning someone in their group comes before them. This challenges the implicit presumption that the white, heterosexual, cisgender male judge is the impartial one (after all, no one ever questions whether a white male judge can hear a case involving a white male litigant, or a non-white person for that matter) and that everyone else is an "other" with respect to impartiality, and that their otherness will cause biased thinking or analysis.[29]

C. Part 2. Overcoming Tangible and Intangible Challenges for Women in the Legal Profession

Justice Abella's career spanned many decades. It began in the 1970s, at a time when very few women were working in the legal profession. As Justice Freda Steel recounted in her remarks on the panel, when she herself started practising law in the 1970s, she lived in a world of men.[30] Garnering laughter from the audience, Justice Steel related a story about how when she was starting out as a litigation attorney, a

28 After the Court of Appeal for Ontario decided *Halpern v Canada (Attorney-General)*, [2003] OJ No 2268, C. Gwendolyn Landolt filed a complaint with the Canadian Judicial Council (CJC). The CJC ruled that the sexual orientation of a judge's children, and indeed whether a judge's children are married or living in a common law relationship, is not, in Chief Justice Richard Scott's view, indicative of any bias on the part of a judge.

29 See, for example, a Scottish case where a Jewish judge was alleged to have been biased in a case dealing with a Palestinian's request for asylum: *Helow (AP) v Secretary of State for the Home Department and Another* (Scotland), [2008] UKHL 62.

30 Freda Steel, "Justice Abella and Women in the Legal Profession" panel, above note 9.

judge greeted the lawyers in the courtroom by saying, "Good morning gentlemen and other member of the Bar!" While admittedly somewhat humourous, it is startling that such a comment was made by a judge just a few decades ago.

Justice Abella became a member of the Ontario Bar in these male-dominated times, in 1972, and was appointed to the Ontario Family Court as a judge, the first female and pregnant judge, in 1976. As Justice Steel related, during those early years, there were significant challenges to working in a male-dominated legal and judicial world. For example, prominent counsel Linda Rothstein explained that in order to fit in, women had to abide by the "Goldilocks Calibration": the clothes they wore, and how they comported themselves, had to meet the oft-unattainable standard of "just right." Women lawyers wore masculine jackets with padded shoulders and long scarves tied as bows (to replicate the male necktie), but never wore trousers. Women's voices were also important — they spoke in lower registers so as not to appear shrill, but they were also expected to speak loudly (but not too loudly) to command respect. Women lawyers were required to be agreeable, but not pushovers. They needed to have ambition, but not too much. And women lawyers were not to disrupt any of these expectations and certainly not draw attention to themselves. Clothing and comportment were symbols of competence and seriousness. Rocking the boat and confronting norms were out of the question.[31]

Yet, Justice Abella proved to be impervious to these norms. In an affront to the constraints placed on women lawyers in the 1970s and thereafter, Justice Abella taught us that "you can practice law and wear your personality."[32] She brought colour, literally and metaphorically, to the courtroom. In fact, as Sana Halwani put it, "she brought her whole self everywhere."[33] Linda Rothstein noted how Justice Abella spoke in her natural voice and hugged those around her at a time when the profession did not make space for the kind of personal warmth she exuded. Indeed, Justice Abella became a role model, mentor, and champion to many talented women jurists. Her authenticity helped create a culture

31 Linda Rothstein, speech, "Justice Abella and Women in the Legal Profession" panel, above note 9.

32 As stated by Sinziana Hennig, one of Justice Abella's former clerks, who spoke at the Banquet Dinner: Sinziana Hennig, Banquet Dinner speech, *The Honourable Rosalie Silberman Abella: A Life of Firsts* (Conference, Ottawa, 12 May 2022).

33 Sana Halwani, speech, "Justice Abella and Women in the Legal Profession" panel, above note 9.

where the unwritten rules that were restrictive and misguided became unnecessary and, in turn, antiquated.

Justice Abella demonstrated that, like a "pas de deux," culture changes law and law changes culture. Her work on employment equity bears this phenomenon out. As Linda Rothstein remarked, this work was important because of its influence on the legal culture and its impact on women.[34] Justice Abella mapped out the arguments that women lawyers were able to make in their lobbying efforts for maternity leave, partnership representation, and fair compensation. Ultimately, as Justice Freda Steel remarked, the entry of women into the profession changed the legal profession itself.[35]

All the panelists agreed that great strides have been made in the legal profession but that notwithstanding, the challenges for women jurists have not disappeared; rather, they have simply evolved. The challenges today are, of course, very different than they were in the 1970s, where it was a question of getting women into the legal profession in the first place. Today, women make up the majority of law students, and there are many examples of extremely successful women jurists.[36] Yet, as Shantona Chaudhury discussed, even women who are younger, and who have entered the profession at a time when glass ceilings have supposedly been broken, face significant challenges.[37] These contemporary challenges are more intangible and often take the form of insidious barriers that are, in many ways, more difficult to fix. One such challenge is reflected in the so-called "Punishment Gap," where the margin of error is much slimmer for women, with a narrower band of acceptable

---

34 *Ibid.*

35 Steel, above note 30.

36 Notably my co-panelists and outstanding panel moderator.

37 Above note 24. Statistics bear out the fact that the percentage of women partners at major law firms has not increased significantly: see, for example, Sylvia Guirguis, "Women in Law: How the Legal Sector Still Fails Female Lawyers and Why True Equality Remains Elusive" *Lexpert* (7 September 2022), online: www.lexpert.ca/legal-insights/women-in-law-how-the-legal-sector-still-fails-female-lawyers-and-why-true-equality-remains-elusive/368855; Robyn Doolittle and Christine Dobby, "Female Partners Earned Nearly 25 Per Cent Less than their Male Colleagues at a Major Toronto Law Firm, Document Shows" (9 February 2021), online: *Globe & Mail* www.theglobeandmail.com/canada/article-female-partners-earn-less-than-male-colleagues-at-big-law-firm/. Further, the continued adherence to the billable hour continues to be a barrier to a better work/life balance for all lawyers: see, for example, Leigh McMullan Abramson, "Is the Billable Hour Obsolete?" (15 October 2015), online: *The Atlantic* www.theatlantic.com/business/archive/2015/10/billable-hours/410611/.

behaviour that we expect from women leaders.[38] Women in positions of authority are subject to more scrutiny,[39] and the repercussions of the Punishment Gap are significant. In the legal profession, as well as in others, it may help explain why women and minorities struggle to rise to the "top" of the profession — the Punishment Gap results in a steeper fall when these individuals "fail" in their professional duties.

The aftermath of the *Bruker* decision is an apt illustration of the Punishment Gap as an intangible challenge for women and other marginalized jurists. Some critics took issue with the decision arguing that Justice Abella unjustifiably used the neutrality of the secular courts to interfere with religion.[40] Others maintained that her decision may not have gone far enough.[41] These criticisms from both sides are not unique to *Bruker*.

---

38 Mark Egan, Gregor Matvos & Amit Seru, "When Harry Fired Sally: The Double Standard in Punishing Misconduct" (2018) Harvard Business School Finance Working Paper No 19-047; Abhishek Parajuli, "The Punishment Gap: How Workplace Mistakes Hurt Women and Minorities Most" *World Economic Forum* (18 June 2019), online: www.weforum.org/agenda/2019/06/the-punishment-gap-how-workplace-mistakes-hurt-women-and-minorities-most/; Brett Beasley, "How Can We Close the Gender Punishment Gap?" *Notre Dame Deloitte Center for Ethical Leadership*, online: https://ethicalleadership.nd.edu/news/gender-punishment-gap/.

39 Tonja Jacobi and Dylan Schweers, "Female Supreme Court Justices Are Interrupted More by Male Justices and Advocates" (11 April 2017), *Harvard Business Review* online: https://hbr.org/2017/04/female-supreme-court-justices-are-interrupted-more-by-male-justices-and-advocates; Maya Yang, "Let Her Finish: Interruptions of Female Justices Led to New Supreme Court Rules" *Guardian* (15 October 2021), online: www.theguardian.com/law/2021/oct/15/us-supreme-court-female-justices-interruptions-sonia-sotomayor.

40 As dissenting Justice Deschamps asserted in *Bruker*, above note 10 at para 132, "secular law has no effect in matters of religious law." Authors who agree with this position and criticize Justice Abella's judgment include F.C. DeCoste, "Caesar's Faith: Limited Government and Freedom of Religion in *Bruker v. Marcovitz*" (2009) 32:1 *Dalhousie Law Journal* 153; M.H. Ogilvie, "*Bruker v. Marcovitz*: (Get)ting Over Freedoms (Like Contract and Religion) in Canada" (2009) 24 *National Journal of Constitutional Law* 173. This is also the view of Christelle Landheer-Cieslak as cited in Louise Langevin et al, "L'affaire *Bruker c. Marcovitz* : variations sur un theme," (2008) 49:4 *Cahiers de droit* 655 at 700–6.

41 See, for example, Joanna Lindenberg, "(Un)Chained Wives: Understanding the *Bruker v. Markovitz* Decision, and Possible Alternative Legal Claims for Jewish Women Who Are Denied a Get" (2010) *Dalhousie Law Journal* 1 at 15–24. While Joseph is favourable to Abella's decision, she does question whether the Supreme Court can push for more state intervention in marriage in the name of gender equality and whether the low amount of the damage award is such that the case is "a symbolic victory, important in law but less so perhaps for the persons involved": see Joseph, above note 10 at 12 & 13.

In fact, Justice Abella faced the same criticism for other judgments, such as *Québec v A*,[42] *Kahkewistahaw First Nation v Taypotat*,[43] and similar section 15 cases in which she was the most aligned with equality-seeking groups but still faced pushback for "not doing enough."[44] Justice Wilson discusses this phenomenon in her paper "Will Women Judges Really Make a Difference?" where she observes that overcoming tangible and intangible challenges as the "first" of your kind comes with pushback on two fronts.[45] Are you doing too much and jeopardizing the legitimacy and "reputation" of jurists who look like you? Or are you not doing enough to "champion" the groups that are often excluded from positions like yours? This manifestation of the Punishment Gap holds women and minorities to a much higher, and often unattainable, standard (as compared to their white male counterparts), and when these individuals fail to meet that standard, they are "punished" disproportionately for otherwise bold or groundbreaking acts such as penning the decision in *Bruker*.

D. Part 3: Resolving the Authenticity-Professionalism Paradox

Throughout her career, Justice Abella disrupted the authenticity-professionalism paradox and, in so doing, helped dismantle harmful norms and barriers for women in the legal profession. This "paradox," which is starting to receive attention in business media outlets[46] such as the Ivey Business School blog, posits that:

> individuals often feel a tension between being their authentic selves and conforming (or at least trying to blend in) to the dominant or pervading culture of an organization. This tension can lead some people to reduce, alter or eliminate the presentation of ethnic, religious, racial, social, economic, educational and other identifiers. At the same time, employees can resent the pressure to "fit the mold" and find themselves at a crossroads.[47]

---

42 2013 SCC 5.

43 2015 SCC 30.

44 See, for example, Jonnette Watson Hamilton & Jennifer Koshan, "*Kahkewistahaw First Nation v Taypotat*: An Arbitrary Approach to Discrimination" (2016) 76 *Supreme Court Law Review* 241 at 258 and 261–262; Jonnette Watson Hamilton & Jennifer Koshan, "Roundtable on *Quebec v A*: Searching for Clarity on Equality" *ABlawg: The University of Calgary Faculty of Law Blog* (5 June 2013), online: https://ablawg.ca/2013/06/05/roundtable-on-quebec-v-a-searching-for-clarity-on-equality/.

45 See Wilson, above note 21 at 507.

46 See, for example, the sources listed in above note 3.

47 See Milani, above note 3.

There is scant commentary on the relationship between authenticity and professionalism in the legal profession specifically, but as demonstrated by the panelists' commentary, there is little doubt that it exists for women lawyers and judges. As Halwani observed, legal professionalism should be about skill and judgment.[48] Yet, women are often judged by the way they look and comport themselves, as opposed to the job they are doing.

Justice Abella's singular rejection of the very existence of the paradox allowed her to be fearless in her role as a judge and, in so doing, inspire other female legal professionals to be equally fearless. As explained by Chaudhury, Justice Abella's role as a "champion" was both general and specific: her authenticity in her judicial role helped make far-reaching strides for women in the legal profession.[49] But her thoughtful, personable nature and approach to mentorship led her to champion women jurists on an individual level as well.

Many of the lessons I have learned from Justice Abella flow from the co-existence of her authenticity and professionalism, as well as her intellectual rigour. First, she taught me that I could, and indeed should, acknowledge my family life in my classroom and not hesitate to inject stories about my children and my husband into my lectures and, here was the real lesson, still be a great professor. And the lesson paid off as, over the years, students ended up loving the anecdotes I would tell them, or insights I would impart, using my family as an example. Years later, they would remind me, for example, of my lecture on the contractual doctrine of mistake using a hilarious exchange between my then-teenage daughter and me about a person called "Fergie," me thinking we were speaking about Sarah Ferguson of the royal family (who had, most relevantly to this story, red hair) and my daughter referring all along to the pop star Fergie (who, of course, is blonde). They never forgot the doctrine of mistake! They also loved my anecdote about a bargain between my husband and me regarding the division of household chores (something along the lines of me agreeing to do carpool while he took out the garbage), which he didn't execute, to illustrate the concept of the domestic contract and its potential unenforceability. Was our bargain a contract? If not, what element was missing? If so, was it enforceable? If not, why not? If so, in what venue — a court of law? Again, the use of a simple but genuine family example not only rendered the concept more accessible, but it also allowed my students to delve into

48 Above note 32.

49 Above note 24.

all the difficult and complex issues surrounding the "domestic agreement," including a feminist critique of it.[50]

As such, the first important lesson that Justice Abella taught all of us is that we can, and indeed should, bring our human side to the workplace and that we must embrace our whole identity and not artificially split it up into the "work self" and the "home self."

The second important lesson is that intellectual rigour necessitates having the courage to try new things outside of one's comfort zone. For Justice Abella, this meant teaching, instead of adjudicating, and, moreover, teaching courses that she herself admitted she had not mastered.[51] In the years she was a Boulton Visiting Professor at McGill, she taught a wide variety of different and difficult courses, showing me that great intellectual rigour includes *intellectual fearlessness*. Perhaps this fearlessness stems from Justice Abella's personal history of being born in a displaced persons camp in post-war Germany to parents who had survived the Holocaust. Halwani, herself an immigrant to Canada, characterized the attitude that comes from such personal history as "take nothing for granted and try everything,"[52] a mindset that Justice Abella certainly adopted and extended to others. Justice Albie Sachs, in the opening panel of the conference, put it this way: "She didn't follow her dreams; she followed her life and the dreams followed."[53] I have personally been influenced tremendously by this attitude and I owe it to Justice Abella's example that during my career, I was open to taking on the teaching of new courses on different topics (which many professors are not willing to do) and to doing new things, like leaving my comfort zone of teaching and entering the world of university administration to become McGill's first woman Dean of Students for six years, or leaving teaching at McGill for two years to work as a senior advisor at the National Judicial Institute. Looking back, these twists and turns in my career have ended up being among the most enriching of my professional life.

---

50 *Balfour v Balfour* [1919] 2 KB 571. For a feminist critique of the domestic agreement, see also Prince Saprai, "*Balfour v Balfour* and the Separation of Contract and Promise" (2017) 37:3 *Legal Studies* 468.

51 Justice Abella described her experience teaching unfamiliar courses in Rosalie Abella, "Rod Macdonald: A Man of Virtue, a Teacher of Virtue, and a Friend of Virtue" in Richard Janda, Rosalie Jukier and Daniel Jutras, eds, *The Unbounded Level of the Mind: Rod Macdonald's Legal Imagination* (Montreal & Kingston: McGill-Queen's University Press, 2015) at 258.

52 Above note 32.

53 Albie Sachs, speech, "International Impact" panel, *The Honourable Rosalie Silberman Abella: A Life of Firsts* (Conference, Ottawa, 12 May 2022).

The *Bruker* decision is instructive in understanding the authenticity-professionalism paradox as well as how expertly Justice Abella resolves it. Many of Justice Abella's judgments highlight how she manages to be both authentic and professional, but this balance shines through in *Bruker* because it demonstrates how carefully she could marry her personal, authentic self and her judicial, professional self. This judgment illustrates, to borrow the words of Justice Albie Sachs, "the confluence of her mind and her heart."[54] Many who have written about the *Bruker* judgment sided with the way the minority judge (another woman, Justice Marie Deschamps) dealt with the case — namely that courts simply should not mix into religion and that secularity of the state means there is a firm line between secular and religious law.[55] In my view, by using the secular law (of contracts) so carefully, ingeniously, and judiciously,[56] Justice Abella managed to walk a very fine, but fair, line in this case. There is genuine creativity and boldness in this decision. And, as explained earlier in the paper, it contains many important lessons for judicial impartiality and the power and potential of a diverse bench.

E. Conclusion

Justice Abella has been a true champion for women in the legal profession. She has broken countless glass ceilings with her myriad of "firsts." But throughout her career, her biggest lesson is that she has simply been herself — an honest, warm, bright woman who has brought so much to her family, her friends, Canadian society, and indeed the world. Justice Louise Charron, speaking at the Conference's banquet dinner, recounted how before she met Justice Abella, Justice McLachlin explained to her that, "you don't meet Rosie, you experience Rosie."[57] There is no doubt that both the Canadian and international legal profession is better for having done so.

54 *Ibid.*

55 See above note 40.

56 See, for example, Jukier and Van Praagh, above note 10.

57 Louise Charron, Banquet Dinner speech, *The Honourable Rosalie Silberman Abella: A Life of Firsts* (Conference, Ottawa, 12 May 2022).

6 Engaging Abella: Humanity, Imagination, and the Legal Profession

MARY LISTON*

A. Introduction

This chapter is an encomium in two parts. Part A is a reflection celebrating the artistic and creative dimensions of Justice Rosalie Abella's career with an eye to reinforcing the importance of the humanities for those who comprise legal profession.[1] Here I am thinking of a multiplicity of actors ranging from arbitrators, decision-makers in government, judges, lawyers, reformers, and educators. These are the people Justice Abella has tellingly called the "players" — the recurring cast of characters — in the legal profession.[2] In this first section, I consider how legal actors profit from a sensibility and set of competencies derived from the humanities, both of which support legal craftship. Skills developed from the humanities also undergird legal actors' capacity to make reasoned and reasonable judgments through the use of pragmatic, principled, and thickly contextualized reasoning. Lastly, I highlight the undeniable importance of narrative skills for persuasive writing. To illustrate these arguments, Justice Abella's powerful dissent in *Alberta v Hutterian Brethren of Wilson Colony* provides a touchstone throughout

---

* Mary Liston is an Associate Professor at the Peter A. Allard School of Law, University of British Columbia. The author wishes to thank the organizers of the conference at which this chapter was first presented, as well as Professor Vanessa MacDonnell for fruitful feedback on the arguments and especially Justice Rosalie Silberman Abella for her remarkable contributions to Canadian jurisprudence and justice.

1 For reflections on Justice Abella's career as a legal professional and the importance of both judging and judicial education, see Chapter 21 in this volume by Rosemary Cairns-Way, "Equality and the Judicial Role: Lessons from Singing in a Choir."

2 Rosalie Silberman Abella, "Lawyers, Judges and Rights" (1998) 36:4 *Alberta Law Review* 990 at 990.

this first section.[3] Part B constitutes a brief eulogy for the passing of a classic age in one field of law in a concurrence deeply imbued with Justice Abella's spirit. In this part, I will consider how the story of Canadian administrative law is framed and narrated and why these skills matter for law and the legal imaginary. Conceiving law as part of the humanities permits us to understand jurisprudence as a kind of collective historical memory and an important — indeed vital — resource to assist with ethical reflection about justice.

B. In Praise of Law and the Humanities

Employing a law and humanities lens, this first part considers several of Justice Abella's attributes that both legal education and legal professionals should value and nurture: artistic sensibility and skill (the legal professional as artist), craftship (the legal professional as craftsperson), the ability to make reasoned and reasonable judgments (the legal professional as an embodied and empathetic person), and narrativity (the legal professional as storyteller and narrator).

1. The Legal Professional as Artist

It is no secret that Justice Abella is a devotee of the arts — dance, film, literature, music, sculpture, theatre — all of it![4] What is less obvious is how this passion for the arts morphs into her love of the law and the legal profession. Earlier in her career, for example, she played an instrumental role in a conference and published proceedings entitled *Justice Beyond Orwell*, which explored various relations between law and justice in light of a portentous year, 1984, by drawing on themes from that novel.[5] To take another example, most people do not depict a courtroom like so: "They say that most people only hear the music, not the lyrics of human events. In the courtroom is where we find humanity's lyrics and lawyers are the instruments that give voice to these lyrics."[6]

3 *Alberta v Hutterian Brethren of Wilson Colony*, 2009 SCC 37, [2009] 2 SCR 567 [*Hutterian*].

4 I will discuss Justice Abella's library a little later on. She and her late husband, Irving Abella, were longtime patrons of many arts, artists (such as Charles Pachter), and institutions (such as the influential publishing house Lester & Orpen Dennys).

5 George Orwell, *Nineteen Eighty-Four* (London: Secker & Warburg, 1949); Rosalie Silberman Abella and Melvin L Rothman, eds, *Justice Beyond Orwell* (Montréal: Éditions Yvon Blais Inc, 1985). This edited collection emerged out of the Canadian Institute for the Administration of Justice's 10th anniversary conference. Two contributions on freedom of expression from this book informed *R v Keegstra*, [1990] 3 SCR 697.

6 Abella, Lawyers, Judges and Rights," above note 2 at 994.

While only an arts aficionado could think of a courtroom in this manner, that is not the most interesting aspect of her analogy. Notice how this quote also reveals Justice Abella's sense of, and sensibilities about, justice. While legal professionals are indeed *instrumental*, their primary function is to be an *instrument* that channels the voice of the affected person. For Justice Abella, it is the person at the heart of the legal issue, the legal subject, who remains both the *author and source* of a claim on justice. She captures an ethical complexity, the puzzle of how a person is simultaneously author and subject, autonomous and vulnerable, free and constrained, in their own legal case and, indeed, in their lives. In law, it is the legal system and the professionals who inhabit it who are tasked with recognizing and enhancing that person's autonomy and dignity instead of reducing them to actual subjecthood.

For those of us who have followed her career, we know on which side of history she lies in this matter. She clearly carries forward the torch that her sisters, Justices L'Heureux-Dubé and McLachlin, raised in the *Cooper* decision, stating that neither the *Charter* nor the law itself is "some holy grail which only judicial initiates of the superior courts may touch."[7] In a constitutional democracy, the law is authored or authorized by the public and in a real sense *belongs* to the affected person individually when their issue is adjudicated. This is one way the legal order (and ultimately the state itself) gains both authority and legitimacy. As legal philosopher David Dyzenhaus suggests, it is through adjudicating rights that the affected person poses this fundamental question: "But, how can that be law for me?"[8] It is the reciprocal duty of the legal system and legal professionals to provide an adequate answer to that question for that person.

The lyricism Justice Abella hears in the courtroom resonates with legal and literary theorist James Boyd White's views on the many intersections between art and law. In his essays on law and legal education, Boyd White suggests that art and law both possess a basic transformative power to convert the raw material of everyday experience and life into something new and different (and, perhaps, better):

> Conversion of this kind is a radical form of human activity, for which our word is art: we convert earth and oil into paintings that may change the imagination; pleasing sounds into music, not always pleasing, but sometimes of incredible power and beauty; human actors and costumes and words into another dimension of reality, on the stage, with another claim on our attention altogether. So in the Law: we convert immediate

7 *Cooper v Canada (Human Rights Commission)*, [1996] 3 SCR 85 [*Cooper*] at para 70.
8 David Dyzenhaus, *The Long Arc of Legality* (Cambridge, UK: Cambridge UP, 2022) at xi.

> experience into the subject of thought of a particular kind, which has at is center the question of meaning: what this event means, and should mean, in the language of the law; and what that language itself means, as a way in which we articulate our deepest values and attain collective being. The life that gives meaning in such a way is itself a life of meaning.[9]

Whether or not such a transformation is beneficial remains a question that the legal professional should always have at the top of their mind.

Law can be about brute power and it necessarily involves political power. But thinkers like Boyd White remind us that law can also positively shape a politico-legal community, how it talks about itself, the way its people talk to each other, and the way its members lead their lives together. At best, law evinces a commitment to a "continuous process of discussion and evolution,"[10] rather than anomie or violence. While we should be mindful of the mundane and jurispathic facets of law, this hopeful and jurisgenerative potential also exists. Justice Abella kept faith with both the good and the bad in law, mindful of the wrongs that law created or sustained but also holding onto the promise of law to recognize and restructure human relations for the better. The possibility for law to transform undergirds a sense of responsibility that goes beyond legal ethics and fosters a commitment to contribute to a way of meaning and living together in a political community aspiring to good governance and good relations.

To my mind, Justice Abella's jurisprudential contributions on matters relating to religious freedom and the constitutive nature of religious identity underscore these points. Cases[11] like *Multani v Commission scolaire Marguerite-Bourgeoys*,[12] *Bruker v Marcovitz*,[13] *Alberta v Hutterian*

9 James Boyd White, *From Expectation to Experience: Essays on Law and Legal Education* (Ann Arbor: U of Michigan P, 2000) at 182.

10 *Reference re Secession of Quebec*, [1998] 2 SCR 217 at para 150.

11 Note that the following list is illustrative, not exhaustive.

12 2006 SCC 6, [2006] 1 SCR 256. Justices Deschamps and Abella co-authored a prescient dissent, which held that a school board's prohibition against a student wearing a ceremonial kirpan at school because it was considered to be a "weapon" constituted an unreasonable violation of freedom of religion and a lack of required accommodation. The dissent is prescient in that it engaged in administrative law review of this body's discretionary decision rather than *Charter* review, thus portending the developments brought by *Doré v Barreau du Québec*, 2012 SCC 12, [2012] 1 SCR 395, a unanimous judgment authored by Justice Abella.

13 2007 SCC 54, [2007] 3 SCR 607 [*Bruker*]. Justice Abella balanced section 2(a) (religious freedom) and section 15 (equality rights) in a non-*Charter* context, as this case involved a husband who wanted to deny his ex-wife a Jewish religious divorce (a *get*) following civil divorce proceedings. Justice Abella held that religious freedom did not discharge his contractual obligations to his ex-wife as he had promised to

Brethren of Wilson Colony,[14] *R v NS,*[15] *Loyola High School v Quebec (AG),*[16] and *Mouvement laïque québécoise v Saguenay (City)*[17] disclose a sensitivity that seeks to discern the whole context, a finely-tuned awareness of the costs that even a skilful balancing of rights requires, and acute attentiveness to the needs of vulnerable persons and communities.[18] In *Hutterian,* for example, the province of Alberta rejected the Hutterites' request not to be photographed for driver's licenses because they believe that the Second Commandment, by forbidding idolatry, prohibited their likeness from being captured. Prior to the introduction of the new requirement by regulation, the Hutterites benefitted from an exemption from a universal photo requirement. This resulted in a seemingly imperviable impasse between the government and the community. The majority

---

provide a *get*. For a rich discussion of this case, see Chapter 5 in this volume: Rosalie Jukier, "Justice Abella: Confronting the Authenticity-Professionalism Paradox."

14 Above note 3.

15 2012 SCC 72, [2012] 3 SCR 726. Justice Abella's concurring judgment held that a Muslim woman's religious belief — that wearing a niqab during court proceedings was mandated — should be respected. This woman ought not be required to remove her niqab in order to testify in a sexual assault case unless revealing her face was directly relevant to the case (e.g., such as where identity was in question). Justice Abella balanced *Charter* guarantees of section 2(a), religious freedom, with section 11(d), trial fairness, differently than the majority. She disagreed with the majority's view that being unable to see the witness's face is acceptable in a fair trial where the evidence is uncontested. Justice Abella contended that in cases involving sexual assault complaints, the evidence will always inevitably be contested, and that complainants and supporting witnesses may therefore be inappropriately forced to choose between participation in the justice system and their sincere religious beliefs.

16 2015 SCC 12, [2015] 1 SCR 613. In her majority judgment, Justice Abella held that Quebec's Minister of Education, Recreation and Sports improperly exercised discretion by requiring Loyola High School's proposed alternative program for teaching a mandatory ethics and religious culture course be entirely secular in its content and delivery. This administrative decision was found to contradict both the statutory objectives of the program as well as freedom of religion under the *Quebec Charter of Rights and Freedoms.*

17 2015 SCC 16, [2015] 2 SCR 3. In her concurring reasons, Justice Abella agreed with the majority that the City of Saguenay's municipal by-law permitting the recital of a Christian prayer at the beginning of each council meeting violated the principle of state neutrality. She disagreed with the majority that judicial review of different aspects of a final decision from the Quebec Human Rights Tribunal could be subject to different standards of review; instead, she held that the reasons of a specialized tribunal must be read as a whole on a reasonableness standard.

18 For a brief analysis of Justice Abella's attentiveness to vulnerability, see Lawrence David, "The Voice of the Vulnerable" *CBA National Magazine* (1 July 2021), online: https://nationalmagazine.ca/en-ca/articles/law/opinion/2021/justice-abella-the-voice-of-the-vulnerable.

decision, penned by Chief Justice McLachlin, weighed in favour in the provincial government, adhering closely to the principle of deference. The decision adverted to, but did not grapple with, the "all or nothing"[19] nature that section 2(a) religious freedom cases frequently seem to pose for public law.

Justice Abella's perceptive dissent best captures the nature of the harm that the minority Hutterian community members felt at the hands of an uncompromising government. She weighed the context very differently to conclude that this universal and mandatory licensing requirement "completely extinguishes"[20] the affected right and therefore did not minimally impair the Hutterites' religious freedom. As many readers will know, this is extremely strong language and, like the loud clash of cymbals in a symphonic performance, commands our attention.

What would it be like to be without this aesthetic dimension of professional responsibility or sense of vocation? Rather bleak. Consider how Charles Darwin describes his life without art:

> In one respect my mind had changed during the last twenty or thirty years. Formerly pictures gave me considerable, and music very intense delight. But now . . . I have almost lost my taste for pictures or music. . . . My mind seems to have become a sort of machine for grinding general laws out of large collections of fact. . . . The loss of these tastes, this curious and lamentable loss of the higher aesthetic tastes, is a is a loss of happiness, and may possibly be injurious to the intellect, and more probably to the moral character, by enfeebling the emotional part of our nature.[21]

If he could live his life again, Darwin vowed that he would read some poetry and listen to some music at least once every week. Looking at the raw material of law, would Justice Abella concur with law student Franz Kafka, whose legal education amounted to, in his words, being force-fed "intellectual sawdust which had been chewed by a thousand mouths before"?[22] The public might very well see these two views as confirmation of law's inner dystopia: machine-like legal professionals

---

19 *Hutterian*, above note 3 at para 61.

20 *Ibid* at para 148.

21 Oliver Sacks, *Musicophilia* (New York and Toronto: Knopf, 2007) at 292, citing Charles Darwin, *The Autobiography of Charles Darwin*, ed Nora Barlow (London: Collins, 1958).

22 Reza Banakar, "In Search of Heimat: A Note on Franz Kafka's Concept of Law" (2010) 22:3 *Law and Literature* at 469, citing Franz Kafka, *Letter to My Father*, trans. Howard Colyer (North Carolina: Lulu, 2008), 63.

surviving solely on intellectual sawdust so that they may continually grind out general laws from large and arbitrary collections of facts, which they impose on hapless, passive legal subjects. I would posit that this is not the vision of law that Justice Abella has in her mind's eye. Her legal order depends on a contextually oriented, dialogic, dynamic, empathetic, pragmatic, and principled set of actors for the practice and creation of law.[23]

Perhaps unsurprisingly, then, dance animates Justice Abella's jurisprudence. In conversation with journalist Paul Wells, she revealed her vision of the judicial authors of several early foundational *Charter* decisions, Justices Brian Dickson and Bertha Wilson: "I call them the Fred and Ginger of the *Charter*. Because they choreographed it. And they did it wonderfully."[24] What a contrast with Darwin and Kafka! Moved by law's constitutive rhythm, Dickson and Wilson are not machines grinding out *Charter* widgets; they are artists and partners full of grace and skill. Unprecedented, one might say. The artist-judge takes dusty legal materials and makes something new out of common ordinary law. Unlike Bartleby the Scrivener, this judge prefers to engage *with* the life of the law, to be in tune with law's imagination, rather than prefer *not to*.[25] This kind of legal professional wants the law to be just, true, good, *and* beautiful and is deeply committed to making it so.

2. *The Legal Professional as Craftsperson*

The legal craftsperson desires law to be of high quality — useful, lasting, and well made. They take pride in their work, the "pride of the craftsman."[26] Lon Fuller, in his classic text *The Morality of Law*, con-

---

23 On how the phrase "alert, alive and sensitive" — first coined by Justice L'Heureux-Dubé in the major Supreme Court of Canada administrative law decision *Baker v Canada (Minister of Citizenship and Immigration)*, [1999] 2 SCR 817 at para 75 — captures several essential attributes of good judging, see Mary Liston, "'Alert, Alive and Sensitive': *Baker*, the Duty to Give Reasons, and the Ethos of Justification in Canadian Public Law" in David Dyzenhaus, ed, *The Unity Of Public Law* (Oxford: Hart Publishing, 2004) 113.

24 Paul Wells, "Rosie Abella said she'd answer questions when she turned 75" *Maclean's* (15 June 2021), online: https://www.macleans.ca/news/rosie-abella-said-shed-answer-questions-when-she-turned-75/.

25 Herman Melville, "Bartleby, The Scrivener: A Story of Wall Street" in *The Piazza Tales* (New York: Dix, Edwards & Co, 1856). Bartleby, employed as a clerk by an elderly lawyer, becomes unproductive after an initial period of intense activity and responds to his employer's requests to work with the now-famous phrase "I would prefer not to."

26 Lon L Fuller, *The Morality of Law* (New Haven and London: Yale University Press, 1964) at 43.

structs a model legal professional (therefore quite different from his allegorical ruler Rex who fails in eight ways to make law) who adheres to two moralities — the morality of duty and the morality of aspiration, together which comprise Fuller's internal morality of law. Drawing on Adam Smith's theory of moral sentiments, Fuller suggests that "[t]he morality of duty 'may be compared to the rules of grammar' while the morality of aspiration may be compared 'to the rules which critics lay down for the attainment of what is sublime and elegant in composition."[27] Rather than relying on the conventional metaphor of the "judge as umpire" which supports the morality of duty, Fuller's dual-duty legal professional also acts like a judge in an artistic field — perhaps a judge like Justice Abella was in 2003 for the Giller Prize.[28] This conception puts judging in a non-positivistic frame. Judging is not only about ascertaining facts and deducing rules of law. It is also more than being an "umpire" in the beautiful game. It is about perceiving context deeply, really *hearing* the parties, and caring about the integrity of the entire legal endeavour. This conception embraces the humanness of law, such that law is like a child whose heritage is shared between two parents: the arts and the sciences.

While exhibiting fidelity to precedent and existing law, the legal craftsperson will also innovate if such innovation points towards improvement and realization of the overarching *telos*, justice. But to do so requires the virtues of candour, transparency, openness, and truthfulness about when and why such innovation is needed.[29] As Justice Abella writes: "Weighing values and taking public policy into account does not impair judicial neutrality of impartiality. Pretending we do *not* take them into account, and refusing to confront our personal views and be open in spite of them, may be the bigger risk to impartiality."[30] Consonant with this claim is the knowledge that interpretation is never about extracting meaning from a text; rather, it is about the reader putting meaning in. This is a complex task and not one without constraints, because an ethic of reading exists based on fidelity to the text(s) that engage our critical attention.[31] Reading

27 *Ibid* at 5.

28 The Giller Prize is a literary award given to a Canadian author — emerging or established — of a novel or short story collection published in English (including translation) from both small independent and large publishing houses.

29 See, for example, Steven J. Burton, *Judging in Good Faith* (Cambridge, UK and New York: Cambridge University Press, 1992).

30 Abella, "Lawyers, Judges and Rights," above note 2 at 995.

31 On the ethics of reading, see this famous exchange between Ronald Dworkin and

carefully and reflectively can be an ethical act, whether it be literature, theology, or caselaw.

Like all artisans, the legal craftsperson is concerned with balance, proportionality, and fit. They are not afraid of complexity and indeed find complexity both fascinating and pleasing — like the complex design of a Gothic cathedral or a Muslim mosque. The legal craftsperson understands that law needs both symmetry and asymmetry in structuring relations, finding both fair and fitting according to the context. They perceive how symmetry and asymmetry undergird conceptions of equality and fairness. This perception underscores the aesthetic dimension of the principles of fairness and proportionality.[32] The legal craftsperson also sees beauty in just social arrangements, what Fuller termed *eunomia,* to which the law can contribute to constructing or restructuring. And, like a skillful modiste, this child of Themis possesses the practical wisdom to know when to alter, amend, hem, re-fashion, tailor, or tuck when it comes to reviewing laws. The overarching criterion is "fit," for that which is fitting has integrity in the Dworkinian sense of the term.[33]

In *Hutterian,* Justice Abella pushed the government to more finely tailor laws in order to recognize and accommodate the valid claims of a different normative minority community. This is partly because she gave equal weight to the individual *and* the collective nature of religious freedom.[34] Here is how she communicated her understanding of their situation: "The harm to the constitutional rights of the Hutterites, in the absence of an exemption, is dramatic. Their inabil-

---

Stanley Fish: Ronald Dworkin, "Law as Interpretation" (1982) 9 *Critical Inquiry* 179 and Stanley Fish, "Working on the Chain Gang: Interpretation in the Law and in Literary Criticism" (1982) 9 *Critical Inquiry,* 201.

32 Elaine Scarry, *On Beauty and Being Just* (Princeton, NJ: Princeton UP, 2001) at 91. Indeed, and as Scarry discusses, the aesthetic and jurisprudential senses of fairness overlap in the sense of finding process and substance pleasing, equitable, streamlined, open, and direct.

33 See Ronald Dworkin, *Law's Empire* (Cambridge, MA: Belknap Press, 1986) at 225: "According to law as integrity, propositions of law are true if they figure in or follow from the principles of justice, fairness, and procedural due process that provide the best constructive interpretation of the community's practice."

34 On the co-existence of plural normative communities — or *nomoi* — see Robert M. Cover, "The Supreme Court, 1982 Term — Foreword: Nomos and Narrative" (1983) 97 *Harvard Law Review* 4. According to Cover, a religious community is a distinct normative community (i.e., *nomos*) which can make valid demands on the democratic constitutional state for recognition and accommodation. See, for example, the description of the Hutterite community as a nomos at paras 164–66 in *Hutterian,* above note 3.

ity to drive affects them not only individually, but also severely compromises the autonomous character of their religious community."[35] Self-sufficiency is understood to be a fundamental feature of this deeply religious community, and the self-sufficiency characteristic of this communal way of life would be irreparably harmed by the denial of a driving licence in the modern age. Contextualizing this, Justice Abella approvingly cited the Alberta Court of Appeal, acknowledging that "certain members must drive regularly on Alberta highways in order to . . . facilitate the sale of agricultural products, purchase raw materials from suppliers, transport colony members (including children) to medical appointments, and conduct the community's financial affairs."[36] To suggest, as the majority did, that members of the Colony could "simply arrange for third party transportation"[37] to assist them not only in daily living but in maintaining a living, functioning community could be considered unreasonable in the extreme. To her mind, the government's decision not to provide an exemption for the 250 affected Hutterites when, at that time, over 700,000 Albertans were not part of the photo database because they did not have driver's licences, appeared arbitrary, unfair, unreasonable, and disproportionate. Would the database truly be compromised by excluding the Hutterites?

In contrast to the majority's perspective, Justice Abella's dissent faced this simple brute fact head on: "[t]here is no evidence that in the context of several hundred thousand unphotographed Albertans, the photos of approximately 250 Hutterites will have any discernable impact on the province's ability to reduce identity theft."[38] Superadded onto this fact was the obstinate policy preference of the government: all of the alternatives presented by the government involved taking a photograph and the various alternatives proposed by the Hutterites were all rejected.[39] Rather than bespoke tailoring and fit, the Hutterites received "one size fits all" treatment. For the dissent, this outcome flew in the face of the proportionality principle because "the benefit of adding the pho-

35 *Ibid* at para 114.

36 *Ibid* at para 164, citing *Hutterian Brethren of Wilson Colony v Alberta*, 2007 ABCA 160.

37 *Ibid* at para 167.

38 *Hutterian*, above note 3 at para 115. *Hutterian* comports with Justice Abella's views that "[w]e must be prepared, when the situation warrants, to experience what Herbert Spencer called 'The Tragedy of the Murder of a Beautiful Theory by a Gang of Brutal Facts'": "Lawyers, Judges and Rights," above note 2 at 995.

39 The Hutterians had proposed that no photograph be taken and that the non-photo driver's licences issued to them be marked "Not to be used for identification purposes," as a compromise.

tographs of the few Hutterites who wish to drive, would be marginal" compared to the nature of the harm to the integrity of their religious beliefs.[40]

The legal professional knows that some laws, such as an uncompromising photo licensing regime, are downright ugly. Indeed, one might increasingly think this about the *Charter*'s section 33 notwithstanding clause, given recent experience. Other flaws, internal to the mind, must be brought to the surface so that their potential influence on judgment can be examined.[41] Justice Abella is aware of the potential mischief that the unexamined, uncritical mind can produce: "The question of almost all judicial decision-making comes down to a question of how you frame the issue, and how you decide which of the available choices should be given more or less weight."[42]

I want to return to the courtroom now, but this time with a different analogy — architectural. Those expounding the morality of duty (and popular culture, apparently) typically portray the courthouse as a brutalist nightmare — concrete, dark, heavy, oppressive, with the judgment of Nemesis looming above, and the weight of the state bearing down on the lowly legal subject. Certainly, that is how Justice Abella portrays the way the Hutterites felt at the hands of the state. Might our

40 *Hutterian*, above note 3 at para 158.

41 Law is increasingly turning to cognitive neuroscience to understand how the brain and the mind work optimally and sub-optimally when thinking or making decisions. This literature has examined agency, analytic frameworks, psychological harm, jury deliberation, procedural problems resulting in miscarriages of justice, judicial and policing biases involving stereotypes, legal reasoning, and promoting empathy in judicial decision-making. For a sample, see: Phoebe C Ellsworth, "Legal Reasoning" in K.J. Holyoak and R.G. Morrison Jr., eds, *The Cambridge Handbook of Thinking and Reasoning*, (Cambridge and New York: Cambridge UP, 2005) 685; Daniel Kahneman, *Thinking, Fast and Slow* (Toronto: Anchor Canada, 2013); Susan A. Bandes, "Remorse and Demeanor in the Courtroom: Cognitive Science and the Evaluation of Contrition" in Jill Hunter et al, eds, *The Integrity of the Criminal Process* (Oxford and Portland: Hart, 2016) 309; Jules Lobel and Huda Akil, "Law & Neuroscience: The Case of Solitary Confinement" (2018) 147:4 *Daedalus* 61; Mary Liston, "Transubstantiation in Canadian Public Law: Processing Substance and Instantiating Process" in John Bell et al, eds, *Public Law Adjudication in Common Law Systems: Process and Substance* (Hart: Oxford, 2016) 213; Nicole E. Negowetti, "Judicial Decisionmaking, Empathy, and the Limits of Perception" (2014) 47:3 *Akron Law Review* 693; Dianne L. Martin, "Lessons about Justice from the Laboratory of Wrongful Convictions: Tunnel Vision, the Construction of Guilt, and Informer Evidence" (2000-02) 70:4 *University Of Missouri-Kansas Law Review* 847; Martha C Nussbaum, *Upheavals of Thought: The Intelligence of Emotions* (Cambridge and New York: Cambridge University Press, 2001).

42 Abella, "Lawyers, Judges and Rights," above note 2 at 994.

sense of justice change to fit us better if our legal actors employed a different modernist style — perhaps one that emphasized horizontality, light, openness, transparency, inclusivity, and space?[43] The mutuality of form and function might then create a law-full room fit for the human being at the centre of the justice system.[44]

The craftsperson is, of course, aware of flaws in any artistic endeavour. Justice Abella's active style of judging has garnered praise but drawn detractors, too.[45] But active judging is not the same thing as judicial activism or politicized judging. Judicial non-transparency, not candour or sincerity, is what warps the model of a judge who starts to appear like a stereotypical Olympic judge in figure skating or soccer, covertly responding to various political pressures.[46] As Justice Abella argues, pretending not to weigh values or take public policy into account and refusing to actually "confront one's personal views and be open in spite of them" constitute a greater danger.[47] Disagree with her, yes, but one cannot say that she hides her true colours.[48]

---

43 I am reminded of Monty Python's Architects Sketch, where John Cleese as the architect Mr. Wiggin designs a Kafkaesque block of residential flats combining classical neo-Georgian features with elements of torture. When questioned whether he truly understands the goals of the project, he responds: "Oh. I hadn't fully divined your attitude towards the tenants." See episode 17 of *Monty Python's Flying Circus*, "The Buzz Aldrin Show," recorded on 18 September 1970 and originally broadcast on 20 October 1970. I am also reminded of the accessibility lessons that modern architecture often ignores, and which disability rights advocate and lawyer David Lepofsky has tirelessly aired.

44 See, for example, Linda Mulcahy, *Legal Architecture: Justice, Due Process and the Place of Law* (Abingdon, UK and New York: Routledge, 2011).

45 See the range of views expressed in Sean Fine, "How Rosalie Abella's Personal History Shaped her Legal Legacy" *Globe and Mail* (26 June 2021), online: www.theglobeandmail.com/canada/article-how-rosalie-abellas-personal-history-shaped-her-legal-legacy/. See also Leonid Sirota, "Delusions of Grandeur: Justice Abella Sets Out a Vision of the Supreme Court as Arbiter of National Values" *Double Aspect* (blog) (6 November 2018), online: https://doubleaspect.blog/2018/11/06/delusions-of-grandeur/.

46 Chad M. Oldfather, "Aesthetic Judging and the Constitution (or, Why Supreme Court Justices Are Less Like Umpires and More Like Figure-Skating Judges)" (2020) 72 *Florida Law Review* 391.

47 Abella, "Lawyers, Judges and Rights," above note 2 at 995.

48 Referring to the *Bruker* decision and the nature of Justice Abella's judicial impartiality, Rosalie Jukier writes: "The decision begged the question of whether a Jewish woman could really be impartial in this case. . . . She could be impartial and have an *open* mind even though she was a Jewish woman herself, and her mind was not *empty* regarding the issues, value, and consequences at play": above note 13 at 7.

3. *The Legal Professional as an Embodied and Empathetic Thinker*

According to moral philosopher Martha Nussbaum, to be a fully rational human being necessarily involves emotional intelligence. In *Poetic Justice*, she argues that a good judge "needs a great deal of non-literary equipment: technical legal knowledge, a knowledge of history and precedent, a careful attention to proper legal impartiality. . . . But in order to be fully rational, judges must also be capable of fancy and sympathy. They must educate not only their technical capacities but also their capacity for humanity."[49] Nussbaum's work on empathy and judgment argues that empathy should be understood as an imaginative reconstruction of another person's experience that does not require us to align or merge our interests with those of the other person. Rather than rejecting emotions, or privileging an embodied rational mind, Nussbaum advocates for a particular reflective position where we can responsively contemplate a situation when we find ourselves balanced between a certain detachment and a certain connection to context and difference. For her, this paradigmatic position is effectively realized when we read literature — and it is a position that is transportable to other disciplines.

In a similar vein, legal theorist Jennifer Nedelsky also emphasizes that judgment involves the mind-body connection, but through the Arendtian-derived concept of an "enlarged mentality."[50] Judgment is a cognitive process distinct from forming an opinion. An enlarged mentality or enlarged thought takes into account the thoughts of others. The judging person must "woo the consent of everyone else in the hope of coming to an agreement"[51] with their perspective. In this model of judging as a basic human capability (which is therefore not restricted only to judges), the enlarged and embodied mentality tacks back and forth between the internal self and knowledge that lies outside the self. Imagination is of crucial assistance in creating this enlarged mentality because it facilitates receptivity or mindfulness, understood as the ability to respond creatively and suspend (pre-)judgment. One aspires to start with non-judgment and to be receptive to the perspectives of others and diverse contexts. This requires being attentive to difference and particulars when imagining the perspective of others. Impartiality

49 Martha C. Nussbaum, *Poetic Justice* (Boston: Beacon Press, 1995) at 121.

50 Jennifer Nedelsky, "Receptivity and Judgment" (2011) 4:4 *Ethics & Global Politics* 231.

51 Nedelsky quoting Arendt quoting Kant in "Judgment, Diversity, and Relational Autonomy" in Ronald Beiner and Jennifer Nedelsky, eds, *Judgment, Imagination, and Politics* (Lanham, Md: Rowman & Littlefield, 2001) at 107.

therefore means taking into account the possible standpoints of others, which means it is distinguishable from choice, idiosyncrasy, opinion, preference, subjective determination, and other like states of mind. Empathy enables the person to imagine another perspective and to care enough to really try to comprehend it. The effort to create an enlarged mentality, which is an exercise in responsibility, is iterative because you must sometimes repeat the process several times in order to truly know and form a reflective judgment that leads to fresh perception and action. The result of this process is a valid and legitimate public claim of agreement with others, and when expressed, it becomes part of public reason. Judgment, understood this way, is clearly of paramount importance for legal professionals.

Legal scholars Anthony Amsterdam and Jerome Bruner similarly argue for the need for law and human sciences[52] to engage with each other: "The insights of the human sciences also help to make the familiar strange again. Studies of the foibles of categorization, of the hidden regularities of narrative structure, of our strange human ways of conveying requests or promises or excuses — these make us sharply conscious of how we manage (or fail to manage) contextual matters that are too often out of sight, out of mind."[53] In order to develop a fresh perspective and distance yourself from convention, habit, opinion, confirmation bias, and standard frames, it is crucial to practice mindfulness. Mindfulness, Amsterdam and Bruner suggest, can be a form of legal pedagogy, but one that is necessarily preliminary to the business of doing law and lawyering.[54] The implications for law schools are significant. According to Amsterdam and Bruner, who follow George Lakoff and Mark Johnson, formal legal pedagogy needs to better understand and teach the effective use of analogy, metaphor, narrative, and rhetoric not only as legal skills but as essential components of our conceptual systems that lay at the core of cognition.[55]

---

52 Human sciences (i.e., history, anthropology, philosophy, neuroscience, sociology, evolutionary biology, etc.) use humanistic, non-positivistic, and interdisciplinary methodological approaches to the study of human phenomena (e.g., human behaviour, culture, experience, expression, nature, environment, and so on).

53 Anthony G. Amsterdam and Jerome Bruner, *Minding the Law* (Cambridge, MA: Harvard University Press, 2002) at 288.

54 *Ibid* at 289. They label it "propaedeutic," or, in the nature of preliminary instruction.

55 George Lakoff and Mark Johnson, *Metaphors We Live By* (Chicago: University of Chicago Press, 1980). See also Douglas Hofstadter and Emmanuel Sander, *Surfaces and Essences: Analogy as the Fuel and Fire of Thinking* (Philadelphia: Basic Books, 2013). On metaphors in law, see Hugo Cyr, "Conceptual Metaphors for an Unfinished Constitution" (214) 19 *Review of Constitutional Studies* 1; Kate Glover,

The constitutive nature of religious identity rests at the core of Justice Abella's mindful reasoning, along with a historically informed understanding of the recurring intolerance exhibited by majorities against religious minorities, both by the larger public and the state itself. She writes:

> Because I am a Canadian, my French-English history since 1867 teaches me to revel in difference and to understand that you can be equal even if you are different. Because I am a Jew, my history teaches me to fear conformity and those who would impose their sameness on my difference.[56]

Looking to earlier *Charter* section 2(a) cases penned by Chief Justice Dickson and to key European human rights jurisprudence on religious freedom, along with this public and personal historical context, she listened *with intent* to the Hutterites' complaint.[57] She concretized their situation, underscoring how the denial of a driver's licence excluded them from the larger community, making them both more isolated and more vulnerable. Not only were they in danger of being made more invisible in their already insular rural community, they were in danger of being shut out and silenced by the operation of the law itself. And if the Hutterites capitulated to the province's demand, their non-voluntary acquiescence would destroy "the integrity of identity"[58] for that particular community. For Justice Abella, such a tragic choice denied the jurisgenerative possibility of a shared identity where the Hutterites could "simultaneously retain that identity *and* be in the mainstream."[59]

The concept of embodied and empathetic cognition has parallels with another methodology or process drawn from medical science. Medicine, like law, invites us to explore our concrete reality and it provides a means of organizing the seemingly chaotic material of life, with its masses of particulars, and account for differences and variables. As a

---

"The Supreme Court in a Pluralist World: Four Readings of a Reference" (2015) 60:4 *McGill Law Journal* 839; and Étienne Cloutier, "A Tale of Two Metaphors: A Narrative Take on the Canadian Constitution" (2019) 64:3 *McGill Law Journal* 447. For a less optimistic view of one foundational metaphor — the constitutional architecture metaphor — see Richard Haigh, "You Don't Need a Metaphor to Know Which Way the Case Goes: The *Senate Reference* and Constitutional Metaphors" (2015) 71 *Supreme Court Law Review* 137.

56 Rosalie Silberman Abella, "Law, Literature, and Identity: Seeking Equality" (2000) 63:1 *Saskatchewan Law Review* 1 at 21 [Abella, "Law, Literature, and Identity"].

57 On the importance of intentional listening to judging, see also Cairns-Way, above note 1 at 12.

58 Abella, "Law, Literature, and Identity," above note 56 at 2.

59 *Ibid* at 21 (emphasis in original).

field of knowledge, law might well look to medicine for insights on how to go about balancing the demands of the abstract-categorical-conceptual with the concrete-contextual-particular. The model I am thinking of here is best expressed by Oliver Sacks through his rediscovery of the "romantic science" dimension of neurological science through the methodology of a case history.[60] When talking about the benefits of a case history methodology, Sacks writes persuasively about how medicine needs to remember that what lies at the heart of the discipline is not only *episteme* and *techne*, but empathy for a real, living human being best expressed through narrative (or, as it is called in medicine, pathography):

> There is no subject in a narrow case history; modern case histories allude to the subject in a cursory phrase ("a trisomic albino female of 21") which could as well apply to a rat as a human being. To restore the human subject at the centre — the suffering, afflicted, fighting human subject — we must deepen a case history to a narrative or tale; only then do we have a "who" as well as a "what", a real person, a patient, in relation to disease — in relation to the physical.[61]

Sacks contrasts impersonal neurological science with a richly *human* science that values the process of patients telling their stories to doctors, narrating their experiences, and outlining their struggles to survive or overcome disease.[62] To my mind, a key analogy exists with law if we think of each case as a case history — that is, a pathology of injustice. When teaching law, for example, one could take a single legal case on

60 Oliver Sacks, *The Man Who Mistook His Wife for a Hat and Other Clinical Tales* (New York: Touchstone, 1998) at xi. A case history approach facilitates a holistic, in-depth, and multi-faceted explorations of complex issues in real-life settings often employing qualitative methods such as interviews.

61 *Ibid* at viii and 174.

62 On the use of narrativity in the health sciences, see: Andrew John Hull, "Fictional Father? Oliver Sacks and the Revalidation of Pathography" (2013) 39:2 *Medical Humanities* 105; Debra Journet, "Forms of Discourse and the Sciences of the Mind: Luria, Sacks, and the Role of Narrative in Neurological Case Histories" (1990) *Written Communication* 171; Hannah Proctor, "Astronomers of the inward: on the histories and case histories of Alexander Luria and Oliver Sacks" (2022) 74 *Studies in Eastern European Thought* 39; and, John Wiltshire, "Deficits and Enhancements: Reflections on the Writings of Oliver Sacks" (1991) 20:4 *Cambridge Quarterly* 304. Sacks's methods are controversial in academic medical circles — for an overview see Leonard Cassuto, "Oliver Sacks: The P.T. Barnum of the Postmodern World?" (2000) 52:2 *American Quarterly* 326, and Daniela Mergenthaler, "Oliver Sacks — A Neurologist Explores the Lifeworld" (2000) 3:3 *Medicine, Health Care and Philosophy* 277.

its own and unfold its "case history" in the medical style.[63] Such a perspective provokes us not only to ask about the facts and the law, but to focus on the optimal remedy (which may lie within law or outside of it). My area of law (administrative law) is infamous for focussing too much on "law office metaphysics"[64] at the expense of the human subject at the heart of a case. By way of contrast, a more Sacksian way of thinking about legal cases prioritizes both back-end thinking on how to access justice and front-end thinking on whether justice has been accessed optimally. Legal professionals, thinking this way, would (as we are now doing to meet the access to justice crisis) look creatively and pragmatically on how the legal system can best serve affected parties. We would want to not only remedy injury, loss, and pain but also invest resources in prevention and mitigation, looking to new technology as well as older techniques like case histories.

Justice Abella's principled pragmatism is attentive to remedies in this way. Her judgment asks why, in this day and age of biometric and fingerprint recognition, an innovative solution to the Hutterian impasse cannot be devised. Could technology not provide an appropriate compromise? Must state neutrality be antagonistic towards religious beliefs? For the Hutterites, the lack of an alternative meant that they had to choose between their conscience governed by religious laws and the state's laws, a choice that necessarily implicated civil disobedience (i.e., driving without a licence).[65] Alternatively, if such a requirement is truly necessary, then governments must, after accommodation attempts, construct a viable justification based on evidence and good reason in order to satisfy the proportionality analysis.

---

63 Legal pedagogy should also be diverse and creative because "[a]cademics are the people who will teach the future lawyers and judges what they need to know and what they need to ask in order to do the justice jobs properly": Abella, "Lawyers, Judges and Rights," above note 2 at 998.

64 Justice Binnie in *Dunsmuir v New Brunswick*, 2008 SCC 9 (CanLII), [2008] 1 SCR 190 at para 122 [*Dunsmuir*]. *Dunsmuir* is a particularly good example of a massive judgment where the protagonist barely appears in it at all. In contrast, the voice of Constable Nicholson makes a prominent appearance in Chief Justice Laskin's judgment in *Nicholson v Haldimand-Norfolk Regional Police Commissioners*, [1979] 1 SCR 311 at 330.

65 For critical commentary on the remedial aspects of the *Hutterian* decision, including the majority's rejection of reasonable accommodation, see Richard Moon, "Accommodation Without Compromise: Comment on *Alberta v. Hutterian Brethren of Wilson Colony*" (2010) *Supreme Court Law Review: Osgoode's Annual Constitutional Cases Conference* 51, online: https://digitalcommons.osgoode.yorku.ca/sclr/vol51/iss1/5; and Sara Weinrib, "An Exemption for Sincere Believers: The Challenge of *Alberta v Hutterian Brethren of Wilson Colony*" (2011) 56:3 *McGill Law Journal* 719.

Finally, Justice Abella's lived experience gives her a particular stance from which to view a legal system — multiperspectival. Her and her family's lived experience as outsiders to, and objects of, a genocidal legal order combined with being an insider in the Canadian legal order have given her an ability to observe (like Kafka) the "internal and external operations of law"[66] as well as the "the precariousness and vulnerability of the normality of daily life."[67] Justice, Rosalie Abella has said, is "the application of law to life, not just the application of laws to facts,"[68] and that task necessarily involves narration and good writing.

4. *The Legal Professional as Narrator and Storyteller*

Good writing is vital for law. Legal writing is now "modernist" in its aesthetic goals, unlike the style of legal writing found in the age of Charles Dickens. Legal professionals would do well to attend to Judge Richard Posner's sage advice that reading highly regarded works of literature known for their good writing can literally improve how judges, lawyers, and government actors' ability to make persuasive arguments and write good decisions.[69] As Posner advocates, legal writing should be unpretentious, clear, concise, logical, and sincere. It should provide justifications for argumentative positions taken and it should know the various audiences it speaks to, tailoring its goals and tone correspondingly. Legal scholar Robin West also suggests that good legal writing should be cognizant of other virtues that literature can provide, such as an awareness of the importance of metaphor, the role of rhetoric, and the power of emotion in the task of constructing persuasive arguments. For West, echoing Nussbaum, writing is one way we can develop empathetic competencies in our thinking.[70]

Justice Abella agrees that "Literature helps us know. It is a constant tutor in human experience."[71] Through literature, we can come to understand an "other." As she herself has put it, good books are

---

66 Banakar, above note 22 at 465.

67 *Ibid.*

68 Paul Wells, "Rosie Abella said she'd answer questions when she turned 75" *Maclean's* (15 June 2021), online: https://www.macleans.ca/news/rosie-abella-said-shed-answer-questions-when-she-turned-75/.

69 Richard A. Posner, "Law and Literature: A Relation Reargued" (1986) 72 *Virginia Law Review* 1351.

70 Robin West, "Economic Man and Literary Woman: One Contrast" (1988) *Mercer Law Review* 867.

71 Abella, "Law, Literature, and Identity," above note 56 at 2.

"where you learn about the human universals,"[72] including the universal experience of being an "other." For Justice Abella: "It was the book [*Les Misérables*] that taught me what injustice looked like."[73] Literature clearly sparked her imagination, and with her imagination she put her mind and her skills to work to craft a better language to express equity and equality, to describe marginalization, to understand the effects of oppression and victimization, and to communicate how it feels to be wronged by another person and by a system built on inequality. Justice Abella brings to her career many insights about the "human universals," but also the particulars gleaned from experiences as a refugee and a member of a marginalized community, a practicing lawyer representing diverse clients, an administrative decision-maker, a commissioner, a law professor, a judge, and a family member. Professor Eric Adams astutely writes: "Her early legal career was a crash course in the experience of legal pluralism . . . . Abella saw that the textures of law — its norms, values, and experiences — were products of human interaction as much as commands of the state."[74] As a lifelong learner in law and literature, Justice Abella has indeed come to understand law as "humanized knowledge."[75]

Literature, both Boyd White and Nussbaum argue, creates space for ethical and moral reflection about law, the power of law, the aspirations of law, and the harms of law. Nussbaum suggests that literature enables the mind to enter a special space, the moral imagination, where the mind can grapple with ethical questions that narratives embody and raise. This space is informed by emotion and reason, which come together through understanding and empathy. Nussbaum believes that literature helps us regulate our emotions so that when we read a narrative, we are using the specific faculty of "rational emotions" — there is therefore no Cartesian separation between mind and body, reason and emotion, when it comes to reading literature.[76]

Perhaps legal cases, when read from this standpoint, can share in this faculty too.[77] Legal storytelling, according to critical race theorists Richard Delgado and Jean Stefancic, can function like literature by opening

---

72 Fine, above note 45.

73 *Ibid.*

74 Eric Adams, "Justice Abella's Overture," Chapter 1 in this volume at 37.

75 Abella, "Law, Literature, and Identity," above note 56 at 3.

76 See Martha Nussbaum, "Rational Emotions" in *Poetic Justice* (Boston: Beacon Press, 1995) 53.

77 See *ibid.*

a window to an alternative or ignored reality.[78] Narrative in law can be used to tell a counterstory that gives voice to silenced minorities, challenges damaging social scripts and framings, and resists dominant narratives.[79] Amsterdam and Bruner suggest that legal argument is not only about logic and precedent — it is also about storytelling.[80] Law must become more aware of its storytelling function generally, but also so that it can better understand the myths, scripts, and stereotypes that inform its jurisprudential stories and then engage in the hard work to eliminate them. Justice Abella came to this understanding through her own experience about the "importance of being able, comfortably, to accept and assert a Jewish identity" but also, importantly, through the writings of Ralph Ellison on the same need in relation to a racialized identity.[81]

She applied these lessons from literature in her legal writing. To take one last example from *Hutterian*, one can see how she framed the plight of the Hutterites differently than the majority, as discussed above. One can also look to how she read the applicable jurisprudence differently from the majority. The case context before Justice Abella resonates with an earlier precedent, the celebrated case of *Roncarelli v Duplessis*.[82] In that seminal case, then Premier of Quebec, Maurice Duplessis (who was also the Attorney General at the time), required the Liquor Commission to revoke restaurateur Frank Roncarelli's liquor licence forever. The action was taken because Roncarelli had been posting bail for his fellow Jehovah's Witnesses, who had been arrested for pamphleteering. Like Justice Rand, whose judgment she follows and uses to frame her analysis, Justice Abella rejected the formalistic distinction between a licence as a "privilege" versus a licence as a "right":

> Moreover, I have difficulty understanding what is meant by a "privilege" in the context of the provision of government services. As long ago as *Roncarelli v. Duplessis*, 1959 CanLII 50 (SCC), [1959] S.C.R. 121, this Court recognized the profound significance a licence may have on an individual's life or livelihood and that the government is required to exercise its power in administering the licensing system in a fair and constitutional manner.[83]

78 Richard Delgado and Jean Stefancic, *Critical Race Theory*, 3rd ed (New York: New York University Press, 2017).

79 *Ibid* at 46–53.

80 Above note 53.

81 Abella, "Law, Literature, and Identity," above note 56 at 18.

82 *Roncarelli v Duplessis*, [1959] SCR 121.

83 *Hutterian*, above note 3 at para 172.

The constitutional burden, according to Justice Abella, lay squarely on the government to provide a justification in proportion to the significant harm the photo requirement imposed on the Hutterian Colony. In her view, deference should not be shown when a government's law, regulation or discretionary licencing decision so infringes a fundamental constitutional right and harmfully intrudes on an individual's or community's way of life.

C. The Story of Canadian Administrative Law

But how does a lawyer tell a "good" — that is, effective, purposeful, persuasive, compelling and factually meticulous, and truthful — story?[84] While others may look to her constitutional or equality cases for examples of telling a good story, I will turn to the surprising area of administrative law and the concurrence penned by Justices Abella and Karakatsanis in the *Vavilov*[85] case. Alexander Vavilov was born in Toronto to parents who turned out to be covert Russian agents working under "deep cover." If this sounds familiar, it is because the family's story partly inspired the spy drama television series *The Americans*. The key question in the case was whether the *Citizenship Act* prevented Vavilov from acquiring Canadian citizenship (which normally would have been assumed at birth in the jurisdiction). Did a proper interpretation of the provisions denying citizenship to children of a diplomatic or consular officer or other representative or employee of a foreign government in Canada apply? They did only if spies were considered to be representatives or employees in Canada of the Russian government. Both the majority and the concurring judgments answered no, overturning the Registrar's decision, which had denied citizenship to Vavilov. In coming to that answer, the Court reworked the administrative law reasonableness framework for the standard of review in order to emphasize the importance of reasons to the Canadian culture of justification in public law.[86]

84 Philip N Meyer, *Storytelling for Lawyers* (New York: Oxford University Press, 2014) at 3.

85 *Canada (Minister of Citizenship and Immigration) v Vavilov*, 2019 SCC 65, [2019] 4 SCR 653 [*Vavilov*].

86 The Supreme Court had previously (but problematically) emphasized this connection in a unanimous decision written by Justice Abella, *Newfoundland and Labrador Nurses' Union v Newfoundland and Labrador (Treasury Board)*, 2011 SCC 62, [2011] 3 SCR 708. For a critical evaluation of this decision, see: Mary Liston, "Deference as Respect: Lost in Translation?" in Paul Daly and Leonid Sirota (eds), *A Decade of Dunsmuir / Les 10 ans de Dunsmuir*, 2018 Special issue of the Canadian

The concurring judgment, co-authored by Justices Abella and Karakatsanis, was certainly driven by the jurisprudential proclivities Abella had previously displayed in administrative law. This is not only because Justice Abella uses literary devices of plot, character, voice, point of view, detail, image, setting, and time. Nor is it because, using Justice Abella's own words, "the passions were primordial, the tensions were timeless, and the consequences were cataclysmic"[87] in this jurisprudential story. It is for these reasons and more.

I will now turn from the genre of encomium to eulogy, shifting into a minor mood. Perhaps D minor, which is, as Spinal Tap's Nigel Tufnel muses, the saddest of all keys.[88] The setting is Justice Abella's judicial office, replete with blazing colour and blaring jazz standards. She follows her usual practice — picking up a pen to write on a blank piece of paper.[89] The story that unfolds is labelled a concurrence, but the spirit of dissent permeates every page.

Vavilov's majority decision neutrally claimed to merely restore coherence to the jurisprudence. The concurrence counters by suggesting that the apparent disagreement is much deeper and concerns two distinct philosophies of administrative law. Framing the issue this way throws down the gauntlet to judge and reader. We must all sit back and think about which philosophy we subscribe to and why. The stakes, it is implied, are high.

Journal of Administrative Law & Practice, 47-54; and, Paul Daly, "Vavilov and the the Culture of Justification in Contemporary Administrative Law" (2021) *Supreme Court Law Review: Osgoode's Annual Constitutional Cases Conference* 100, online: https://digitalcommons.osgoode.yorku.ca/sclr/vol100/iss1/13 .

87 Abella, "Lawyers, Judges and Rights," above note 2 at 990.

88 Rob Reiner (director), *This is Spinal Tap* (Embassy Pictures, 1984).

89 Several of Justice Abella's former law clerks describe her writing method as follows:

> We had the great honour of . . . witnessing the focus and care she pours into each handwritten judgment (and yes, it's with pen and paper that she begins nearly all her work). We watched as her reasoning and prose would emerge, slowly and carefully, into its final polished form. Every word in an Abella judgment is not just written but considered, crossed out, revised, mulled over, and written again. Long before it was in fashion, Justice Abella stripped Latin and legalese from her reasoning, so as to make it accessible to Canadians from all walks of life.

See Jeremy Opolsky, Sana Halwani, Sinziana Hennig & David Matyas, "As Her Former Clerks, Justice Rosalie Silberman Abella's Legacy Is Deeply Personal" *Torys* (29 June 2021), online: https://www.torys.com/Our%20Latest%20Thinking/Publications//2021/06/as-her-former-clerks-justice-rosalie-silberman-abellas-legacy-is-deeply-personal/.

The concurrence then spun a "home grown"[90] tale about the evolution of Canadian administrative law, replete with recognizable tropes (e.g., deference, expertise, privative clauses, separation of powers) and the pantheon of landmark cases, powered by an epic cast of characters, both judicial (e.g., the noble Justice Dickson, the stalwart Justice Wilson, the shrewd Justice Iacobucci, the brothers Justices Bastarache and Lebel, a bemused Justice Binnie, and the magisterial Lord Bingham) and professorial (e.g., the villainous Albert V. Dicey, the sage David Mullan, the provocateur Harry Arthurs, the felicitous Felix Frankfurter, and the dynamic duo of Dyzenhaus and Daly). The majority, they said, was doing "more than ushering in a simplified next act"; rather, it was rewriting "the whole script, reassigning to the courts the starring role Dicey ordained a century ago."[91]

Rolling back the clock was the theme, but the feeling was far from nostalgic:

> [198] Forty years ago, in *Canadian Union of Public Employees, Local 963 v. New Brunswick Liquor Corp.*, 1979 CanLII 23 (SCC), [1979] 2 S.C.R. 227, this Court embarked on a course to recognize the unique and valuable role of administrative decision-makers within the Canadian legal order. Breaking away from the court-centric theories of years past, the Court encouraged judges to show deference when specialized administrative decision-makers provided reasonable answers to legal questions within their mandates. Building on this more mature understanding of administrative law, subsequent decisions of this Court sought to operationalize deference and explain its relationship to core democratic principles. These appeals offered a platform to clarify and refine our administrative law jurisprudence, while remaining faithful to the deferential path it has travelled for four decades.
>
> [199] Regrettably, the majority shows our precedents no such fidelity.[92]

The majority was said to turn its back on forty years of change, beginning in 1979 when Canadian administrative law both modernized and nativized itself. The concurrence issues a declaration that "[t]he rule of law is not the rule of courts. A pluralist conception of the rule of law recognizes that courts are not the exclusive guardians of law, and that others in the justice arena have shared responsibility for its

---

90 *Vavilov*, above note 85 at para 210.

91 *Ibid* at para 229.

92 *Ibid*.

development, including administrative decision-makers."[93] The downgrading of expertise and privative clauses are indeed unfortunate plot turns, but it is the elevation of the statutory appeal as an indicator of correctness on the civil (not administrative law) standard that is the real kicker — an amazing twist not unlike, for those of us old enough to remember, the "Dream Season" of the 1980s TV show *Dallas.*[94] The companion case of *Bell Canada*[95] is the practical application of the story told in *Vavilov,* but without the happy ending. Whether or not you agree with the moral of the tale told by the concurring judges, while reading it, an MRI image of your brain should be lit with fireworks as the neural network is activated.

Perhaps while penning their view, the concurrence looked up and glanced at out towards our neighbour to the south to have a look at what was happening politically and legally in administrative law there. There, rearguard defences attempted to justify an administrative state under siege. In cases like *West Virginia v Environmental Protection Agency,*[96] the US Supreme Court seems determined to employ a variety of doctrines — separation of powers, non-delegation, major questions, unitary executive — that will delegitimize and dismantle the "fourth branch" of government.[97] The jurisprudence followed fast on the heels of the Trump administration, which was hell bent on challenging administrative actors and undermining their independence. A new political and social reality has emerged in the United States. Will *Vavilovian* jurisprudence be affected by these developments?

---

93 *Ibid* at para 241. On the irreducible plural nature of law, see Margaret Davies, "The Ethos of Pluralism" (2005) 27:1 *Sydney Law Review* 87.

94 Plot spoiler alert! The TV series *Dallas* was infamous for a number of plot surprises. In addition to the much parodied cliffhanger, "Who Shot J.R.?," the entire narrative of season 9 — the "Dream Season" — was later disclosed to have been a dream of one of the characters with the end result that one of the deceased characters turned out to actually still be alive.

95 *Bell Canada v Canada (Attorney General),* 2019 SCC 66, [2019] 4 SCR 845 [*Bell Canada*]. The concurrence agreed with the result in *Vavilov,* while Justices Abella and Karakatsanis are in full dissenting mode in *Bell Canada.*

96 *West Virginia v Environmental Protection Agency,* No 20-1530, 142 S Ct 2587 (2022). In brief, the Supreme Court of the United States majority concluded that Congress could not delegate power to the Environment Protection Agency using broad terms in the *Clean Air Act.* Employing the major questions doctrine, the majority stated that Congress must make itself very clear when it authorizes executive agencies to address major political and economic questions.

97 Jonathan H. Adler, "A Rearguard Defense of the Administrative State" Cato Institute (2021), online: www.cato.org/regulation/summer-2021/rearguard-defense-administrative-state.

The legal imaginary of *Vavilov*'s concurrence is not coloured by nostalgia. It does not make the elementary mistake of believing that progress is inevitable. It expresses through law a historical memory and is, in a very real sense, archival. That may not be a bad thing. Times will change again. The story can be picked up and re-told years later. And then, as Thomas King recommends, "Want a different ethic? Tell a different story."[98]

D. Engaging Abella

Regarding style, poet Mary Oliver writes: "Dancing with Mr. Emerson is not much like dancing with Mr. Blake; certainly it is not like dancing with Mr. Pope or Ms. Dickinson. Each poet, following the abiding rules *more than less*, writes differently from all other poets. . . . All significant poets have a distinctive style."[99] The same can be said about judges. Dancing with Justice Abella is certainly not like dancing with Justices Wilson, Dickson, L'Heureux-Dubé, Binnie, Côté, Wagner, or any other.

Rosalie Abella is multiply engaging, and I have tried to engage with those many dimensions. I use the words "engage" and "engaging" deliberately and in all of their key senses — to attract and keep someone's attention and interest, to try to understand somebody, to do a particular task, to begin to work, and to enter into conversation or debate. I don't know if Justice Abella is a fan of *Star Trek* in any of its iterations, but, if she is, to me she is the epitome of a Picardian imperative: "Engage!"[100] She engages people, life, work, experience, and historical memory. By being embracing, she is also disarming in all senses of that word. As Professor Rosalie Jukier describes it, Justice Abella's *style* of judging has always been accessible constructive, and collaborative.[101] Even in dissent, she is respectful and collegial.

Shortly after she retired from the bench in July 2021, she donated 1000 books, personally curated, and many from her Supreme Court office, to the Faculty of Law's library at the University of Toronto. These books constitute an important part of Justice Abella's legacy, because they helped make her who she is as a person and as a legal actor. But there is another important legacy that this gift represents, and that is the

98 Thomas King, *The Truth About Stories* (Toronto: Anansi, 2003) at 164.

99 Mary Oliver, *Rules for the Dance* (New York: Houghton Mifflin, 1998) 79.

100 Gene Roddenberry, *Star Trek: The Next Generation* (United States: Paramount Domestic Television, 1987–94). I will leave it to others to speculate on the aptness of the others: "Make it so!" and "Tea, Earl Grey, hot."

101 Jukier, above note 13 at 4–5.

importance of the humanities for learning and teaching law. More precisely, why "law *and* humanities" is as valuable an approach to understanding law as the more conventional doctrinal, economic, historical, philosophical, sociological, or anthropological approaches. As a legal professional cognizant of the past, fully present in the here and now, and imagining a better future, she has bequeathed a legacy exemplifying the life of the mind and putting the legal imagination to dream and to work. Let us hope that Justice Abella will, post-retirement, still "wander freely in the fields of the law"[102] called *nomia*.

102 Abella, "Lawyers, Judges and Rights," above note 2 at 990.

PART 2

Justice Abella's Jurisprudence — Empirical Analysis and Constitutional Law

7 Abella by the Numbers

STEPHEN BINDMAN AND KEENAN MACNEAL*

A Supreme Court of Canada career as illustrious as Justice Rosalie Silberman Abella's cannot be reduced to numbers. The impact of one landmark judgment or one stinging dissent may not be felt for years and may outweigh numerous other rulings.

Nevertheless, Justice Abella's career can be *described* in numbers. A quantitative analysis of her time on the Court and the decisions she wrote provide insight into her perspectives and positions, her preferences and her pet peeves. Such a review highlights how Justice Abella differed from her colleagues on the Court and demonstrates how she evolved as a justice over time. While the numbers cannot capture the entirety of Justice Abella's significance in Canadian law, we hope this review serves as a useful complement to the other chapters in this book, which explore in detail her jurisprudence across various areas of the law.

Rather than count cases manually, as many other analysts have done, our research team from the uOttawa Public Law Centre and the Legal Technology Lab created a database of all Supreme Court decisions from 1975 to the end of 2021 using data licensed from CanLII.[1] There were

---

* Stephen Bindman is a Visiting Professor and Executive in Residence at the University of Ottawa Faculty of Law (Common Law Section), and Keenan MacNeal is a graduate of the Faculty and currently counsel at Peacock Linder Halt & Mack in Calgary. The authors thank Professors Adam Dodek, Vanessa MacDonnell, and Carissima Mathen (as she then was) and research assistant Kelley Humber (as she then was) for their comments on earlier drafts. We wish to acknowledge the support of the Social Sciences and Humanities Research Council provided to the *Judging Equality Judgments* project, an innovative research initiative of the uOttawa Public Law Centre and Legal Technology Lab which applies legal data analytics to qualitative studies of Supreme Court of Canada jurisprudence.

1 The Canadian Legal Information Institute (canlii.org) is a non-profit organization created and funded by the Federation of Law Societies of Canada in 2001 on behalf of its fourteen member societies. It provides access to court judgments from all Canadian

a total of 4,142 judgments in the database. Computerization facilitated efficient filtering, searching, counting, and comparison across the dataset. Much of the analysis below would have been functionally impossible without these tools, most notably the "cinnamon words" analysis, which required counting every instance of every word found in almost fifty years of Supreme Court decisions.

A. How Do You Measure a Year in the Life (of Abella)?[2]

Table 7.1 summarizes Justice Abella's career at the Supreme Court of Canada. She was appointed to the country's top court on 30 August 2004 and retired on her seventy-fifth birthday on 1 July 2021. Like all retiring justices, she had six months to complete her reserved judgments. Our research shows she sat on approximately 932 cases.[3] In 205 of those cases (23 percent), she authored reasons. Of those, 53 (26 percent) were for a unanimous court and 64 (31 percent) were dissents. On average she wrote 12 judgments in each full year she was a justice — from a low of 8 in 2021 to a high 18 in 2015.

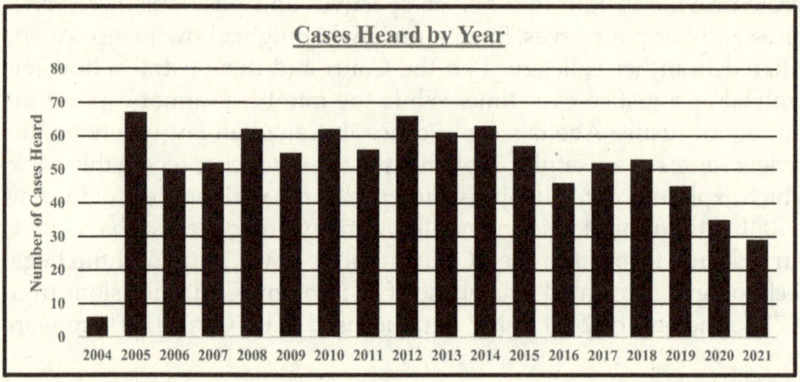

Figure 1

courts, including the Supreme Court of Canada, federal courts, and the courts in all Canada's provinces and territories. It also contains decisions from many tribunals nationally and the consolidated statutes and regulations of every jurisdiction in Canada.

2 For suggestions on alternative measures, see "Seasons of Love," *Rent (Original Broadway Cast Recording)* (Recording: DreamWorks, 1996).

3 The exact number of cases depends on how cases are counted. For example, if the Court hears two cases together raising the same issues, some may count that as two cases and others as one. We adopt a definition of "case" in which multiple appeals that are heard together and decided together are a single case; this matches the organization used by CanLII. For instance, *R v Ipeelee*, 2012 SCC 13, is one case in our data, despite the decision being related to two separate appeals.

Table 7.1. Summary of Justice Abella's Career at the Supreme Court of Canada

Year	Cases Heard	Opinions Authored	Unanimous Judgments Written	Dissenting Judgments Written
2004	5	0	0	0
2005	71	10	4	5
2006	50	10	3	2
2007	52	13	4	1
2008	62	10	4	1
2009	55	14	4	2
2010	60	10	3	3
2011	55	11	2	3
2012	64	11	3	6
2013	61	12	4	4
2014	62	15	6	7
2015	59	18	4	6
2016	47	11	5	2
2017	53	13	3	5
2018	53	13	1	4
2019	54	15	8	0
2020	38	11	1	1
2021	31	8	5	1
TOTAL	932	205 (22% of cases)	64 (31% of opinions)	53 (26% of opinions)

Figure 2 shows Justice Abella's agreement with her co-panellists.[4] For example, of the 383 cases she sat on with Chief Justice Wagner, she agreed with him in 86 percent of the cases.

She agreed most with Justice Andromache Karakatsanis — 91 percent of the time. (She had a similar agreement rate with Justice Jack Major but sat on fewer cases with him.) Her lowest rate of agreement, at 66 percent, was with Justice Suzanne Côté, though it should be noted that, as discussed below, Justice Côté has an unusually high rate of dissent in general.

4 "Agreement" was defined as being on the same "side" of a case, either agreeing with the majority or dissenting from it. For example, the author of a concurrence would be considered to agree with the author of the majority judgment.

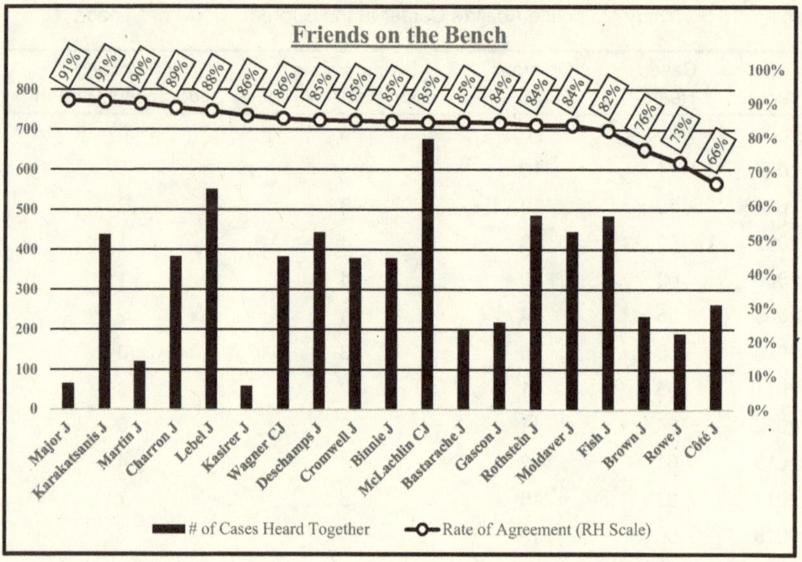

Figure 2

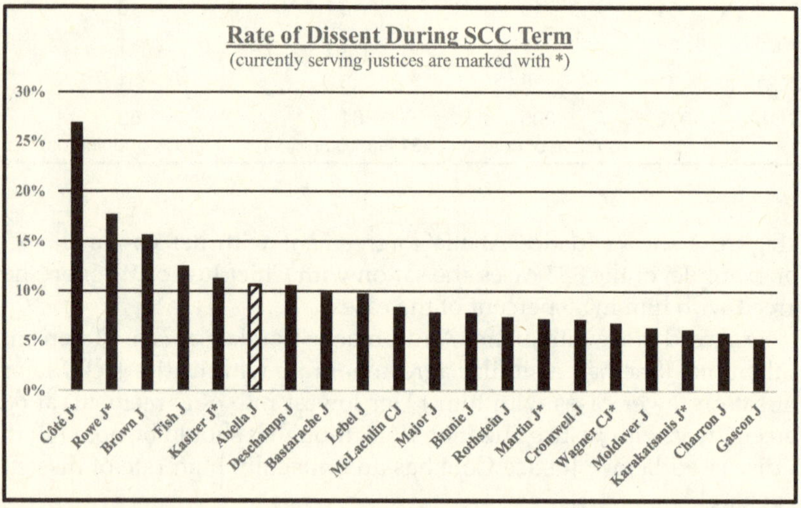

Figure 3

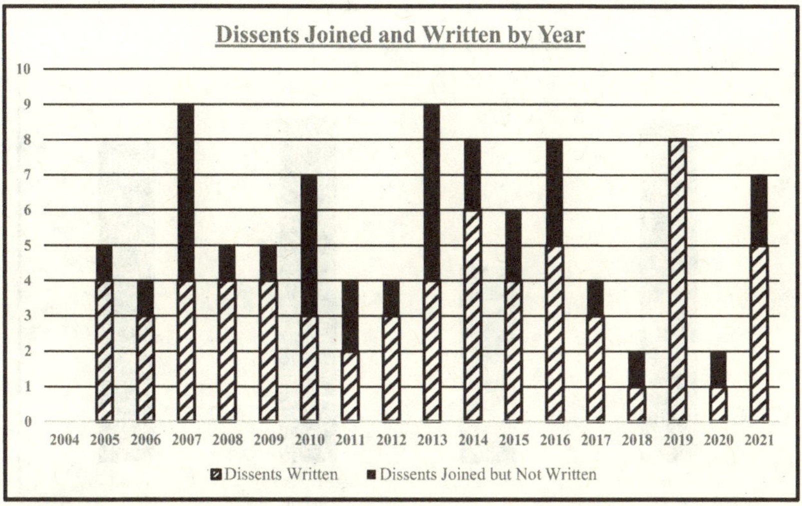

Figure 4

Figure 3 shows Justice Abella's rate of dissent compared to her colleagues. Overall, she dissented from the majority in 10.6 percent of cases she heard. Of the colleagues she sat with, only Justices Suzanne Côté (26.9 percent), Malcolm Rowe (17.7 percent), Russell Brown (15.7 percent), and Morris Fish (12.6 percent) had higher dissent rates.[5] In 24 cases, Justice Abella was the only dissenter. Figure 5, below, shows the number of dissents authored and joined by Justice Abella by year.

Figure 5 divides her dissents by four broad areas of law (constitutional, criminal, other public law, and private law).[6] The results show that she was much less likely to dissent in criminal cases. Justice Abella was also less likely to author opinions in criminal law cases, both compared to other areas of law (Figure 6) and compared to her colleagues (Figure 7).

5 Although Justice Nicholas Kasirer also had a slightly higher dissent rate, he had only sat on 71 cases by the end of 2021.

6 Because some cases are included in multiple categories (e.g., both constitutional and criminal) and other cases are uncategorized, the sums of the numbers of cases indicated in Figure 6 do not match the totals shown in Table 7.1.

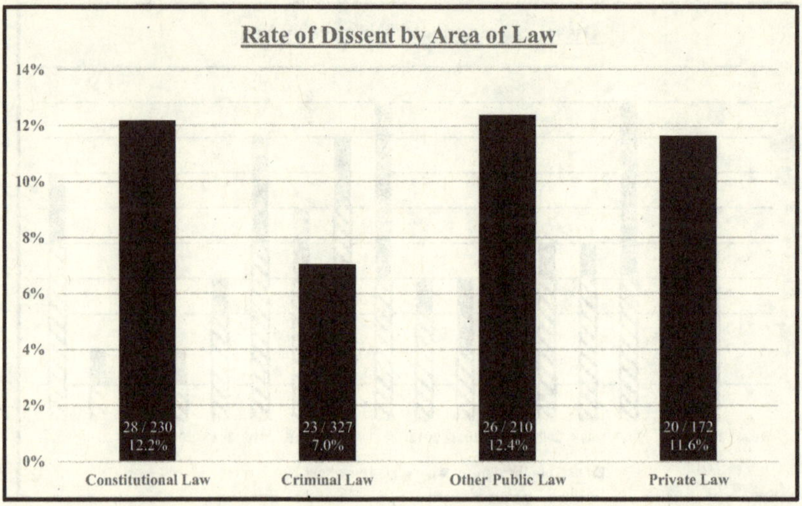

Figure 5

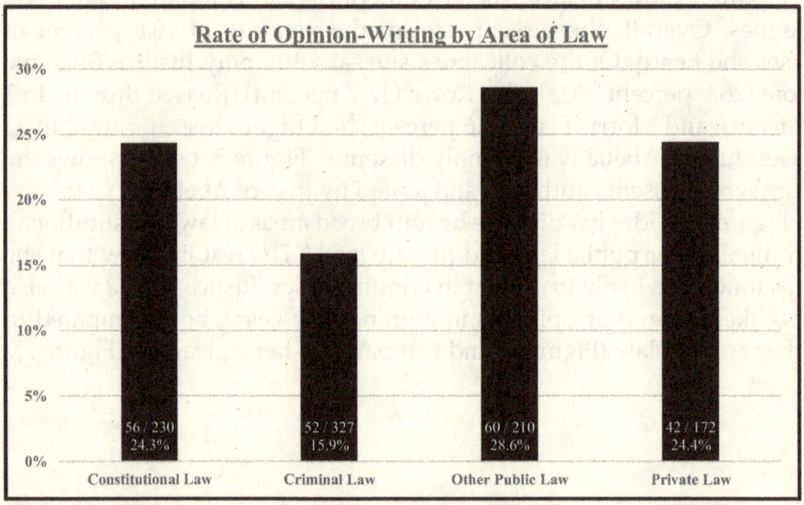

Figure 6

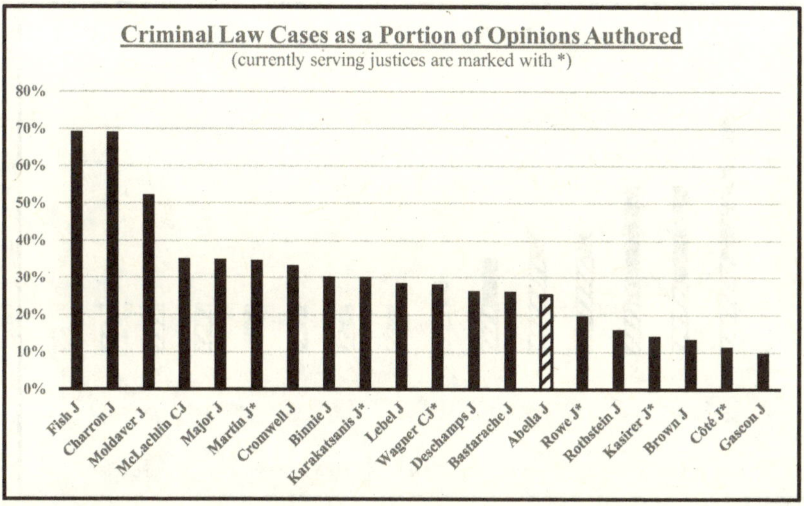

Figure 7

Justice Abella often co-authored opinions with other justices, as shown in Figure 8. She co-wrote reasons with one or more other justices in 56 cases (27 percent). Justice Andromache Karakatsanis was Justice Abella's most frequent writing partner. Together they penned 10 opinions (seven majority and three dissenting). Other common writing partners were Justices Michael Moldaver and Richard Wagner (seven each) and Thomas Cromwell and Beverley McLachlin (five each). Despite their philosophical differences, she also co-wrote one opinion with Justice Suzanne Côté and two with Justice Malcom Rowe. Despite their high rate of overall agreement, Justice Abella and Justice Martin authored no opinions as a duo. She also co-wrote judgments with more than one other judge — sometimes as many as eight.[7]

Justice Abella delivered significantly fewer decisions from the bench than the other justices (Figure 9), although most from-the bench rulings are delivered by the senior judge presiding. Her average written opinion contained 5371 words, slightly less than the 5550 words

7 Some of the group joint decisions are anomalies, however. For example, in *TD Bank v Young*, 2020 SCC 15, eight justices signed a two-paragraph majority judgment to Justice Côté's fifty-nine-paragraph dissent. In *Reference re Supreme Court Act*, ss 5 and 6, six judges signed a majority judgment with only Justice Moldaver in dissent.

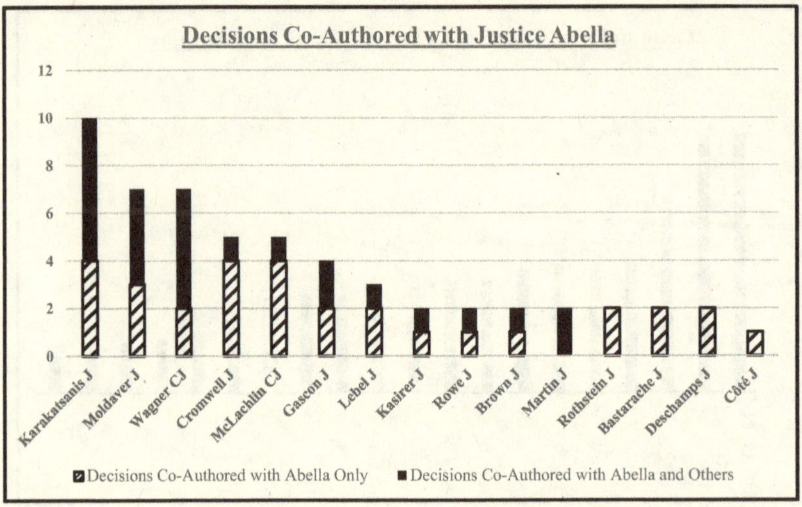

Figure 8

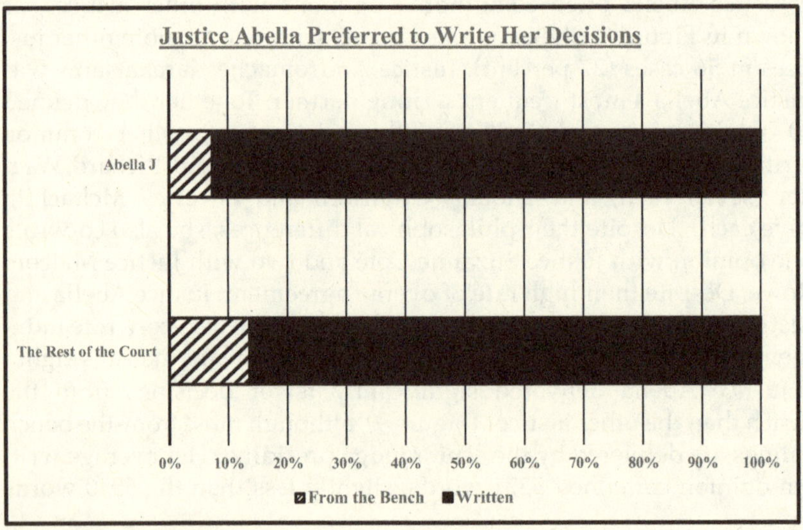

Figure 9

used in the average non-Abella written opinion in our data. However, Abella's median[8] written opinion was wordier than the median opinion written by her colleagues (4758 versus 4309 words). This suggests that Justice Abella wrote somewhat longer judgments in general but avoided extremely long opinions that would pull up her overall average.

The longest majority decision authored by Justice Abella, *Council of Canadians with Disabilities v VIA Rail Canada Inc*,[9] had 22,535 words (also her longest sole-authored opinion). Her longest concurrence was in *Canada (Minister of Citizenship and Immigration) v Vavilov*,[10] co-written with Justice Karakatsanis, at 18,045 words. Justice Abella's longest dissent, co-written with Justice Kasirer, was in *Ward v Quebec*,[11] at 13,122 words.

Justice Abella wielded an expansive vocabulary as a writer, using 24,846 unique words across her written opinions.[12] The number of unique words used by a judge is closely related to the total number of words written by that judge[13]; the more text one writes, the more opportunities there are to use new words. Figure 10 compares the number of unique words used to the total words used for each justice in our data.

---

8 The median is the middle value in a data set. For instance, the median of {1,3,100} is 3. Medians are less influenced by outliers than averages.

9 *Council of Canadians with Disabilities v VIA Rail Canada Inc*, 2007 SCC 15.

10 *Canada (Minister of Citizenship and Immigration) v Vavilov*, 2019 SCC 65.

11 *Ward v Quebec (Commission des droits de la personne et des droits de la jeunesse)*, 2021 SCC 43.

12 "Words" included all sequences of characters bounded by spaces, line breaks, or begin/end characters, and thus were <u>not</u> limited to English words. "Vocabulary" in this section refers exclusively to the range of words used by each justice in their written SCC opinions; the justices are presumed to have much larger actual vocabularies. Numbers and punctuation marks were removed from the text prior to counting.

13 The correlation is extremely strong ($R^2 > 0.9$). R^2 represents, on a scale from 0 to 1, the degree to which variation in one metric can be explained using another metric, with 0 meaning the second metric has no explanatory power and 1 meaning that all variation in the first metric can be explained using the second metric. An $R^2 > 0.9$ means that total text authored explains more than 80% of the variation in vocabulary size between justices; the more words a judge has written in total, the more unique words we should expect to find. For comparison, this is a stronger relationship than the connection between the size of someone's foot and their height ($R^2 \approx 0.7$). The relationship better fits a square root curve ($F = 439$) than a logarithmic curve ($F = 135$), meaning that a judge's total vocabulary is better predicted by taking the square root of the total number of words authored than the logarithm of the total number of words. A square root curve grows much faster than a logarithmic curve, especially at higher values.

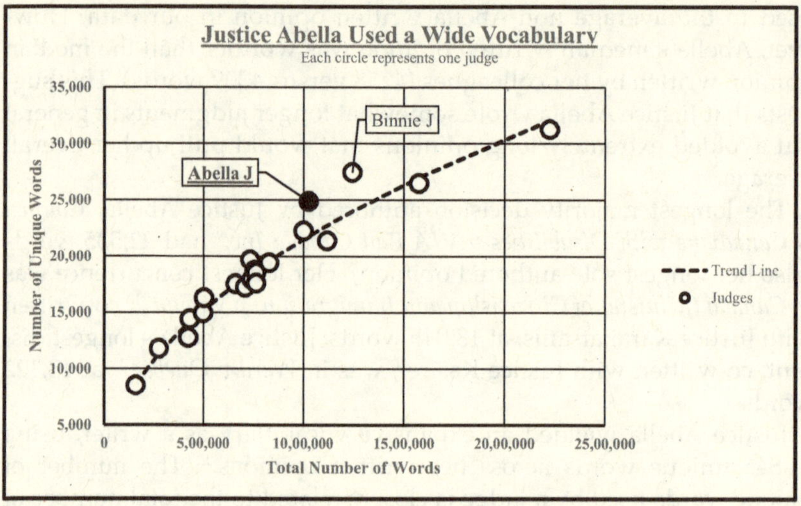

Figure 10

Justice Abella used a markedly wider vocabulary given her total written output compared to the rest of the Court; only Justice Binnie used a larger vocabulary, by this measure.

B. How Do You Find a Word that Means Abella?[14]

We have so far described Justice Abella's time on the Supreme Court using metadata: the number of cases heard, number of decisions authored, etc. This section will instead apply quantitative techniques to the text of her opinions. Justice Abella authored more than 200 decisions, totaling approximately one million words, during her time on the Court. Those words were selected and ordered with great care.[15] By comparing the collection of decisions Justice Abella authored with those of the Court's other judges, we can attempt to find quantitative insights into not just her writing style but the topics and ideas she cared about most. The numbers show what made Justice Abella unique.

14 With apologies to Rodgers and Hammerstein, the answer will be neither *flibbertigibbet* nor *will-o-the-wisp* (see "Maria," *The Sound of Music* (Recording: Argyle Enterprises & 20th Century Fox, 1965)).

15 Justice Abella has often described hand-writing dozens of drafts of her judgments.

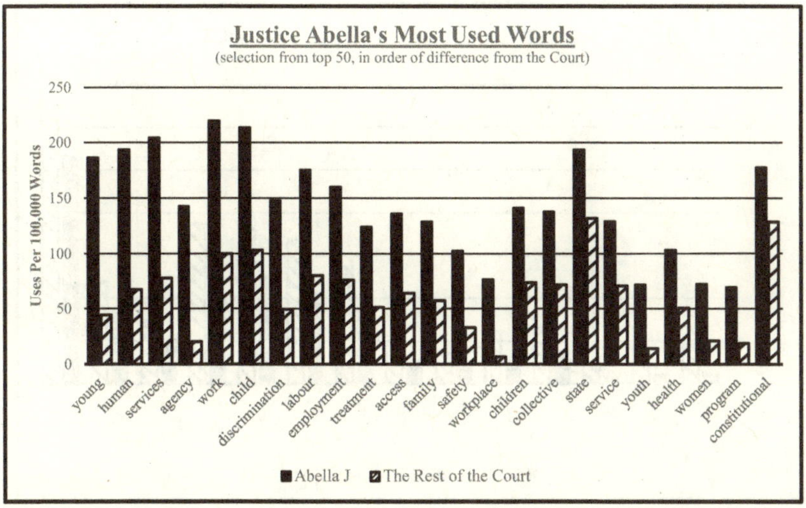

Figure 11[16]

The following analysis borrows heavily from the concept of "cinnamon words" developed by data journalist Ben Blatt in his book "Nabokov's Favourite Word is Mauve."[17] "Cinnamon words" are words used by an author at a much higher rate than those words are used in a reference body of work. It is a quantitative method to find an author's favourite words; the term "cinnamon words" is a reference to *cinnamon* being Ray Bradbury's favourite word.[18]

In Blatt's book, he applies the technique to the works of famous authors, discovering that Nabokov's most used word, comparatively, was *mauve*.[19] We applied this technique to Justice Abella's opinions on the Supreme Court, using the remaining opinions of the Court as the benchmark for comparison.[20] In addition to cataloguing Jus-

16 The selected terms are a curated list selected by the authors. The full list can be found in the appendix.

17 Ben Blatt, *Nabokov's Favourite Word is Mauve* (New York: Simon & Schuster, 2018).

18 *Ibid.*

19 Some notable author/cinnamon word results: Ernest Hemingway and *cognac*; Agatha Christie and *inquest*, Dan Brown and *masonic*; Jane Austen and *civility*.

20 All SCC cases from 1975 on. A case was considered authored by Justice Abella if she wrote it alone or with one or more other justices. Names and other proper nouns are used at unusually high frequencies for the number of cases they appear in; a single opinion may use the parties' names dozens of times, and those uses may be the only occurrence of those words across the whole dataset. To compensate, words

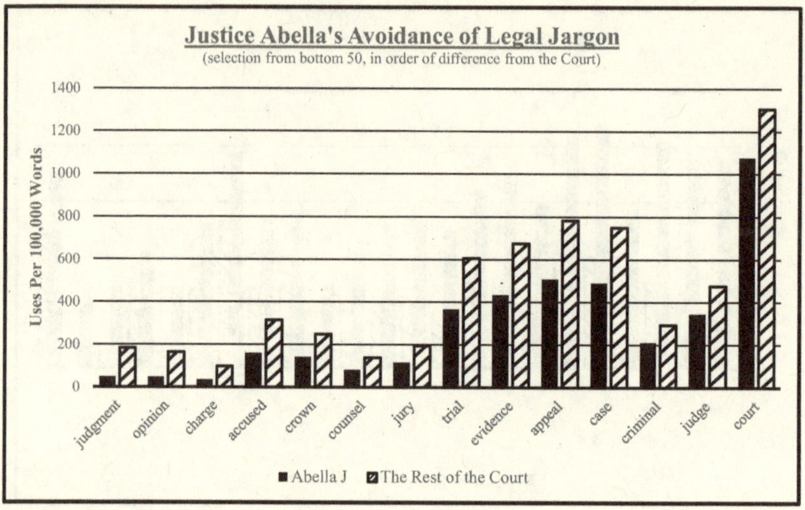

Figure 12

tice Abella's most used words[21] compared to the Court's, we also compiled the fifty words she used least — an "anti-cinnamon word" analysis.

Justice Abella's most used terms demonstrate the breadth and coherence of her jurisprudential impact. Her interest in law related to human rights, especially the rights of children (*human, young, child, discrimination, family, children, youth, women*), working conditions (*work, labour, employment, safety, workplace, collective*), and the functioning of the state (*services, treatment, access, agency, state, service, health, program, constitutional*) are all evident in the results.[22]

While Justice Abella's "cinnamon words" largely point to the areas of law where she was most active, her stylistic choices are clearer in what

---

used less than five times across three different cases were removed from the data prior to analysis. Punctuation was also removed. All analysis was completed in R, with heavy use of the stringr, dyplr, and quanteda libraries.

21 For clarity, the terms relating to "used more" and "used less" in the following section always refer to Justice Abella's use of a word compared to the rest of the Court.

22 Justice Abella's most used word, *para,* should not be overinterpreted: the transition from citing pages in the Supreme Court Reports to citing paragraph numbers started in the mid-1980s and was complete by the mid-1990s, and thus much of her apparent preference for the term is an artifact of when she served. Her least used word, *supra,* is likewise an artifact of changing citation practices; during Justice Abella's tenure, the term was used only four times across all justices.

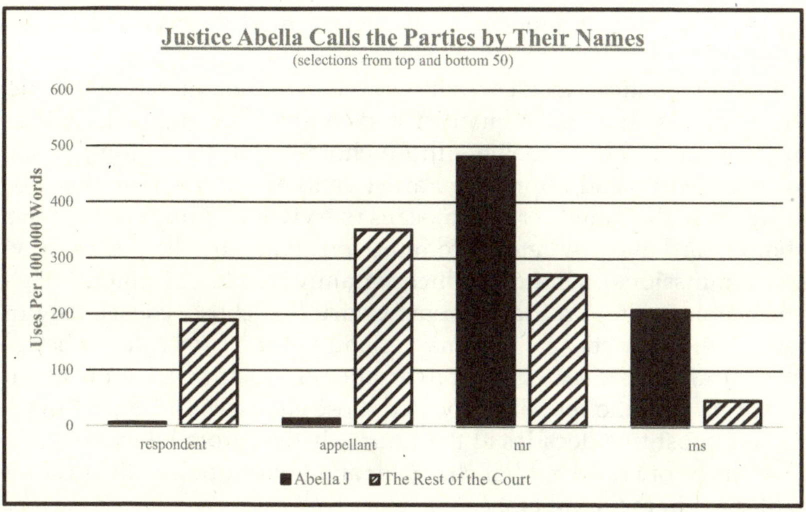

Figure 13

words she used least. Most notable is her avoidance of legal jargon and references to legal procedure; among her least used words are *judgment, opinion, accused, Crown, charge, counsel, trial, evidence, case, jury, fact, issue, judge,* and *court*. Many of these terms are most frequently used in a criminal context, so the disparity is largely explained by Justice Abella's less frequent decisions in criminal cases.

But not all. Among Abella's least favorite legal jargon were the terms *appellant* and *respondent,* which she used at 1/30th the frequency of the rest of the Court. Justice Abella instead referred to parties before the Court by their surnames: *Mr.* and *Ms.* are among the words she used most compared to the Court. The latter of these prefixes is another meaningful stylistic choice. *Mrs.* is used by Abella exclusively in quotations or paired with *Mr.*[23]

Justice Abella avoided *first, second, one* and *two*; she does not like lists. She also shunned the use of *thus* and *however* to connect ideas. Instead, she preferred *also,* her seventh most-used word. Abella avoided the "judicial register": *indeed, regard, upon, although, now.* She used the word

23 See, for example, *Bruker v Marcovitz*, 2007 SCC 54 at para 68 (". . . in his words: 'Mrs. Bruker harassed me . . .'"); *R v Craig*, 2009 SCC 23 at para 5 ("At the time of the offence, *Mr. and Mrs.* Nguyen resided . . ."). *R v Szczerbaniwicz* is an interesting example. Justice Abella, writing for the majority, includes "Mrs." twice, both in quotations. The dissent, by Justice Binnie, uses "Mrs." twenty-one times, despite containing fewer overall words.

rule less than her colleagues but outpaced them in her usage of the word *impact*.

In short, Justice Abella's writing style was not merely aesthetic. Modern tools allow us to quantify and contrast her linguistic choices on the Court, and we believe those choices give us a glimpse into her perspective and approach. Earlier chapters in the book describe her roots as the daughter of Holocaust survivors, family court judge, labour board and law reform commission chair, and the head of several commissions on inquiry, which certainly may have influenced her word choices later on the Supreme Court. She chose, consciously or not, to call the parties by their names and not their roles, to exchange the clinical *first/second* for the conversational *also*, to speak more about the *impact* than the *rule*. She repeated those choices hundreds of times across almost two decades at the Court, distinct from her colleagues. How she wrote reflected her character and her outlook — the proof is right there in the numbers!

Appendix A: Justice Abella's Most Used Words Compared to the Court

Numbers are in uses per 100,000 words and are listed in descending order of difference between Justice Abella's usage rate and the Court's. "The Rest of the Court" includes all Supreme Court of Canada cases from 1975 to the end of the 2021 term, except those authored by Justice Abella. Words used fewer than five times and words used in fewer than three separate cases were removed prior to analysis.

Table 7.2. Justice Abella's Most Used Words Compared to the Court

	Word	Justice Abella	The Rest of the Court		Word	Justice Abella	The Rest of the Court
1	*para*	715	339	26	*family*	128	57
2	*Mr.*	481	270	27	*safety*	102	33
3	*Canada*	517	338	28	*workplace*	76	7
4	*Ms.*	208	46	29	*Canadian*	256	187
5	*young*	186	44	30	*convention*	93	26
6	*international*	188	54	31	*children*	141	74
7	*also*	472	344	32	*ability*	104	37
8	*human*	193	67	33	*collective*	137	72
9	*services*	204	78	34	*article*	113	47
10	*agency*	142	20	35	*pay*	125	62
11	*work*	220	100	36	*state*	194	132
12	*v*	798	680	37	*order*	410	349
13	*copyright*	135	18	38	*Evans*	68	7
14	*child*	214	103	39	*production*	88	27
15	*protection*	204	101	40	*age*	98	39
16	*information*	253	151	41	*service*	129	71
17	*discrimination*	148	49	42	*youth*	72	14
18	*via*	97	2	43	*health*	103	51
19	*labour*	175	80	44	*analysis*	174	122
20	*impact*	130	38	45	*women*	72	21
21	*based*	208	123	46	*freedom*	128	78
22	*employment*	160	76	47	*explained*	86	35
23	*religious*	107	28	48	*program*	69	19
24	*treatment*	124	51	49	*constitutional*	178	128
25	*access*	136	64	50	*adult*	59	11

Appendix B: Justice Abella's Least Used Words Compared to the Court

Numbers are in uses per 100,000 words and are listed in descending order of difference between the Court's usage rate and Justice Abella's. "The Rest of the Court" includes all Supreme Court of Canada cases from 1975 to the end of the 2021 term, except those authored by Justice Abella. Words used fewer than five times and words used in fewer than three separate cases were removed prior to analysis.

Table 7.3. Justice Abella's Least Used Words Compared to the Court

	Word	Justice Abella	The Rest of the Court		Word	Justice Abella	The Rest of the Court
1	*supra*	5	207	26	*counsel*	80	139
2	*respondent*	6	189	27	*however*	171	293
3	*appellant*	13	351	28	*jury*	116	194
4	*page*	8	152	29	*trial*	365	605
5	*land*	16	89	30	*evidence*	433	675
6	*indeed*	14	72	31	*appeal*	507	784
7	*present*	32	132	32	*case*	488	749
8	*thus*	31	126	33	*said*	128	189
9	*judgment*	48	183	34	*must*	342	490
10	*opinion*	48	163	35	*power*	133	189
11	*upon*	69	223	36	*criminal*	210	292
12	*charge*	35	98	37	*within*	168	233
13	*regard*	30	82	38	*judge*	345	475
14	*trust*	31	84	39	*time*	222	295
15	*stated*	60	145	40	*fact*	214	284
16	*although*	47	112	41	*issue*	231	306
17	*point*	56	129	42	*first*	199	257
18	*rule*	76	175	43	*two*	183	233
19	*matter*	77	160	44	*may*	477	607
20	*now*	49	100	45	*general*	213	268
21	*accused*	159	313	46	*court*	1075	1306
22	*question*	174	334	47	*one*	350	425
23	*might*	61	118	48	*made*	288	349
24	*second*	82	144	49	*view*	276	327
25	*crown*	142	247	50	*s*	1132	1263

8 Her Fundamentals: Justice Abella and Section 2(b) of the *Charter*

JAMIE CAMERON*

A. Introduction

Rosalie Abella's legendary aspirations for human rights all but define her, but should not overshadow other parts of her *Charter* legacy.[1] For instance, she earned praise for her approach to fundamental freedoms in her dissenting opinions in *Alberta v Hutterian Brethren of Wilson Colony* and *R v NS*, as well as for her majority opinion constitutionalizing the right to strike in *Saskatchewan Federation of Labour v Saskatchewan*.[2] Nor did it surprise when Justice Abella formed part of the majority opinion that supported equality and dignity values over freedom of religion in *Law Society of British Columbia v Trinity Western University*.[3] In comparison, her section 2(b) jurisprudence has attracted less scholarly attention.[4] For example, Justice Abella's most influential section 2(b)

---

* Professor Emerita, Osgoode Hall Law School. I thank Stephen Bindman, Gerald Chan, and Vanessa MacDonell for inviting me to participate in "A Life of Firsts: A Celebration of a Remarkable Career and Legacy." And words cannot easily convey my gratitude and thanks to Justice Abella for what I have learned from her and for the myriad ways she has informed and enriched my experiences as an academic and occasional advocate at the Supreme Court.

1 *Canadian Charter of Rights and Freedoms*, Part I of the *Constitution Act, 1982*, being Schedule B to the *Canada Act 1982* (UK), 1982, c 11.

2 *Alberta v Hutterian Brethren of Wilson Colony*, [2009] 2 SCR 567 (invalidating mandatory photo ID for driver's licenses as a violation of the section 2(a) rights of Wilson Colony Hutterites); *R v NS*, [2012] 3 SCR 26; (upholding a witness's right under section 2(a) to wear a niqab while testifying in court); *Saskatchewan Federation of Labour v Saskatchewan*, [2015] 1 SCR 245 (constitutionalizing the right to strike under section 2(d)).

3 [2018] 2 SCR 293 [*Trinity Western University*] (upholding the Law Society's decision not to approve TWU's proposed law school). Five members of the Court, including Justice Abella, wrote a joint majority opinion.

4 Justice Abella has written many decisions on section 2's other fundamental freedoms, including section 2(a), which address freedom of conscience and religion,

decision, *Doré v Barreau de Quebec*, is celebrated and debated more for its approach to administrative decision-making under the *Charter* than for expressive freedom.[5] Elsewhere, her section 2(b) jurisprudence has for the most part been quietly received. To some degree, that changed with her dissenting opinions in the Court's monumental section 2(b) decisions in *City of Toronto v Ontario*[6] and *Ward v Quebec*.[7]

If unexpected, Justice Abella's section 2(b) legacy is singular and true. It may be a surprise to learn that, with the exception of Justice Beverley McLachlin, she has written more opinions on freedom of expression and the press than any other member of the Court.[8] This jurisprudence, comprising five majority opinions, two concurrences, and nine dissenting opinions — most of which support section 2(b) — is unapologetically Abellian.[9]

One of the hallmarks or fundamentals of Abella's approach to law is balancing, which serves as the bedrock principle of her *Charter* interpretation. Though balancing is closely associated with the *Doré* administrative law test, the final or "narrow" proportionality balancing step under the section 1 *Oakes* test played a principal role in her section 2(b) decision-making. There, Justice Abella brought the deleterious consequences of violating section 2(b) to the forefront, and more often than

---

and section 2(d), which guarantees freedom of association. On section 2(a), for example, see Howard Kislowicz, "Reaching to See Through Another's Eyes: Justice Abella's Religious Freedom Jurisprudence," Chapter 9 in this volume.

5 2012 SCC 12 [*Doré*].

6 [2021] SCC 34 [*City of Toronto*] (rejecting a section 2(b) challenge to Ontario legislation re-structuring Toronto City Council during a municipal election).

7 2021 SCC 43 [*Ward*] (rejecting a human rights claim and upholding the expressive freedom of a stand-up comedian).

8 While Justice McLachlin signed twenty section 2(b) decisions in twenty-seven years at the Supreme Court, Justice Abella wrote sixteen in a seventeen-year period. Justice McLachlin's opinions on expressive freedom between 1990 and 2000 are especially notable. See Appendix 1, Section 2(b) opinions of Justice Abella, 2004–2021 and Appendix 2, Section 2(b) opinions of Justice McLachlin, 1990–2018.

9 *R v Bryan*, [2007] 1 SCR 527; *R v National Post*, [2010] 1 SCR 477; *Toronto Star Newspapers Ltd v Canada*, [2010] 1 SCR 721 [*Toronto Star*]; *Ontario (Public Safety & Security) v Criminal Lawyers' Association*, [2011] 1 SCR 815; *Malhab v diffusion Metromedia CMR Inc*, [2011] 1 SCR 214 [*Malhab*]; *Crookes v Newton*, [2011] 3 SCR 269; *Doré*, above note 5; *AB v Bragg Communications Inc*, [2012] 2 SCR 567; *Alberta (Information and Privacy Commissioner) v UFCW, Local 401*, [2013] 3 SCR 733 [*UFCW*]; *Ernst v Alberta Energy Regulator*, [2017] 1 SCR 3; *R v Vice Media Canada Inc*, [2018] 3 SCR 374 [*Vice Media*]; *Denis v Côté*, [2019] 3 SCR 482; *Bent v Platnick*, 2020 SCC 23; *CBC v Manitoba*, 2021 SCC 33; *City of Toronto*, above note 6; *Ward*, above note 7. See Appendix 1, Section 2(b) opinions of Justice Abella, 2004–2021.

not, doing so led to the conclusion that the infringement was disproportionate.[10] To some extent, proportionality balancing ameliorated the problems of the contextual approach, which dominates the section 2(b) jurisprudence and leads to a finding of justified limits under section 1, in large part because it discounts the value of expressive content.[11] Discussion of the deleterious consequences of infringing section 2(b) is somewhat beside the point under a methodology that essentially preempts that step. In practice, the contextual approach's subjective assessment of expressive content determines the outcome and displaces proportionality balancing, which should be a critical step in the analysis. Justice Abella enhanced the role of that step, determining what proportionality required in the circumstances through analysis that was evidence based and even handed in its assessment of the interests at stake.

Her second fundamental is a provocative duality in her conception of expressive freedom, which separated section 2(b)'s core democratic functions from its "civil liberties" objectives — in principle, protecting the former but not the latter. While Justice Abella was quick to intervene when section 2(b)'s democratic rights and press interests were at risk, she took a different view when the civil liberties protected by section 2(b) were set up against "human rights." While both are "crucial mainstays of our democratic catechism," human rights have primacy over civil liberties in what she describes as the "conceptual battle of the constitutional titans."[12] Though she likely would not have supported

10 Examples include *R v Bryan*, *Toronto Star*, and *UFCW*, *Ibid.*

11 In brief, the contextual approach is a section 1 mechanism that tests the expressive content at stake against section 2(b)'s abstract, aspirational values. The purpose of this exercise is to determine whether expressive activity is of low or high value, and uses that assessment to lower the standard of justification for low-value expression, allowing limits to be readily upheld. This approach was determinative in most cases, rendering the final step of proportionality balancing effectively irrelevant and little more than a formality. See generally Jamie Cameron, "Renewing Freedom of Expression, Part Two: From the Contextual Approach to Proportionality Balancing," in Brian Bird & Derek Ross, eds, *Supreme Court Law Review, 2nd Series, Volume 112: Rights, Freedoms and their Limits: Reimagining Section 1 of the Charter*" (Toronto: LexisNexis Canada Inc, 2023) 121 (explaining the relationship between the contextual approach and the final stage of proportionality balancing under section 1).

12 Rosalie Silberman Abella, "Freedom of Expression or Freedom from Hate: A Canadian Perspective" (2017) 40 *Cardozo Law Review* 503 at 508. In "International Law and Human Rights: The Power and the Pity" (2010) 55 *McGill Law Journal* 871, at 878, she explains, "Civil liberties is about treating everyone the same; human rights is about acknowledging people's differences so that they can be treated as equals. Civil liberties is only about one individual; human rights is about how individuals are treated because they are part of a group. Civil liberties is a concept of rights

section 2(b) in the earlier *Charter* decisions on hate propaganda and Holocaust denial, because these issues engage the guarantee's civil liberties entitlements, she had little opportunity prior to *Ward v Quebec* to embed the primacy of human rights into her interpretation of section 2(b)'s guarantee of expressive freedom.[13] Instead, Justice Abella's legacy centers on her devotion to section 2(b)'s democratic objectives and guarantee of a free press.

Shortly before her tenure on the Court ended, Justice Abella's dual conception of section 2(b) entitlement crystallized fortuitously in *City of Toronto* and *Ward*.[14] In *City of Toronto*, she forcefully defended section 2(b)'s rights of democratic participation when the province of Ontario enacted legislation that re-constituted City Council during a municipal election in *City of Toronto*. Then she and Justice Kasirer wrote a joint dissent that just as fiercely maintained that the human rights claim of a disabled teenage boy should prevail over a stand-up comedian's right of expressive freedom in *Ward*. While all nine judges enforced section 2(b) once, no member of the Court protected or rejected expressive freedom in both decisions.[15] Justice Abella was at the center of deeply contested conceptions of section 2(b), and *City of Toronto* and *Ward* are her capstone opinions, culminating and defining her legacy under this section of the *Charter*.

By her own account, Justice Abella never sought a civil liberties legacy. At the same time, she was deeply committed to the support and promotion of the *Charter*'s democratic values. Those conceptual dynamics generated a jurisprudence that was unequalled in its protection of the

---

that requires the state *not* to interfere with our liberties; human rights, on the other hand, cannot be realized *without* the state's intervention" (emphasis in original). She goes on to discuss human rights and civil liberties as the "crucial mainstays" of our "democratic catechism." See also Rosalie Silberman Abella & Matthew Diller, "A Conversation with the Honourable Rosalie Silberman Abella and Dean Matthew Diller" (2018) 87 *Fordham Law Review* 843 at 846 ("human rights primacy").

13 *R v Keegstra*, [1990] 3 SCR 697; *Canada (Human Rights Commission) v Taylor*, [1990] 3 SCR 892; *R v Zundel*, [1992] 2 SCR 731.

14 *City of Toronto*, above note 6, was decided on 1 October 2021 and *Ward*, above note 7, on 29 October 2021. Justice Abella completed her work at the end of 2021, six months after she retired on her seventy-fifth birthday.

15 The juxtaposition of these decisions raises questions about the nature of the claim and about why all members of the Court granted the section 2(b) claim in one but not the other; the question, in other words, is whether there is a conception of expressive freedom that explains why one claim failed and the other succeeded. See Jamie Cameron, "Section 2(b) Solitudes: *City of Toronto* and *Ward v Quebec*" *Centre for Free Expression* blog (10 February 2022), online: https://cfe.ryerson.ca/blog/2022/02/freedom-expression-and-charter-1982-2022-part-1-5.

guarantee's democracy-enhancing objectives, but selective or uneven in supporting section 2(b)'s principal civil liberties goal of protecting expressive freedom.

B. Abella's Fundamentals: Proportionality Balancing

Justice Abella's *Charter* jurisprudence revolved around a concept of balancing and included a distinctive role for *Charter* balancing in administrative decision making. While its merits cannot be discussed in any detail here, it is important to distinguish *Doré* balancing in administrative law from proportionality balancing under section 1. Though the two are closely related, it is open to question whether *Doré*'s standard of asking whether the decision-maker was "alive to the issues" squares with the requirements of *Oakes* or can be described as a robust form of review.[16] In this, the issue at stake in *Doré* may be a case in point. There, the Court upheld the Barreau's decision to reprimand a lawyer for writing a highly inflammatory but private letter to a judge who had denounced him in open court.[17]

Key to this discussion is how Justice Abella re-calibrated the section 1 analysis to demand that real work be done under the final stage of the *Oakes* test, to incorporate and elevate section 2(b)'s underlying values in the analysis. In doing so, she heightened the role of deleterious consequences, drawing the harm arising from the infringement of section 2(b) directly into the balancing of interests. Two examples of this proportionality balancing that stand out in her section 2(b) jurisprudence are *R v Bryan*[18] and *Alberta (Information and Privacy Commissioner) v United Food and Commercial Workers, Local 401 (UFCW)*.[19]

16 See, for example, *Ktunaxa Nation v British Columbia*, [2017] 2 SCR 386 at para 144 per Moldaver J, concurring, and upholding the decision where the Minister did not expressly address it but was "alive" to the substance of Ktunaxa's section 2(a) right; *Law Society of British Columbia v Trinity Western University*, above note 3 at paras 54 & 55 (per the Court's anonymous majority opinion, stating that the Benchers were "alive to the issues" and made a decision that reflected proportionality balancing, despite providing no reasons).

17 *Doré*, above note 5 at para 71, stating that the decision to reprimand "cannot be said to represent an unreasonable balance of expressive rights with statutory objectives." But compare *Groia v Law Society of Upper Canada*, [2018] 1 SCR 772, finding the Law Society's conclusion that a lawyer's in-court remarks violated standards of civility and constituted professional misconduct to be unreasonable; Justice Abella joined Justice Moldaver's majority reasons.

18 Above note 9 (dissenting opinion).

19 Above note 9 (joint majority opinion with Justice Cromwell).

In *R v Bryan*, a closely divided Court upheld Parliament's prohibition on the transmission of federal election results from some parts of the country, while the voting continued in others as a justified limit on freedom of expression.[20] The *Canada Elections Act* adopted a model of staggered voting hours in different time zones to reduce the risk that a release of early election results in eastern Canada could influence voting in western provinces and even affect the outcome. The early transmission of election results raised other issues, such as informational equality and the perceived fairness of an election. In the absence of evidence, the Court's majority opinion, written by Justice Michel Bastarache, was prepared to conclude that informational inequality — for example, when election results are only available in some parts of Canada — affected public confidence in elections, treating that view as the "logically direct result of the requirement that elections be fair."[21] In addition, Justice Bastarache's majority opinion found that the interest in releasing election results in eastern Canada prior to the close of polls elsewhere lay "at the periphery of the section 2(b) guarantee."[22] That conclusion is an example of the contextual approach, because it shows how limits on expression can be justified by discounting the value of freedom of expression at stake.

On proportionality balancing at the final stage of *Oakes*, Justice Bastarache responded to Justice Abella's reference to "clear and convincing evidence," declaring that the state has no higher onus to meet than on the "salutary benefit" stage of the tests. He found no evidence that the harm arising from the ban was "of a quality or character manifestly superior" to the goal of electoral fairness; in other words, the harm to section 2(b) did not outweigh the objective of election fairness.[23] Under his calibration of the interests at stake, the magnitude of a ban temporarily delaying the release of election results for two to three hours was "extremely small."[24] Justice Morris Fish wrote concurring reasons, which concluded that a minor delay in transmitting election results "at

20 See the *Canada Elections Act*, SC 2000, c 9, section 329. Justice Bastarache wrote the majority opinion upholding section 329, and Justice Fish added a concurrence in a 5–4 vote in which Justice Abella wrote the minority opinion for four members of the Court.

21 *R v Bryan*, above note 9 at paras 22 and 14 (per the majority opinion, explaining that the "true objective" of the provisions is to ensure informational equality by measures that address the perception of unfairness when some voters have access to information that is denied to others).

22 *Ibid* at para 30.

23 *Ibid* at para 51.

24 *Ibid* at paras 48 and 51.

least" had the merit of "addressing the perception of unfairness caused by the information balance alone."[25] Although the harm to informational equality was "resistant to precise measurement," he upheld the prohibition because the deleterious effects of delaying the release of results were minimal.[26]

Justice Abella's attention to the evidence of harm is telling.[27] Her dissenting opinion placed a sharp focus on proportionality balancing and the issue of harm, studying it from both sides.[28] She maintained that the salutary benefits of a prohibition must meet a standard of "clear and convincing evidence" and found that the mere fact of informational equality was not sufficient to warrant the infringement.[29] In her view, the staggered-hours model ameliorated the risk that voters might know the outcome of the election before casting their ballot.[30] She explained that the harm of suppressing "core political speech," even for a short time, was profound. Under her analysis, the speculative, hypothetical, and unsubstantiated harm to electoral fairness was far outweighed by the deleterious consequences for a core democratic right.

The balance in *Bryan* was between the relative benefits and consequences of a two- to three-hour delay in transmitting results and the early release of information about results from only thirty-two of 308 House of Commons seats. Under Justice Abella's analysis, the evidence on harm balanced in favour of expressive freedom on both sides of the proportionality equation. First, the unsubstantiated harm arising from unequal but temporary access to results from some ridings did not establish the salutary benefits of the restriction. Second, the violation of section 2(b) was not trivial or minor in nature, but constituted a serious interference with expressive activity, which is at its apex during a democratic election.[31] Under that view of the evidence, the balance

25 *Ibid* at para 66.

26 *Ibid* at paras 66 and 80.

27 While Justice Bastarache's discussion of proportionality balancing was four paragraphs and Justice Fish's was fourteen, Justice Abella's extended over twenty-six paragraphs.

28 She repeated and emphasized the question of harm more than twenty-five times in her reasons.

29 *Ibid* at para 110.

30 *Ibid* at para 89 (stating that without a ban, the only results that would be known to voters outside Atlantic Canada would be for the thirty-two Atlantic ridings, or 32 of 308 seats in the House of Commons).

31 "News is news precisely because of its immediacy, especially during an election." *Ibid* at para 128.

between the benefits and consequences of the section 2(b) violation was not close.

The majority opinion written by Justices Abella and Cromwell in *UFCW* also demonstrated how proportionality balancing and its discussion of deleterious consequences could serve as the doctrinal forum for embedding section 2(b)'s values — the reasons for protecting the guarantee — in the section 1 analysis.[32] In *UFCW*, the *Privacy Information Protection Act* (*PIPA*) was applied to a labour union that was photographing individuals, including members of the public, who crossed the picket line during a strike. [33] The Court unanimously invalidated *PIPA* in its entirety because the statute failed the demands of proportionality balancing.[34] The legislation was overbroad in several respects, but rather than linger on minimal impairment, the Abella/Cromwell opinion focused on proportionality and the deleterious consequences of violating section 2(b). In the circumstances, the privacy law interfered with labour expression, which the Court described as a "particularly crucial form of expression."[35] Moreover, *PIPA*'s deleterious effects weighed heavily in the balance because labour relations objectives are "at the core of protecting expressive activity under section 1."[36] The proportionality analysis in *UFCW* grounded a conclusion that the deleterious consequences of overbroad legislation were disproportionate to the benefits of the privacy legislation.[37]

For much or most of the *Charter*'s first forty years, the final stage of the proportionality analysis was not a serious or developed part of the section 1 test. *Bryan* and *UFCW* show how a robust approach to proportionality balancing can enhance protection for section 2(b) and change outcomes by drawing the underlying values of expressive freedom into the discussion of deleterious consequences. By shifting the focus to the question of balancing, this approach proposes a heightened role for section 2(b) values in section 1 analysis.

By drawing section 2(b)'s values into proportionality balancing, Justice Abella's opinions in *Bryan* and *UFCW* affirmed the importance

32 Above note 9.

33 Signs posted in the area warned that images of those who crossed the line could be posted on a website. *Ibid* at para 4.

34 *Ibid*. This discussion is the centrepiece of the *UFCW* decision, extending from paras 20 to 38 of a forty-two-paragraph opinion.

35 *Ibid* at paras 28 and 35.

36 *Ibid* at para 28.

37 Notably, *UFCW* is one of only two decisions after 2000 that invalidated statutory provisions under section 2(b) of the *Charter*. The other was *Greater Vancouver Transportation Authority v Canadian Federation of Students*, [2009], 2 SCR 295.

of expressive freedom and marked a step in the right direction. As such, her approach to proportionality balancing stands out in a jurisprudence that tends to give scant consideration under section 1 to the freedom interests at stake. In each instance, her evidence-based model of proportionality balancing offset to some extent the one-way and transparently outcome-oriented elements of the contextual approach. *Bryan* demonstrated that Justice Abella would not tolerate a violation of section 2(b) where the deleterious consequences for expressive freedom were grave and the salutary benefits were speculative or hypothetical in nature. Although the balancing worked in section 2(b)'s favour in *Bryan* and *UFCW*, a lingering concern is that open-ended balancing can lack rigour and work against the entitlement. To prevent that, proportionality balancing must be principled and evidence based.[38]

Justice Abella was a champion of balancing that, in her conception, was versatile and creative. That creativity included *Doré* balancing and proportionality balancing under section 1, as well as the harmonized approach she proposed in *Vice Media*.[39] There, in a case dealing with production orders against the press, her concurring opinion recognized the constitutional status of the press and media, treated sections 8 and 2(b) as co-equal entitlements, and proposed a harmonized approach to search warrants and production orders seeking access to newsgathering materials that required formal analysis under s.2(b) as well as s.8. It was not sufficient, in her view, simply to roll the violation of section 2(b) into section 8 and its analysis of the reasonableness of search and production orders against the press and media. Significantly, she found an independent breach of section 2(b) that required its own discussion. In particular, she would have required the deleterious consequences of

38 Elsewhere I have proposed an overhaul of section 2(b) methodology that, among other things, abandons the contextual approach and recalibrates the proportionality analysis by entrenching key principles. First is a reminder that the purpose of proportionality balancing is to require the state to justify an infringement that has passed the other parts of the *Oakes* test. As such, it imposes a final and distinctive burden on the state to explain why the salutary benefits justify the violation. Second, the Court must also consider the deleterious consequences of the violation, not only for the expressive activity at stake but to expressive freedom more generally. In doing so, the Court must incorporate the section 2(b) analysis into the discussion to fairly consider the scope and gravity of the violation. See Jamie Cameron, "Resetting the Foundations: Renewing Freedom of Expression Under Section 2(b) of the Charter" (2022) 105 *Supreme Court Law Review* (2d) 120.

39 *Vice Media*, above note 9. This is discussed at greater length below.

the violation to be identified and weighed against the salutary benefits of compelling the disclosure of newsgathering materials.[40]

Justice Abella's solicitude for freedom of the press and media is found in other section 2(b) decisions as well. Also worth noting is her solo dissent in *R v National Post*, which took a robust approach to the Wigmore common law test for balancing the competing interests in compelling the disclosure or protecting the confidentiality of a journalist-source privilege.[41] There, her approach — which was granular, evidence based, and probing — led to a conclusion that the interest in protecting the privilege should prevail against the state's interest in access to confidential source information.

C. Justice Abella and the Duality of Expressive Freedom

No other member of the Court worked harder to entrench democratic and press rights under section 2(b) than Justice Abella, but she took a different view of expressive content that targeted vulnerable groups or individuals. This dichotomy reached a pinnacle in her back-to-back dissenting opinions in *City of Toronto* and *Ward*. She could hardly have been more protective of section 2(b) in *City of Toronto*, and scarcely more determined to uphold limits on expressive freedom in *Ward*. These outcomes, which may seem disparate, pivot around two centrepiece principles: on one hand, Justice Abella's unwavering support for democratic values, and on the other, her steadfast conviction that human rights such as equality and dignity of the person have primacy over civil liberties, including freedom of expression.

1. Section 2(b)'s Democratic Core

Justice Abella's faith in democracy is reflected in a significant jurisprudence that protected section 2(b)'s democracy-affirming purposes. As discussed, the *Bryan* dissent heightened the role of deleterious consequences in proportionality balancing to protect core section 2(b) expression related to the electoral process. In *Toronto Star*, Justice Abella was alone in defending the open court principle from a mandatory publication ban on information disclosed at bail proceedings.[42] The majority opinion upholding the ban canvassed its salutary benefits, finding that

40 *Ibid* at para 142.

41 Above note 9; this is discussed at greater length below.

42 Above note 9. A publication ban on bail hearing information is mandatory under section 517 of the *Criminal Code*, at the request to the accused: *Criminal Code*, RSC 1985, c C-46, section 517.

while not a "perfect outcome," the mandatory ban represented a "reasonable compromise."[43] In dissent, Justice Abella again focused on proportionality balancing, finding that while concerns about pre-trial publicity and delay could be attenuated, the interference with open court was profound. In finding the ban unconstitutional, she emphasized the role transparency plays in maintaining the public's trust and confidence in the justice system.[44] In the absence of a more compelling rationale, she was not prepared to compromise the open court principle.

On any view, Justice Abella's most important contribution to section 2(b)'s democratic objectives came near the end of her judicial career, in *City of Toronto*. There, she did not mince words in challenging the majority opinion's conclusion that the *Better Local Government Act* (BLGA), which restructured Toronto City Council during a municipal election, did not violate section 2(b)'s rights of democratic participation. Despite the unavoidable disruption of a democratic election that was underway, the majority opinion maintained that restructuring City Council did not violate section 2(b) because the *BLGA* did not prohibit or regulate electoral expression. In formal terms, the purpose of the *BLGA* was to restructure City Council, and its collateral or incidental effects on electoral expression did not engage section 2(b). Chief Justice Richard Wagner and Justice Russell Brown agreed that the *BLGA*'s impact on electoral expression "superficially resemble[d] a negative claim," but characterized the challenge as an attempt to impose a positive obligation on government — to maintain the status quo and preserve the effectiveness of electoral expression in the pre-*BLGA* municipal campaign.[45]

Conceptualizing the claim as positive or negative was the pivot in *City of Toronto*. From the majority's perspective, provinces can change the rules for municipal elections "as they wish," and any suggestion that section 2(b) requires the temporary constitutionalization of the existing framework during a municipal election was "constitutionally dubious, nonsensical, and even futile."[46] As the majority explained, the purpose of the *Baier* doctrine, which governs affirmative entitlements under section 2(b), is to shield positive claims from *Irwin Toy* and its low-threshold standard of breach.[47]

43 *Toronto Star*, above note 9 at para 60.

44 *City of Toronto*, above note 6 at para 65.

45 *Ibid* at para 32.

46 *Ibid* at paras 33 & 34.

47 *Ibid* at para 18. Under *Irwin Toy*, there is a *prima facie* breach of s.2(b) whenever the government interferes with an individual's attempt to convey meaning. *Irwin Toy Ltd v Quebec*, [1989] 1 SCR 927. In *Baier v Alberta* the Court imposed a higher

Reliance on *Baier v Alberta* and the construct of positive rights enabled the majority in *City of Toronto* to raise the threshold for breach to a near-invincible standard of "radically frustrating" expression. Under that restatement of the *Baier* doctrine, expressive activity need not be "absolutely impossible" to ground a claim but must at least be "effectively precluded." In this way, the majority imposed "an exceedingly high bar that would be met only in extreme and rare cases."[48] In refusing to acknowledge that transforming City Council during an election had serious and irreversible consequences for electoral expression, the majority opinion's conclusion flew in the face of the evidence. Raising the standard enabled the majority to minimize an evidentiary record that demonstrated the myriad ways the *BLGA*'s restructuring of City Council undermined and transformed section 2(b)'s rights of participation in an electoral process. The majority's suggestion that it might radically frustrate section 2(b) if the province declared that the election campaign would only be two days long shows how extreme the interference must be to warrant section 2(b)'s attention.[49]

Justice Abella's dissent did not flinch from the responsibility of enforcing section 2(b) in the face of the government's disrespect for, and disruption of, an extant election process. In the circumstances, she felt it was just as important to call the government out for its heavy-handed interference in the municipal election as it was to protect the doctrinal integrity of section 2(b) from the majority's narrow conception of entitlement. Justice Abella centered her discussion of the section 2(b) values at stake on the "reciprocal relationship between the democratic responsibilities of elected municipal officials and the rights of those who elected them."[50] She explained that an election involves a process of "reciprocal deliberative engagement" that warrants robust protection because it is integral to section 2(b)'s democratic purposes.[51] State interference with a stable election period and process of reciprocal discourse strikes at the heart of section 2(b)'s democratic values. Justice Abella's review of the evidence made it clear that redrawing the number, size, and boundaries of

---

standard for breach under s.2(b) for positive rights or affirmative entitlements. See *Baier v Alberta*, [2007] 2 SCR 673, adapting the positive rights doctrine from *Dunmore v Ontario* and section 2(d) of the *Charter* and applying it to section 2(b).

48 *City of Toronto*, above note 6 at para 27. This is how *City of Toronto* upgraded the "substantial interference" test to create a new and much more onerous standard of breach.

49 *Ibid.*

50 *Ibid* at para 120.

51 *Ibid* at para 128.

Toronto's electoral wards during the election unjustifiably interfered with the rights of all participants to engage in meaningful political discourse.[52]

In light of that evidence, Justice Abella found there was no scope whatsoever for positive rights analysis or for *Baier v Alberta*, which she described as having "no relevance to the legal or factual issues in this case."[53] Moreover, elevating the threshold for breach added a "gratuitous hurdle" that made it harder to prove a breach of "this core aspect of section 2(b) than other expressive activities."[54] In other words, the majority opinion raised the standard, making it harder to establish a violation of the democratic rights that define section 2(b)'s core purposes. In such circumstances, it could not have been clearer to Justice Abella that the foundational framework in *Irwin Toy* applied and that the *BLGA*'s interference with expressive rights that attach to an electoral process was "precisely" the kind of claim that is governed by *Irwin Toy*.[55]

Three years after the election took place, the Abella minority found that the *BLGA*'s violation of section 2(b) could not go unanswered.[56] It was important for the flaws in the majority opinion to be placed under analytical scrutiny and exposed. Justice Abella's *City of Toronto* minority opinion posed a powerful counterpoint to the majority's convoluted reasoning, which rejected section 2(b)'s role in promoting democratic governance and accountability.[57]

2. *Freedom of the Press: "A Distinct Constitutionally Protected Right"*[58]

By merely "including" freedom of the press in freedom of expression and not clearly granting it its own status, section 2(b) added a wrinkle that reinforced the Court's reluctance to grant a free press independent status as a *Charter* guarantee. Forty years on, the section 2(b)

---

52 She demonstrated that the *BLGA* necessarily interfered with the section 2(b) rights of a large metropolitan electorate, reviewing the evidence and detailing the ways in which restructuring City Council mid-election disrupted the process: see *ibid* at paras 136-47 (reviewing the evidence of consequences for candidates and members of the electorate).

53 *Ibid* at para 148.

54 *Ibid* at para 156.

55 *Ibid* at paras 156 and 151.

56 The minority opinion would have granted a remedy restoring the trial judge's declaration that the timing of the Act violated section 2(b) of the *Charter*. See *ibid* at 186.

57 The discussion on unwritten constitutional principles also featured prominently in the majority and minority opinions, but is not addressed here.

58 *Vice Media*, above note 9 at para 123.

jurisprudence acknowledges the critical role of the press and media in a functioning democracy, but it has refused to "constitutionalize" it. This is despite the text of section 2(b) and the role the press has played in the evolution of freedom of expression doctrine, including the open court principle.[59] The Court's decisions that are specific to the press are few in number and confer a modicum of protection but stop short of treating it — and its newsgathering activities — as a constitutional entitlement.[60]

The Court's foremost advocates of constitutional status for the press were Justices McLachlin and Abella. As the only member of the Court to find a breach of section 2(b) and protect the press from police warrants, Justice McLachlin led the way in the 1991 search warrant cases.[61] Not only did she develop a functional conception of the press, but she proposed a standard of justification to govern the state's access to newsgathering materials.[62] Several years later, Justice Abella dissented twice on her own to protect confidential journalist sources from being disclosed to the state.

In *R v National Post*, the Court considered whether a journalist-source privilege protected a reporter's confidential source from a production order against the press.[63] Justice Binnie's majority opinion rejected a *Charter* analysis and maintained that Wigmore's generic common law test for privilege adequately protected confidential journalist-source relationships. Without supporting a constitutional privilege under section 2(b), Justice Abella conducted a rigorous form of Wigmore balancing, which included a nuanced analysis of the evidence, and held that the confidential information — a brown envelope enclosing a disputed bank statement — should be protected from disclosure to the authorities. After identifying "demonstrable and profound injury" to the journalist-source relationship, she found, in contrast, that the countervailing benefits of disclosure ranged from "speculative to negligible."[64] If it is disappointing that she did not conduct a section 2(b) analysis, it is admirable that she was the only member of the Court who protected the work

59 Section 2(b) guarantees freedom of expression, including freedom of the press and other media of communication.

60 See *CBC v Lessard*, 3 SCR 421 [*Lessard*]; *CBC v New Brunswick*, [1991] 3 SCR 459 [*New Brunswick*]; *R v National Post*, above note 9; *Globe & Mail v Canada*, [2010] 2 SCR 592; *Vice Media*, above note 9; *Denis v Côté*, above note 9. Note that this case was decided under the *Journalistic Sources Protection Act* (*JSPA*) and not section 2(b) of the *Charter*. See discussion below in this chapter.

61 *Lessard*, above note 60; *CBC v New Brunswick*, above note 60.

62 *Lessard*, above note 60 at 455.

63 Above note 9.

64 *Ibid* at para 131.

of an investigative journalist who was the leading reporter on Shawinigate[65] and the question of corruption in the Prime Minister's Office.

Justice Abella also dissented alone in *Denis v Côté*, which arose under the federal government's newly enacted *Journalistic Sources Protection Act* (*JSPA*).[66] There, the Chief Justice's majority opinion provided a framework for the *JSPA*'s interpretation and returned the issue to the lower court, without disposition, pending completion of a further investigation into the source of leaks to the media.[67] Pointing to "fundamental legal errors" in the lower court's application of the *JSPA*, at the expense of the journalist's rights, Justice Abella saw no reason to extend the proceedings and would have set aside the subpoena and disclosure order against the journalist.[68]

Justice Abella's concurring reasons in *Vice Media* stand out because there she spared no effort in urging the Court to recognize a distinct constitutionally protected right for the press.[69] There had been little attention to that issue for some years and it was not raised in the appeal. Justice Abella was forceful, nonetheless, explaining why the press has distinct and independent status under section 2(b) and stating that a "vigorous, rigorous, and independent press holds people and institutions to account, uncovers the truth, and informs the public," providing the information necessary for informed debate.[70] Without providing newsgathering activities with protection from interference, "public access to the fruits of the media's work is diminished, as is the public's ability to understand, debate and form opinions on the issues of the day, thereby impairing its ability to participate meaningfully in the democratic process."[71] As she observed, granting the press section 2(b) status is "merely recognizing explicitly something this Court has repeatedly gestured towards."[72]

65 Shawinigate was the name given to the scandal that arose from an investigative reporter's articles on then Prime Minister Chretien's interest in a property that received a loan from the Business Development Bank of Canada. The specific issue in *National Post* was whether the newspaper was required to produce a brown envelope allegedly containing evidence about the BDBC account. For discussion, see Jamie Cameron, "Of Scandals, Sources and Secrets: Investigative Reporting, *National Post* and *Globe and Mail*," (2011), 54 S.C.L.R. (3d) 233.

66 SC 2017, c 22.

67 *R v National Post*, above note 9 at paras 32–57 (providing a comprehensive discussion of the background to the *JSPA* and its framework for protecting confidential sources).

68 *Ibid* at para 73.

69 See, for example, *Vice Media*, above note 9 at paras 123, 125, 149, 141, and 145.

70 *Ibid* at para 125.

71 *Ibid* at para 127.

72 *Ibid* at para 122.

The *Lessard* framework, which was established in 1991, was problematic because section 2(b) was subordinated to section 8 and incorporated into the analysis for determining the question of reasonable search. Under this framework a search warrant against the press did not violate s.2(b) and was analyzed as a matter of search and seizure under s.8. Justice Abella maintained that the press was no longer a "backdrop" to a section 8 analysis that, without analysis under s.2(b), did not sufficiently respect the media's enhanced status.[73] She situated the breach under section 2(b) and required that violation to be justified specifically, and on its own. To do so, she proposed a "rigorously protective harmonized analysis" that presupposed dual breaches of the *Charter*, under section 2(b) as well as under section 8. Proportionality balancing was the key to this approach, which added a section 2(b) branch to the section 8 analysis of production orders against members of the press. Her model required analysis of whether the state's beneficial interests in compelling access to newsgathering materials outweighs the harmful impact a production order would have on the press.[74] Her point was that doctrinally, orders affecting newsgathering activities would have to be justified as a violation of section 2(b) and not treated merely as an aspect of reasonableness under section 8.

Justice Abella's model for proportionality balancing under section 1? hardly proposed a radical change in *Charter* interpretation. As she observed, granting the press section 2(b) status is "merely recognizing explicitly something this Court has repeatedly gestured towards."[75] Moreover, and in the face of the obvious — that police orders against the press violate freedom of the press — she felt the *Lessard* framework warranted reconsideration. Yet having concluded that its adjustments to that framework sufficiently protected the press, the majority opinion held firm and refused to join issue on the section 2(b) status of the press.[76]

The 5–4 division on this issue in *Vice Media* came close to constitutionalizing freedom of the press and media under section 2(b). In pushing this issue to the forefront, Justice Abella's concurring opinion has

73 *Ibid* at paras 141 and 133. This framework bypasses the violation of section 2(b) but considers press-specific factors in determining the reasonableness of a search against the press under section 8.

74 *Ibid* at paras 142 and 145.

75 *Ibid* at para 122.

76 Justice Moldaver stated that the status of the press was not joined as an issue in the appeal and should not be addressed for that reason. In addition, he confirmed the *Lessard* framework under section 8 and, in doing so, considered it unnecessary to consider whether orders against the press also violate section 2(b). *Ibid* at paras 102–5.

positioned the Court to take the next step. As her reasons demonstrate, it is incomprehensible that the jurisprudence refuses to accept the constitutional status of a free press that is guaranteed by the text of the *Charter*.

D. Civil Liberties and Human Rights: "The Conceptual Battle of the Constitutional Titans"[77]

Justice Abella has never disguised her aspirations for the protection of human rights, including at the expense of expressive freedom. Though reflected in her dissenting opinion in *Malhab v Diffusion Metromedia* and her remarks on bullying in *AB v Bragg Communications*, this view is less developed in her section 2(b) jurisprudence. Just before leaving the Court, she co-wrote a dissenting opinion with Justice Kasirer in *Ward v Quebec*, which protected the dignity rights of a disabled teenager from a stand-up comedian's expressive freedom to target the boy. These reasons defended that position fiercely, and not without a hint of judicial fury.

The issue these two decisions expose is different because it is focused on the harm associated with expressive activity. In *Malhab*, which arose under the civil law, the Court dismissed a class action in defamation against a talk radio host who made on-air and highly disparaging remarks about Arabic and Creole-speaking cab drivers in Montreal. The majority opinion by Justice Deschamps described views that were "extravagant" and "undoubtedly serious and infuriating" as an "extreme, irrational, and sensationalist generalization."[78] She found no injury to the reputation of individual cab drivers, though, because an ordinary person would not believe those views apply to all those in a class of about 1100 drivers. In her view, the putative ordinary person would "brush aside implausible allegations without connecting them with the group's members personally" and, despite finding the comments annoying, would not apply the "insults, abuse and offensive accusations to each taxi driver personally."[79]

Justice Abella's dissent began by acknowledging that assessing the issue of harm caused by words is "the most complicated of barometers."[80] Rather than the "popularity, influence, or insensitivity" of expressive activity, the issue in *Malhab* was instead about "highly stigmatizing remarks" that were "blatantly racist" and constituted an attack on

77 Abella, "Freedom of Expression or Freedom from Hate," above note 12 at 508.

78 *Malhab*, above note 9 at paras 90 and 92.

79 *Ibid* at paras 76 and 82.

80 *Ibid* at para 95.

vulnerable communities.[81] As she explained, such comments "deliberately vilify vulnerable people," "diminish dignity and are an invitation to contempt."[82] No other member of the Court agreed that words defaming a vulnerable group also defamed every member of the group.

In *AB*, open court was at issue in civil proceedings that involved a minor who was a victim of cyberbullying and sought anonymity and a publication ban to protect her identity.[83] The Court held that the victim's interests could be protected by an anonymity order and found that a publication ban was unnecessary as a result.[84] What stands out in *AB* is Justice Abella's extensive discussion of bullying and its consequences for young victims. Absent evidence of AB's vulnerability, she cited and relied on sources that documented the inherent vulnerability of children, especially those who are victims of sexualized cyberbullying. Protecting an especially vulnerable class of victims was her central concern, and in that, *AB* fully aligns with her core values. The same imperative to protect the vulnerable resurfaced in *Ward*.[85] The issue there was whether Mike Ward's comedy routine, which ridiculed and insulted Jeremy Gabriel, a teenage boy with some celebrity status, violated the Quebec *Charter of Human Rights and Freedoms* and its right to the safeguard of one's dignity.[86]

There is a hard edge in the majority and minority reasons in *Ward* that attests to the intensity of competing conceptions of section 2(b) among members of the Court. In explaining why the human rights claim failed, the majority opinion of Chief Justice Wagner and Justice Coté was forceful to the point of provocative, adopting an analogy to hate speech and setting a threshold for limits on expression that employed the language of incitement.[87]

The dissent by Justices Abella and Kasirer was hardly less insistent in upholding the human rights claim. They explained that *Ward* was not about freedom but about rights, and that conception of the

---

81 *Ibid* at paras 95 and 107.

82 *Ibid.*

83 *AB v Bragg Communications*, above note 9.

84 *Ibid* at paras 28–30. First, the relative unimportance of a sexual assault victim's identity was a complete answer to open court's concerns about anonymity, and once the victim's identity was protected, a publication ban was unnecessary.

85 *Ward*, above note 7.

86 Section 4 of the Quebec *Charter* states that "[e]very person has a right to the safeguard of his dignity, honour and reputation," and section 3 states that "[e]very person is the possessor of fundamental freedoms . . . including freedom of expression." *CQLR*, c 12.

87 On *Saskatchewan (Human Rights Commission) v Whatcott*, [2013] 1 SCR 467 [*Whatcott*] and the analogy to hate speech, see *Ward*, above note 7, at paras 62–78; on the standard of incitement, see paras 6, 83, 108 & 109.

issue framed the analysis throughout.[88] There was little semblance of the balancing that is so emblematic of Justice Abella's jurisprudence, and that is because the dissenting opinion's framework of values was decisively weighted against expressive freedom. Justices Abella and Kasirer reverted to the contextual approach, incorporating it into the proportionality balancing and stating that Ward's comedy routine was "only peripherally connected to the core values underlying freedom of expression."[89] That assessment made it unnecessary to discuss the deleterious consequences of upholding the human rights claim, not only for Ward and stand-up comedy but for expressive freedom more generally. The dissenting opinion's analytical matrix made it inevitable that Ward's valueless expressive activity would be found "completely disproportionate" to the harm suffered by its target.[90]

The victim's status as a disabled child was an aggravating and inflammatory factor. Though the high-impact rhetoric of the dissent was driven by those facts, the Abella-Kasirer opinion rejected the analogy to hate speech and supported broader restrictions on expression. The analysis of hate speech and the Court's decision in *Whatcott* was a key issue in *Ward*. In *Whatcott*, the Court unanimously upheld a human rights prohibition on hate speech, but severed the words "ridicules, belittles or otherwise affronts the dignity of" from the provision as an impermissible violation of section 2(b).[91] In doing so, the Court explained the distinction between hate speech and expressive content that is repugnant, excluding hurtful or offensive representations that belittle or attack the dignity of a minority group from the scope of hate speech.[92]

The dissent in *Ward* maintained that the prohibition on speech could be broader under Quebec's human rights law because *Whatcott* addressed a different provision with a different objective.[93] From that perspective, it is questionable whether the Abella-Kasirer standard of "a contemptuous affront to the individual's dignity" in *Ward* is consistent with *Whatcott*'s conclusion that more than an affront to dignity is

---

88 *Ibid* at para 117 (stating that this was not "primarily" a case about artistic freedom, but a case about the rights of vulnerable and marginalized individuals).

89 *Ibid* at para 217.

90 *Ibid.*

91 *Ibid* at paras 93 & 94.

92 *Ibid* at para 51 (stating that hate speech legislation does not prohibit debate about the merits of reducing the rights of vulnerable groups in society) and para 90 (stating that representations belittling a minority group or jokes, ridicule, or insults *attacking its dignity* may be hurtful and offensive, but do not justify an infringement of expressive freedom; italics added).

93 *Ibid* at para 156.

required to justify limits on section 2(b) of the *Charter*.[94] Under the *Ward* dissent, freedom of expression is subject to a relatively open-ended concept of dignitary interests, and that is troubling.

Justice Abella once said that "[f]or democracy to work, we must never forget how the world looks to those who are vulnerable."[95] That is the moral value and core belief she responded to in *Malhab*, *AB*, and *Ward*. She did not advocate or promote a "civil liberties" interpretation of section 2(b), and she was consistent and transparent about her scale of values. Even so, diminishing expressive freedom as the vestige of an outdated conception of rights based on civil liberties undermines the core principle that freedom of expression was entrenched in the *Charter* and Quebec *Charter* "so as to ensure that everyone can manifest . . . all expressions of the heart and mind, however unpopular, distasteful or contrary to the mainstream."[96] That promise requires and depends on a framework of analysis that is evidence based and prepared, in principle, to protect expressive content that offends competing interests, including equality and dignity of the person.

E. A Parting Benediction

In *Saskatchewan Federation of Labour*, Justice Abella wrote with pride that it was "the time" to give the right to strike its "constitutional benediction" under section 2(d) of the *Charter*.[97] It is also time for this reflection to end, on a benedictory note of another kind.

Justice Abella was a writerly judge whose opinions brim with vitality, passion, and personality. She placed her imprimatur on all her *Charter* jurisprudence, including section2(b). The section 2(b) imprimatur is punctuated with an exclamation mark (!) for her unwavering support for the guarantee's democratic-affirming objectives, as well as an asterisk (*) for her lower threshold of harm for freedom and expression that targets the vulnerable. Though I hold — and defend — a different conception of freedom, I agree with Justice Abella that "[y]ou can get some very good ideas even from people you disagree with."[98] That has unquestionably been my experience in offering this reflection on her section 2(b) jurisprudence. More than that, there is much to learn and admire in Justice Abella's loyalty to a moral conception of justice that

94 *Ibid* at para 163.

95 Abella, "Freedom of Expression or Freedom from Hate," above note 12 at 522.

96 *Irwin Toy Ltd v Quebec*, [1989] 1 SCR 927 at 968 [*Irwin Toy*].

97 *Saskatchewan Federation of Labour v Saskatchewan*, above note 2 at para 3.

98 Abella & Diller, above note 12 at 850.

repeatedly asked her to be fearless and place herself in a minority of one, not only under section 2(b) but whenever and as required.

To me, a short exchange that took place during oral argument in *Denis v Côté* says much. As an intervenor with just five precious minutes for oral argument and frustrated by that, I rushed to answer a question that had interrupted my submission. As I reached a verbal frenzy, I felt eyes on me and looked up from my notes to see Justice Abella patiently waiting. While I did my best to worsen the situation with an awkward apology, she replied with a friendly and matter-of-fact quip that, "[oh well] I knew I'd still be here when you finished." Once again, I have finished. And once again, Justice Abella is still here. She and her legacy are embedded in the evolution of the *Charter* — forming part of its narrative arc — and will ever be a vital part of the *Charter* and its conception of rights.

Appendix 1

Section 2(b) opinions
Justice Abella, 2004–2021

1. *R v Bryan*, [2007] 1 SCR 527
2. *R v National Post*, [2010] 1 SCR 477
3. *Toronto Star Newspapers Ltd. v Canada*, [2010] 1 SCR 721
4. *Ontario (Public Safety & Security) v Criminal Lawyers' Association*, [2011] 1 SCR 815 (with McLachlin CJ)
5. *Malhab v diffusion Metromedia CMR Inc*, [2011] 1 SCR 214
6. *Crookes v Newton*, [2011] 3 SCR 269
7. *Doré v Barreau du Quebec*, 2012 SCC 12
8. *AB v Bragg Communications Inc*, [2012] 2 SCR 567
9. *Alberta (Information & Privacy Commissioner) v UFCW, Local 401*, [2013] 3 SCR 733
10. *Ernst v Alberta Energy Regulator*, [2017] 1 SCR 3
11. *R v Vice Media Canada Inc*, [2018] 3 SCR 374
12. *Denis v Côté*, [2019] 3 SCR 482
13. *Bent v Platnick*, 2020 SCC 23
14. *CBC v Manitoba*, 2021 SCC 33
15. *City of Toronto v Ontario*, [2021] SCC 34
16. *Ward v Quebec*, [2021] SCC 43 (with Kasirer J)

Appendix 2

Section 2(b) opinions
Justice McLachlin, 1990–2018

1. *Rocket v Royal College*, [1990] 2 SCR 232
2. *R. v Keegstra*, [1990] 3 SCR 697
3. *Canada (Human Rights Commission) v Taylor*, [1990] 3 SCR 892
4. *Canada v Committee for the Commonwealth of Canada*, [19991] 1 SCR 139
5. *Lavigne v OPSEU*, [1991] 2 SCR 211
6. *CBC v Lessard*; 3 SCR 421
7. *CBC v New Brunswick*, [1991] 3 SCR 459
8. *R. v Zundel*, [1992] 2 SCR 731
9. *Dagenais v CBC*, [1994] 3 SCR 835
10. *RJR MacDonald v Canada*, [1995] 3 SCR 199
11. *R. v Lucas*, [1998] 1 SCR 439
12. *R. v Sharpe*, [2001] 1 SCR 45
13. *RWDSU v Pepsi-Cola Canada*, [2002] 1 SCR 156 (with LeBel J)
14. *Harper v Canada*, [2004] 1 SCR 827
15. *City of Mtl v 2952-1366 Quebec Inc*, [2005] 3 SCR 141 (with Deschamps J)
16. *Grant v Torstar*, [2009] 3 SCR 640
17. *Ontario (Public Safety & Security) v CLA*, [2011] 1 SCR 815 (with Abella J)
18. *R. v Khawaja*, [2012] 3 SCR 555
19. *BC Freedom of Info and Privacy Ass'n v BC*, [2017] 1 SCR 93
20. *Law Society BC v TWU*, [2018] 2 SCR 293

9 Reaching to See Through Another's Eyes: Justice Abella's Religious Freedom Jurisprudence

HOWARD KISLOWICZ*

A. Introduction

When religious individuals and communities come to court seeking to vindicate their religious freedom, there is a momentous encounter. It is a meeting of cultures,[1] of legal traditions;[2] for some, it is even a meeting of sovereignties[3] or different forms of faith.[4] The encounter presents both great opportunity and significant risk. The opportunity is for the law to dwell in the "real living" of "meeting,"[5] to honour the relations between communities, and to develop in conversation with diverse perspectives. The risks are that the law will fail to understand the perspective of religious minorities, misrecognize[6] them, send messages of exclusion and alienation, or lose track of its own core commitments.

Justice Rosalie Silberman Abella's religious freedom jurisprudence reveals the voice of a judge who sees the opportunity presented by the encounter. Her judgments bear the hallmarks of a person willing to do the hard work of attempting to see the world from unfamiliar

---

* Associate Professor, Faculty of Law, University of Calgary.

1 Benjamin L. Berger, *Law's Religion: Religious Difference and the Claims of Constitutionalism* (Toronto: University of Toronto Press, 2015) ch 3.

2 Howard Kislowicz, "Sacred Laws in Earthly Courts: Legal Pluralism in Canadian Religious Freedom Litigation" (2013) 39 *Queen's Law Journal* 175.

3 Perry Dane, "Master Metaphors and Double-Coding in the Encounters of Religion and State" (2016) 53 *San Diego Law Review* 53.

4 Steven D. Smith, "Believing Like a Lawyer" (1998) 40 *British Columbia Law Review* 1041–1138.

5 Martin Buber, *I and Thou*, Ronald Gregor Smith, trans (Edinburgh: T&T Clark, 1937) at 11.

6 Charles Taylor, "The Politics of Recognition" in Amy Gutmann, ed, *Multiculturalism* (Princeton: Princeton University Press, 1992).

perspectives, recognize the litigants before her as whole people with their own horizons of meaning, and allow the law to be transformed by the experience. Litigation presents structural barriers to the kinds of transformational dialogue that can emerge between individuals: the power differential is stark, and one party must render judgment. Nevertheless, Justice Abella's decisions make the most of these encounters by demonstrating the two central skills of cross-cultural communication: respect and self-awareness.[7] Because she enters the dialogue in this way, she can translate the stories told by litigants into terms meaningful to Canadian law. This is a remarkable achievement.

In this chapter, I highlight moments in four of her judgments — two in dissent, two in writing for the majority[8] — that demonstrate Justice Abella's strengths in cross-cultural communication. Part B elaborates on respect and self-awareness, two central skills of cross-cultural communication. Part C draws on Justice Abella's dissent in *Hutterian* as an example of respect in cross-cultural communication. Part D examines self-awareness, from two perspectives. The dissent in *NS* serves as model of self-awareness in the sense of allowing an encounter to highlight the inconsistencies in one's own legal tradition. The majority judgment in *Loyola* demonstrates a more nuanced form of self-awareness in the balance it strikes between making room for religious objections to certain forms of teaching while also holding firm to core state values. Part 5 discusses the translation of religious obligations into civic obligations using the example of *Bruker v Marcovitz*, in which Justice Abella recognized that individuals are often subjects in multiple legal systems and sometimes need to use both to protect their interests.

B. Encounter/Communication

Whenever people communicate, they participate in a "a symbolic process by [which they] create shared meanings."[9] Creating such shared meanings across cultural boundaries is challenging, and this is inherent

7 Howard Kislowicz, "Faithful Translations? Cross-Cultural Communication in Canadian Religious Freedom Litigation" (2014) 52:1 *Osgoode Hall Law Journal* 141–89.

8 In dissent: *Alberta v Hutterian Brethren of Wilson Colony*, [2009] 2 SCR 567; *R v NS*, [2012] 3 SCR 726 [*NS*]; for the majority [*Hutterian*]: *Loyola High School v Quebec (Attorney General)*, [2015] 1 SCR 613; *Bruker v Marcovitz*, [2007] 3 SCR 607.

9 Houman A Sadri & Madelyn Flammia, *Intercultural Communication: A New Approach to International Relations and Global Challenges* (New York: Bloomsbury Academic, 2011) at 10.

in much religious freedom litigation. As Benjamin Berger argues, we can think of the meeting of law and religion as a cross-cultural encounter.[10] Religious worldviews, as cultures, can shape the way people "understand, regulate and structure their individual and collective lives."[11] We might likewise think that "the constitutional rule of law is, itself, a cultural system . . . composed of sets of symbols, categories of thought, and particular practices that lend meaning to experience."[12] Some might go further to argue that the encounter between law and religion is akin to a meeting between faiths. Though Canadian law does not explicitly profess to belong to a particular religious tradition,[13] some have argued that there are faith-like aspects to the Anglo-American legal tradition. Central to this claim is the observation that, in judicial opinions, "the law" somehow exists as a "less visible but overarching reality" that "cannot be seen directly" and "cannot be fully reduced to human comprehension."[14] In either case, there is an obstacle to understanding, as the parties in dialogue may not share crucial assumptions about the world and/or perspectives on the meanings attributed to actions and events.

Given these challenges, the skills of respect and self-awareness are necessary for effective communication to occur. Respect is crucial in order to accurately understand and absorb the message another is relaying without discounting or recasting its meaning. Respect, in this context, means encountering another in the recognition that both are whole people,[15] each a separate "center of meaning."[16] As Elizabeth M. Pope and Aliki Nicolaides write in their study of interfaith dialogue, drawing on the work of Martin Buber, "transformative learning" is best achieved when dialogue partners are engaged in "I-Thou" relationships,[17] "in

---

10 Berger, above note 1 at 105–7.

11 Bhiku Parekh, *Rethinking Multiculturalism: Cultural Diversity and Political Theory* (Houndmills: Macmillan Press Ltd, 2000) at 143.

12 Benjamin L Berger, "The Cultural Limits of Legal Tolerance" (2008) 21 *Canadian Journal of Law and Jurisprudence* 245 at 246.

13 At least, not anymore. In *Saumur v City of Quebec*, [1953] 2 SCR 299 at 327, Justice Rand held: "The Christian religion, its practices and profession, exhibiting in Europe and America an organic continuity, stands in the first rank of social, political and juristic importance."

14 Smith, above note 4 at 1114; see also Howard Kislowicz, "Law, Faith, and Canada's Unwritten Constitution" (2020) 25:1 *Review of Constitutional Studies* 19.

15 Mordechai Gordon, "Listening as Embracing the Other: Martin Buber's Philosophy of Dialogue" (2011) 61:2 *Educational Theory* 207 at 208.

16 James Boyd White, *Justice as Translation: An Essay in Cultural and Legal Criticism* (Chicago: University of Chicago Press, 1990) at 257.

17 Elizabeth M Pope & Aliki Nicolaides, "Becoming Thou as Transformation in Interfaith Dialogue" (2021) 40:2 *International Journal of Lifelong Education* 115 at 116.

which each person affirms the other's basic difference and still stands firm in his or her own being."[18] As a listener, we must respond "to the other as a whole person and creat[e] a space in which the other can speak his or her own words and meaning";[19] we must keep an "ear out for places of silence, erasure, misrecognition."[20] Importantly, however, this "does not imply approval; it means accepting the other with his or her difference and uniqueness."[21]

There are limits to how closely communication in the litigation setting can approximate this idealized kind of exchange. A true "I-Thou" relation is "utterly without telos, aim, or intention."[22] By contrast, participants in litigation all have aims that go beyond communication: litigants seek a particular outcome, judges seek to resolve a dispute justly. Moreover, there is a power differential between the court and the parties, and communication is usually mediated through counsel, which can inhibit a full exchange.[23] But striving for this form of understanding is essential for good judgment. To accurately and justly address a litigant's claim, the judge must fully comprehend it. Of course, some of this burden must be shouldered by the litigant, who may rely on counsel to translate their claim into terms recognized by law. Nevertheless, if courts are to accord the litigants before them the equal treatment of the law, judges must also bridge that gap by attempting to understand litigants' arguments on their own terms rather than imposing their own view of the world on the parties. This can yield a result more attuned to the specific context of each case.

Inherent in this aspiration is the second crucial skill in cross-cultural communication: self-awareness.[24] A self-aware listener acknowledges themself as a full person, complete with their own normative commitments, preferences, and preconceptions. Recognizing the cultural contingency of these can help allay the distortion or prejudgment of the

---

18 Gordon, above note 15 at 209.

19 *Ibid* at 207.

20 Lisbeth Lipari, "Listening for the Other: Ethical Implications of the Buber-Levinas Encounter" (2004) 14:2 *Communication Theory* 122 at 122.

21 Gordon, above note 15 at 209.

22 Lipari, above note 20 at 125–26; See also Gordon, above note 15 at 210.

23 See Gordon, above note 15 at 211: "Some relationships . . . by their very nature can never unfold into complete mutuality."

24 See Richard Brislin & Tomoko Yoshida, *Intercultural Communication Training: An Introduction* (Thousand Oaks, California, 1994) ch 2; Brooks Peterson, *Cultural Intelligence: A Guide to Working with People from Other Cultures* (Yarmouth, Me: Intercultural Press, 2004) at 89–92; David C. Thomas & Kerr Inkson, *Cultural Intelligence: Living and Working Globally*, 2nd ed (San Francisco, CA: Berrett-Koehler Publishers, 2009) ch 3.

speaker's message. As Wendy Brown has argued, the term "culture" is often deployed asymmetrically: "Though 'culture' is what nonliberal peoples are imagined to be ruled and ordered by, liberal peoples are considered to have culture or cultures."[25] Effective communicators avoid this view, instead learning to become comfortable with ambiguity and multiple perspectives on the same issue.[26] In the litigation context, this is especially important for judges, given their power to issue orders that affect the lives and legal rights of the parties before them, with whom they must communicate. Judges must come to recognize that they "inevitably [see and judge] from a particular situated perspective"[27] and "can never see [things] with any eyes except [their] own."[28] When confronted with an unfamiliar perspective, a self-aware judge will attempt to see their own perspective and the perspective of the legal system they serve with some distance, without taking its normative assumptions as "natural" or beyond culture. This leads to a fuller and more faithful understanding of the litigant's claim.

As developed below, Justice Abella's judgments in the religious freedom context stand out as exemplary in displaying the values of respect of self-awareness, which allows her to engage in the delicate work of translation.

C. Respect

The quality of respect is shown strongly in Justice Abella's dissenting reasons in *Hutterian*. At issue was Alberta's decision to make driver's licence photos universally mandatory as an effort to combat identity fraud. Though driver's licences in Alberta have included photographs since 1974, there had been an exemption available for some thirty years for those who objected on religious grounds to being photographed.[29] The exemption was used by a subset of Hutterites, who understand

25 Wendy Brown, *Regulating Aversion: Tolerance in the Age of Identity and Empire* (Princeton: Princeton University Press, 2006) at 150; See also Charles Taylor, "Conditions of an Unforced Consensus on Human Rights" in Joanne R. Bauer & Daniel A. Bell, eds, *The East Asian Challenge for Human Rights* (Cambridge: Cambridge University Press, 1999) 124 at 143.

26 Brislin & Yoshida, above note 24 at 31 and 40.

27 Martha Minow, *Making All the Difference: Inclusion, Exclusion, and American Law* (Ithaca: Cornell University Press, 1990) at 52.

28 Benjamin N. Cardozo, *The Nature of the Judicial Process* (New Haven: Yale University Press, 1921) 13, as cited in Masua Sagiv, "Cultural Bias in Judicial Decision Making" (2015) 35:2 *Boston College Journal of Law & Social Justice* 229 at 232.

29 *Hutterian*, above note 8 at para 117.

the biblical prohibition on graven images set out in the Second Commandment as forbidding all photography. With the removal of the exemption, Hutterites who objected to being photographed had to choose between violating their religious beliefs to obtain a driver's licence or forgoing the ability to drive on public highways.

The respect shown by Justice Abella was first evident in her attempt to see the situation from the Hutterite perspective. Before the case reached the courts, Alberta had proposed two accommodations to the Hutterian Brethren: 1) a licence that would be stored in a sealed envelope and 2) a proposal that the licensee sit for a digital photograph to be stored in the province's database but be provided with a photoless licence. Justice Abella notes that these proposals missed the mark because they failed to consider why the Hutterian Brethren objected to the photo requirement in the first place. "The Wilson Colony members rejected these alternatives since they both required them to contravene the religious prohibition against having their photograph taken."[30] She also rejected the characterization of the colony members as uncompromising, emphasizing that they made their own proposal to alleviate the province's concerns with identity fraud that motivated the law. "Their proposal was that there be a photoless licence with a stamp indicating that the licence could not be used for identification purposes."[31]

Justice Abella even more clearly demonstrates respect for the Hutterite litigants by fully recognizing the impact that the change in the law had on the religious life of the Hutterite community. Unlike the Supreme Court majority, for whom the effect on the community was something to be considered under the proportionality analysis,[32] Justice Abella foregrounded this concern by considering it as an aspect of the rights infringement:

> The harm to the constitutional rights of the Hutterites, in the absence of an exemption, is dramatic. Their inability to drive affects them not only individually, but also severely compromises the autonomous character of their religious community.[33]

30 *Ibid* at para 123.
31 *Ibid*.
32 *Ibid* at para 31.
33 *Ibid* at para 114. At paras 130–31, Justice Abella emphasized the collective aspects of religious freedom with reference to caselaw from the SCC and the European Court of Human Rights.

In Justice Abella's understanding, there were two religious freedom problems created by the regulation. Not only did the law affect the Hutterites' practice of refraining from photography, it also impacted their communal living. She noted that Hutterites "believe in communal property and live together in religious colonies. The colonies attempt to be self-sufficient, and members of the community operate motor vehicles in order to fulfill their responsibilities to the community."[34] In her view, the majority of the Court failed "to appreciate the significance of their self-sufficiency to the autonomous integrity of their religious community."[35] Seeing the matter from this perspective highlighted the "indirect coercion"[36] worked by the universal photo requirement. One might also observe a commonality in Justice Abella's reasoning with her expressive freedom jurisprudence as described in Jamie Cameron's chapter in this volume. As Cameron notes, a distinctive feature of Justice Abella's approach in that context is to integrate the values of expressive freedom into her proportionality analysis under section 1 in order to highlight the magnitude of the harm to a constitutional right. Likewise, in *Hutterian* Justice Abella draws on the values of religious freedom — which include allowing claimants to advance a subjective understanding of their religious practices — to fully account for the severity of the rights infringement and require direct proof of the benefits promised by the infringing state action. Here, Justice Abella found that Alberta's case amounted to "a web of speculation,"[37] insufficient to justify the serious infringement.

In sum, Justice Abella arrived at the opposite conclusion as the majority in part because she made the effort to view the dispute from the unfamiliar perspective of the Wilson Colony members. This transformed the character of the claim and may have compelled the analysis that followed. This kind of respectful engagement is essential to understanding the arguments of religious minority litigants and stands in stark contrast to the majority's understanding of the harm to Hutterites as "impos[ing] costs in terms of money and inconvenience."[38] This view misses half the objection raised by the claimants, while Justice Abella's view captured it faithfully and therefore subjected it to a scrutiny more reflective of the dignitary interests engaged in the dispute.[39]

34 *Ibid* at para 118.

35 *Ibid* at paras 164–67.

36 *Ibid* at para 170.

37 *Ibid* at para 154.

38 *Hutterian*, above note 8 at para 102.

39 For a thorough and compelling argument on how treating human dignity as the animating norm of the legal system drives up the justificatory demands for rights

Importantly, Justice Abella never implied that she can easily and fully know what it is to be a member of the Hutterite colony, which would suggest, as Emily Kidd White argues, "a lack of humility, and / or curiosity about the other" in its denial of deep and unbridgeable gaps between perspectives.[40] Nor did she reason from a position of imagining what she would do were she a member of a Hutterite colony, which would ignore how deeply context shapes perspective.[41] Instead, she honoured the claim by paying respectful attention to how it was articulated.

D. Self-Awareness

The typical narrative of religious diversity often emphasizes the value of tolerance. As Wendy Brown has written, however, when we speak about diversity in the language of tolerance, our gaze is drawn to behaviours and ideas of which we disapprove.[42] As we focus on which of these we will tolerate, we reinforce existing power relations by suggesting that the decision to tolerate is at the sole discretion of the tolerator, putting the tolerated in a precarious and subservient position. Relatedly, the focus on the behaviours of others can draw our attention away from troubling aspects of our own practices. The asymmetry in this relation can serve as a barrier to cross-cultural communication that is best remedied by developing a strong sense of self-awareness. When we are willing to turn our gaze inward, we can find points of commonality, or aspects of our own views that we would prefer to revise.

Justice Abella's dissenting judgment in *NS* is a model of this quality. The question in *NS* was whether a complainant in a sexual assault trial could, while testifying, wear a niqab (a veil worn by some Muslim women that covers the whole face except the eyes).[43] The two accused objected, arguing that this would compromise their fair trial rights.

---

infringements, see Jacob Weinrib, *Dimensions of Dignity: The Theory and Practice of Modern Constitutional Law*, Cambridge studies in constitutional law (Cambridge, United Kingdom: Cambridge University Press, 2016) ch 7.

40 Emily Kidd White, "On Emotions and the Politics of Attention in Judicial Reasoning" in Ed Amalia Amaya and Maksymilian Del Mar (2020) *Virtue, Emotion and Imagination in Law and Legal Reasoning*, (Oxford: Hart Publishing, 2020) 101, online: https://digitalcommons.osgoode.yorku.ca/scholarly_works/2827 at 107.

41 *Ibid*. For an example of how this kind of reasoning can go awry, see *Hutterian Brethren of Wilson Colony v Alberta*, [2007] 2007 ABCA 160 at para 116. Here, Justice Slatter engaged in some biblical interpretation to demonstrate that the accommodation offered by Alberta was meaningful. This approach failed to honour the potentially distinct worldview of the colony members.

42 See Brown, above note 25 at 186–88.

43 *NS*, above note 8.

Justice Abella's reasons began by recognizing the strength of the accused's position, holding that "the assessment of a witness' demeanour is easier if it is based on being able to scrutinize their whole demeanour — face, body language, voice, etc." She notes, as well, that in the Canadian legal tradition, "we *expect* to see a witness' face when he or she is testifying."[44] However, instead of seeing an unfamiliar practice and dwelling on the way it clashes with expectations, Justice Abella turned inward and examined existing practices in the Canadian legal tradition.

She started her inward-looking analysis by considering the various ways courts routinely accept limitations on their ability to see a witness's facial expressions in the name of other important interests: "we have come to use screens for children, interpreters for those without facility in our official languages, and a myriad of other means to facilitate a witness' ability to give evidence in the courtroom."[45] She also highlighted the limited utility of demeanour evidence for establishing credibility, which Canadian courts and the Canadian Judicial Council had previously noted.[46] Perhaps most incisively, she then drew an analogy to witnesses with "physical or medical limitations that affect a judge's or lawyer's ability to assess demeanour. A stroke may interfere with facial expressions; an illness may affect body movements; and a speech impairment may affect the manner of speaking."[47] It is nearly impossible to imagine a Canadian judge disqualifying a complainant from testifying because of facial paralysis, so Justice Abella asks why the niqab should be treated differently, given the constitutional right of religious freedom.

Engaging with the niqab pushed Justice Abella to develop a stronger awareness of aspects of the Canadian legal tradition that may have previously gone unnoticed. Her reasoning demonstrates how engagement with another can help a person to better see unstated assumptions of one's own traditions and, in turn, make the unfamiliar less strange. Thus, Justice Abella realized that the wearing of a niqab is "only a partial obstacle to the assessment of demeanour," leaving available other forms of bodily and verbal expression.[48] It is only because of her openness to this aspect of the encounter that Justice Abella could achieve this insight. And though her view did not carry the day, it is difficult now to

44 *Ibid* at para 91 (emphasis in original).
45 *Ibid* at para 92; see also paras 102 and 104–05.
46 *Ibid* at paras 99–101.
47 *Ibid* at para 103.
48 *Ibid* at para 106 and 108.

doubt its persuasiveness, given the routine use of masks in courtrooms during the COVID-19 pandemic.[49]

It would be plausible to read this account as one that equates understanding the perspective of a religious minority individual or community with the validation of their religious freedom claim. It is true that building cross-cultural understanding often results in more space being made for religious difference. However, we also see in Justice Abella's jurisprudence the ability to commit to an encounter without losing sight of one's own (here, the state's) priorities.

This quality is best demonstrated in *Loyola*. In that case, Loyola High School sought an exemption from teaching a new Ethics and Religious Culture curriculum developed by Quebec's Ministry of Education.[50] In the school's view, the curriculum's "normative pluralism" was inconsistent with its Catholic commitments.[51] Initially, Loyola argued that teaching about religious and ethical systems, including Catholicism, from a neutral perspective "would be incompatible with Catholic beliefs."[52] At the Supreme Court, Loyola narrowed its objection. It accepted the curricular requirements of teaching about other world religions from a "neutral" perspective. However, it still asserted its right to "teach the *ethics* of other religious traditions from the perspective of the Catholic religion," and "to teach Catholic doctrine and ethics from a Catholic perspective."[53]

Justice Abella's response clearly understands the gravamen of Loyola's objection to the decision. Requiring a Catholic institution to teach about Catholic religious traditions and ethics from something other than a Catholic perspective "seriously impairs its Catholic identity."[54] Moreover, the decision undermined the curriculum's goal of encouraging respect for and openness to others because it assumes that "engagement with an individual's own religion on his or her own terms can simply be presumed to impair respect for others."[55]

However, the decision is equally notable for its insistence that the state has a legitimate interest in advancing the core values of "equality, human

49 See, for example, *R v MacKinnon*, 2021 ONSC 2749, a murder trial held during the COVID-19 pandemic in which the court allowed witnesses to wear face masks. The court reasoned that "the substance of a witness' evidence, and its relationship to the other evidence in a trial, are better guides to assessing credibility and reliability than a witness' demeanour" (at para 69).

50 *Loyola High School v Quebec (Attorney General)*, above note 8 at paras 24–27.

51 *Ibid* at para 29.

52 *Ibid* at para 31.

53 *Ibid* (emphasis in original).

54 *Ibid* at para 70.

55 *Ibid* at para 69.

rights and democracy."[56] It follows that the state can validly promote the development of a "pluralist, multicultural democracy" by "ensuring that students in *all* schools are capable, as adults, of conducting themselves with openness and respect as they confront cultural and religious differences."[57] This meant that Quebec could require Loyola to teach about other religious and ethical perspectives "in a neutral, historical and phenomenological way."[58] Justice Abella recognized the delicacy of teaching alternative ethical frameworks in a religious school, noting that "Catholicism's answer to ethical questions . . . will sometimes conflict with the approach taken by the ethics of other religions."[59] But these difficulties would not negate the "immense public importance" of fostering openness and respect for other worldviews.[60]

So we see in Justice Abella's reasons in *Loyola* a different side of self-awareness from what we see in *NS*. In *NS*, Justice Abella looked inward at the Canadian legal system and found its tradition of requiring witnesses to testify with their faces showing to be inconsistently applied and without sufficient justification to warrant excluding the niqab. In *Loyola*, however, she identified core beliefs of the Canadian state and legal system that should not be compromised in an encounter with a religious community. Still, her willingness to partially vindicate Loyola's claim shows the seriousness and care of her engagement.

E. Translation

A final moment to highlight in Justice Abella's religious freedom jurisprudence is a case in which she assisted in the translation of religious legal norms to judicially enforceable norms. In *Bruker v Marcovitz*,[61] Bruker sought damages from her former husband, Marcovitz. The husband had agreed, in the context of a separation agreement, to provide a *get* (Jewish religious divorce), but for a period of fifteen years failed to provide one. The consequences for Bruker were that she could not remarry within her Orthodox Jewish community, and any children she might have had during that period would have faced similar challenges.[62] While Marcovitz

56 *Ibid* at para 47.

57 *Ibid* at para 48 (emphasis in original).

58 *Ibid* at para 71. At the SCC, Loyola said it was prepared to teach about other religions in this manner, but not other ethical perspectives (para 70).

59 *Ibid* at para 73.

60 *Ibid* at para 74.

61 *Bruker v Marcovitz*, above note 8.

62 *Ibid* at para 4.

eventually provided the *get*, Bruker sought damages for the period of non-compliance. The question was whether the promise to provide a religious divorce was judicially enforceable.

For the dissenting justices, enforcing the contractual clause was too grave an intervention in religious matters, given that Bruker's civil rights were not affected by Marcovitz's failure to provide a *get*.[63] For Justice Abella and the majority, however, individuals were free to choose to convert their religious obligations into civil ones.[64] Justice Abella recognized that people often understand themselves to be legal subjects in more than one legal tradition, and sometimes live their lives at the intersection of these systems. To leave Bruker without a remedy failed to take into account that her ex-husband "freely entered into a valid and binding contractual obligation and [sought] to have it set aside based on *ex post facto* religious compunctions."[65] Further, as seen above in her *Loyola* reasons, Justice Abella took the view that she had the obligation to draw on "our constitutionally and statutorily articulated commitments to equality, religious freedom and autonomous choice in marriage and divorce,"[66] which weighed in favour of enforcing the obligation.

To be sure, the choice to enforce this obligation is complicated. According to some interpretations of Jewish Law, a *get* provided under civic compulsion is not valid because it must be provided freely.[67] Moreover, while the dispute in *Bruker* seems to be between two individuals, it also speaks more broadly to the norms of the Orthodox Jewish community of which the parties were members. All the harms that Bruker suffered and for which she was compensated had to do with how her community treated her before Marcovitz provided the *get*. Justice Abella was aware of this, of course, and was careful to explain that the challenge posed by Orthodox Jewish divorce law is one that leaders of the Canadian Orthodox Jewish community have recognized and sought the assistance of Canadian law to address.[68] Members of that community,

---

63 *Ibid* at para 131.

64 *Ibid* at para 51. See Rosalie Jukier & Shauna Van Praagh, "Civil Law and Religion in the Supreme Court of Canada: What Should we Get out of *Bruker v. Marcovitz*?" (2008) 43 *Supreme Court Law Review* (2d) 381 at 395–96.

65 *Bruker v Marcovitz*, above note 8 at para 79.

66 *Ibid* at para 80.

67 See Rabbi Michael J. Broyde, "The 1992 New York Get Law" (1995) 29 *Tradition* 5; Adrienne Barnett, "Getting a 'Get' — The Limits of Law's Authority?" (2000) 8:2 *Feminist Legal Studies* 241 at 252; Lisa Fishbayn, "Gender, Multiculturalism and Dialogue: The Case of Jewish Divorce" (2008) 21:1 *Canadian Journal of Law and Jurisprudence* 71 at 87.

68 *Bruker v Marcovitz*, above note 8 at para 81.

and Orthodox Jewish women in particular, were the motivating forces behind the addition to the *Divorce Act* of a provision that allows courts to dismiss an application and strike any proceeding of a spouse who has not removed barriers to religious remarriage.[69] So, in doing the challenging work of translating religious obligations to civil ones, Justice Abella pursued a controversial path, but did so with some sensitivity to the communities affected and all the interests at play.

F. Conclusion

Of the many legacies Justice Abella leaves Canadian law on her retirement, her approach to engagement with religious minority perspectives is a valuable inheritance. Her judgments show great care and respect for unfamiliar views, a willingness to re-evaluate the practices of Canadian law, and the courage to stand firm on core commitments. Even if we may only see the world through our own eyes, Justice Abella's jurisprudence shows that the attempt to look through another's, even briefly, can reveal important truths.

69 Jukier & Van Praagh, above note 64 at 407; *Divorce Act*, RSC 1985, c 3 (2nd Supp), s 21.1.

10 Equality and Equity: An Essay in Honour of Justice Rosalie Abella

MARTHA MINOW*

A. Introduction

"[E]very person counts morally," writes philosopher Thomas Scanlan.[1] Translating this into actual practices requires effort; societies have yet to achieve systems that allow all individuals to matter for their own sake and therefore to be able to access equal rights and reach their full potential. This causes harm not only to the impacted individuals and their loved ones, but also to all of humanity,[2] because human beings are not only unique individuals but also interconnected to form a web of community.[3] Laws should recognize and protect individuals while also helping to combat inequalities that stem often from human-made

* 300th Anniversary University Professor, Harvard University. Thanks to Maroussia Levesque and Liz Walsh for crucial research assistance and discussions.

1 Thomas M. Scanlon, "When Does Equality Matter?" https://law.yale.edu/sites/default/files/documents/pdf/Intellectual_Life/ltw-Scanlon.pdf. In this context, to "count morally" means to have moral standing, as in: "an individual has moral standing for us if, when making moral decisions, we feel we ought to take that individual's welfare into account for the individual's own sake and not merely for our benefit or someone else's benefit": Claire Andre & Manuel Velasquez, "Who Counts?" (1991) 4:1 *Issues in Ethics*, online: www.scu.edu/mcae/publications/iie/v4n1/counts.html.

2 Joshua Castellino, "Equality Matters: Why and So What?" *Trans European Policy Studies Association* (Co-funded by the Europe for Citizens Programme of the European Union) (July 2021), online: https://tepsa.eu/analysis/equality-matters-why-and-so-what/.

3 Marié P. Wissing, Lusilda Schutte & Angelina Wilson Fadiji, "Cultures of Positivity: Interconnectedness as a Way of Being," in Irma Eloff, ed, *Handbook of Quality of Life in African Societies*. International Handbooks of Quality-of-Life 3-22 (2019), online: https://doi.org/10.1007/978-3-030-15367-0_1.

decisions and practices. Yet even discussions about equality can generate disagreements and debates.

In recent discourse about combatting inequality in the United States, the terms "equality" and "equity" have become weapons in polarized political arguments as people argue over the precise meaning and apparent implications of each word.[4] Political volleys over terminology obscure decades of litigation, policy, and academic work, including pioneering writing and thinking by Justice Rosalie Silberman Abella. It is frequently argued that the term "equality" implies only simplistic plans to treat everyone alike regardless of historic and current differences and experiences, but conceptions of equality and equal treatment can move well beyond that. What is needed is a framework "of laws and policies that are responsive to individual and structural differences in people's circumstances" and that can be used to advance truly individualized accommodations attentive to background, group membership, and social structures.[5] This framework should honor individual choice while staying mindful of systemic patterns.

Justice Abella's work laid important groundwork that can aid in crafting a such framework, both within Canada and in other nations, including the United States. In this chapter, I will examine current approaches to the idea of equity and equality, including the importance thereof and the barriers we face in achieving it. Although Justice Abella and others have taken important strides, there is still much work that remains to be done, especially around judicial and policy remedies and around public understanding of why equity and equality benefit everyone.

1. *Equality versus Equity: The Apparent Problem*

"Equality" as a normative goal means treating likes alike; equality before the law very often means treating all people the same. Someone charged with violating the law should receive the same presumption of innocence and the same opportunities for defence whether that someone holds high public office or has no job, and regardless of the individual's race, gender, wealth, or background. Some call this "formal equality."

---

4 Because of intense debates, there are no simple definitions of each term; this paper will explore the range of meanings they have come to signify.

5 Martha Minow, "Equality vs. Equity" (2021) 1 *American Journal of Law and Equality* 167, online: https://direct.mit.edu/ajle/article/doi/10.1162/ajle_a_00019/107229/EQUALITY-VS-EQUITY.

Yet in common practice, "equality" means ignoring people's different starting points and conditions. The right to counsel means something quite different for someone able to find and pay for the most effective lawyers than it does for someone dependent on an overworked public defender on a state salary. The legacies of slavery and displacement of Indigenous persons; the social and legal imposition of gender-based and sex-based roles in work, family, and public life; exclusion and degradation based on religion, language, national origin, or disability; crushing daily effects of poverty; all these realities and more can affect the consequences that seemingly equal laws and policies can have for people. Even seemingly neutral and even-handed rules and practices can have deeply different effects for different people, depending on individual situations and influenced by these larger patterns. The idea of treating everyone the same inspired author Anatole France's observation that, "The law, in its majestic equality, forbids rich and poor alike to sleep under bridges, to beg in the streets, and to steal their bread."[6] Treating people the same when they are situated differently can produce very different results.[7]

6 Anatole France, *The Red Lily* (Le Lys Rouge) (1894), quoted in Andrew Sepielli, "The Law's 'Majestic Equality'" (2013) 32 *Law and Philosophy*, 673–700, online: https://doi.org/10.1007/s10982-012-9165-y.

7 Outside the scope of this essay but quite related are claims of positive rights — access to health care, land, housing, water, court expenses, or other resources that are beyond the reach of some individuals due to their poverty or low income. The South African Constitutional Court has ruled in favour of some claims for positive rights while subjecting the remedies to tests of reasonableness or other limitations and focussing on processes for developing access to the needed resources. The remedy in the face of claims of people lacking homes was not for the court to order creation of homes but instead to require the government to devise plans to create housing. See, for example, *Trustees For the Time Being of the Biowatch Trust v Registrar, Genetic Resources and Others* [2009] ZACC 14 (government must bear court costs for litigants who successfully show that the state has failed to fulfill its constitutional and statutory obligations); *The Government of the Republic of South Africa and Others v Grootbroom and Others* [2000] ZACC (unhoused people waiting for adequate shelter have a right for access to adequate housing, requiring the state to take reasonable action to ensure progressive realization of this right). Even that court, though, has denied some such claims. See, for example, *Thiagrai Soobramoney v Minister of Health* (Kwazulu-Nata), CCT 32/97 (1997) (no constitutional violation in government failure to provide access to kidney dialysis on a non-emergency basis to a low-income person); *Lindiwe Mazibuko and Others v City of Johannesburg and Others* (2009) (claim of access to water under the constitution did not entitle claimant to immediate fulfilment of the right, only to reasonable and progressive fulfillment by local authorities of the obligation to ensure everyone has access to sufficient water).

Moreover, judgments about who deserves "the same treatment" and who does not often reflect old assumptions that can perpetuate false or unfair conclusions. Some elements of difference should not be made to matter, but some aspects of difference should call for different treatment. Determining which path to follow makes the work of courts challenging when they are presented with questions about equality and equity. Does a traditional law entitling male but not female descendants to inherit property upon the death of their parent contravene equality protections?[8] Does an American citizen who does not live in a state of the country have a claim to the same social security benefits as one who does live in a state?[9] Do permanent residents who are not citizens of the nation or of a state have a claim to social security benefits?[10] Should the same criminal sentence apply to an adolescent who commits a crime that is imposed when an adult commits that offense?[11] And should a ban on use of marijuana apply the same way to people who have a religious ritual calling for its use as it does to people without that religious

---

8 *Bhe and Others v Khayelitsha Magistrate and Others* (2004) (South Africa Constitutional Court) (Black Administration Act disallowing women and nonmarital children from inheriting held unconstitutional).

9 *United States v Vaello-Madero*, (2022), online: www.scotusblog.com/case-files/cases/united-states-v-vaello-madero/ (the Supreme Court ruled that the constitution does not require Congress to extend Supplemental Security Income benefits to residents of Puerto Rico because they have a different relationship in terms of taxes and benefits to the United States than do citizens in states and than do noncitizens in territories that negotiated for such benefits).

10 *Khosa and Others v Minister of Social Development* (2004), online: https://collections.concourt.org.za/bitstream/handle/20.500.12144/2210/Full%20judgment%20(168%20Kb)-1344.pdf?sequence=1&isAllowed=y) (the Constitutional Court found the requirement of citizenship unreasonable for permanent residents who fled Mozambique during the 1980s civil war and obtained permanent resident status in South Africa because the exclusion was unreasonable, discriminatory, and an infringement on the right to equality and because of the importance the constitution places on protecting vulnerable peoples).

11 *Centre for Child Law v Minister for Justice and Constitutional Development and Others*, 2009(2) SACR 477 (CC)2009(6) SA 632 (CC)BCLR 1105 (CC) (individualized assessment rather than flat minimum sentences required for sixteen- and seventeen-year-olds). The United States Supreme Court has one the one hand required individualized assessments for juveniles facing sentences of life without parole, but with new members of the court, it has limited the application of this decision. See *Jones v Mississippi; Montgomery v Louisiana; Miller v Alabama*. See also *Roper v Simmons and Graham v Florida* (death penalty against juveniles for crimes committed before they reach the age of eighteen and life without parole for juveniles convicted of nonhomicide crimes are both unconstitutional).

claim?[12] Courts at different times and in different places have given different responses to such questions.

Calls for "equity," on the other hand, increasingly reflect hopes for answers that address systemic inequalities and achieve results in the direction of "substantive equality."[13] Sometimes, this may mean overcoming historic significance given to a "difference" that does not justify different treatment. Hence, in light of changing views about sex roles, female and male descendants should all be entitled to inherit from a parent. Will similar changes lead to rejecting differences in legal status as a basis for eligibility for government social security benefits? At other times, emphasizing a difference may be what "substantive equality" seems to require, as in exempting adolescents from the same stringent punishment assigned to an adult for the same crime or accommodating use of a banned substance for religious reasons. For some, in the United States, "equality" means identical treatment, regardless of the circumstances of different individuals or groups, while "equity" calls for attention to differences in lived experiences and situation. Substantive equality often means redressing historic disadvantages including race, gender, disability, religion, and economic class.

---

12 Compare *Minister of Justice and Constitutional Development and Others v Prince*, Cct 109/17 ACC 30 (2018) (prohibition on marijuana possession and use in homes and other appropriate places unconstitutional discrimination against the Rastafarian community; Parliament required to amend the law and interim relief accorded making use of cannabis lawful by adults in private spaces and permitting cultivation of cannabis for private consumption) with *Employment Div v Smith*, 494 US 872 (1990) (rejecting claim to religious accommodation for members of a Native American nation seeking permission to use peyote in a religious ceremony).

13 On substantive equality in Canadian law, see *Fraser v Canada (Attorney General)*, 2020 SCC 28 and the work of Margot Young, such as Margot Young, "Unequal to the Task: 'Kapp'ing the Substantive Potential of Section 15" (2010) 50 *Supreme Court Law Review* (2d) 183. Very related is Justice Abella's approach to "systemic equality," examined in Charles Tremblay Potvin, "Les suites du Rapport Abella au regard de l'élaboration du concept de discrimination systémique dans la jurisprudence canadienne," Chapter 2 in this volume. The meanings of the term equity, as examined here, are complex and multiple. It is worth noting that this was the term proposed by ultra-conservative factions in the United Nations so that state parties could avoid being bound by the strictures of women's equality under international conventions — specifically, the *Convention on the Elimination of All Forms of Discrimination Against Women* (see, for example, Alda Facio and Martha I Morgan, "Equity Or Equality For Women? Understanding CEDAW's Equality Principles" (2009) 60:5 *Alabama Law Review* 1133 (2009). Yet in the United States, the term has been embraced by advocates critical of formal equality who view "equity" as a more capacious and ambitious term.

Spurred in no small part by the analysis of Justice Abella, Canadian jurisprudence generally includes within its equality protections the services and benefits that are required to enable equal outcomes despite unequal prior conditions faced by different individuals and groups.[14] The Canadian idea of "equality of condition, not just equality of opportunity"[15] proceeds with the recognition that people start off from different positions, so achieving equality requires attention to people's actual positions and staring points.[16]

Distinguishing when "same treatment" is called for and when instead substantive equality calls for distinct treatment demands consideration of history and current facts on the ground. In the field of education in the United States, laws used the race of students in assigning individuals to racially segregated public schools. Those practices did not only segregate students by race, they also ensured more resources to schools reserved for whites than to other schools. Yes, dismantling the school assignment laws did not alter prior, ongoing, and real disparities in resources and in expectations. As a factual matter, public school funding in much of the United States relies predominantly on local property taxes that, again as a factual matter, reiterate patterns of advantage and disadvantage. Variations between local communities and between states in taxed wealth and in tax levels produce stark per-pupil spending differences, and states and communities with lower-valued property cannot make up the difference even if they adopt taxes at a higher level than other communities.[17] And disparities in per-pupil funding are highly correlated with disparities in educational outcomes.[18] These

14 Government of Canada, *Jordan's Principle: Substantive Equality Principles*, online: www.sac-isc.gc.ca/eng/1583698429175/1583698455266; Justice Claire L'Heureux-Dubé, "It Takes A Vision: The Constitutionalization of Equality in Canada," 14 *Yale Journal of Law & Feminism* 363 (2002), online: https://digitalcommons.law.yale.edu/cgi/viewcontent.cgi?article=1197&context=yjlf.

15 William Little, *Introduction to Sociology*, 2d Canadian edition, 2013, online: https://opentextbc.ca/introductiontosociology2ndedition/chapter/chapter-9-social-inequality-in-canada/. "Equity of condition" does not mean a permanent commitment to identical outcomes as much as an effort to make "equal opportunity" genuine and not rigged based on past privileges and disadvantages. Canadian law reflects contributions by many, notably including Rosalie Silberman Abella; see note 26.

16 William Little, above note 15, explains that "[s]ubstantive equality seeks to address the inequalities that stem from an individual's particular circumstances, to help put them at the same position and give them the same opportunities as others."

17 Bruce Baker, "The Unequal State of Public Education in the United States" *The Century Foundation* (25 June 2020) 13, online: https://production-tcf.imgix.net/app/uploads/2020/06/24185424/1bruce-baker_-fn.pdf.

18 *Ibid* at 12–13.

practices and results persist even though race-based student assignments are illegal.

Spending disparities are in fact associated with differences in the racial composition of the schools.[19] Even as courts rejected legally enforced racial segregation, conscious and unconscious racial biases persisted or grew worse. Racial disparities in identification of students with special needs, in disciplinary practices, and in school enrollments amplify different patterns of funding and student achievement. Many non-white students remain stuck in schools marked by concentrated poverty, fewer resources, and lower test scores than schools predominantly composed of white students.[20] Equal opportunity in terms of access to excellent teachers and materials would be an advance but would not address the deeper patterns producing differences such as contrasting qualities of facilities, different school expenditure levels, different percentages of students in poverty, different distribution of students having or lacking parents with the time or background to provide enrichment and guidance, and different rates of school discipline and community-level risks of violence. Identical per-pupil expenditures, even if achievable, would not address potentially greater costs of educating students with special needs.

One analysis by the National High School Society of Scholars calls for both equality and equity in schooling. It defines equality to mean: "every student gets the same resources and opportunities . . . the same quality of and abundance of materials and facilities, and/or the same quality of instruction," while describing equity as assurance "that every student gets the opportunities and resources they need depending on their situation."[21] To combine identical distribution of resources with the ability to adapt to unique circumstances suggests a baseline of identical resources that can be modified with extra resources to overcome challenging patterns and problems. In the context of public-school finance, evening the tax base through state and federal grants can allow districts with higher concentrations of poverty to generate per-pupil expenditures comparable to those in wealthier districts. At the same

---

19 Robert Bifulco & Sarah Souders, "Racial Disparities in School Poverty and Spending: Examining Allocations Within Metropolitan Areas" (2024) 10:1 *AERA Open* 1–20, online: https://files.eric.ed.gov/fulltext/EJ1455261.pdf.

20 Martha Minow, *In Brown's Wake: Legacies of America's Educational Landmark* (New York: Oxford University Press, 2010) 7.

21 Sarah Zoloff, *Equality vs. Equity in Education: Why Both Are Essential in Today's Classrooms* (4 January 2024), online: https://www.nshss.org/resources/blog/blog-posts/equity-vs-equality-in-education-why-both-are-essential-in-today-s-classrooms/.

time, further funding support is necessary to ensure genuine learning opportunities for students with special needs and those encountering other learning challenges.[22]

It is this extra level that is often signaled by the turn to "equity." Justice and fairness, in this sense, require more than colour-blindness, gender-blindness, or other impositions of the "same treatment" when it ignores historic causes of and influences on disparities in opportunities and outcomes within society.[23] Precisely because historic patterns of privilege and disadvantage took decades to take hold, altering their impact on current and future lives takes work and requires an active approach. Whether the patterns reflect intentional or accidental actions matters less than the mere fact that, regardless of motivation, they shape people's options and experiences.

One example involves the norms and practices of sorting men and women into different jobs, the social expectations that historically assign care of children and other dependents to women, and differences in years and hours of employment history associated with gender.[24] Seeking "equity" is one way to challenge these norms and practices; challenging discrimination and seeking equal protection under national and local laws may also offer ways to object to persistent wage gaps associated with gender.

The idea that "equality" is an empty concept is an old objection, and it has been joined more recently by arguments stating that confused and incoherent notions of equality permeate judicial treatments.[25] Yet in

22 Emily Brixey, *Cracking the Code on Funding Schools Equitably*, EdNote (29 January 2021), online: https://www.ecs.org/cracking-the-code-on-funding-schools-equitably/.

23 Code for America, *Our Vision for DEI*, online: www.codeforamerica.org/diversity (work with governments, design, and tech firms). For a very similar definition, see YBoston, *Beyond the DE& I Acronym: What Are Diversity, Equity, and Inclusion?* YBoston (26 March 2016) (quoting Fatima Dainkeh).

24 Robin Bleweis, *Quick Facts About the Gender Wage Gap*, Center for American Progress (24 March 2020), online: www.americanprogress.org/article/quick-facts-gender-wage-gap/; Anna Louie Sussman, "How to End 'Women's Work': New Zealand is Pursuing a Century-Old Idea to Close the Gender Pay Gap" *New York Times* (13 November 2020), www.nytimes.com/2020/11/13/opinion/women-pay-gender-gap.html? (drawing on 1919 International Labor Organization constitution citing "the principle that men and women should receive remuneration for work of equal value").

25 For the older claim, see Peter Westen, "The Empty Idea of Equality" (1982) 95 *Harvard Law Review* 537, online: https://www.jstor.org/stable/1340593?seq=1; for the newer claim, see R. George Wright, "Equal Protection and the Idea of Equality" (2016) 34 *Minnesota Journal of Law & Inequality* 1.

order to find resources under the general rubric of equality to challenge exclusions, subordination, and denials of opportunity on the bases of race, ethnicity, gender, disability, citizen status, or other grounds, we need not first resolve contests over competing philosophic ideas about needs, just deserts, distribution, and oppression. For many, overcoming systemic discrimination remains the goal, whether they use the label "equality" or "equity.

B. Individual Accomodations and Systemic Change

Redressing inequality cannot be accomplished through simple or static answers like "treat likes alike." Instead, laws and policies should respond to individual differences in people's circumstances while addressing structural and categorical treatment. Both the unique circumstances of each individual and underlying structures of disadvantage contribute to inequality. In order to achieve equity, it is also necessary to enable enforcement and to acknowledge potential fallout without flinching from what justice requires.

Rosalie Silberman Abella, serving as Chair of the Royal Commission on Equal in Employment in 1984, explained such problems with clarity:

> The goal of equality is more than an evolutionary intolerance to adverse discrimination. It is to ensure, too, that the vestiges of these arbitrarily restrictive assumptions do not continue to play a role in our society . . . It is not a question of whether this discrimination is motivated by an intentional desire to obstruct someone's potential, or whether it is the accidental by-product of innocently motivated practices or systems. If the barrier is affecting certain groups in a disproportionately negative way, it is a signal that the practices that lead to this adverse impact may be discriminatory.[26]

---

26 Rosalie Silberman Abella, *Equality in Employment: A Royal Commission Report* (Ottawa: Commission on Equality in Employment, 1984), online: https://publications.gc.ca/site/eng/471737/publication.html. For further exploration of developments in Canada, see Anthony Robert Sangiuliano, "Substantive Equality As Equal Recognition: A New Theory of Section 15 of the Charter" (2015) 52 *Osgoode Hall Law Journal* 601, online: http://digitalcommons.osgoode.yorku.ca/ohlj/vol52/iss2/9. See *Fraser v Canada (Attorney General)*, 2020 SCC 28 (rejecting on equality grounds pension plan devised for job-sharing due to adverse impact on women and children with the effect of reinforcing, perpetuating, or exacerbating disadvantage); *R v Kapp*, 2008 SCC 41 (finding legally protected advantages for Indigenous fishing rights compatible with the Charter of Fundamental Rights and Freedoms despite an antidiscrimination clause); *Andrews v Law Society of British Columbia*, [1989] 1 SCR 143) (equality provision successfully invoked by an individual qualified

This shift from examining the *intentions* of those in power to assessing the *effects* of practices and systems is critical to moving from the status quo and making equality more than an abstract and unachieved ideal. The Supreme Court of Canada applied this approach in its first effort to interpret the equal rights guaranteed by the *Canadian Charter of Rights and Freedoms*.[27]

Scholars writing after now-Justice Abella's earlier analysis include Owen Fiss, Reva Siegel, and Cass Sunstein, who have framed equality itself as the tool to undo and overcome subordination and caste.[28] Racially disparate results — whether in employment, education, or other sectors — offer a reason to investigate whether and how people begin at different "starting points." Disparate results can also prompt thinking about changing systems to produce something approximating equality of outcomes despite the different starting points and circumstances of individuals.[29]

---

for admission to the bar but facing exclusion as a noncitizen of Canada). For a detailed treatment of the elements of equality analysis influenced by Justice Abella, see Charles Tremblay Potvin, above note 13. For a critique of Canadian equality jurisprudence, see Judy Fudge, "Substantive Equality, the Supreme Court of Canada, and the Limits to Redistribution" (2007) 23 *South African Journal on Human Rights* 235.

27 Paul Wells, "Rosie Abella said she'd answer questions when she turned 75" *Maclean's* (15 June 2021), online: macleans.ca / news / rosie-abella-said-shed -answer-questions-when-she-turned-75 / . Actual application of the concept of substantive equality in Canada can still involve disputes, given the flexibility in meanings. For example, the Supreme Court of Canada has allowed continued use of explicit, status-based distinctions on several occasions and treated them as non-discriminatory despite their obvious subordinating effects (see, for example, *Hodge v Canada (Minister of Human Resources Development)*, 2004 SCC 65 (exclusion of separated common-law spouses from Canada Pension Plan death benefits upheld as non-discriminatory even in a context involving abuse).

28 Owen Fiss, "Another Equality: The Origins and Fate of Antisubordination Theory" (2004) 20 *Issues in Legal Scholarship*, online: https: / / law.yale.edu / sites / default / files / documents / faculty / papers / Fiss_AnotherEquality.pdf; Reva B. Siegel, "Equality Talk: Antisubordination and Anticlassification Values in Constitutional Struggles Over Brown" (2003–04) 117 *Harvard Law Review* 1470; Cass R. Sunstein, "The Anticaste Principle" (1993) 92 *Michigan Law Review* 2410. See Isabel Wilkinson, *Caste* (New York: Random House, 2020).

29 See Brian Barry, Why Social Justice Matters (2005); Richard J. Arneson, Does Social Justice Matter? Brian Barry's Applied Political Philosophy, 117 Ethics 391 (April 2007), http: / / ezp-prod1.hul.harvard.edu / login?url=https: / / www.jstor.org / stable / 10.1086 / 511732. See also Equity vs. Equality: 20 Differences!, Public Health Notes (site created by Sandesh Adhikar), https: / / www.publichealthnotes.com / equity-vs-equality / .

No less significant is the idea, again articulated by Justice Abella, that the disproportionate impact of existing structures is a clue to possible underlying discrimination, but that is not the end of the analysis. Designing meaningful remedies that can actually be implemented, anticipating and dealing with resistance to reforms, and preparing for what will be an ongoing and never-finished task are three further dimensions of just responses to persistent inequalities.

1. Determining the Appropriate Remedy

Remedying inequalities is more challenging than simply acknowledging that there is a problem. Unique individual contexts and broad patterns and structures require very different responses. Helping an individual obtain educational assistance, compensating for discrimination in employment, or granting other individualized remedies for discriminatory experiences will do little to alter the larger situation that affects many other people. The capacity of legislatures and courts to devise meaningful remedies also differs and reflect the constraints of each institution: legislatures require political compromises; courts require compliance or cooperation from other branches and actors.

Remedies for unequal treatment experienced by an individual may call for individualized accommodations. There are those who argue that individualized tailoring means disuniformity — and that it is therefore unfair. Compare, though, issues of disuniformity with the alternative of one-size-fits-all treatments that can systemically disadvantage or burden members of minority or marginalized groups.

In certain circumstances, however, there can be disadvantages to tailoring responses to individual circumstances. Individualized remedies are expensive to design and to implement, and the resulting costs may defeat the overall policy goal.[30] Such accommodations often take far longer to achieve, when a more standardized remedy could be implemented more quickly and therefore be more helpful to the person in need; a timely but imperfect remedy, after all, is better than a remedy that comes too late. For example, devising individualized assessments of the needs of individuals following natural disasters may require so much time and expense that aid would not be available to people in those emergency circumstances. In such situations, issuing uniform cheques may be better than devising tailored support. And getting the cheques out quickly may be more valuable and

30 For further discussion, see Minow, "Equality vs. Equity," above note 5.

meaningful to those with urgent needs than fitting the amounts to the specific circumstances.

Widescale remedies can also be an important way to avoid further ostracizing someone who requires accommodation. An across-the-board retirement age, for example, avoids judgments about a specific person that could potentially be more hurtful.[31] The impact of universal benefits as opposed to individualized ones is therefore always a factor to consider.[32]

Even in situations where individualized remedies are ideal, they are also not enough in of themselves. Large-scale systemic changes are also necessary. Case-by-case accommodations — such as those that have been undertaken for years in the contexts of religious, racial, or disability discrimination — make all the difference for the individuals involved. But do such individualized accommodations alter systemic biases in norms and practices? Indirectly and over time, there may be change, but individualized accommodations are neither targeted nor well-designed to tackle structural changes in rules, practices, and attitudes that exclude or burden some people based on their needs, identities, or backgrounds. Systemic racism builds different treatments of people based on their perceived race into the patterns of practices and rules used in laws, institutions, and people's conscious and subconscious acts. Individualized responses may well leave these patterns in place, addressing exceptional issues and individual problems rather than structural failures.

2. *Levelling Up or Levelling Down?*

Conceptually, some may think a remedy for inequality comes with removing the advantages of some rather than with extending those same advantages to those who lack them.[33] When a court finds a constitutional violation on the basis of equality, the design of a remedy will further express the content and scope of the claim to equal treatment. Simply announcing that a violation of equal treatment has occurred without also providing an effective remedy is a failure. Yet another

31 See Fred Schauer, *Profiles, Probabilities, and Stereotypes* (Cambridge, MA: Harvard University Press, 2006).

32 Samuel R. Bagenstos, "Universalism and Civil Rights (and Notes on Voting Rights after *Shelby*)" (2014) 123 *Yale Law Journal* 2838.

33 For a glimpse of related philosophical debates, see Nils Holtug, "Egalitarianism and the Levelling Down Objection" (1974) 58 *Analysis* 166, online: www.jstor.org/stable/3328488.

kind of failure results from a narrow view of "equal treatment" — one that "levels down" by removing the benefit offered to some rather than "levelling up" by extending it to those who were excluded.[34] "Levelling down" rather than "levelling up" exposes what Peter Westen dubbed the "empty idea of equality:" an "equality" that lacks any substantive commitments.[35] A broader, substantive view calls for a remedy that "levels up" by extending the benefit to the excluded class.[36]

Consider the proper remedy for a father's objection on sex discrimination grounds when an employer provides maternal leave to employees who are mothers but does not provide paternal leave. The father's objection of unequal treatment could be resolved by the employer ending maternal leave. This would constitute levelling down. Levelling up, on the other hand, would ensure parental leave to any employee, and in the contexts of adoption and foster care as well as childbirth. A fuller, more inclusive remedy would involve family and dependent care leave and encompass situations with an ill or elderly parent of an employee.[37] For another example, consider religious objections to a ban on the use of marijuana when members of a particular religious group claim its use is part of a religious practice. One remedy would be accommodation solely for members of the religious group, but another, broader

---

34 See, for example, Deborah L. Brake, "When Equality Leaves Everyone Worse Off: The Problem of Leveling Down in Equality Law" (2004) 46 *William & Mary Law Review* 512; Tracy A. Thomas, "Leveling Down Gender Equality" (2019) 42 *Harvard Journal of Law & Gender* 177.

35 Westen, above note 25. Kent Greenawalt rejects this view as depending on too restrictive a conception of equality; see Kent Greenawalt, "How Empty Is the Idea of Equality," (1983) 83 *Columbia Law Review* 1167, online: https://scholarship.law.columbia.edu/faculty_scholarship/82. In a similar spirit, but turning to conceptions beyond equality, Dean Erwin Chemerinsky defends equality as necessary but not sufficient; see Erwin Chemerinsky, "In Defense of Equality: A Reply to Professor Westen" (1983) 81 *Michigan Law Review* 575. On leveling up and leveling down, see Larry S. Tempkin, "Inequality" (Spring 1986) 15:2 *Philosophy and Public Affairs* 99, online: https://www.jstor.org/stable/2265381; Brake, above note 34; Louis Michael Seidman, "The Ratchet Wreck: Equality's Leveling Down Problem" *Georgetown University Law Center* (30 November 2020), online: https://scholarship.law.georgetown.edu/cgi/viewcontent.cgi?article=3348&context=facpub.

36 See Mark C. Gillespie, "Note: Level-Up Remedies for Religious Discrimination" (2021) 44 *Harvard Journal of Law & Public Policy* 961. See also sources cited in above note 34.

37 Mary Beth Ferrante, "Your Company Should Get Rid of its Maternity Leave Policy" *Forbes* (12 August 2019), online: www.forbes.com/sites/marybethferrante/2019/08/12/your-company-should-get-rid-of-its-maternity-leave-policy/?sh=1c1f379a1fce.

remedy — adopted by South Africa's Constitutional Court — would require allowing marijuana use in private for any adult.[38]

C. Anticipating Resistance to Change

Remedies for unequal treatment that level up are more ambitious and more costly than those that level down. This by itself could trigger opposition and backlash. If history is a guide, valiant and hard-won struggles overcoming inequality can be eviscerated. The Reconstruction Amendments to the United States Constitution ended slavery and were supposed to guarantee equal protection of the law and voting rights for previously enslaved men, but their effect was foreshortened by changes in the judiciary, reflecting political backlash.[39]

Proponents of the current rash of state legislation in the United States seek to halt public school teaching about the history of race and racism, and to minimize controversy and sources of discomfort in classrooms.[40] But where is the concern for discomfort that Black students and other students of colour will experience, missing truthful examinations of US history and practices?[41] The current movement against "critical race theory" in schooling is in fact a reaction against efforts to remedy omissions and gaps when US schools teach about history and society without addressing racism or the contributions of Black Americans to the nation.

As these examples indicate, risks of backlash are real. Reactionary responses can torpedo not only specific remedial efforts but larger movements for political change or for knowledge itself. Resistance to remedial efforts should be anticipated on a broad scale. Such responses can be purely emotional, but they are often coaches in an attempt at logic. In the United States, for example, some arguments against inequality remedies

---

38 *Minister of Justice and Constitutional Development and Others v Prince*, above note 12.

39 Eric Foner, *The Second Founding: How the Civil War and Reconstruction Remade the Constitution* (New York: W.W. Norton, 2019); Peter S. Canellos, *The Great Dissenter: The Story of John Marshall Harlan, America's Judicial Her* (New York: Simon & Schuster, 2021).

40 Catherine Stout & Thomas Wilborne, "CRT Map: Efforts to Restrict Teaching Racism and Bias Have Multiplied Across the US" *Chalkbeat* (1 February 2022), online: https://www.chalkbeat.org/22525983/map-critical-race-theory-legislation-teaching-racism (comparing thirty-six states adopting laws restricting such teachings and seventeen encouraging such teaching).

41 Stephanie Wolf & Jess Clark, "As Legislators Push So-Called Anti-CRT Bills Citing Discomfort, Black Students Ask Whose Feelings Matter?" *WFPL* (radio) (March 21, 2022), online: https://wfpl.org/as-legislators-push-so-called-anti-crt-bills-citing-discomfort-black-students-ask-whose-feelings-matter/.

can assert competing moral and legal principles. A familiar argument is that liberty and equality are at odds — and thus, that more equality will impair liberty. Those who see these two foundational ideals as clashing actually adopt particular frames of analysis, but there are other frameworks that open avenues for joint pursuit of liberty and equality. Treating liberty and equality as in tension with one another usually means treating pre-existing distributions of resources as natural or given. Libertarians, free-market defenders, and anti-communists in particular have helped formulate liberty and equality as eternally or inevitably opposed to one another.[42] Those who stress the incompatibility of liberty and equality often have advantages that might be altered if there were more measures to achieve equality. They might argue that equality of results, if enforced, would involve grave losses of liberty and individuality. An obvious rejoinder asks, whose freedom precisely is then being defended? Is the freedom of those burdened by existing unequal treatment not as worthy as the liberty of those with powers and privileges?[43]

Recognizing such risks should not halt pursuit of equality but should help to inform the campaigns, outreach, defence, and communication by those seeking redress for inequalities. One approach, which is important but under-utilized, involves emphasizing how all people are harmed by ongoing inequality. See, for example, Heather McGhee's powerful analysis, which offers detailed evidence of the costs of racism for all.[44] She shows the prevalence of a mindset among white people that gains for people of colour come at the expense of whites. This implicit narrative of a zero-sum game helps to perpetuate the current status

42 See Danielle Allen, "Liberty and Equality Aren't Mutually Exclusive" *Washington Post* (17 October 2014), online: www.washingtonpost.com/opinions/liberty-equality-arent-mutually-exclusive/2014/10/17/d9df36ba-55fb-11e4-809b-8cc0a295c773_story.html.

43 See Nancy LeTourneau, "The Ongoing Struggle Between Two American Ideals: Liberty and Equality" *Washington Monthly* (18 June 2020), online: https://washingtonmonthly.com/2020/06/18/the-ongoing-struggle-between-two-american-ideals-liberty-and-equality/. Canada, too, has wrestled with tension between liberty and equality while working to maintain commitment to both values. Hence, the Canadian courts assume if that the claimant has liberty to exercise choice in relation to their condition, then a state action that discriminates based on that choice must be consistent with equality. See, for example, Sonia Lawrence, "Choice, Equality and Tales of Racial Discrimination: Reading the Supreme Court on Section 15" in Sheila McIntyre & Sandra Rodgers, eds, *Diminishing Returns: Inequality and the Canadian Charter of Rights and Freedoms* (Markham, Ontario: LexisNexis Canada Inc, 2006) 115.

44 Heather McGhee, *The Sum of Us: What Racism What Racism Costs Everyone and How We Can Prosper Together* (New York: Random House, 2021).

quo.[45] However, McGee also demonstrates policies hurting people of colour also do a great deal of harm to white people. For example, slavery benefitted a narrow slice of the white population while contributing to the suppression of wages for white workers and failures of investment in public services. And in a classic levelling-down remedy, claims against racial segregation in public swimming pools led communities to eliminate the public pools altogether.[46]

Overcoming the zero-sum mindset requires showing how discriminatory structures impair society as a whole. As Justice Ruth Bader Ginsburg maintained, gender stereotypes also harm everyone.[47] When women's pay rises to match men's salaries, families do better. Foreclosed educational opportunities for girls means businesses never developed, scientific discoveries never made, and other accomplishments never reached given what those girls could achieve over their lifetimes. The perpetuation of gender roles and stereotypes also means that boys and men are punished when they do not conform to patriarchal ideals of masculinity. The same point applies to other disadvantaged groups. When people with disabilities are denied educational and work opportunities, their families and their communities miss out on all they could contribute. Diversity in terms of race, sex, gender, and disability improves workplaces, juries, and knowledge-building for all. Including arguments such as these in defences of remedies for inequality will not halt backlash but can strengthen the political and legal context for the work against inequality.

D. Conclusion: Equality as Vigilant Inquiry

Effective responses to inequalities require vigilance and continual efforts. Justice Abella explained why:

> Equality is evolutionary, in process as well as in substance; it is cumulative, it is contextual, and it is persistent. Equality is, at the very least, freedom from adverse discrimination. But what constitutes adverse

45 See *ibid.*

46 Jeff Wiltse, *Contested Waters: A Social History of Swimming Pools in America* (Chapel Hill: University of North Carolina Press, 2010); Andre Toren, "Segregated Pools" *USA Today* (1 February 2021), online: www.usatoday.com/story/sports/2021/02/23/segregated-public-pools-has-lasting-effect-black-america/4539339001/.

47 Melissa Block, "Pathmarking the Way: Ruth Bader Ginsburg's Lifelong Fight for Gender Equality" *NPR* (24 September 2020), online: www.npr.org/2020/09/24/916377135/pathmarking-the-way-ruth-bader-ginsburgs-lifelong-fight-for-gender-equality.

> discrimination changes with time, with information, with experience and with insight. What we tolerated as a society 100, 50, or even 10 years ago is no longer necessarily tolerable. Equality is thus a process, a process of constant and flexible examination, of vigilant introspection, and of aggressive open-mindedness.[48]

Stereotypes become outmoded. Exclusions become no longer acceptable. Political and social movements help change people's minds. What once seemed lawful can become no longer acceptable. Only when equality is understood as evolutionary does it become clear that efforts toward it must be persistently ongoing. Courts can play critical roles in redressing inequalities. Indeed, judicial enforcement has been key to successes in redressing racial discrimination and segregation in the United States, even in the face of opposition.[49]

Yet judicial interpretations can hollow out the concept of equality and make remedies for inequalities more remote. Justice Abella has showed through her thinking, persistence, and example how to make courts and law tools for recognizing individuals and for overcoming inequalities. Thank you, Justice Abella, for teaching us that "you cannot be equal unless you acknowledge how different people are."[50]

---

48 Rosalie Silberman Abella, "The Dynamic Nature of Equality" in S. L. Martin & K. E. Mahoney, eds, *Equality and Judicial Neutrality* (Toronto: Carswell, 1987) 3.

49 Douglas S. Reed, "Twenty-Five Years After Rodriguez: School Finance Litigation and the Impact of the New Judicial Federalism" (1998) 32 *Law & Society Review* 175 (energetic state judicial intervention achieves more equitable results in school funding and can proceed despite public opposition).

50 Rosalie Silberman Abella & Matthew Diller, "A Conversation with the Honourable Rosalie Silberman Abella and Dean Matthew Diller" (2018) 87 *Fordham Law Review* 843.

11 The Pursuit of Reconciliation: Justice Abella's Contribution to Drawing Back the Curtain on Canada's (Hi)storied Relationship with Indigenous Peoples

AIMÉE CRAFT*

A. Introduction

Interpreting Canada's constitution is a daunting task, as are the legal obligations that arise from such interpretation. There is no guidebook, only sets of interpretive principles, many aimed at decoding often unwritten and ever-evolving concepts. Canadian Aboriginal law is no exception. The evolution of the constitutional rights jurisprudence that defines the exercise of Indigenous rights in Canada is sui generis and multidimensional. The interpretation of section 35 of the *Constitution Act, 1982* in particular has been complicated and sometimes ambiguous, as the Supreme Court of Canada has sought to define the scope of Treaty and Aboriginal rights, set out a test for establishing Aboriginal title, frame the duty to consult and accommodate, establish legal tests to prove the existence Aboriginal rights, understand Treaty rights, and explain the justification for infringing those constitutionally protected rights, to name only a few.

The "legal fictions"[1] that inform Canadian Aboriginal law have shaped the historied interpretation of Canada's constitution in several ways, according to Professor John Borrows. First, the twin doctrines of discovery and of terra nullius, by which the Crown purported to establish British sovereignty by claiming underlying title to "unoccupied" lands, have influenced Canada's property laws and land tenure systems. Secondly, and equally problematic, are the legislated assertions that

---

* Associate Professor, University of Ottawa, Faculty of Common Law. With special thanks to Jayna Greene (Research Assistant).

1 John Borrows, "Canada's Colonial Constitution" in John Borrows & Michael Coyle, eds, *The Right Relationship: Reimagining the Implementation of Historical Treaties* (Toronto: University of Toronto Press, 2017) 17 at 18.

Indigenous peoples had (and continue to have) "inferior legal status,"[2] giving rise to the need to enfranchise and assimilate them through discriminatory government policies and practices. These legal fictions have been perpetuated by Canadian Aboriginal law jurisprudence.

The inclusion of section 35 in the *Constitution Act, 1982* marked a new era in Crown-Indigenous relationships in Canada, where existing treaty and Aboriginal rights were both recognized and affirmed. As the Supreme Court jurisprudence evolved, the Court identified accompanying rights, obligations, and sets of duties, including fiduciary obligations, ancillary rights, and the duties to uphold the honour of the Crown, to consult and accommodate, and to advance reconciliation. Borrows suggests that Canada's legal system mingles together positive and negative aspects of Canada's creation in both "complementary and inconsistent ways."[3] The application of the principle of reconciliation in Supreme Court jurisprudence emerges as a stark example, as it has been applied in ways that "advance Indigenous thought and practice" but also in ways that perpetuate the notion that Indigenous thought and practice are frozen in time, unable to evolve in the same way that non-Indigenous rights have.[4] Recent caselaw has aimed to acknowledge Indigenous and Crown relationships, the duties of the honour of the Crown, and the duties of reconciliation between nations.

Recent Supreme Court jurisprudence, to which Justice Abella made meaningful contributions, was built on the body of earlier cases in what is a relatively young area of the common law, and it intends to enhance our legal understanding of the underlying constitutional principles and duties that characterize Canadian Aboriginal law. In her final address to the Supreme Court of Canada, Justice Abella told the story of her journey to the bench and spoke of the importance of breathing life into the law:

> Judges could no longer be defenders of the status quo. We had to accept that justice was the application of law to life, not just the application of laws to facts.[5]

---

2 *Ibid* at 19–20.

3 *Ibid* at 19.

4 Aimée Craft, "Thawing the Frozen Rights Theory: On Rejecting Interpretations and Resurgence that Define Indigenous Peoples as Frozen in a Precolonial Past" in *Reconciliation and Resurgence* (forthcoming, University of Toronto Press).

5 Rosalie Silberman Abella, "The Honourable Rosalie Silberman Abella Bids Farewell to the Supreme Court" (webcast delivered at the Supreme Court of Canada 21 May 2021), online: www.scc-csc.ca/judges-juges/webcast-webdiffusion-farewell-aurevoir-rosalie-silberman-abella-eng.aspx.

Abella's commitment to this statement is clear, as her legacy has been described as one that "breathe[s] life into Canada's most treasured values."[6] Justice Abella's decisions have contributed to re-storying parts of Canadian Aboriginal law in ways that better reflect the long-standing relationships of Indigenous people with the Crown, the fiduciary obligations aligned with the honour of the Crown, and the current imperative of reconciliation.

This paper examines four of Justice Abella's decisions in the area of Canadian Aboriginal law. Whether writing for the Court in *Daniels v Canada*;[7] for the majority in *Newfoundland and Labrador (Attorney General) v Uashaunnuat (Innu of Uashat and of Mani-Utenam)*[8] and *R v Morris*;[9] or in a minority judgment (dissenting on the issue of consultation and accommodation) in *Mikisew Cree v Canada* (Governor General in Council) (2018),[10] Justice Abella's decisions in this area of law are characterized by her habitual thoughtful reasoning, clear writing, and attention to equity and equality. She has meaningfully contributed to Canadian Aboriginal law, especially by enhancing the Court's reliance on two constitutional determinations: that the honour of the Crown applies to all of the Crown's dealings with Indigenous peoples and that the purpose of section 35 of the Constitution is reconciliation. In focusing specifically on the themes of the honour of the Crown and reconciliation, these four decisions exhibit Justice Abella's strong commitment to these principles in different contexts.

In the seminal *Daniels v Canada* judgment, Justice Abella affirmed that reconciliation with all of Canada's peoples is a goal of Parliament and reminded the Crown of its obligations to act honourably as a fiduciary to Canada's Métis population, as established in *Manitoba Métis Federation*. In Justice Abella's minority opinion (with Justice Martin concurring) in the 2018 *Mikisew Cree v Canada (Governor General in Council)* case, she asserted that the Crown has an obligation, grounded in its duty to act honourably, to consult proactively on legislation that may infringe Aboriginal or treaty rights. In the *R v Morris* decision, co-written by Justices Deschamps

6 Lawrence David, "The Voice of the Vulnerable" *Canadian Bar Association* (1 July 2017), online: nationalmagazine.ca/en-ca/articles/law/opinion/2021/justice-abella-the-voice-of-the-vulnerable.

7 *Daniels v Canada (Indian Affairs and Northern Development)*, 2016 SCC 12, [2016] 1 SCR 99 [*Daniels*].

8 *Newfoundland and Labrador (Attorney General) v Uashaunnuat (Innu of Uashat and Mani-Utenam)*, 2020 SCC 4 [*NL v Uashaunnuat*].

9 *R v Morris* 2006 SCC 59, [2006] 2 SCR 915 [*R v Morris*].

10 *Mikisew Cree First Nation v Canada (Governor General in Council)*, 2018 SCC 40, [2018] 2 SCR 765 [*Mikisew Cree First Nation*].

and Abella for the majority, the Court breathed life into the "meaningful diminution" framework for treaty infringements, suggesting that a *prima facie* infringement of treaty rights includes anything but an insignificant interference with that right.[11] This conceptualization of the infringement spectrum contributed significantly to the 2021 *Yahey v British Columbia* decision of the British Columbia Supreme Court that the Crown breached its duty to act honourably in diligently implementing the promises of Treaty 8.[12] Finally, in *NL v Uashaunnuat*, Justice Abella, writing for the majority, confirmed that the sui generis nature of Aboriginal rights means their interpretation cannot be confined by civil or common law principles of property law and "ownership." To do so would place undue burden and strain on Indigenous litigants, thereby limiting their access to justice, which ultimately results in a violation of the honour of the Crown.

This paper suggests that Justice Abella's decisions have held the Crown accountable for its overarching constitutional obligations through the recognition of positive duties attached to section 35 of the *Constitution Act 1982*, including the Crown's fiduciary duties, the duty of consultation and accommodation, the honour of the Crown, and the imperative of reconciliation. Practically, these duties have engaged the corresponding obligations to ensure Indigenous access to justice, engage consultation in the legislative context, and uphold and protect the right to Indigenous ways of life grounded in treaty relationships and rights.

B. Positive Duties Attached to Section 35 of the *Constitution Act 1982*

While the honour of the Crown was previously considered to be an interpretive principle used in the context of treaty interpretation litigation, the honour of the Crown was elevated during Justice Abella's time to a constitutional imperative, which that gives rise to obligations on the Crown that are enforced by the courts. According to the Court, the honour of the Crown is a principle that governs all the Crown's conduct in its dealings with Indigenous peoples. As an overarching constitutional duty, "the law assumes that the Crown always intends to fulfill its solemn promises, including constitutional obligations."[13]

11 *Ibid* at para 93.

12 *Yahey v British Columbia*, 2021 BCSC 1287 (CanLII), paras 77, 104, 484–85, and 528 [*Yahey*].

13 *Manitoba Métis Federation Inc v Canada (AG)*, 2013 SCC 14 at para 77 [2013] 1 SCR 623 [*Manitoba Métis Federation*]. See also Aimée Craft, "The Honour of the Crown and Hydroelectric Development in Manitoba" in Jill Blakley & Aimée Craft, eds, *"In*

The Supreme Court clarified the doctrine of the honour of the Crown and its scope in the *Manitoba Métis Federation* decision.[14] The Court stated that the honour of the Crown is integral to reconciliation and that the Crown must act honourably as it fulfills all promises made under section 35.[15] Furthermore, the Court affirmed that the honour of the Crown must guide the Crown's actions at all times during consultation, treaty interpretation, fulfillment of other constitutional obligations, and negotiation of claims.[16] Following the *Manitoba Métis Federation* reasoning, in *Daniels v Canada*, penned by Justice Abella for the majority, the Court addressed a long-standing struggle faced by Métis in Canada. The Court placed importance on Canada's commitment to reconciliation in this decision, writing that "reconciliation with *all* of Canada's Aboriginal peoples is Parliament's goal."[17] *Daniels* clarified the Métis and non-Status Indians are "Indians" for the purposes of section 91(24) of the *Constitution Act 1867*, as well as being "Indians" for the purposes of the *Indian Act*. Prior to this decision, federal and provincial governments both claimed they did not have jurisdiction when Métis would seek government support, funding, or assistance. Their requests would often fall victim to a "jurisdictional tug of war."[18] Justice Abella explained that it would be "constitutionally anomalous" if the Métis were to be excluded from the definition of "Indian" under section 91(24), as they would be the only Indigenous group to be included under section 35 grouping of "Aboriginal Peoples of Canada" but excluded under section 91(24).[19] She also highlighted inconsistencies in the Crown's historical application of section 91(24), emphasizing that the Crown had legislated over Métis out of convenience in the past and had subjected Métis to assimilative policies, including various *Indian Act* prohibitions, and sent Métis children to residential schools.[20] Justice Abella aimed to ensured that the federal government could not use the impacts of divisive identity policies to deny Métis inclusion under section 91(24).[21]

Our Backyard": The Legacy of the Keeyask Experience in Northern Manitoba (Winnipeg: University of Manitoba Press, 2022) 321.

14 *Manitoba Métis Federation*, paras 65–83.

15 *Ibid*, paras 68 and 78.

16 Craft, above note 4, citing *Haida Nation v British Columbia* (Minister of Forests), 2004 SCC 73, [2004] 3 SCR 511 at para 16 [*Haida Nation*].

17 *Ibid* at para 37.

18 *Daniels*, above note 7 at para 15.

19 *Ibid* at para 35.

20 *Ibid* at paras 30, 32 & 37.

21 Krista Nerland, "Supreme Court Says Federal Government Has Legislation Power of the Métis and Non-status Indians" *Olthuis Kleer Townshend LLP* (2016), online:

Furthermore, according to Justice Abella in *Daniels*, the fiduciary obligations owed to the Métis had already been settled in law. She decided not to grant the second declaration sought by the applicants, which declared that there was a fiduciary duty owed by the Crown to the Métis, because the declaration was merely "restating settled law" and therefore "lack[ed] practical utility."[22] According to Justice Abella, the declaration was unnecessary because jurisprudence from *Delgamuukw v British Columbia* and *Manitoba Metis Federation* had already established that the Crown has a fiduciary obligation to Indigenous peoples, including the Métis.

In addition to framing the larger concepts of the honour of the Crown and reconciliation, and affirming the fiduciary obligations of the Crown, Justice Abella expanded upon those principles in other cases to engage positive duties, including the duty of legislators to consult about where proposed laws would potentially impact constitutionally protected rights, although that view has yet to be endorsed by a majority of the Court.

C. The Duty to Consult on Proposed Legislation

In her *Mikisew Cree* minority opinion, Justice Abella stressed that if the government intends to enact legislation that could potentially affect section 35 rights, a duty to consult and accommodate will arise, and that this duty flows from the honour of the Crown.[23]

The origin of the *Mikisew Cree* claim stemmed from Parliament introducing two pieces of omnibus legislation[24] that amended Canada's environmental protection regime, prior to any consultation with Mikisew Cree First Nation (MCFN).[25] In response, MCFN brought an application for judicial review to the Federal Court, claiming they were owed a duty to consult before the legislation was enacted since the amendments could impact their Aboriginal and Treaty rights.[26] After a Federal Court of Appeal decision determined that ministerial actions in a

---

www.oktlaw.com/supreme-court-says-federal-government-legislative-power-metis-non-status-indians/.

22 *Daniels*, above note 7 at para 53.

23 *Mikisew Cree First Nation*, above note 10 at para 54.

24 Bill C-38 (enacted as the *Jobs, Growth and Long-term Prosperity Act*, SC 2012, c 19), which received royal assent in June 2012. Later that year, the Minister introduced Bill C-45 (enacted as the Jobs and Growth Act, 2012, SC 2012, c. 31), which received royal assent in December 2012.

25 *Mikisew Cree First Nation* above note 10 at paras 5–7.

26 *Ibid* at para 9.

legislative capacity are exempt from judicial review, MCFN appealed to the Supreme Court.[27] A majority of the Supreme Court dismissed the appeal, concluding that the doctrine was "ill-suited for legislative action"[28] and that parliamentary sovereignty, parliamentary privilege, and the separation of powers precluded the obligation to consult on proposed legislation, regardless of the potential impact of that legislation on Treaty and Aboriginal rights.

Justice Abella indicated that although parliamentary privilege and constitutional commitments to Parliamentary sovereignty "are central to ensuring that the legislative branch of government is able to do its work without undue interference, these concepts cannot displace the honour of the Crown."[29] Therefore, she held, consulting with Indigenous peoples where their constitutional rights are at stake was required. She explained that "the obligation arises because it would not be honourable to make important decisions that have an adverse impact on Aboriginal and treaty rights without efforts to consult, and if appropriate, accommodate those interests."[30] In Justice Abella's view, to suggest (as the majority did) that the duty to consult does not apply in the context of legislative decision-making is to say that the honour of the Crown does not extend to the legislative sphere:

> Endorsing such a void in the honour of the Crown would create a corresponding gap in the s.35 framework, leaving Aboriginal rights-holders vulnerable to the same government objectives carried out through legislation, rather than executive action.[31]

She also noted that the inherent flexibility embedded in the duty to consult doctrine could address issues within the legislative context. The triggering of a duty to consult would only occur where the Crown contemplates enacting legislation it knows could potentially impact an existing Aboriginal right. Depending on the extent to which it would potentially interfere with the right, it would be placed somewhere on the *Haida* spectrum of consultation, one end of which requires only basic notification and some discussion, while the other end requires in-depth

---

27 *Ibid* at para 11.

28 *Ibid* at para 32 in the judgment of Chief Justice Wagner and Justices Karakatsanis and Gascon.

29 *Ibid* at para 55.

30 *Ibid* at para 62.

31 *Ibid* at para 79.

accommodation or consent of a Nation.[32] Furthermore, Justice Abella stressed that a duty to consult challenge would not automatically invalidate the legislation in question.[33] Instead, applying the doctrine in the legislative context would encourage the federal and provincial Crowns to proactively consult Indigenous peoples on legislation that could potentially affect their rights, prior to infringements arising. Justice Abella noted that this distinguished this legislative application of the duty to consult from the *Sparrow* infringement and justification framework, thereby guaranteeing that all efforts would be made to ensure that infringements of constitutionally protected rights would not arise as a result of legislative action (or inaction).[34] If a majority were to adopt reasoning similar to Justice Abella's dissent in this case, it could lead to a broader application of the doctrine: all decisions being made by the Crown that may impact Aboriginal and treaty rights would engage a positive and proactive duty to consult.[35]

D. A Framework for Infringing Treaty Rights

At issue in the *R v Morris* case was whether the valid provincial legislation found in BC's *Wildlife Act*[36] preventing night hunting interfered with the Tsartlip First Nation's (TFN) right to hunt at night with illuminating devices.[37] Charges were laid against the appellants for violating sections 27(1)(d) and 29 of BC's *Wildlife Act*, which prevented hunting with a firearm during prohibited periods, as well as any form of dangerous hunting.[38] Writing for the majority, Justices Abella and Deschamps concluded that night hunting is a protected TFN treaty right since it recognizes that "the Saanich Nation would be 'at liberty to hunt over the unoccupied lands; and to carry on [their] fisheries as formerly.'"[39] The majority first considered whether the provisions of the *Wildlife Act* in question infringed TFN's treaty rights and then determined whether the impugned provisions were valid under the division of powers.[40] Regarding the dangerous hunting provision, the Court concluded that

32 *Ibid* at para 96.
33 *Ibid*.
34 *Ibid*.
35 *Ibid* at para 62.
36 *Wildlife* Act, SBC 1982, c 57.
37 *R v Morris* above note 9 at paras 1–4.
38 *Ibid* at para 6.
39 *Ibid* at para 2.
40 *Ibid* at paras 14–15.

"there is no treaty right to hunt dangerously."[41] Therefore, this second limit did not impair a treaty right. However, the Court did conclude that the broad prohibitions found in section 27 on night hunting went above what was necessary to regulate unsafe hunting and infringed TFN's treaty rights.[42]

In the decision, the Court examined the common law's treaty infringement framework as delineated in *Sparrow* and *Gladstone*.[43] The justices wrote that a *prima facie* infringement of a treaty right will require a "meaningful diminution" of the right, which "includes anything but an insignificant interference."[44] A year prior, the Court in *Mikisew Cree First Nation v Canada (Minister of Canadian Heritage)* interpreted treaty infringement differently, suggesting that a First Nation could demand a *Sparrow* justification if they retained "no meaningful right" to hunt over their traditional territories.[45] Therefore, the majority's conclusion in *Morris* indicated a notable development in treaty interpretation caselaw and confirmed that unlawful infringements can arise where there is a reduction in the ability to exercise the right, not only where the is no meaningful right remaining.

Following this line of reasoning, Justice Burke of the British Columbia Supreme Court, in the *Yahey v British Columbia* case, relied on the "meaningful diminution" standard set out in *Morris* and other treaty interpretation precedents to conceptualize treaty infringement as a spectrum.[46] In that case, a treaty-protected right to preserve Blueberry River First Nation's (BRFN) way of life was established and the meaningful diminution standard was applied. Justice Burke determined that "the focus of the infringement analysis — and consideration of whether 'no meaningful right remains' — should be on whether the treaty rights can be *meaningfully* exercised, not on whether the rights can be exercised *at all*."[47] Using this rationale, she concluded that the BRFN's treaty right to maintain their way of life had been infringed, since the members of the First Nation could not meaningfully exercise their rights due to the cumulative effects of development in Treaty 8.[48] Additionally, Justice

41 *Ibid* at para 14.

42 *Ibid*.

43 *Ibid* at paras 51–53.

44 *Ibid* at para 53.

45 *Mikisew Cree First Nation v Canada (Minister of Canadian Heritage)* 2005 SCC 69, [2005] 3 SCR 338 at para 48.

46 *Ibid* at para 485.

47 *Ibid* at para 540.

48 *Ibid* at paras 657, 1116 & 1117.

Burke established that by failing to implement the treaty promise, the province violated the honour of the Crown, holding the Crown to a high standard when it comes to the management of cumulative effects and the diligent implementation of treaty promises.[49]

While the honour of the Crown requires that infringements of treaty rights be held to a high level of scrutiny, the process of challenging breaches through litigation has proven to be costly, lengthy and risk laden. According to Justice Abella's view, the honour of the Crown, coupled with the imperative of reconciliation, requires facilitating access to justice issues for Indigenous litigants.

E. The Honour of the Crown Requires Access to Justice

The 2020 *Newfoundland and Labrador (Attorney General) v Uashaunnuat* decision suggested that a positive duty or function of the honour of the Crown includes facilitating access to justice for Indigenous litigants.[50] The majority saw this decision as an opportunity to rely on the imperatives of reconciliation and the honour of the Crown to ensure access to justice for Indigenous peoples.[51]

The Innu of Uashat, of Mani-Utenam, and of Matikmekush-Lac John all occupy the Nitassinan, their traditional territory that straddles the Quebec-Labrador border. The IOC Megaproject resulted in numerous open-pit mines in the Nitassinan region, which the Innu respondents claimed were constructed without their consent and infringed their rights to use and enjoy their territory as they have since time immemorial.[52] The mining companies claimed the action was outside of the jurisdiction of Quebec courts, given that part of the claim concerned "real rights over property situated in Newfoundland and Labrador (NL)."[53] The Attorney General for NL agreed with the companies and appealed the Superior Court and the Quebec Court of Appeal decision. Both of those decisions dismissed the motion to strike, finding that Quebec was the proper jurisdiction to hear the claims of the Innu in this case.[54]

The Supreme Court of Canada reversed the Québec Court of Appeal decision in a joint decision by Justice Abella, Chief Justice Wagner, and Justice Karakatsanis for the majority. They stressed the importance of

49 *Ibid* at paras 1779 and 1786.

50 *NL v Uashaunnuat*, above note 8 at paras 51–52.

51 *Ibid* at para 23.

52 *Ibid* at para 6.

53 *Ibid* at paras 9 and 10.

54 *Ibid* at paras 12–13.

the honour of the Crown in protecting section 35 rights and explained that "whether we are dealing with the assertion of sovereignty or the resolution of rights or title claims, the honour of the Crown is always at stake."[55] The majority linked the honour of the Crown to access to justice, finding that it is not only inequitable to make Indigenous applicants litigate a dispute in multiple jurisdictions, but it also violates the honour of the Crown because it places undue strain and financial burden on Indigenous applicants, hence restricting their access to justice.[56] Justice Abella drew on the *Trial Lawyers Association of British Columbia v British Columbia (Attorney General)* framework, which affirms that "access to justice is fundamental to the rule of law."[57] The Court took this point and coupled it with the Crown's fiduciary obligation to Indigenous peoples and its obligation to fulfill its duties honourably. In their view, it requires flexible interpretation of jurisdictional rules; otherwise, it could prevent Indigenous Peoples from being able to assert their constitutional rights, thereby "undermin[ing] the twin constitutional imperatives" of the honour of the Crown and access to justice.[58]

F. Conclusion

Early cases in Canadian Aboriginal law employed the term "reconciliation" in the context of reconciling Indigenous interests and rights against the broader objectives of Canadian society. This impoverished view of reconciliation effectively froze Indigenous rights, thought, and practice in time and claimed to justify Crown infringements of Aboriginal and treaty rights.[59] It left Indigenous peoples in a position of doing the reconciling alone. Earlier cases did not apply reconciliation in the context of a "mutually respectful relationship," whereas in *Daniels*, Justice Abella found mutual respect to be imperative to advancing the Crown-Indigenous relationship in Canada.

While it was extremely difficult to choose just four of Justice Abella's decisions to examine, the ones outlined demonstrate her commitment

55 *Ibid* at para 22.

56 *NL v Uashaunnuat*, above note 8 at para 52.

57 *Ibid* at para 47, citing *Trial Lawyers Association of British Columbia v British Columbia (Attorney General)*, 2014 SCC 59, [2014] 3 SCR 31 at para 39 [*Trial Lawyers*].

58 *NL v Uashaunnuat*, above note 8 paras 50 and 52.

59 See Craft, Aimée, "Neither Infringement nor Justification — The SCC's Mistaken Approach to Reconciliation" in B. Gunn and K. Drake, eds, *Renewing Relationships: Indigenous Peoples and Canada* (University of Saskatchewan Native Law Centre, 2019) 59.

to a more robust constitutional interpretation of section 35. As colleagues in this volume have pointed out, Justice Abella's contributions to the common law in Canada are numerous, and her commitment to equity, equality, and social justice has become a defining aspect of her jurisprudential legacy. Justice Abella's judgements have addressed fundamental principles, including Indigenous access to justice, the sui generis nature of Aboriginal rights, application of the duty to consult, equality rights for Indigenous people, and the importance of reconciliation based on mutual respect. She has recognized how the interpretation and application of law "can either make life easier or harder for people"[60] and has reminded the public that "we're far from resolving the consequences of our frequently shameful and misguided treatment of Indigenous people."[61]

Justice Abella has interpreted Canadian Aboriginal law principles in a way that advances the rights of Indigenous people while continuously holding the Crown accountable to its duty to act honorably. Her decision-making has emphasized reconciliation in a way that strengthens the relationship between the common law and Indigenous legal traditions. By doing so, Justice Abella has countered some of the "legal fictions" that have historically dominated the common law system, making that system inaccessible for Indigenous peoples. Justice Abella's legacy is apparent across Canada's legal landscape, and this area is no exception: she helped to breathe life into Canadian Aboriginal law by setting the stage for the pursuit of both redress in the Crown's relationship with Indigenous Peoples in Canada and a form of reconciliation born out of mutual respect.

60 Sean Fine, "How Rosalie Abella's Personal History Shaped her Legal Legacy" *The Globe and Mail* (26 June 2021), online: www.theglobeandmail.com/canada/article-how-rosalie-abellas-personal-history-shaped-her-legal-legacy/.

61 Joseph Mathieu, "Justice Abella Cites Work Undone with Indigenous Peoples, Minorities, and the Poor" *Carleton Newsroom* (11 December 2017), online: https://newsroom.carleton.ca/archives/2017/12/11/justice-abella-cites-work-undone-with-indigenous-peoples-minorities-and-the-poor/.

PART 3

Justice Abella's Jurisprudence — Labour and Employment Law

12 Dignity at Work in Justice Abella's Jurisprudence: Recognizing Worker Vulnerability and Power Imbalance

COLLEEN BAUMAN*

A. Introduction

In *Saskatchewan Federation of Labour v Saskatchewan*, a foundational and transformative decision from the Supreme Court of Canada on the constitutional right to strike, Justice Abella held that "collective action at the moment of impasse is an affirmation of the dignity and autonomy of employees in their working lives." She added that collective action "promotes equality in the bargaining process" and works to address "the deep inequalities that structure the relationship between employers and employees, and the vulnerability of employees in this context."[1] These themes of enhancing dignity at work, on the one hand, while recognizing the vulnerability of workers and the imbalance of power between employers and employees on the other, provide a useful lens through which to review Justice Abella's jurisprudence on the law of work in all its many facets.

Within labour law in cases such as *SFL* and *Ontario (Attorney General) v Fraser*,[2] these themes have played a central role in the evolution of Justice Abella's section 2(d) *Charter* jurisprudence. In this respect, she can be seen as the inheritor of Chief Justice Brian Dickson's legacy.[3] These

---

* Colleen Bauman is a Partner at Goldblatt Partners LLP where she practices union-side labour law and constitutional and administrative law. Special thanks to Seema Shafei for her invaluable research assistance in preparing this article and for her helpful and insightful edits. Thank you also to Husna Sarwar for her edits and comments.

1 *Saskatchewan Federation of Labour v Saskatchewan*, 2015 SCC 4 at paras 54–55 [*SFL*].

2 *Ontario (Attorney General) v Fraser*, 2011 SCC 20 [*Fraser I*].

3 *Reference Re Public Service Employee Relations Act (Alta)*, [1987] 1 SCR 313 at 368 [*Alberta Reference*].

themes of respecting the dignity of work in light of worker vulnerability also play a prominent role in her employment law jurisprudence, in cases such *Evans v Teamsters Local Union No 31*[4] and *Wilson v Atomic Energy of Canada Ltd*.[5] These cases make room for the potential of law to protect the dignity of workers in the face of unequal bargaining power, even within the context of individual employment contracts. Similarly, the contract law case *Uber Technologies Inc v Heller*[6] examined the rights of "gig workers" who are amongst the most precarious workers in the contemporary economy. Justice Abella's recognition of the glaring inequality of bargaining power between the gig workers and Uber was key to finding the contract in question unconscionable. These themes can also be found in her work on equality, much of which has been focused on helping employees achieve equity in their workplaces, including her seminal *Report on the Commission on Equality in Employment*[7] and decisions such as *Quebec (Attorney General) v Alliance du personnel professionnel et technique de la santé et des services sociaux*[8] and *Fraser v Canada (Attorney General)*.[9]

Justice Abella has actively used her decisions to redress the imbalance of power between workers and their employers. Her decisions and writings have provided us with strong language to advocate for those seeking to confront the vulnerable position of workers, particularly those who are marginalized or precariously employed. Throughout her jurisprudence, she laid a foundation for the future of law to appropriately address the everchanging economic hardships and realities of workers today.

B. Dignity, Vulnerability, and Power at Work

The notions of dignity at work, the vulnerability of workers, and the inherent imbalance of power in the employment relationship are of course not novel but rather foundational to labour rights both in Canada and internationally. For example, in its 1948 *Declaration concerning the aims and purposes of the International Labour Organisation*, the International Labour Organization [ILO] recognized the fundamental right of all people to "to pursue both their material well-being and

4 *Evans v Teamsters Local Union No 31*, 2008 SCC 20 [*Evans*].

5 *Wilson v Atomic Energy of Canada Ltd*, 2016 SCC 29 [*Wilson*].

6 *Uber Technologies Inc v Heller*, 2020 SCC 16 [*Uber*].

7 Rosalie Silberman Abella, *Report of the Commission on Equality in Employment*, Supply and Services Canada, Ottawa, 1984 [Abella Report].

8 *Quebec (Attorney General) v Alliance du personnel professionnel et technique de la santé et des services sociaux*, 2018 SCC 17 [*Alliance*].

9 *Fraser v Canada (Attorney General)*, 2020 SCC 28 [*Fraser II*].

their spiritual development in conditions of freedom and dignity, of economic security and equal opportunity."[10] More recently, the ILO's 1998 *Declaration of Fundamental Principles and Rights at Work* identifies fundamental rights at work, including the right to collective bargaining, as "go[ing] to the essence of human dignity at work, touching upon bedrock values of freedom and equality."[11]

Indeed, as emphasized by the academic Sharon Bolton, "the concept of dignity lies at the heart of the study of work." In her view, dignity at work encompasses "structures and practices that offer equality of opportunity, collective and individual voice, safe and healthy working conditions, secure terms of employments and just rewards."[12] Beyond being a human characteristic, dignity is realized through organizational structures and practices. It is via work that "most of us secure much of our self-respect and self-esteem" and the "integrity of our identities."[13]

On the other side of the equation, some of the barriers to achieving dignity at work include both the inequality of bargaining power between workers and their employers and, frequently, the vulnerability of workers, particularly those who find themselves in precarious or non-standard employment. As explained by David Beatty, from an economic perspective, "the essence of bargaining power lies . . . in one's ability to withhold or deny something of value to another," which, in the context of the individual employment contract, results in a "dramatic imbalance in the equivalence of the exchange and the resulting bargaining powers of the participants."[14] Of course, the desire to remedy this imbalance has led to the enactment of various statutory regimes to govern collective bargaining "as a means of restoring the consensual root of the employment relationship."[15] In the North American context, this has meant the *Wagner Act* model of collective bargaining, which Brian Langille has described as "shift[ing] away from the common law narrative of freedom of contract to the narrative of correcting for inequality of

10 International Labor Organization, "Declaration and Resolution (Selected) of the International Labor Conference" (1944) 38:4 *American Journal International Law* 203 at 203–16.

11 Anne Trebilcock, "The ILO Declaration on Fundamental Principles and Rights at Work: A New Tool" in Roger Blanpain & Chris Engels, eds, *The ILO and Social Challenges of the 21st Century: The Geneva Lectures* (The Hague: Kluwer, 2001) 105 at 107.

12 Sharon Bolton "Dignity in and at Work: Why it Matters" in Sharon Bolton, ed, *Dimensions of Dignity at Work* (Amsterdam: Elsevier, 2007) 3 at 8–9.

13 David Beatty, "Labour is not a Commodity" in Barry J. Reiter and John Swan, eds, *Studies in Contract Law* (Toronto: Butterworths, 1980) 314 at 324–25.

14 *Ibid.*

15 *Ibid* at 336.

bargaining power." This model resulted in a new distribution of rights, obliterating those at common law.[16]

However, while the collective bargaining model is an essential means of redressing the imbalance of power in the employment context, it is also a very limited tool that benefits only those employees who are unionized. For non-unionized employees, factors such as "[Employment Insurance] reforms, the NAFTA agreement, the behavior of the minimum wage, the unemployment rate, and [declining] unionization," among others, have in fact "eroded worker bargaining power, thereby diminishing workers' ability to secure wage gains in tandem with productivity growth."[17]

Indeed, evidence of growing income inequality and worker vulnerability is not hard to find, particularly with the rise of precarious employment in recent years. As recognized by the Ontario *Changing Workplace Review*, the forms of precarious employment are many and include not only "a temporary worker, or a part-time worker who wants a full-time job but is working in a minimum wage or low-aid job without a pension or benefits," but also those who may technically be in "standard employment," such as "a low-paid employee, earning somewhat above minimum wage in a full-time job without a pension or benefits" or "a single mother who works part-time for low wages without a pension or benefits because she cannot work full-time due to her child care responsibilities." These workers experience precarity and "real vulnerability" daily.[18] Troublingly, there is also a gender-based and racialized dimension to this precarity and vulnerability in the labour market.[19]

As can be seen in Justice Abella's labour, employment and workplace equality jurisprudence discussed below, she has been alive to the vulnerability, precarity, and relative powerlessness of workers in these contexts, seeking to use the law to provide redress and to achieve dignity at work for all employees. While the expansive approach adopted by the

16 Brian Langille, "The Condescending Constitution (or, The Purpose of Freedom of Association is Freedom of Association)" (2016) 19 *Canadian Labour and Employment Law Journal* 335 at 346.

17 Mathieu Dufour & Ellen Russell, "Why Isn't Productivity More Popular? A Bargaining Power Approach to the Pay/Productivity Linkage in Canada" (2015) 28 *International Productivity Monitor* 47 at 61.

18 C. Michael Mitchell & John C. Murray, *Changing Workplaces Review* (Ontario: Ontario Ministry of Labour, 2017) at 6–7.

19 See Ron Saunders, "Defining Vulnerability in the Labour Market" (2003) *Canadian Policy Research Networks Incorporated*, Research Paper W-21; Nicole S. Bernhardt, "Racialized Precarious Employment and the Inadequacies of the Canadian Welfare State" (2015) *Journal of Workplace Rights* 1 at 1–13.

Court to the freedom of association under section 2(d) of the *Charter* has provided fruitful ground for achieving workplace dignity in unionized workplaces, she has similarly sought to use employment law, contract law, and equality principles to address worker vulnerability in non-unionized environments.

C. Labour Law Jurisprudence

In Justice Abella's labour and section 2(d) *Charter* jurisprudence, these goals of equality of bargaining power and dignity at work are given full bloom. Indeed, the Court's freedom of association jurisprudence is now firmly rooted in the vocabulary of empowering the vulnerable and marginalized to address power imbalances.[20] In many ways, her decision in *SFL* marks the culmination of the Court's section 2(d) jurisprudence evolution. Giving the right to collectively bargain a meaningful enforcement mechanism with the recognition of the right to strike shifted the balance of power between employer and employee.

To understand the transformative impact of the decision in *SFL*, it is necessary to look back at the Supreme Court's first labour trilogy, which interestingly was decided at the same time Justice Abella served as the Chair of the Ontario Labour Relations Board. With the enactment of the *Charter* in 1982, the first section 2(d) challenges had wended their way up to the Supreme Court by 1987. Although labour rights advocates had high hopes for a robust and meaningful interpretation of freedom of association rights from the start, the decisions of the majority frequently took a "legalistic, ungenerous, [and] indeed vapid"[21] approach to section 2(d).

In contrast, Chief Justice Dickson, in dissent in the *Alberta Reference*, offered an expansive vision for the freedom of association in section 2(d), one that was grounded in international law[22] and an understanding of labour relations history, where "workers have combined to overcome the inherent inequalities of bargaining power in the employment relationship and to protect themselves from unfair, unsafe, or exploitative working conditions."[23] Notably, his interpretation of section 2(d) also recognized the fundamental importance of work to one's "sense of identity, selfworth," "emotional wellbeing," and

20 Jennifer Koshan, "Inequality and Identity at Work" (2015) 38:2 *Dalhousie Law Journal* 473 at 493.

21 Chief Justice Dickson in *Alberta Reference*, above note 3 at para 81.

22 *Ibid* at paras 57–72.

23 *Ibid* at para 23.

personal dignity, as well as the role that association plays in workers' ability to overcome their vulnerability as individuals in order to achieve "fair wages, health and safety protections, and equitable and humane working conditions."[24] Seen in this light, Chief Justice Dickson held that the provisions of the Alberta *Public Service Act*, which prohibited strikes, infringed section 2(d) of the *Charter*.

It was Chief Justice Dickson's mantle that Justice Abella and the majority of the Supreme Court were to pick up almost thirty years later in second labour trilogy, which overturned the previous trilogy and expanded upon Dickson's dissent. The groundwork for the new trilogy had been previously laid in *Health Services and Support-Facilities Subsector Bargaining Association v British Columbia*,[25] in which a majority of the Supreme Court, including Justice Abella, held that collective bargaining was protected under section 2(d) of the *Charter*, thereby giving meaning to labour rights as human rights. Following Chief Justice Dickson, the majority recognized that the values of "human dignity, equality, liberty, respect for the autonomy of the person and the enhancement of democracy" complemented and promoted the protection of collective bargaining by giving workers "the opportunity to influence the establishment of workplace rules and thereby gain some control over a major aspect of their lives, namely their work."[26]

The first decision in the new trilogy was *Mounted Police Association of Ontario v Canada (Attorney General) (MPAO)*,[27] a challenge under section 2(d) of the *Charter* to federal legislation that prevented Royal Canadian Mounted Police (RCMP) members from unionizing or engaging in collective bargaining. In the *MPAO* decision, a majority of the Supreme Court held that this legislation was unconstitutional. Building on the Dickson dissent and *BC Health Services*, the majority's decision again recognized that vulnerable groups, by associating with each other, are empowered "to right imbalances in society," which in turn "protects marginalized groups and makes possible a more equal society."[28]

The second decision in the new labour trilogy was *Meredith v Canada (Attorney General)*,[29] a constitutional challenge to the federal govern-

24 *Ibid* at paras 91–92.

25 *Health Services and Support-Facilities Subsector Bargaining Association v British Columbia*, 2007 SCC 27 [*BC Health Services*].

26 *Ibid* at paras 81–82.

27 *Mounted Police Association of Ontario v Canada (Attorney General)*, 2015 SCC 1 [*MPAO*].

28 *Ibid* at para 58.

29 *Meredith v Canada (Attorney General)*, 2015 SCC 2 [*Meredith*].

ment's *Expenditure Restraint Act*,[30] which imposed a 1.5 percent cap on wage increases in the public sector from 2008 to 2010 and resulted in negotiated and scheduled wage increases for RCMP members being rolled back without prior consultation. While the majority of the Court found these wage restraint measures constitutional, Justice Abella, writing in dissent, disagreed. In particular, she found that the lack of meaningful consultation with RCMP members about the unilateral wage rollbacks constituted an unjustified infringement of section 2(d). In particular, she noted that "[e]nsuring fair wages is among the key purposes of collective bargaining" and that, as held by Chief Justice Dickson in dissent in *Alberta Reference*, collective bargaining allowed workers associating together to negotiate with their employers on a more level playing field:[31]

> Throughout history, workers have associated to overcome their vulnerability as individuals to the strength of their employers. The capacity to bargain collectively has long been recognized as one of the integral and primary functions of associations of working people. While trade unions also fulfil other important social, political and charitable functions, *collective bargaining remains vital to the capacity of individual employees to participate in ensuring fair wages, health and safety protections, and equitable and humane working conditions.*

The culmination of the Court's section 2(d) jurisprudence evolution was Justice Abella's decision in *SFL*, which constitutionalized the right to strike, the "powerhouse" of collective bargaining,[32] providing workers with a meaningful mechanism to shift the balance of power in the employment relationship. With this decision, she gave full meaning to the promise of the Dickson dissent in the *Alberta Reference*, finding that the right to strike is an indispensable component of the right to collective bargaining. As such, the right to strike was constitutionally protected under section 2(d). Like Chief Justice Dickson, Justice Abella grounded her decision in international law and labour history, recognizing that the right to strike is an "affirmation of the dignity and autonomy of employees in their working lives" that "promotes equality in the bargaining process."[33] Rejecting the false equivalence between employer and employee relied upon by the minority, she emphasized "the deep

---

30 *Expenditure Restraint Act*, SC 2009, c 2, s 393 [*ERA*].

31 *Meredith*, above note 29 at para 53.

32 *SFL*, above note 1 at para 55.

33 *Ibid* at paras 54–55.

inequalities that structure the relationship between employers and employees, and the vulnerability of employees in this context," noting the "fundamental power imbalance which the entire history of modern labour legislation has been scrupulously devoted to rectifying" and that the value of the strike is that it permits employees "to engage in negotiations with an employer on a more equal footing."[34] Thus, this recognition of the imbalance of power and worker vulnerability on the one hand and a desire to affirm dignity at work on the other are central to the recognition of the right to strike as deserving of constitutional protection.

This desire to address the structural inequalities in employment relationships for vulnerable workers is also apparent in Justice Abella's dissent in *Ontario (Attorney General) v Fraser*,[35] a case involving the rights of some of the most marginalized of workers: farm workers, most of whom are migrants. For these workers, their precarious immigration status puts them at significant risk, not only for the violation of their labour rights but also for the loss of their jobs and immigration status whenever they seek to assert their labour rights.[36]

Fraser I involved a challenge to the Ontario *Agricultural Employee Protection Act (AEPA)*,[37] which was enacted in response to *Dunmore v Ontario (AG)*,[38] where the Supreme Court found that the exclusion of farm workers from Ontario's *Labour Relations Act* violated section 2(d) of the *Charter*. Problematically, the *AEPA* provided agricultural workers only with a right to make "collective representations" to their employer and did not include any requirement for the employer to bargain in good faith with the workers or any provision for a meaningful dispute resolution mechanism. As a result, the statutory labour regime applicable to the most vulnerable and marginalized of workers was effectively toothless. While the majority found, in a pre-*MPAO* decision, that these very minimal *AEPA* provisions satisfied the requirements of section 2(d) because they allowed for "dialogue" between the employer and employees, Justice Abella rejected such an impoverished view of the freedom of association and the protection provided by section 2(d).

34 *Ibid* at paras 54–57.

35 *Fraser I*, above note 2.

36 Jill Hanley et al, "Protecting the Rights of Migrant Farmworkers in Quebec: To What Extent Can Unionization Overcome the Effects of Precarious Immigration Status?" (2020) 15:2 *Journal Rural & Community Development* 122 at 126.

37 *Agricultural Employees Protection Act*, SO 2002, c 16 [*AEPA*].

38 *Dunmore v Ontario (AG)*, 2001 SCC 94 [*Dunmore*].

In her dissent in *Fraser I*, Justice Abella J noted that the *AEPA* lacked any of the section 2(d) linguistic markers established by the Court in *BC Health Services*, including terms such as negotiate, meet, good faith, engage, exchange, dialogue, consultation, discussions, consideration, accommodation, union, or bargaining.[39] Furthermore, though the *AEPA* had been enacted nine years earlier, there was no evidence of any negotiations, let alone a successfully negotiated collective agreement. In addition, she found the lack of statutory protection for majoritarian exclusivity — which is the routine model for labour statutes in Canada — particularly troubling given the extreme vulnerability of agricultural workers, who are "among the most economically exploited and politically neutralized individuals in our society."[40] In Justice Abella's view, allowing for multiple representatives instead of exclusive representation effectively nullified the ability of already marginalized farmworkers to have a "unified and . . . cogent voice in attempting to mitigate and ameliorate their relentlessly arduous working conditions."[41] While innovative labour relations models were possible under section 2(d), "eliminating a fundamental protection for the most vulnerable of workers is nullification, not innovation."[42]

As reflected by both her seminal decision in *SFL* and her dissent in *Fraser I*, Justice Abella's vision for labour rights in the *Charter* has continuously been grounded in a recognition of worker vulnerability and the inherent imbalance of power between workers and their employers. Her decisions have sought to level the playing field so that the structures and practices that can make the attainment of dignity at work a reality can flourish.

D. Employment Law Jurisprudence

These same themes of vulnerability, inequality of bargaining power, and the importance of workplace dignity are not restricted just to Justice Abella's labour law jurisprudence, where they have a long and extensive history, but can also be seen in her decisions in the employment law context. Historically, employment contract law has been understandably criticized as being "incapable of regulating the personal work relationship to protect the worker's dignity in circumstances of unequal bargaining power," in contrast to labour law with its accompanying statutory regulation of workplace relationships, which has been seen

39 *Fraser I*, above note 2 at para 330.
40 *Ibid* at paras 343–49.
41 *Ibid* at para 350.
42 *Ibid* at para 351.

as *the* means to truly address the inequality of power inherent in the individual relationship of employment.[43] However, even in the context of private contracts of employment, Justice Abella has sought to use the law to address bargaining power inequality and worker vulnerability.

Her dissent in *Evans v Teamsters Local Union No 31* is an example of this approach. This case involved an individual employee's duty to mitigate[44] when he was terminated after twenty-one years of employment. The employee, Evans, was subsequently offered a term-limited contract by the same employer. The majority of the Court found that by rejecting the term contract, the employee had failed to mitigate.

Justice Abella, in a strongly worded dissent, disagreed, holding that there was no question that it was the employer who had breached the contract of employment and was at fault for dismissing Evans without cause or notice. In her view, the majority decision had wrongly focussed on the employee's obligations to his former employer, instead of focussing on the employer's breach of contract. As well, she held that the majority was wrong to have found no difference between terminating an employee with sufficient notice, which is not a breach of contract, and terminating an employee without notice but then subsequently offering a new limited term contract of employment. Rather than viewing this situation strictly through the formalistic lens of contract law, she again relies on the themes of worker vulnerability, inherent lack of bargaining power, and the importance of work to self-identity, ultimately finding that these two situations are not analogous, thereby rejecting the approach of the majority. As she explained:

> [E]mployment contracts [are] a unique subset of contracts marked by an inherent imbalance of bargaining power, making the wholesale, uncritical acceptance of principles from contract law inappropriate.
>
> Because of the inherent imbalance in bargaining power, the central role that work plays in the individual's sense of identity, and the recognition that "[t]he point at which the employment relationship ruptures is the time when the employee is most vulnerable and hence, most in need of protection", this Court has sought to "encourage conduct that minimizes the damage and dislocation (both economic and personal)" inherent in the termination of employment.[45]

43 Alan Bogg, "Labour Law Is a Subset of Employment Law" Revisited (2020) 43:2 *Dalhousie Law Journal* 479 at 481.

44 In employment law, the duty to mitigate is the legal principle that requires one to take reasonable steps to find alternative employment in order to limit losses post-dismissal.

45 *Evans*, above note 4 at paras 96–97.

This desire to provide meaningful protections to non-unionized employees when they are terminated and when they are most vulnerable also animates her majority decision on the merits in *Wilson v Atomic Energy of Canada Ltd.* At issue in this case was whether section 240 of the *Canada Labour Code* provided "unjust dismissal" protection to federally regulated non-unionized employees, or whether those employees could instead be dismissed without cause but with reasonable notice. Looking to the legislative history of the provision, Justice Abella held that the entire purpose of the statutory scheme was "to ensure that non-unionized federal employees would be entitled to protection from being dismissed without cause" and that to only provide notice instead would "completely undermin[e] this purpose by permitting employers, at their option, to deprive employees of the full remedial package Parliament created for them."[46] In addition, she found that the remedies for terminated employees under the *Code* in fact "reflect[ed] those generally available in the collective bargaining context" and that reinstatement was "utterly inconsistent with the right to dismiss without cause." Notably, she held that a more restrictive common law regime cannot take precedence over a contradicting benefit-granting statutory regime.[47]

While technically a contract law case, the rights and vulnerabilities of non-unionized gig workers were at the heart of the Supreme Court's decision in *Uber v Heller*.[48] How to provide meaningful employment rights for precarious low-wage workers in the gig economy is one of the most challenging contemporary problems facing labour advocates today. According to the 2016 census data, 8 percent of Canadians are now engaged in some form of gig work. At the same time, there has been increasing demand for protections for gig workers amidst a growing recognition of the "often-exploitative nature of precarious gig work."[49]

Uber started with a class action brought on behalf of Uber drivers claiming the right to be paid the minimum wage, as well as other minimum statutory employment standards such as overtime and vacation pay. Class actions have increasingly become an effective legal means to enforce minimum labour standard protection for non-unionized

46 *Wilson*, above note 5 at para 39.

47 *Ibid* at paras 63 and 67.

48 *Uber*, above note 6.

49 Laura Lam & Kam Phung Lam, "How Should Canada Design Policies to Protect Gig Workers?" *Policy Options* (27 September 2021), online: https://policyoptions.irpp.org/magazines/septembe-2021/how-should-canada-design-policies-to-protect-gig-workers/.

employees who have been unable to access the benefits of unionization.[50] In this case, however, when the representative plaintiff began work for Uber, he had to sign a standard form agreement, which contained an arbitration clause requiring disputes to be resolved through arbitration in the Netherlands. Thus, at issue before the Supreme Court was whether this clause was either enforceable or unconscionable and invalid.

In applying the unconscionability doctrine, the vulnerability and lack of bargaining power for these precariously employed workers was again a key factor in the majority decision, jointly written by Justices Abella and Rowe. Rejecting Uber's arguments for a more stringent four-part test, they accepted that the doctrine of unconscionability requires showing both an inequality of bargaining power and a resulting improvident bargain, explaining that a "bargain is improvident if it unduly advantages the stronger party or unduly disadvantages the more vulnerable."[51] Moreover, they explained that there was no need to have "proof that the stronger party knowingly took advantage of the weaker" to establish unconscionability.[52]

Applying these principles to Mr. Heller's situation, they noted the "significant gulf in sophistication between Mr. Heller, a food deliveryman in Toronto, and Uber, a large multinational corporation," finding in particular that he was "powerless to negotiate any of [the contract's] terms" and that "the arbitration clause makes the substantive rights given by the contract unenforceable by a driver against Uber."[53] Thus, by refusing to enforce the clause, the majority recognized the inherent vulnerability and lack of bargaining power of these workers, thereby allowing them to continue with their class action, where arguments about their employment status and right to employment standards protections will be front and center. While the decision is a notable step forward for the rights of precarious workers, much work remains to be done on this front since, as Patricia Hughes notes, their situation "often leaves them . . . outside the legal and human rights protections afforded Canadian workers who enjoy 'standard employment'" and "remains part of the unfinished business of Canadian substantive equality policy."[54]

---

50 Louis Sokolov & Colleen Bauman, "Common Cause: Employment-related Class Actions in Canada" (2011) 53 *Supreme Court Law Review* 249 at 250.

51 *Uber*, above note 6 at para 74.

52 *Ibid* at para 84.

53 *Ibid* at paras 93–95.

54 Patricia Hughes, "Remedying the Experiences of Vulnerable Workers: Links with Employment Equity" in Carol Agocs, ed, *Employment Equity in Canada: The*

E. Employment Equality Jurisprudence

Much of Justice Abella's equality jurisprudence and writing has been focused on the world of work and helping individuals to achieve dignity at work. In the face of the inherent vulnerability of many workers, she has recognized the need for systemic changes in order to achieve equality in employment.

In her landmark *Equality in Employment* Report, which has had an immeasurable impact on the development of human rights and employment law and policy, Justice Abella addressed inequality in employment on the basis of gender, visible minority status, disability, and Indigenous identity. Calling her task a "process of redistributive justice," she found that to "create equality of opportunity, we have to do different things for different people" and that we "have to systematically eradicate the impediments to these options according to the actual needs of the different groups, not according to what we think their needs should be."[55] This principle of treating different people in accordance with their differences is now recognized as an essential part of equality rights. In practice, it requires "identifying the specific barriers affecting particular groups and implementing policies and practices that apply to their specific needs," and in the circumstances of vulnerable workers, it "necessitates exploring the approaches that work for each group."[56] As discussed by Brian Langille in his chapter in this collection, equality under the law requires a "good, i.e., rational, reason for treating people differently" if the law is to speak "rationality to power."[57]

Recognizing this fact, Justice Abella called in her report for systemic remedies, which acknowledge "that by and large the systems and practices we customarily and often unwittingly adopt may have an unjustifiably negative effect on certain groups in society,"[58] and for the implementation of programs for affirmative action, which will benefit affected individuals by "providing dignity."[59] Addressing themes that would reappear in her Supreme Court jurisprudence in cases such as *Alliance*, she unequivocally emphasized that "[e]qual pay is an integral

Legacy of the Abella Report (Toronto: University of Toronto Press, 2018) 176 at 177 [*Hughes*].

55 Abella Report, above note 7 at 4.

56 Hughes, above note 54 at 189–90.

57 Brian Langille, chapter 13 in this volume 236.

58 Abella Report, above note 7 at 9.

59 *Ibid* at 18.

element in the implementation of employment equity" and "must be included in any undertaking by employers to make the practices in the workplace more equitable." Indeed, it is this recognition that governments must be proactive in remedying inequality that underlies much of pay equity legislation.[60] Similarly, in her Report, she noted that the long-term negative impact that precarious part-time work can have on benefits such as pensions "increases the vulnerability of women,"[61] because women are over-represented in this area. This is a theme she would later return to in *Fraser II*.

In *Alliance*, Abella the judge was given the opportunity to examine in detail the very type of systemic remedial program that she had called for in her *Equality in Employment* Report. In *Alliance*, however, she found the way it had been implemented served to exacerbate rather than address the discriminatory treatment it was designed to remedy, as it condoned rather than rectified the power imbalance between employer and employee.

At issue in *Alliance* was Quebec's *Pay Equity Act*,[62] which was amended in 2009 to remove the continuous obligation on employers to make pay equity adjustments to wages. It replaced it with pay equity audits, which would be conducted every five years and removed any obligation on the employer to pay retroactive employee compensation, unless the employer acted in bad faith, arbitrarily, or with discrimination. It was these amendments that were challenged by a number of unions as being contrary to section 15.

Writing for the majority, Justice Abella found that the amendments were contrary to section 15(1) of the *Charter*, were not protected by section 15(2), which applies to ameliorative programs, and were not justified under section 1. In particular, she held that the amendment scheme served to codify systemic discrimination by undervaluing the claimants' work and privileging the employer, furthering the power imbalance between them, which she described as "one of the key drivers of pay inequity."[63] As she explains:

> Although the scheme purports to address systemic discrimination, it in fact codifies the denial to women of benefits routinely enjoyed by men — namely, compensation tied to the value of their work. Men receive this compensation as a matter of course; women, under this scheme,

60 Hughes, above note 54 at 188.

61 Abella Report, above note 7 at 175.

62 *Pay Equity Act*, RSQ 1996 c 43.

63 *Alliance*, above note 8 at para 38.

> are expected to endure five-year periods of pay inequity, and to receive equal compensation only where their employer voluntarily acts in a non-discriminatory manner, or where they can meet the heavy burden of proving the employer engaged in deliberate or improper conduct. The scheme thus places barriers along the path to equal pay for women. And it correspondingly tolerates undervaluation of women's work whenever women cannot clear the specific hurdle of proving that they should be paid equally not merely because they are equal, but because their employer acted improperly. . . . In this way, the scheme, by privileging employers, reinforces one of the key drivers of pay inequity: the power imbalance between employers and female workers. By tolerating employer decision-making that results in unfair pay for women, the legislature sends a message condoning that very power imbalance, further perpetuating disadvantage.[64]

Thus, even in the context of her equality jurisprudence, we see Justice Abella again returning to the theme of the inherent power imbalance in the employment relationship to justify, in part, her finding of systemic discrimination.

In *Fraser II*, her final section 15 equality decision before her retirement from the Supreme Court, Justice Abella explored the long-term impact of adverse effects discrimination on vulnerable woman workers in part-time employment situations. This case involved a policy of the RCMP, which denied members who had participated in a job-share program the option to buy back full-time pension credits, because pursuant to the pension regulations, they were classified as part-time. In contrast, full-time RCMP members who were suspended or who took unpaid leave had the option to buy back their pension credits for those periods. Notably, the majority of the members who had participated in the job-share program were women who had done so due to their childcare responsibilities.

Justice Abella wrote for the majority and held that the policy, while neutral on its face, constituted adverse effects discrimination. She rejected any suggestion that the program was not discriminatory because the complainants had voluntarily chosen to participate in it, finding that the notion of choice for these women was in fact illusory and outside of their control.[65] Returning to themes of the vulnerability of workers employed in part-time or precarious work which

64 *Ibid.*

65 *Fraser II*, above note 9 at para 91.

she had identified thirty-five years earlier in the *Equality in Employment* Report, she found that, as identified by the Law Commission of Ontario, women were more likely to be engaged in precarious work than men and were over-represented in part-time and temporary work. This, in turn, was related to them being primarily responsible for caregiving, which contributed to the precarity of their employment situation.[66]

Moreover, as recognized by the International Labour Organization, increased periods of part-time work in turn resulted in lower pension benefits for women, which led to "women accumulat[ing] disadvantages that pile up at older ages."[67] Furthermore, this structural inequality within pension plans contributes to the feminization of poverty.[68] Thus, connecting the dots between vulnerability, precarious work, and structural inequality, she concluded that the policy, by preventing women who had participated in job sharing programs from buying back pension credits, constituted adverse effects discrimination contrary to section 15 of the *Charter*, which was not saved by section 1.

As these two cases demonstrate, the themes of the power imbalance between workers and employers and the vulnerability of workers in precarious employment, which are front and center in Justice Abella's labour jurisprudence, also play a key role in her equality jurisprudence, where she relies upon them to support her findings of structural inequality. As recognized in her *Equality in Employment* Report, it is necessary on the path to employment equity to eliminate those systemic impediments to equality of opportunity at work. It is only through such measures that dignity at work will be achieved.

F. Conclusion

Throughout her jurisprudence, Justice Abella consistently sought to fulfill the promise of dignity of work. By being alive to the vulnerability, precarity, and powerlessness of workers, not only in her labour law rulings but also in her employment law and equality law jurisprudence, Justice Abella helped to meaningfully advance the law as a tool for achieving dignity at work for all employees. At the same time, her judgments also provided guidance with respect to how to address new

66 *Ibid* at para 102.
67 *Ibid* at para 111.
68 *Ibid* at para 112.

issues in labour and employment law, such as the emergence of the gig economy and the growth of precarious work. Going forward, the law must continue to recognize "the deep inequalities that structure the relationship between employers and employees" in these contexts and seek to "affir[m] the dignity and autonomy of employees in their working lives."[69]

69 *SFL,* above note 1 at paras 54–57.

13 Speaking Rationality to Power

BRIAN LANGILLE*

A. "There Isn't Any Why."

One of the most terrifying, and important, passages in Orwell's *1984* is when Winston speaks to his tormentors, in the person of O'Brien, about the purpose of their tyranny: "I understand how: I do not understand why."[1] Northrup Frye has captured the essence of the response Winston receives: he "is told that there isn't any why. The tortures and spying are not means to an end; they are the ends; the object of power is power; the reason for torture is torture."[2]

Such purposeless power is what law is not. "Why" matters in law. All of the time. "Why" is basic to law. Here is the best way I can think of putting this: law speaks rationality to power. The idea of speaking rationality to power (SRTP) is legal bedrock. On this view, law is not mindless — it is a rational, purposeful, human endeavour. Coming to understand the conditions required for living as equals under law, and not unequals under senseless and arbitrary power, can be seen as one of humanity's great moral and intellectual accomplishments. It is one that has occasionally been observed in operation in the world — even if often, or perhaps always, imperfectly.

All of our specific laws are part of this grand legal project. All laws, no matter what else they accomplish, or try to accomplish, are also law. They are instantiations, the embodiment, the quotidian reality of law's

---

* Faculty of Law, University of Toronto.

1 George Orwell, *1984* (New York: RosettaBooks, 2002) at 300.

2 Northrop Frye, "The Authority of Learning" in *Northrop Frye's Writings on Education*, vol 7, ed by Jean O'Grady & Goldwin S. French (Toronto: University of Toronto Press, 2000) at 569. See Orwell, above note 1 at 302–6. See also Primo Levi, *Survival in Auschwitz* (New York: Touchstone Books, 1958) 29: "There is no why here."

project of life under rational, and not senseless and arbitrary, power. Our laws, including, for example, our labour laws, are where the grand project of law shows up in our daily lives and where "Why" really matters, every day, all of the time.[3]

The core of the rationality demanded by the idea of law "speaking rationality to power" is the demand of equality under law. This is so because the idea of equality is not the idea that all must be treated the same, but rather that we must have a good, i.e., rational, reason for treating people differently. (This is "structural" in our basic ideas about "equality," "fairness," "treating like cases alike," the impartiality of judges, the "rule of law," and all the rest.)

The purpose of this paper is to show that while these ideas are deeply embedded in our law, they are not yet fully grasped, and that this defect can and should be corrected.

In making these points, I will proceed in the following way. First, I show how the idea of law speaking rationality to power is embedded, as it should be, in Canadian law — and that this has been true for some time in both our public law and our private law. Second, I will discuss the once "received wisdom" about the nature and limits of SRTP in our law, which flow from the legal basis upon which it was originally introduced into the Canadian legal system. This was the method of "interpretation" in both private and public law. Third, I will show that this approach and its limits are, considering recent developments, no longer in existence as a matter of private law. SRTP is now inescapable in our private law. As a result, that law is now fully "law." Fourth, I will point out the (incongruous) fact that this (needed) revolution has not yet taken place in our public law — and why this failure matters. I do so by referring to a disgraceful and real example in the form of a relatively recent Ontario statute. Fifth, I will attribute this failure in our public law to the confusion of SRTP with another important but narrower idea: "speaking truth to power" (STTP). This confusion is at least partially the result of Supreme Court of Canada decisions, which can and should be reversed. Finally, I will point out the

3 This is a very basic idea and one we should never lose sight of — whether we are dealing with our common, statutory, or constitutional law. Recall Fuller and Perdue's paraphrasing of Nietzsche's observation, "[t]he most common sort of stupidity is to forget what it is one is trying to do" (L.L. Fuller & William R. Perdue Jr, "Reliance Interest in Contract Damages: 1" (1936) 46:1 *Yale Law Journal* 52 at 52). Nietzsche's exact words are: "During the journey we commonly forget its goal. Almost every profession is chosen and commenced as a means to an end but continued as an end in itself. Forgetting our objects is the most frequent of all acts of stupidity." (Friedrich Wilhelm Nietzsche, *Human, All-Too-Human*, 2nd ed, translated by R.J. Hollingdale (Cambridge: Cambridge University Press, 1996) at 360).

real puzzle this exposes: How is it possible that our public law has failed us, while private law has seen the light, even though public law alone is expressly equipped and charged with the demand of equality, which is at the heart of SRTP? I will try to do all of this in a rather old-fashioned, humble, and legal way — by looking at cases.

And here is the reason for delivering these ideas at a conference honouring the inspired and inspiring career of Justice Rosalie Abella. It is my view that at the legal core of her many contributions to our law is her unrelenting and eloquent pursuit of the idea of substantive equality. She was fearless when Canadians really needed someone to "speak truth to power" — the truths of disadvantage, powerlessness, and exclusion. I believe that, as important as her insights are, there remains one more step in her thinking which, now after her retirement, falls to others to take. This is the idea that speaking truth to power is a subset of the larger idea of speaking rationality to power. I do believe that the example she set for those who follow should inspire them to continue down the legal path she blazed — towards this necessary conclusion about the full meaning of the idea of substantive equality.

B. SRTP Is Deeply Embedded in Canadian Public Law — The Cases of *Roncarelli v Duplessis* and *Smith & Rhuland Ltd v Nova Scotia*

All Canadian lawyers — as well as many other Canadians — are familiar with the following facts in the case of *Roncarelli v Duplessis.*[4] The Premier of Quebec, Jean Duplessis, ordered a permanent revocation of Roncarelli's restaurant liquor licence to punish him for undertaking a perfectly legal and political activity — providing bail for Jehovah's Witnesses arrested during a period of "bitter controversy" between them and Roman Catholics in Quebec (and during a campaign by the Catholic Church to end their proselytizing.)[5] The premier, in revoking the liquor licence, relied upon legislation providing that the government "may cancel any permit at its discretion."[6] In striking down and giving remedy for this exercise of this "discretion" by the Premier, and in one of the most famous Canadian legal judgments of all time, Justice Ivan Rand, regarded by many as one of Canada's greatest judges, wrote as follows:

> A decision to deny or cancel such a privilege lies within the "discretion" of the Commission; but that means that decision is to be based upon a

4 [1959] SCR 121, 16 DLR (2d) 689 [*Roncarelli*].

5 *Ibid* at 131–33.

6 *Ibid* at 139.

> weighing of *considerations pertinent* to the object of the administration. In public regulation of this sort there is no such thing as absolute and untrammelled "discretion", that is that action can be taken on any ground or for any reason that can be suggested to the mind of the administrator; no legislative Act can, without express language, be taken to contemplate an unlimited arbitrary power exercisable for any purpose, however capricious or irrelevant, regardless of the nature or purpose of the statute. Fraud and corruption in the Commission may not be mentioned in such statutes but they are always implied as exceptions. "Discretion" necessarily implies good faith in discharging public duty; there is always a perspective within which a statute is intended to operate; and any clear departure from its lines or objects is just as objectionable as fraud or corruption. Could an applicant be refused a permit because he had been born in another province, or because of the colour of his hair? The ordinary language of the legislature cannot be so distorted. To deny or revoke a permit because a citizen exercises an unchallengeable right totally *irrelevant* to the sale of liquor in a restaurant is equally beyond the scope of the discretion conferred.[7]

In a very real way, this is the only case we need to read to see and understand the basics of the idea that the law "speaks rationality to power." Not "truth to power," but rationality.

There are a few important structural points regarding this idea of "speaking rationality to power" worth noting.

First, this is a simple case of statutory interpretation. It is about what a "legislative Act . . . can be taken to contemplate."[8] Nothing more. But nothing less than that.

Second, only one phrase was up for interpretation in *Roncarelli*: "*may . . . at its discretion*."[9] There is a clear grant of a discretion in that phrase. The only issue is the legal meaning of that idea.

Third, the word "may" cannot be interpreted as granting an "unlimited arbitrary power."[10] The proper interpretation is that discretion is impliedly structured and constrained in two ways. First, by fraud and corruption in its use. As Justice Rand explains in the decision, "[f]raud and corruption in the Commission may not be mentioned in such statutes but they are always implied as exceptions."[11] Second, it is con-

7 *Ibid* at 140–41 [emphasis added].
8 *Ibid* at 140.
9 *Ibid* at 139, 155, 166, and 182 [emphasis added].
10 *Ibid* at 140.
11 *Ibid*.

strained by the purpose of the legislation creating the discretion and of which the discretion is a part. This is the demand of fidelity to purpose, and violation of this demand "is just as objectionable as fraud or corruption."[12] Fidelity to purpose, or rational pursuit of legislative purpose, means taking into account considerations "*pertinent*" to that purpose (and not taking into account "*irrelevant*" considerations). So, "[c]ould an applicant be refused a permit because he had been born in another province, or because of the colour of his hair?"[13] Recall above: this is simply a matter of statutory interpretation: "The ordinary language of the legislature cannot be so distorted."[14]

Fourth, we should get one issue out of the way at the outset: interpretation here is not, as often thought, a matter of whether to "read language into" the statute (or contract) to qualify and constrain what is an obviously unlimited discretionary power. The issue is not *whether* to "read in," if one insists on using that turn of phrase. The issue is *what* to read in. That is, there will be "reading in" no matter what decision is reached in the case. When we see the word "may" (and whether followed or not by words such as "in its discretion") the issue is genuinely one of interpretation — figuring out what the word "may" means. The basic choice in our cases is between reading the word "may" as followed by the words: (1) *even if* the legal power/discretion is exercised in bad faith, arbitrarily, and taking into account irrelevant consideration while ignoring relevant ones, etc.; or (2) *only if* the legal power/discretion is exercised in good faith, rationally, taking into account the relevant considerations and ignoring the irrelevant ones.

Neither the words "even if..." nor "only if..." appear on the page of the statute (or contract) in any of our cases. Yet the results of our cases all depend on which of these two interpretations to adopt. The question is: *which* set of words is implied there? On our law's well-understood and accepted (purposive, objective) approach to both statutory and contractual interpretation, we have never had a difficult time in concluding, correctly, that the words to be read in are "only if," not "even if." That is what happens in *Roncarelli*, right before our eyes.

"Only if," not "even if," is critical. It is the demand that the exercise of power be constrained by rational reasons. It is the demand that there be a "Why." It is the very essence of the idea of law. It is law speaking rationality to power. It is the denial of O'Brien's words to Winston in 1984.

12 *Ibid.*
13 *Ibid.*
14 *Ibid.*

Fifth, this simple idea of statutory interpretation — "no legislative Act can, without express language, be taken to contemplate an unlimited arbitrary power exercisable for any purpose, however capricious or irrelevant, regardless of the nature or purpose of the statute"[15] — leads to a very simple conclusion in favour of Roncarelli: "To deny or revoke a permit because a citizen exercises an unchallengeable right totally *irrelevant* to the sale of liquor in a restaurant is equally beyond the scope of the discretion conferred."[16]

These very basic ideas on clear display in *Roncarelli* have also been applied in other leading cases. In *Smith & Rhuland Ltd v Nova Scotia*,[17] the Supreme Court spoke rationality to power six years before *Roncarelli*, with Justice Rand again delivering a beautiful and important judgment.

In *Smith & Rhuland*, the Nova Scotia Labour Relations Board had denied certification of a union for the workers at the Smith & Rhuland shipyard on the basis that a union leader was a member of the Communist Party.[18] But there was nothing illegal at all about being a member of the Communist Party. As Justice Rand noted, the union official could legally run for, and be elected, premier of the province on that ticket.[19]

The reasoning of *Smith & Rhuland* foreshadows completely that of *Roncarelli*. The statutory language in question provided that "[t]he Board may certify" a union, provided the normal preconditions regarding such matters (such as majority support) were met, as they were in this case.[20] The Court overturned the Labour Relations Board's refusal to certify the union on the basis that the Board's discretion was not unfettered and that the political views of a union's leadership were an irrelevant factor in deciding whether to exercise this discretion.

Every step of *Roncarelli* is marked out in *Smith & Rhuland*, providing a clear view of what was to come. This is a case of statutory interpretation. There is a grant of discretion. But such discretion has its "limits," and a grant of legislative discretion is tempered by the purposes of the statute. This purpose generates the rationality we require by identifying factors relevant, and irrelevant, to that purpose and identifying which factors are required in order to determine what is a rational exercise of

15 *Ibid*.

16 *Ibid* [emphasis added].

17 [1953] 2 SCR 95, [1953] 3 DLR 690 [*Smith & Rhuland*]. (There was a dissent — but also based on SRTP.)

18 *Ibid* at 96. Importantly, this occurred in 1953, the era of "McCarthyism," when such an allegation had a very specific political and cultural resonance.

19 *Ibid* at 97.

20 *Ibid* at 96.

the discretion and what is not. Recall the conclusion in *Roncarelli* quoted above. Here it is again with the facts of *Smith & Rhuland* added for comparison: "To deny or revoke [a liquor permit / certification of a union] because a citizen exercises an unchallengeable right totally irrelevant to [the sale of liquor in the province / protecting worker freedom of association] is equally beyond the scope of the discretion conferred."[21]

In *Smith & Rhuland*, the relevant exercise of discretion was struck down as irrational. That is, the Court concluded that the decision to deny certification was based on irrelevant reasons (legitimate political affiliation) and was not simply limited to those considerations relevant to the grant of power / discretion — here, recognition of a trade union as the representative of a group of workers — such as majority status of the union. To repeat:

> I am unable to agree, then, that the Board has been empowered to act upon the view that official association with an individual holding political views considered to be dangerous by the Board proscribes a labour organization. [*Irrelevant consideration*] . . . there must be some evidence that, with the acquiescence of the members, it has been directed to ends destructive of the legitimate purposes of the union, before that association can justify the exclusion of employees from the rights and privileges of a statute designed primarily for their benefit. [*Relevant consideration*][22]

C. SRTP Is Also Embedded in Our Private Law

The administrative law decisions *Roncarelli* and *Smith & Rhuland* find a private law parallel in *Greenberg v Meffert*,[23] a 1985 Ontario Court of Appeal decision which is receiving, I am pleased to report, increasing recognition in our law.[24] *Greenberg* involved a contractual dispute between Greenberg, a real estate agent, and Meffert, his manager at his former agency, regarding the following clause in Greenberg's employment contract:

> In the event that a listing is sold after the sales agent's employment is terminated, any commission he or she receives *will be at the sole discretion of*

21 *Roncarelli*, above note 4 at 141.

22 *Smith & Rhuland*, above note 17 at 100 [emphasis added].

23 *Greenberg v Meffert*, [1985] OJ No 2539 (QL), 1985 CanLII 1975 [*Greenberg*].

24 See discussions of *Wastech Services Ltd v Greater Vancouver Sewerage and Drainage District*, 2021 SCC 7 [*Wastech*] and *Bhasin v Hrynew*, 2014 SCC 71 [*Bhasin*], below.

> *the company*, and the commission earned on the listing will be disbursed at the company's discretion. . . . It is understood that all listings shall be the property of the company and that you shall be entitled to commission or other remuneration only if you are an agent of the company on the date the property is sold or listed.[25]

In the summer of 1980, Greenberg obtained a real estate listing for a property in Ottawa. He then did substantial work on the listing — completed inspections, prepared materials for purchasers, and facilitated negotiations with a purchaser brought in by a co-worker.[26] However, by the time the sale went through, Greenberg was no longer an employee of the real estate agency. Upon his departure, his manager and co-worker conspired that the commission would be split between them in what the court termed a "kick-back arrangement."[27] As a result, Greenberg received nothing for his labours. When Greenberg asked for his share of the commission, the company invoked its discretion under the clause in his employment contract and refused to pay any commission.

The Court of Appeal rejected an interpretation of the contract that conferred unbridled discretion on the company. Instead, it interpreted "sole discretion" as subject to two constraints: an implied term of reasonableness and an obligation to perform the contract in good faith. These are precisely Justice Rand's two limits in *Roncarelli*. The court wrote:

> If this provision is to have purpose and substance, the discretion must be exercised in a reasonable way, not arbitrarily or capriciously but for good reason. Simple fairness dictates that construction, and particularly so where the exercise of the discretion can result in a windfall to the company. It can keep for itself a commission which but for the termination it would not have obtained, while the agent whose listing led to the sale receives nothing. In this employment relationship, based as it is upon a splitting of commissions, I think it only fair and just, and not too onerous, to require the employer company to show that in the circumstances relevant to the transaction its decision was not unreasonable. . . .
>
> Apart altogether from the question of reasonableness, a discretion must be exercised honestly and in good faith. That proposition is so fundamental as to require no elaboration. The collusive conduct here clearly deprived the discretion of those qualities and contaminated the decisional

25 *Greenberg*, above note 23 at para 3 [emphasis added].

26 *Ibid* at paras 4–5.

27 *Ibid* at para 25.

> process. That patently improper conduct vitiated not only the reasonableness required in the objective criteria, but the good faith and honesty required whether the discretion is objective or subjective. In either case the decision to deprive the appellant of any commission was not made honestly and in good faith and cannot stand. Fair dealing is implicit in the contract. The clause in issue, in my opinion, ought not to be construed so as to shield the company's improper exercise of discretion from any review.[28]

Greenberg makes clear that, as in public law, discretion at private law is constrained by the requirements of proper reasons and good faith.[29] As in our public law, this was a matter of "interpretation" (here, at private law of the contract).[30] The words "only if…" are there. On the basis of this interpretation of the contractual terms, the court found that the company exercised its discretion in an improper manner, that this was simply a breach of contractual terms, and that Greenberg was entitled to his share of the commission. The facts of the case were easy. This was a bad faith case — the employer received a "bribe" or a "kick-back"[31] to exercise its discretion on bad faith and irrelevant grounds to divert a commission which, on the reasonable and relevant reason (work done on the sale), would have gone to the plaintiff.

D. Beyond Interpretation — There Is, Now, Always a "Why" at Common Law

Both our public and private law discipline discretion in the same way. Both speak rationality to power. (The idea of legal equality is brought to bear.) And both do so by requiring that the words "only if" be seen as in place. And both have done so as a matter of legal interpretation. And therein lies the point — a point noted in our public and private law cases — in both *Roncarelli* and *Greenberg*. For example, all of Justice Rand's wonderful judgment is prefaced by the following words: "[N]o legislative Act can, *without express language*, be taken to contemplate an

---

28 *Ibid* at paras 24–26.

29 The Supreme Court has relied on similar considerations in *Communications, Energy and Paperworkers Union of Canada, Local 30 v Irving Pulp & Paper Ltd*, 2013 SCC 34 and *Association of Justice Counsel v Canada (AG)*, 2017 SCC 55, to find that, in the collective bargaining context, managerial conduct not expressly constrained by a collective agreement must still be consistent with the collective agreement and based in rational considerations.

30 *Greenberg*, above note 23 at para 13.

31 *Ibid* at para 25.

unlimited arbitrary power exercisable for any purpose, however capricious or irrelevant, regardless of the nature or purpose of the statute."[32]

There is a more difficult and critical question we must face. It is one to which some of our best legal theorists have been attuned for some time:[33] What if the drafter of the statute, or contract, "pre-empts" and suppresses the implication of the words "only if" by specifically and expressly using the words "even if"? What then?

That is a very basic legal question. It is a challenge to the very idea of SRTP. It is a command to submit to arbitrary power — to the absence of law. It is what O'Brien is saying to Winston in 1984: "There isn't any why." Is that something the law can countenance?

If SRTP rests legitimately but solely on "interpretation" and implication, that foundation will be unable to support the legal weight placed on it by such a use of explicit language. So we are forced to look ourselves in the mirror and ask: is "interpretation," as legitimate as it is, the sole legal underpinning of SRTP in our law? Or is there something more basic going on, which would ban such language as a matter of "law"? That is, does law, when explicitly challenged as such, continue to speak rationality to power? Or does it pack up its meagre interpretive resources and quietly leave town?

This is precisely the question we, unfortunately and amazingly, came very close to having to answer in the Supreme Court decision in *CUPE v Ontario (Ministry of Labour)*,[34] a 2003 public law case. In that case, the Ontario government pushed us to the brink of this sheer legal precipice precisely by writing a "law" granting a discretion (in the appointment of labour arbitrators) followed by the words "even if." The question did not have to be answered at the Supreme Court. But it was starkly posed and haunts the decision. As in *1984*, chillingly so. I discuss how and why this is so below.

However, in 2021, we came to the same precipice and stared into the same jurisprudential chasm, but from another direction. This may be the most interesting point about the idea of SRTP in Canada now. The Supreme Court very recently answered this most vital question about

32 *Roncarelli*, above note 4 at 140 [emphasis added].

33 See David Dyzenhaus, *Hard Cases in Wicked Legal Systems: Pathologies of Legality*, 2nd ed (Oxford: Oxford University Press, 2010). Dyzenhaus, writing in the context of apartheid South Africa, discusses a line of caselaw in which the Appellate Division forced the hand of the legislature to complete the sentence "even if…" and deployed the principle of equality to mitigate the effects of statutory provisions permitting differentiation between races.

34 2003 SCC 29 [*CUPE*]. See the discussion below.

the legal foundation of SRTP as a matter of private law in *Wastech Services Ltd v Greater Vancouver Sewerage and Drainage District*.[35] The answer to the question is that the law does not pack up and leave town — it stands its ground and continues to speak rationality to power. In the face of "even if." There is more to SRTP than interpretation. It is basic to law.

Wastech is, in my view, simply a reprise of *Greenberg* but, importantly, coming after the Supreme Court's 2014 *Bhasin* decision establishing the general operating principle of good faith in contractual performance.[36] As in *Greenberg*, it is a case about a contractually granted discretion. As in *Greenberg*, the issue was simply the proper legal interpretation of that discretion. As in *Greenberg*, the discretion was contained in a long-term relational[37] contract, in this case for dealing with municipal waste. The contract stipulated that the City could in its "*absolute discretion*" allocate how much waste was to be delivered by the contractor to various sites. Such allocations could have an impact on the contractor's profits because of different travel times and distances. The contractor argued that a specific exercise of this discretion by the City, which had just such a (negative) impact on its earnings, was a breach of contract. The Court agreed, as in *Greenberg*, that the discretion was not absolute and was disciplined, legally, by the requirements of honesty, reasonableness, and good faith. Unlike *Greenberg*, dishonesty was not in play. But, as in *Greenberg*, the ideas of good faith, purpose, and reasonableness were very much in play. The contours of reasonableness of any exercise of the discretion are established by its purpose. Purpose, as in our prior cases, gives us the tools to determine relevant and irrelevant considerations to be taken or not taken into account in advancing that purpose.[38] With these in hand, we can then ask: Is this exercise of discretion a lawful one or not? (On the facts of *Wastech*, the exercise of discretion, on this SRTP standard, was found to be lawful and not a breach of contract). The legal path followed here is the path followed in *Greenberg*. (And, let us not forget, *Roncarelli*.)

---

35 Above note 24.

36 Above note 24.

37 To use Ian McNeil's very important idea — something the Supreme Court now correctly borrows and invokes a lot — but without, curiously, giving Ian MacNeil any credit — see, for example, *Wastech*, above note 24 at para 2. For MacNeil see, for example, "The Many Futures of Contracts" (1974) 47:3 *Southern California Law Review* 691.

38 In the terms used in *Wastech*, above note 24 at para 75, exercises of discretion ("choices"), which are either "connected" or "unconnected" to the purpose.

Nothing new.

But here is the novel and critical point for our purposes. *Wastech* is post *Bhasin*, and as *Wastech* notes:

> In *Bhasin v. Hrynew*, Cromwell J. observed that the exercise of contractual discretion is one circumstance in which courts have found a duty of good faith performance exists in a manner consonant with the "organizing principle" from which this and other good faith duties derive: "parties generally must perform their contractual duties honestly and reasonably and not capriciously or arbitrarily" . . . . However, *Bhasin* does not explore the source or content of the specific duty to exercise discretion in good faith, which matters were not at issue in that appeal.[39]

Wastech undertakes just that exploration — by, as we have just noted, faithfully following *Greenberg* and setting out now available and fuller reasons for the ideas expressed in that case. *Greenberg*, and the whole field of contractual discretion, under the *Bhasin* umbrella from the beginning (as noted in the passage just quoted), is simply given a warm welcome followed by a lengthy explication of the consequences of being brought under the *Bhasin* way of thinking. The basic idea is that while it is true that there is nothing new in *Wastech*'s legal approach to interpretation of contractual discretion — it really is just *Greenberg* (and *Roncarelli*) — there is a critical consequence of *Greenberg* being given the "*Bhasin* treatment." It is that now the duty of good faith/reasonable (purposive) exercise of contractual discretion is a *rule of law*. It is no longer simply a result of (valid) legal interpretation. No longer an interpretive *choice* between "even if" and "only if." This is because you cannot contract out of it. You cannot use the words "even if." They are banned.[40] The Court hammers this point home several times, including as follows:

> Overall, then, like the duty of honest performance, the duty to exercise contractual discretion in good faith is *not an implied term, but a general doctrine of contract law that operates irrespective of the intentions of the parties* (*Bhasin*, at para. 74). This places the two duties on the same footing, and conforms to the general assumption that parties do not intend discretion to be completely unconstrained (see *Bhasin*, at para. 45). Just like the duty of honest performance, the duty to exercise contractual discretion in good

39 *Wastech*, above note 24 at para 1.

40 *Ibid* at paras 91–92 (following *Bhasin*, above note 24 at para 74).

> faith, as described herein, should be understood to be obligatory in all contracts. Parties who provide for discretionary power *cannot contract out* of the implied undertaking that the power will be exercised in good faith, i.e., in light of the purposes for which it was conferred.[41]

There must always be a "why" at common law.

E. Is There Always a "Why" in Our Public Law as Well?

We now know that SRTP is not simply a matter of interpretation. It is that. But there is also something beyond interpretation. Irrational, non-purposive exercises of discretion are simply illegal as a matter of private law. The words "even if" are off the table. *Wastech* is an important case in and of itself — as a matter of our private law of contract. But it raises the further, critical, and obvious question: what is the import of *Wastech* for the public law of SRTP?

And in contemplating that question, the following ideas come into view. When we, as we must and will, answer this question as a matter of public law, and answer it in the same way as in our private law, that is, outlawing "even if" as a legislative qualifier for the use of public (as well as private) authority, we will be forced to find a public law basis for so doing. It seems reasonably clear that in order to answer the public law question that loomed in *CUPE v Ontario (Ministry of Labour)*, we will need to find a legal limit on legislative power. The obvious vehicle is via an express constitutional limit. The best way to understand SRTP is that it is, at its core, the demand of the idea of equality. So section 15 of the *Canadian Charter of Rights and Freedoms* should be the key. But will our current Supreme Court use that key?

The problem is, as has been clear for a long time, that the Supreme Court does not view "equality" as enshrining the idea of SRTP.[42] That is to say, rather than understanding the idea of equality as the demand for good, rational, relevant reasons for treating people differently, the Court "reads down" section 15 to the status of a non-discrimination clause, that is, a regime of prohibited reasons (and a very short list, at that). In other words, the Court has been concerned to hobble SRTP — to limit it to the narrower legal idea of speaking truth (the truth of a specific and short list of sources of disadvantage) to power (STTP). Here is the provocative idea — our line of SRTP cases just reviewed may just be the law

41 *Wastech*, above note 24 at 94 [emphasis added].

42 See Brian Langille, "The Freedom of Association Mess: How We Got into It and How We Can Get out of It" (2009) 54:1 *McGill Law Journal* 177.

we need to unlocking section 15 from its current shackles and setting it free as a constitutional ideal. That is the idea this paper advances.

But first, a critical point — this is not a matter of abstract legal speculation. It is a very real problem in our public law, as revealed in *CUPE v Ontario (Ministry of Labour)*.

Here is the basic starting point. This case is simply *Roncarelli* or *Smith & Rhuland* over again. (And the reasoning in the case tracks exactly Justice Rand's reasoning in those two decisions, which we have traced above.) A statute granted a minister a discretion regarding the appointment of persons to serve as arbitrators to determine the content of collective agreements between hospital employers and their employees, in a legal framework of "binding interest arbitration" — that is, a framework in which the normal ways of settling contractual terms (withholding performance until terms are agreed — what is called in collective bargaining "striking" or "locking out") were banned.

The ministerial discretion regarding the appointment of arbitrators (upon the failure of the parties to agree to a chair of a three-person board) was broadly expressed in the statute as follows:

> Where the two members appointed by or on behalf of the parties fail within ten days after the appointment of the second of them to agree upon the third member, notice of such failure shall be given forthwith to the Minister by the parties, the two members or either of them and *the Minister shall appoint* as a third member *a person who is, in the opinion of the Minister, qualified to act.*[43]

The Court correctly and explicitly saw that the question it was facing was just the question it faced in *Roncarelli* (and *Smith & Rhuland*), stating "the central issue in this case is statutory interpretation"[44] and then going to say:

> The Minister does not claim an absolute and untrammelled discretion. He recognizes, as Rand J. stated more than 40 years ago in *Roncarelli v. Duplessis,* [1959] S.C.R. 121, at p. 140, that "there is always a perspective within which a statute is intended to operate."
>
> The decision in *Roncarelli,* despite the many factual differences, foreshadows, in part, the legal controversy in this case. There, as here, the governing statute conferred *a broad discretion* which the decision maker

43 *Hospital Labour Disputes Arbitration Act*, RSO 1990, c H.14, s 6(5) [emphasis added].

44 *CUPE*, above note 34 at para 90.

> was accused of exercising to achieve an *improper purpose*. In that case, the improper purpose was to injure financially (by the cancellation of a liquor licence) a Montreal restauranteur whose activities in support of the Jehovah's Witnesses were regarded by the provincial government as troublesome. Here, the allegations of improper purpose behind the unions' challenge are that the Minister used his power of appointment to influence outcomes rather than process, to protect employers rather than patients, and, as stated by the Court of Appeal, to change the appointments process in a way "reasonably" seen by the unions as "an attempt to seize control of the bargaining process" . . . .
>
> The exercise of a discretion, stated Rand J. in *Roncarelli*, "is to be based upon a weighing of *considerations pertinent* to the object of the [statute's] administration" (p. 140). Here, as in that case, it is alleged that the decision maker took into account *irrelevant considerations* (e.g., membership in the "class" of retired judges) and ignored *pertinent considerations* (e.g., relevant expertise and broad acceptability of a proposed chairperson in the labour relations community).
>
> In this case, the "perspective within which a statute is intended to operate" is that of a legislative measure that seeks to achieve industrial peace by substituting compulsory arbitration for the right to strike or lockout. The "perspective" is another way of describing the policy and objects of the statute.[45]

This is, explicitly, Justice Rand's approach. And in applying the approach, Justice Binnie, writing for the majority, tracks Justice Rand's every move. He begins, correctly, by articulating the statutory purpose, "A *fundamental purpose and object* of the *Hospital Labour Disputes Arbitration Act*, R.S.O. 1990, c. H.14 ('*HLDAA*'), was to provide an *adequate substitute for strikes and lockouts*.[46] To achieve the statutory purpose, as the Minister himself wrote on February 2, 1998, 'the parties must perceive the system as neutral and credible.'"[47]

And this statement of purpose leads to the identification of the relevant considerations to take into account in an exercise of the ministerial discretion to select the persons to act as arbitrators: "I would . . . affirm

45 *Ibid* at paras 91–94 [emphasis added].

46 Note that this is a fundamental insight into the role of all arbitration — both rights and interest. See the foundational arbitration decision of Bora Laskin in *Polymer* — the key to "understanding arbitration" in Canada. *Re Polymer Corporation and Oil, Chemical, and Atomic Workers International Union, Local 16-14* (1959), 10 LAC 51, 59 CLLC at paras 18 and 159 (ON LA), aff'd [1961] OR 176 (H Ct J), aff'd [1961] OR 438 (CA), aff'd (*sub nom Imbleau v Laskin*) [1962] SCR 338.

47 *CUPE*, above note 34 at para 49 [emphasis added].

the fundamental principle underpinning the Court of Appeal's judgment that the HLDAA *required the Minister to select arbitrators from candidates who were qualified not only by their impartiality, but by their expertise and general acceptance in the labour relations community*."[48]

As in all our leading cases, both public and private, purpose instructs us on the relevant/pertinent considerations to be taken into account, and as a result, the irrelevant and not pertinent ones are also made evident. The facts of the case were clear — the minister had strayed mightily from the considerations relevant to the purpose for which the discretion was granted. This was to such an extent that, as Justice Binnie put it, there was an "active disclaimer" of the relevant considerations.[49] The legal result was the striking down of the exercise of discretion. A very simple, indeed textbook, application of *Roncarelli* and *Smith & Rhuland*. Why then do we dwell upon it?

Here is our reason for doing so. Only in the light of that decision can we understand a most remarkable (and regrettable) episode in Canadian law. The Supreme Court's opinion upheld the decision of the Ontario Court of Appeal, which had also struck down the exercise of discretion. But following the Court of Appeal decision, the same Ontario government passed another law — the *Back to School Act (Toronto and Windsor)*.[50] It was enacted, as Justice Binnie put it, "apparently in response to the decision of the Ontario Court of Appeal in this case."[51]

The key provision for our purposes is the following:

> (4) In appointing a replacement arbitrator, the Minister may appoint a person who,
>
> (a) has *no* previous experience as an arbitrator;
>
> (b) has *not* previously been or is not recognized as a person mutually acceptable to both trade unions and employers;
>
> (c) is *not* a member of a class of persons which has been or is recognized as comprising individuals who are mutually acceptable to both trade unions and employers.
>
> (5) In appointing a replacement arbitrator, the Minister *may depart from* any past practice concerning the appointment of arbitrators or chairs of arbitration boards, whether established before or after this Act comes

48 *Ibid* [emphasis added].

49 *Ibid* at para 82.

50 SO 2001, c 1 [*Back to School Act*], as repealed by *Good Government Act*, SO 2009, c 33, Schedule 20, ss 5(1)(4) & 6 and, I think, never if fact used after a change in government.

51 *CUPE*, above note 34 at para 81.

into force, without notice to or consultation with any employers or trade unions.[52]

What will we now make of that sort of "law." We would say that looks "Putin-esque" or "Orban-esque." Pick your favourite elected autocrat. This is because it is a statutory overruling of *Roncarelli*. It is "law" as Duplessis understood it, not Rand. It is an express instruction to ignore the relevant considerations. It is the legislature saying, "even if..." Remarkably, scarily, it specifically lists the relevant factors — which have just been identified by the Court — in order to expressly repudiate them. This is an express repudiation of speaking rationality to power. This is *1984*. This is O'Brien explaining the facts of life to Winston. The purpose of discretion is discretion. The purpose of power is power. It is not disciplined by rationality. There isn't any why. There is no law.

If this law is a valid law, then the law is available as a smokescreen, a façade, for whatever power wishes to do to us, for whatever reasons. What is so very scary about this "law" is that this is what it is saying, on its face. (Would you have drafted it if so instructed? I am pretty sure Justice Abella would not have and, if ordered to do so, would have quit on the spot.)[53]

To call the *Back to School Act* "law" is, to rely on Orwell again: doublespeak.

F. A Unified Law, of Law?

Here is the punchline — a cat already out of the bag. The public "law" stunt pulled in the *Back to School Act* is, as we have seen, what *Wastech* prohibits at private law. As a matter of law, you cannot escape law. You cannot contract out of law. You cannot escape SRTP. There must always be a "why." The words "even if" (that is, the words of the *Back to School Act*), are banned.

In our public law, as I read it, this is a point we have not achieved. In the remaining parts of this essay, I ask why this is so — and whether it should continue to be the case. My answer to this second question is "no."

The central point has already been mentioned[54] — the guarantee of equality, which is at the heart of SRTP, is currently unable to come to our

52 SO 2001, c 1, ss 11(4) & (5) [emphasis added].

53 Like a ship leaving a sinking rat.

54 See, for example, Langille, above note 42.

public law rescue. On my long-held view,[55] this is because the notion of speaking truth (the truth of exclusion, power imbalances, disadvantage) to power, which is the animating norm of our anti-discrimination law, has usurped speaking rationality to power as the ("current") "animating norm" of section 15.[56] Although clear for a while, this is now perfectly explicit following Justice Abella's summing up of her views, and those of the Supreme Court, in in her comprehensive judgment in *Fraser v Canada (AG)*. It is also, to my mind and for the cause of SRTP, very unfortunate.

But it may be that the lead of *Wastech* — and the threat exposed by legislation such as the *Back to School Act* — will be the long-awaited call to action for which section 15 has been so patiently waiting. That is the line of thought developed here. One initial point. Mr. Roncarelli, the Smith and Rhuland shipyard workers, and the hospital employees in *CUPE v Ontario* are not to be identified by a "listed or analogous ground." The idea of STTP is important. But it is a subset of a bigger idea — SRTP. SRTP is not the enemy of STTP. It is the basis of STTP — its "animating norm," if you will. That norm is the idea of equality — of having good, rational reasons for exercises of power, for making distinctions, for classifying, for exercising discretion — when dealing with people via laws. STTP is an important instantiation and intervention of SRTP in our "private"[57] lives based on the idea of "prohibited" or "deemed irrelevant" reasons. But as *Roncarelli* and *Smith & Rhuland* show, our public law needs to do more. (And as *Wastech* shows, so does our private law — at least when people are administering/performing/exercising discretion within an established legal (contractual) framework/relationship.) It requires the full idea of equality — the demand for relevant reasons (and not "merely" a short list of prohibited ones).

So here is the pointed question: what is the law now? Would a new version of the *Back to School Act* — a law that explicitly negates *Roncarelli* — be valid law? Would it be constitutionally valid law? (If it is not law, it is hard to see how it is constitutionally valid.)

---

55 *Ibid*.

56 *Fraser v Canada (AG)*, 2020 SCC 28 at para 48 [*Fraser*].

57 Important even if only deployed in limited sphere, such as employment or accommodation, and then often incompletely and asymmetrically — i.e., applicable to employers hiring but not employees choosing employers, or shop owners but not their customers. See, for example, *BC Human Rights Tribunal v Shrenk*, 2017 SCC 62 at para 116 per McLachlin CJ.

I think, on the specific facts of this case, we could now see a constitutional path that would avoid this most critical of questions. We could say that such a piece of legislation is now simply covered and banned by the holding in *Saskatchewan Federation*,[58] containing as it does an especially bad arbitration clause and thus resulting in a violation of 2(d)'s right to strike. But what if it were Premier Duplessis passing a law to the same effect after the decision in *Roncarelli*? Or the premier of Nova Scotia after *Smith & Rhuland*? Or, to take one of the countless hypotheticals we can all think up, the Prime Minister explaining how COVID unemployment benefits would be distributed? Does the law allow itself to be O'Brien letting Winston in on how the lawless operate?

The problem with the *Back to Schools Act* is not that it is a law that violates section 2(d) and cannot be justified under section 1 — it is that it is not a law.

Isn't it section 15 that needs to carry this burden, which only it can carry? If such a terrifying case came forward, would this be the moment when the current animating norm of section 15 — STTP — would give way to the SRTP? Is it possible that the current Supreme Court can come to see that STTP is a subset of SRTP? When the right case comes along, when facts come along that cannot be transmogrified into existing limited constitutional conceptions (such as STTP), it will have to.

At some point, the Supreme Court will have another, but this time, "Charter" *Roncarelli*. Will it have a Justice Rand?

That is the question. I think there is some reason for hope. And there is a very interesting and very instructive case at hand. It is a case that allows us to see clearly that STTP, as important as it is, is indeed derived from an even more basic idea. It is the 1944 decision of the Supreme Court of the United States, *Steele v Louisville and Nashville Railway*.[59] This is a case we shall have to keep our eyes on. Most labour lawyers know that in this case the concept of a union's "duty of fair representation" was judicially created. It is a wonderfully important case. But most folks misread it. Because it was a case, as recognized by the US Supreme Court, of overt racism — overt discrimination against Black workers by both employer and union — we "read" it as a STTP case. It is not. It could not legally be. It is a SRTP case. It is an equality case. It is

58 *Saskatchewan Federation of Labour v Saskatchewan*, 2015 SCC 4 [*Saskatchewan Federation*].

59 323 US 192 (1944) [*Steele*].

Roncarelli. It is the case which, if we needed one, shows that STTP does all the work, and covers the ground, of STTP. It is precisely the case we will need as we go forward.

Now, in Canada, we would treat *Steele* as a STTP case — under human rights law — with the current, limited, STTP understanding of section 15. But as *Steele* makes plain on reading, this is not what did, or could, happen in 1944. While the US Supreme Court was clearly alert to, and deeply offended by, the racial realities of what was occurring, it had no STTP basis for legal action. *Steele* occurred ten years before *Brown v Board of Education*.[60] And twenty years before the *Civil Right Act of 1964*.[61] Also well before any US state had passed anti-discrimination legislation. There was at that time no legal prohibition against racial discrimination — common law, statutory, or constitutional.[62] Careful readers have made this point.[63]

But the US Supreme Court did act — and did so in on basic legal principles. On the basis of SRTP. The logic of *Roncarelli*. The issue was simply the interpretation of a labour statute which, on the Wagner Act Model, clearly gave a union "exclusive power" over the terms and conditions of the Black workers' employment. But, as for Justice Rand, that power is disciplined by the logic of SRTP — that it is a very basic legal idea ("a principle of general application"[64]) that such power is disciplined by law, by a duty to exercise power for rational reasons — taking into account *relevant* reasons for treating workers differently (differing levels of skill, seniority, working conditions, and so on) and not taking into account *irrelevant* reasons (race). It is pure *Rocarelli*. It is pure SRTP. It is pure equality. This is the idea Martin Luther King had clearly in view: "I have a dream that my four little children will one day live in a

60 347 US 483 (1954).

61 78 Stat 241.

62 The same was true in Canada, as *Christie v York*, [1940] SCR 139, [1940] 1 DLR 81 makes all too clear.

63 See, for example, James E. Jones, Jr, "The Origins of the Concept of the Duty of Fair Representation" in Jean T. McKelvey, ed, *The Duty of Fair Representation: Papers from the National Conference on the Duty of Fair Representation* (Ithaca, NY: New York State School of Industrial and Labor Relations, 1977) at 25 and 27. See also Morgana Kellythorne, "Toward a Theory of the Duty of Fair Representation" (2003) 9 *Appeal: Review of Current Law and Law Reform* 32 at 33: "The trade union in question excluded black members of the bargaining unit and denied them seniority rights. The Supreme Court was faced with a dilemma, as it sought to combat this blatant racism without the assistance of anti-discrimination legislation, which did not yet exist."

64 *Steele*, above note 59 at para 10.

nation where they will not be judged by the colour of their skin but by the content of their character."[65]

I think it is plain that for some writers about equality, such an understanding of this basic legal idea is too abstract. The preferred wording is "formal." But I think this is simply wrong — and this is the point of reading *Steele*. The idea of SRTP, which is the idea of legal equality, does not do anything but place STTP on its proper foundation and carry its important weight.

The idea is that *Steele* stands as a beacon of hope — shining its light across the deep waters that still, in some minds, lie between STTP and SRTP.

G. "Where Have You Gone, Rosie Abella? Our Nation Turns Its Lonely Eyes to You."[66]

One of the best lines of political reporting I have ever read was in the *Guardian* a long time ago: "A shiver ran along the government front benches today, looking for a spine to run up."[67] Rosie Abella was, obviously, not on those benches. She has spine to spare.

But Justice Abella has left the Supreme Court. I know that had she been on the Court in the 1950s, she would have stood with Justice Rand. And I cannot help but think that we will, some day, and perhaps soon, need her sort of backbone when a new version of the *Back to Schools Act* surfaces.

That is when the ideas here advanced will come clearly into view. That is when we will clearly see that the point of legal equality is not simply to prohibit perverse reasons — but to demand relevant reasons. That is when we will see that law demands there must always be a why. That is when we will need to declare that the words "There isn't any why" and "Even if" are not possible under law.

That is when we will need, to use Dr. King's words, the content of Rosie's character. I admire that content. I admire it to the point of seeing her as being quite able, when faced with a real need, to rethink her ideas about equality and about "speaking rationality to power," and to see the

65 Eric J. Sundquist, *King's Dream: The Legacy of Martin Luther King's "I Have a Dream" Speech* (New Haven: Yale University Press, 2009) at 15–16.

66 With apologies, and thanks, to Simon and Garfunkel's "Mrs. Robinson."

67 For Oliver Brown's original comment about the SNP's victory in the 1967 Hamilton by-election, see Tom Devine, "The Sixties in Scotland: A Historical Context" (2013) 20 *Scottish Cultural Review of Language and Literature* 23 at 37. Variations of his comments are often used by journalists and politicians.

legal evolution from speaking truth to power to speaking rationality to power as part of "the arc bending toward justice."[68] And I do mean this as a very large tribute to one of the greatest judges in the history of Canada. It is a tribute to an alive and independent mind. And that, on my view, is the greatest tribute an academic can offer.

Thank you, Rosie, for deserving it.

68 She is careful to say, in *Fraser*, that STTP is the "current" animating norm; see *Fraser*, above note 56 at para 48. Perhaps a good way to mark this evolution might be to say: we now see that the truth the law speaks to power is rationality. (I thank David Dyzenhaus for this formulation.)

PART 4

Justice Abella's Jurisprudence — International Law, Immigration and Refugee Law, and Children's Rights

14 Justice Abella's Global Impact

HAROLD HONGJU KOH*

A. Introduction

I love pretty much everything about Rosalie Silberman Abella, as a judge and as a person. We first met decades ago, introduced by mutual friends on the University of Toronto Law Faculty. Accompanied by her brilliant husband Irv, she delivered a memorable Anderson Lecture at Yale Law School, and she has since annually attended several decades of our yearly Global Constitutionalism Seminar, a convening of constitutional court judges from around the world. Over the years, our friendship has only deepened and grown as we have had joyous reunions in Toronto, Ottawa, New Haven, New York, and Cambridge, Massachusetts. Her emails pop up in my inbox regularly, and she delivers a riveting lecture to my Yale Law students every fall.

Those experiences taught me that Rosie's life has been marked by four qualities: joy, courage, humanity, and a global vision. Remarkably, her loving Jewish family rose from shattered lives in Europe to raise a Canadian daughter full of light and joy. When I first visited Rosie at the Supreme Court of Canada and looked up to where one usually sees portraits of grim, bewigged jurists, I saw instead a huge picture of Fred Astaire and Ginger Rogers dancing halfway to the stars. I witnessed her courage vividly each fall for a quarter of a

* Sterling Professor of International Law and former Dean, Yale Law School; former Legal Adviser (2009–13), Senior Advisor (2021), and Assistant Secretary of State for Democracy, Human Rights and Labor (1998–2001), US Department of State. This tribute is a lightly edited and footnoted version of remarks originally delivered on 12 May 2022 at the panel on "Justice Abella's International Impact" at a conference entitled "A Life of Firsts," held in Ottawa, Canada. I am grateful to Professors Richard Albert, Preston Lim, and Gib van Ert for their invaluable suggestions.

century at Yale Law School's judicial seminar, where she fearlessly took on famous judges from around the world, always urging them to do more for human rights.

Justice Abellas's humanity is on display everywhere she goes. When I asked the wonderful man who drove me to the airport for many years which of his Yale Law passengers had been nicest to him, he singled out Rosie and Irv. They had charmed him and kept him awake on a late-night drive from New Haven to Ottawa, singing Broadway showtunes and asking him kind questions about his family. And at the end of a long graduation ceremony a few years ago, Rosie, having just received a coveted honorary degree from Yale University, told her life story to our graduates and their families. In just five minutes, she reduced all of us to tears. As one graduating student sobbed to me afterwards, searching for the words: "Justice Abella is just so, so, so . . . human!" Not a quality that she, as a law student, had come to expect in a judge.

Although I could speak endlessly of Rosie's personal qualities, I am here today to talk about her global vision. "International law," she once wrote, "is a work in progress."[1] As part of the written law they must interpret, domestic courts construe treaties to which many nations are party. And as Justice Abella also noted, "Canadian courts, like all courts, play an important role in the ongoing development of international law."[2] Justice Abella eloquently described customary international law as "the common law of the international legal system — constantly and incrementally evolving based on changing practice and acceptance."[3] In a globalizing world, she recognized, domestic judges must understand their work as interpreting this conventional and customary law against a rapidly changing global background. In particular, "[c]ourts in liberal democracies," she noted, "are increasingly grappling with the domestic effect of international human rights law."[4]

This global perspective has placed Justice Abella at the heart of two central jurisprudential debates: First, what is the proper role of domestic courts in interpreting international law? And second, what is the proper role of international law in the evolution of Canadian public

---

1 *Thibodeau v Air Canada*, 2014 SCC 67 at para 134, Abella J, dissenting [*Thibodeau*] (adding that in her view, Article 29 of the *Montreal Convention* should be interpreted in a way that is respectful of the protections given to fundamental rights, including language rights, in domestic legislation" at para 167).

2 *Nevsun Resources Ltd v Araya*, 2020 SCC 5 at para 70 [*Nevsun*].

3 *Ibid* at para 74.

4 Thibodeau, above note 1 at para 134.

law? These issues help determine how being a part of a globalizing world defines what it means to be a Canadian today. And not surprisingly, on both issues, Rosie has emerged not just as a national, but a worldwide, judicial leader.

B. Domestic Courts and International Law

Justice Abella addressed the first question — the proper interpretation of international law as part of Canadian law — at some length in 2020 case *Quebec (Attorney General) v 9147-0732 Québec inc*. She argues first that Canadian judges should apply a "generous, purposive and contextual approach" interpretation so that the *Canadian Charter of Rights and Freedoms* could grow and adapt to changing realities.[5] As part of that interpretive approach, purpose must remain "the 'central' consideration when interpreting the scope and content of a *Charter* right."[6] Second, Justice Abella argues that to understand that purpose, constitutional court judges from every country must talk continuously with one another, as she did each fall with judicial colleagues at Yale's Global Seminar. "Since Canada's rights protections emerged from the same chrysalis of outrage as other countries around the world," she wrote, "it is helpful to compare Canada's [human rights provisions] with . . . what and how laws and decisions have been applied on related questions by other countries and institutions," which "is part not only of an ongoing global judicial conversation, but of the epistemological package constitutional courts routinely rely on."[7]

Third, Rosie espoused a judicial vision that focused intensely not just on human rights but on the rights and aspirations of ordinary human beings. In the *Quebec (Attorney General)* case, she argued that a law whose purpose "is to confer protection on a 'singularly human level' . . . is meant to protect human dignity and respect the inherent worth of individuals."[8] In *Divito v Canada (Public Safety and Emergency Preparedness)*, she argued eloquently that having human rights is what it means to be Canadian:

> The protection for citizens in [the law under review], like most modern human rights protections, had its origins in the cataclysmic rights violations of WWII. . . . Without the ability to enter one's country of citizenship,

5 2020 SCC 32 at para 73 [*Quebec (Attorney General)*].

6 *Ibid* at para 80.

7 *Ibid* at paras 98 and 107.

8 *Ibid* at para 135.

> the "right to have rights" . . . cannot be fully exercised. [And so] the right of a Canadian citizen to enter and to remain in Canada is therefore a fundamental right associated with citizenship.[9]

Similarly, she authored the landmark opinion in the 2015 case *Saskatchewan Federation of Labour v Saskatchewan*, constitutionalizing the collective right to strike and reasoning that "the ability to engage in the collective withdrawal of services in the process of the negotiation of a collective agreement is therefore, and has historically been, the 'irreducible minimum' of the freedom to associate in Canadian labour relations."[10]

Nor was that the first time Justice Abella tackled the issue. In the 2014 *Febles v Canada (Citizenship and Immigration)* case, she insisted on a "good faith interpretive approach [that] mandates not divorcing the text of [a treaty] from its human rights purpose."[11] The intention of state parties must therefore be discerned by using a "good faith approach" not only to the words at issue, but also to the context, history, object, and purpose of the treaty as a whole. This requires a generous interpretive approach sensitive to the humanity of the person whose human rights are at issue.[12]

To show how relevant Justice Abella's interpretive approach is to today's most pressing international law issues, allow me to cite the

9 *Divito v Canada (Public Safety and Emergency Preparedness)*, 2013 SCC 47 at para 21 [*Divito*].

10 *Saskatchewan Federation of Labour v Saskatchewan*, 2015 SCC 4 at para 61 [*Saskatchewan Federation of Labour*]. See also para 62 ("Canada's international human rights obligations also mandate protecting the right to strike as part of a meaningful process of collective bargaining" and 75 ("This historical, international, and jurisprudential landscape suggests compellingly . . . that a meaningful process of collective bargaining requires the ability of employees to participate in the collective withdrawal of services for the purpose of pursuing the terms and conditions of their employment through a collective agreement"); see also James J. Brudney, "The Right to Strike as Customary International Law" (2021) 46 *Yale Journal of International Law* 1 at 11 (citing the Saskatchewan decision as a "[n]otable national court decision . . . affirming the existence of this right as constitutionally imbedded, based in part in ILO [International Labor Organization] norms").

11 *Febles v Canada (Citizenship and Immigration)*, 2014 SCC 68 at para 130, Abella and Cromwell JJ, dissenting.

12 *Ibid* at paras 130–31. Justices Abella and Cromwell, dissenting, argued that a "relentlessly exclusionary — and literal — approach would contradict both the 'good faith' approach to interpretation required by the *Vienna Convention*, as well as the *Refugee Convention's* human rights purpose" and urged careful attention to the sympathetic personal circumstances of the claimant.

recent Ukraine genocide case before the International Court of Justice.[13] In February 2022, Vladimir Putin invaded Ukraine in a naked act of aggression and atrocity. He claimed as a fact that Ukraine, not Russia, was committing genocide against its own citizens, and as a matter of law, that the Genocide Convention thus entitled him to use force against Ukrainian civilians to prevent genocide. Before the International Court of Justice, Ukraine argued successfully on provisional measures that these claims had no basis in either fact or law and insisted, as Justice Abella has done, on a purposive, contextualized, human rights-based, good faith interpretation of the international law instrument in question. Although that contentious litigation continues at this writing,[14] in March 2022 the World Court adopted Justice Abella and Ukraine's interpretation in a near-unanimous binding provisional measures order, concluding that Russia's actions were therefore *prima facie* illegal and must cease.

C. International Law and Canadian Public Law

That brings us to Justice Abella's second question: what should the proper role of international law be in the evolution of Canadian public law? Not only should domestic courts learn from each other, she argued, they must also interpret international human rights law in a way that respects the protections given to fundamental rights in domestic law. For that reason, she argued in *Thibodeau* that an international treaty should be interpreted not to bar a damage award for breach of language rights during international carriage by air.[15] In *RS v PR* (2019), Justice Abella argued — perhaps reflecting the cardinal principle that governed her own marital relationship — that "[t]he violation of the principle of spousal equality would be manifestly incompatible with public order as understood in international relations," such that a foreign judgment that contradicted those conceptions would not be recognized in Quebec.[16]

---

13 *Allegations of Genocide Under the Convention on the Prevention and Punishment of the Crime of Genocide (Ukraine v Russian Federation)*, Order of 16 March 2022, [2022] ICJ Rep 211.

14 See Juliette McIntyre, Kyra Wigard & Ori Pomson, *Goliath vs David (and Friends): A Recap of the Preliminary Objections Hearings in Ukraine v Russia*, 2 October 2023, online: www.ejiltalk.org/goliath-vs-david-and-friends-a-recap-of-the-preliminary-objections-hearings-in-ukraine-v-russia/?utm_source=mailpoet&utm_medium=email&utm_campaign=ejil-talk-newsletter-post-title_2.

15 *Thibodeau*, above note 1 at para 167.

16 *RS v PR*, 2019 SCC 49 at para 129 (including within such unenforceable foreign judgments a decision made under art 1096 of the Belgian *Civil Code in this case*).

In *Kazemi Estate v Islamic Republic of Iran* (2014), Justice Abella dissented from the majority's ruling that the State Immunity Act immunized two Iranian officials from claims of torture because of their official status.[17] "[H]ow can torture be an official function for the purpose of immunity under international law when international law itself universally prohibits torture," her dissent asked, arguing that the majority's view posed challenges "for the integrity of international law."[18] She would have answered instead that "[t]he very nature of the prohibition as a peremptory norm means that all states agree that torture cannot be condoned" and that thus, "concerns about any interference with sovereignty which may be created by acting in judgment of an individual state official who violates this prohibition, [must] necessarily shrink.[19]

In March 2020, Justice Abella issued her most important international ruling in *Nevsun Resources Ltd v Araya*, holding that Canadian corporations may be sued in tort for violations of international human rights law that occur abroad.[20] The *Nevsun* plaintiffs sued a Canadian company that owned a mine in Eritrea, claiming that by conscripting them into forced labor, the Eritrean military had subjected them to compensable breaches of customary international law prohibitions against forced labor, slavery, crimes against humanity, and cruel, inhuman, or degrading treatment.[21] The defendant moved to strike the customary international law claims as having no reasonable prospect of success. But writing for the Court, Justice Abella disagreed. Her words are worth quoting at length:[22]

> Modern international human rights law is the phoenix that rose from the ashes of World War II and declared global war on human rights abuses. Its mandate was to prevent breaches of internationally accepted norms. Those norms were not meant to be theoretical aspirations or legal luxuries, but moral imperatives and legal necessities. . . .
>
> The past 70 years have seen a proliferation of human rights law that transformed international law and made the individual an integral part of this legal domain, reflected in the creation of a complex network of conventions and normative instruments intended to protect human rights and ensure compliance with those rights. The rapid emergence of human

17 *Kazemi Estate v Islamic Republic of Iran*, 2014 SCC 62, Abella J dissenting.

18 *Ibid* at para 173.

19 *Ibid* at para 229.

20 *Nevsun Resources Ltd v Araya*, 2020 SCC 5 [*Nevsun*].

21 *Ibid* at paras 3–5.

22 *Ibid* at paras 1, 107 & 108.

> rights signified a revolutionary shift in international law to a human-centric conception of global order. The result of these developments is that international law now works not only to maintain peace between states, but to protect the lives of individuals, their liberty, their health, and their education. The context in which international human rights norms must be interpreted and applied today is one in which such norms are routinely applied to private actors [including corporations].

Justice Abella's *Nevsun* opinion is a landmark for at least three reasons. First, it resolved under Canadian law a question that the US Supreme Court has repeatedly failed to answer under US law: namely, that as a matter of Canadian law, international human rights norms impose corporate tort liability for gross human abuses.[23]

Second, her ruling recognized that there should be a domestic law remedy for this international law right,[24] holding that domestic courts could develop "a civil remedy in domestic law for corporate violations of the customary international law norms adopted in Canadian law."[25]

---

23 In *Sosa v Alvarez-Machain*, 542 US 692 (2004), the US Supreme Court had recognized an implied cause of action under the Alien Tort Statute (ATS) for well-established norms of human rights law. But the Second Circuit subsequently held in *Kiobel v Royal Dutch Petroleum*, No 06-4800 (2d Cir 2011) that corporate liability for human rights violations was not well-established enough to meet the *Sosa* standard. The Supreme Court then granted certiorari to decide the corporate liability question, but instead disposed of the case by limiting the ATS cause of action to claims that "touch and concern" the territory of the United States: *Kiobel v Royal Dutch Petroleum*, 59 US 108 (2013). The Court then again granted certiorari to decide the corporate liability question in *Jesner v Arab Bank, PLC*, 584 US __ (2018), but again avoided the question by limiting the ATS cause of action to US corporations. In *Nestle v Doe*, 593 US __ (2021), the Court for a third time took up the corporate liability issue, but again failed to resolve the question, holding instead that application of the ATS cause of action would be impermissibly extraterritorial.

24 *Nevsun*, above note 20 at para 120.

25 *Ibid* at para 122. Applying the doctrine of "adoption" (or "incorporation" in English law), which the Court traced to William Blackstone's *Commentaries* (para 87), Justice Abella argued that norms of customary international law are fully integrated into and form a self-executing part of Canadian domestic common law, absent conflicting law and subject to legislative revision (para 94). The norms alleged to have been breached in this case prohibiting crimes against humanity, slavery, forced labour, and cruel, inhuman, and degrading treatment were all found to be well established as *jus cogens* in customary international law (paras 99–103), in some cases "regardless of whether the perpetrator is a state" (para 105), and they were therefore potentially applicable to corporations (para 111). The majority thus concluded: "it is not 'plain and obvious' that corporations today enjoy a blanket exclusion under customary international law from direct liability for violation of 'obligatory, definable, and universal norms of international law,' or indirect liability

As she argued, "since customary international law is part of Canadian common law, a breach by a Canadian company can theoretically be directly remedied."[26] At the same time, Justice Abella wisely acknowledged that every nation must decide whether and how its own legal system should provide redress for corporate violations of those norms, leaving to the trial court on remand to decide whether to recognize new domestic common law torts against slavery based on customary international law or, because of the gravity of the offenses, to apply customary international law directly to the defendant's conduct.[27]

Third, Justice Abella's ruling in *Nevsun* added Canada to a growing list of nations recognizing the possibility of corporate liability for human rights violations abroad. In 2017, the UK Supreme Court, in *Vedanta Resources PLC v Lungowe,* allowed claims to go forward against a UK corporation and its Zambian subsidiary seeking damages for toxic emissions from a mine in Zambia.[28] Just weeks later, a Dutch district court in The Hague held in *Kiobel v Royal Dutch Shell* that it had jurisdiction over claims by widows of activists executed in Nigeria alleging that Dutch and UK parent companies and their Nigerian subsidiary were accessories to the unlawful arrests, detentions, and executions.[29] So even while the US Supreme Court has repeatedly limited the availability of suits against corporate defendants, Canada, under Justice Abella's leadership, and other democratic nations have moved in the opposite direction, recognizing the availability of corporate liability for human rights violations against parent companies domiciled in those countries.

---

for their involvement in . . . 'complicity offenses.'" (para 113). Since the customary international law norms raised by the Eritrean workers form part of the Canadian common law, and Nevsun is a company bound by Canadian law, the Eritrean workers' customary international law claims should be allowed to proceed.

26 *Ibid* at para 127.

27 *Ibid* at paras 127–29.

28 *Vedanta Resources PLC and another (Appellants) v Lungowe and others (Respondents),* [2019] UKSC 20 (UK) (observing that the parent company may have intervened sufficiently in the management of the mine to have assumed a duty of care under Zambian common law or fault-based liability under Zambian legislation).

29 *Kiobel v Royal Dutch Shell,* C-09-540972-HA ZA 17-1048 (NL). The Dutch suit involved the same plaintiffs as the US *Kiobel* case, but alleged violations of fundamental rights under Nigerian law, rather than customary international law. In March 2022, The Hague court dismissed Esther Kiobel's civil case due to insufficient evidence to link Shell to the bribing of witnesses to give false testimony at the trial of the "Ogoni Nine." Kiobel initially said she would appeal the decision, but she ended up not doing so. See "Nigeria: Dutch Court Rejects Suit of "Ogoni Nine' Widows Against Shell," *Aljazeera* (23 March 2022), online: www.aljazeera.com /news/2022/3/23/dutch-court-rejects-suit-of-nigerian-widows-against-shell.

D. Conclusion

Let me close with this story: one night in New Haven, Connecticut, I went to dinner with the late Professor Irving Abella, who had just delivered a brilliant visiting lecture at Yale's history department. A lively Yale women's singing group entered the restaurant and started singing Broadway songs.

Saying "Rosie would love this," Irv pulled out his phone and called her at her Ottawa chambers, holding up his phone so that she could also listen to the young women exuberantly singing. When the song ended, Rosie shouted, "I love you both! I've been here working on this depressing opinion, but for the last few minutes, I've been dancing along with you, transported to a better world."

That is the vision of Justice Abella that will stay with me: a path-breaking justice in her chambers — ever mindful of the horrors her family escaped and her love of her adopted country — grappling with the gritty reality of the world that is, but still able to dance joyfully to the music of a better world she can imagine. It is Rosie's unique lifelong ability to deal with what is, while transporting us to where we should be, that will ensure Justice Abella's lasting global impact for many decades to come.

15 Understanding *Nevsun* Through an Equality Lens

YOUSUF AFTAB AND ELINOAM ABRAMOV*

A. Introduction

Justice Abella's landmark decisions have fundamentally changed "Canada's legal landscape and the lives of everyday Canadians."[1] Her legacy is built on a creative, empathetic, and relentless pursuit of equality and dignity for all. *Nevsun Resources Ltd v Araya*[2] is the archetype of her innovative reasoning. The case established for the first time that corporations could be held civilly liable for human rights violations under customary international law. In so doing, it charted a new frontier in the burgeoning discipline of corporate human rights responsibility.

At first blush, *Nevsun* seems emblematic of global legal trends in business and human rights norms. The majority's reasoning, however, marks a radical departure from core principles underlying developments in corporate human rights responsibility across civil and common-law jurisdictions. The departure creates significant conceptual and practical uncertainties for theorists and practitioners alike. But it is precisely such uncertainty that may inspire a reconception of how law can best advance justice. Rather than being just another business and human rights decision, Justice Abella's *Nevsun* reasoning may be better understood as a critique of the common law and a plea to adapt

---

* Yousuf Aftab is a Partner at Steptoe LLP, based in New York. He clerked for Justice Abella from 2006 to 2007. Elinoam Abramov is an International Associate at Steptoe LLP. We are indebted to Joseph Ho, Amelie Rigoll, and Stobo Sniderman for their invaluable help. All errors are ours.

1 Andromache Karakatsanis & Sheilah L Martin, "The Joy of Judging with Justice Rosalie Silberman Abella" (2021) 105:3 *Judicature* 89 at 90.

2 *Nevsun Resources Ltd v Araya*, 2020 SCC 5, [2020] 1 SCR 166 [*Nevsun*].

customary international law to the modern era — all woven together by the very threads that animate her equality jurisprudence.

This article traces this argument in three stages. Part I summarizes the decision in *Nevsun* and highlights its significance in the field of business and human rights. Part II explores the dissonance of *Nevsun* with the broader trends in business and human rights law. Part III outlines Justice Abella's substantive equality jurisprudence and draws on two underlying principles — a purposive approach to judicial interpretation and the privileging of the rights-holder perspective — to conclude that *Nevsun* can be better understood through the prism of this jurisprudence.

B. *Nevsun Resources Ltd v Araya*

Nevsun concerned a claim by three Eritrean refugees who were conscripted through the Eritrean National Service Program to work at the Bisha Mine, owned by the Canadian company Nevsun Resources Ltd. The plaintiffs claimed that they were victims of forced labour, violence, and cruel, inhumane, and degrading treatment. Specifically, the plaintiffs brought two claims: a tort action and a claim based on customary international law. Nevsun argued that the plaintiffs' claims should be struck out because they would require adjudicating the lawfulness of Eritrea's conduct — triggering the act of state doctrine — and because no common law claim for damages against a corporation for customary international law exists under Canadian law. In a 5–4 decision, the Supreme Court of Canada rejected both arguments and ruled that the claims could proceed to trial on the merits. Shortly after, the parties reached a settlement.

Justice Abella's majority decision was based on two principal holdings. First, the Court refused to import the English act of state doctrine, often used by corporations to bar liability, into Canadian law.[3] Second, and more importantly, Justice Abella ruled that claims against corporations for breaches of customary international law could constitute a legitimate cause of action under Canadian common law.

To reach this conclusion, the majority first determined (1) that the allegations against Nevsun concerned breaches of peremptory norms of customary international law; and (2) that such norms are automatically and directly incorporated into Canadian law, as in "virtually all states," unless expressly abrogated by statute.[4] More notably from the perspective of business and human rights law, the majority held, for the first

3 *Ibid* at para 57.

4 *Ibid* at para 88.

time, that corporate actors (not only state actors) can face common-law liability for breaches of customary international law.

This reasoning rested on an understanding of how international human rights law has evolved from a state-centric to an individual-centric regime: "a central feature of the individual's position in modern international human rights law is that the rights do not exist simply as a contract with the state. . . . They are discrete legal entitlements, held by individuals, and are 'to be respected by everyone.'"[5] The crux of the issue before the Court was whether these "discrete legal entitlements" could afford individual civil remedies under Canadian common law. The Court held that "it is not 'plain and obvious' that corporations are immune from such liability."[6] While recognizing that a private right of action against corporations under customary international law was novel, the Court emphasised that other nations had not excluded the possibility and noted that the holding was consistent with the Government of Canada's policy to ensure that Canadian companies respect international human rights abroad.[7] Corporations may thus be liable under the common law for violations of "obligatory, definable and universal norms of international law."[8]

Importantly, Justice Abella found that "a breach by a Canadian company can theoretically be *directly* remedied based on a breach of customary international law."[9] The Court essentially recognized breaches of customary international law as a new tort.[10] The majority justified the creation of this tort based on the fact that "customary international law norms . . . [are] inherently different from existing domestic torts" due to their gravity, public nature, and impact on global rights.[11] As such, these breaches are not merely amalgams of existing tort claims; in light of their severity, they warrant a new, standalone claim.

In a preview of *Nevsun*'s potentially radical implications, Justice Abella paid particular attention to the issue of remedy: "Customary international law norms . . . [are] of a more public nature than existing domestic private torts since violation of these norms 'shock[s] the conscience of humanity.'"[12] Civil remedies may be insufficient to

5 *Ibid* at para 110.
6 *Ibid* at para 128.
7 *Ibid* at para 115.
8 *Ibid* at para 188.
9 *Ibid* at para 127 [emphasis added].
10 *Ibid* at para 233.
11 *Ibid* at para 124.
12 *Ibid*.

address such harm. The majority reasoned that the nature of corporate violations of international human rights under customary international law may be of such import as to warrant "different and stronger"[13] remedies commensurate with the moral opprobrium associated with the norms at issue.

Nevsun thus represents novelty in three ways: (1) corporations may be direct duty-bearers of human rights obligations under customary international law; (2) corporations may face civil liability under the Canadian common law for breaches of their obligations under customary international law; and (3) courts may need to conceive new types of remedy — beyond "typical tort claims" — to address the public nature and gravity of such harms.

C. Understanding *Nevsun* from the Business and Human Rights Perspective

Justice Abella's innovations in *Nevsun* challenge conventional understandings of customary international law and the common law. They also cut against the grain of evolving corporate human rights responsibility across jurisdictions. The dissonance lies in three premises underlying the decision: first that international human rights law applies directly between private actors, second that corporate groups can be treated as a unitary whole, and third that corporate responsibility for international human rights is independent of corporate governance.

The cornerstone of the majority's reasoning is that there has been a shift within international law, blurring the distinction between public and private human rights responsibilities. This premise is controversial. Authoritative commentary on international human rights has focused on individuals' rights *vis-à-vis* government. The United Nations Human Rights Committeee has opined that the International Covenant on Civil and Political Rights does not have "direct horizontal effect [as between private actors] as a matter of international law."[14] As the Supreme Court dissent highlights, even John Ruggie, the lead drafter of the UN Guiding Principles on Business and Human Rights (Guiding Principles), has concluded that "uniform and consistent state practice establishing

13 *Ibid* at para 129.

14 United Nations Human Rights Committee, *General Comment No 31 [80]: The Nature of the General Legal Obligation Imposed on States Parties to the Covenant*, UN Doc CCPR/C/21/Rev.1/Add.13 (26 May 2004) at para 8, online: www.refworld.org/legal/general/hrc/2004/en/52451 [*General Comment 31*].

corporate responsibilities under customary international law" has not yet been established.[15]

Nevsun also erodes the distinction between the Canadian parent company and its Eritrean subsidiary, challenging fundamental tenets of corporate theory. The concept of separate corporate personality is foundational to corporate law in many jurisdictions.[16] Separate legal personality allows "companies to structure management of diverse regional risks and responsibilities across a global organisation."[17] While recent legal developments have challenged this concept's contours and permeability,[18] none have done away with the concept completely.

The evolution of legal corporate human rights responsibility in other jurisdictions has been linked to the practical implications of the corporate form. In the United Kingdom, for instance, the plaintiffs in *Vedanta Resources v Lungowe*[19] argued that the UK-based parent company Vedanta owed a duty of care to individuals injured most directly by the wrongdoing of its Zambian subsidiary, KCM. The UK Supreme Court agreed — but only on the condition that the parent exercised a sufficient level of involvement and control over its subsidiary.[20] That is, the *de jure* separateness of Vedanta and KCM endured; it could be pierced for specific claims based on the particular facts in any given case. By contrast, possibly because of how it was argued, neither the majority nor the minority opinions in the *Nevsun* ruling considered the implications of the corporate form. Nevsun appeared to be treated as one entity, with either uniform obligations across the corporate group or all human rights obligations flowing to the Canadian parent. Either way, the decision creates uncertainty in the heart of the corporate human rights responsibility, as the role of corporate structure in shaping responsibility under customary international law remains unaddressed.

Perhaps most importantly, *Nevsun* is at odds with the approach to corporate human rights responsibility animating litigation and legislation in Canada and across the globe. The UN Guiding Principles are the source of these developments. One of their major practical contributions is to recognize the inherent difference between states and businesses as

---

15 *Ibid* at para 190.

16 Yousuf Aftab & Jonathan Drimmer, "ESG and the Future of Resource Company Governance" in the Rocky Mountain Mineral Law Foundation, *67th Annual Rocky Mountain Mineral Law Institute* (2021) at 20-3.

17 *Ibid* at 20-14.

18 *Ibid*.

19 *Vedanta Resources v Lungowe*, 2019 UKSC 20 [*Vedanta*].

20 *Ibid* at para 61.

the duty-bearers of human rights. States are expected to "*respect, protect and fulfil* the human rights of individuals within their territory and/or jurisdiction."[21] Businesses have a more limited duty to "*respect* human rights."[22] "Respect" is defined by corporate governance — that is, it refers to the strength of policies and procedures companies put in place to identify and address human rights risks. In effect, businesses are held to a standard of best efforts. The Guiding Principles thereby translate amorphous corporate responsibility into a practical compliance structure familiar to businesses from the corruption, money-laundering, and health and safety contexts. This structure has a built-in defence of due diligence to allegations of corporate human rights malfeasance.

This distinction between public and private human rights responsibility is integral to the reasonableness and efficacy of the Guiding Principles. States may face a suite of positive and negative obligations to meet their human rights commitments under international law. By contrast, businesses are handed obligations — particularly due diligence and remedy — tied to their involvement with human rights impacts and sensitive to their institutional constraints. They are not public actors with public responsibilities, so their primary obligation is to *try their best* to do no harm.

This governance-based approach is also reflected in caselaw. In the United Kingdom, litigation against businesses for extraterritorial human rights wrongs has largely been framed in negligence terms, with plaintiffs alleging that the corporate defendant did not implement reasonable risk-management measures.[23] So too in Canada.[24] Thus far, court decisions in these jurisdictions have focused on the preliminary question of whether the parent company may owe a duty of care to plaintiffs affected most directly by a foreign subsidiary. The standard of care in such contexts remains largely unexplored.

---

21 United Nations Office of the High Commissioner for Human Rights, *Guiding Principles on Business and Human Rights: Implementing the United Nations "Protect, Respect and Remedy" Framework* (New York and Geneva: United Nations, 2011), GP 1 Commentary, online: www.ohchr.org/Documents/Publications/GuidingPrinciplesBusinessHR_EN.pdf [emphasis added].

22 *Ibid*, GP 11 [emphasis added].

23 See, for example, *Guerrero v Monterrico Metals plc*, [2009] EWHC 2475 (QB); *Okpabi and others v Royal Dutch Shell plc and another*, [2018] EWCA Civ 191, [2018] Bus LR 1022; Vedanta.

24 See, for example, *Choc v Hudbay Minerals Inc*, [2013] OJ No 3375, 2013 ONSC 1414, 116 OR (3d) 674 (Ont SCJ); *Garcia v Tahoe Resources Inc*, [2015] BCJ No 2431, [2016] 3 WWR 169 (BCSC); *Das v George Weston Ltd*, [2017] OJ No 3542, 2017 ONSC 4129 (Ont SCJ).

The Dutch case *Milieudefensie et al v Royal Dutch Shell PLC*[25] addressed the standard of care issue in the context of climate litigation framed as a human rights claim. The plaintiffs argued that Shell has a duty of care to take action to reduce its greenhouse gas emissions based on Article 6:162 of the Dutch Civil Code, which was informed by the European Convention on Human Rights and the Guiding Principles. The District Court drew on Guiding Principle 13(a), which obligates businesses to "avoid causing or contributing to adverse human rights impacts through their own activities,"[26] to order that Shell reduce its direct greenhouse gas emissions across its portfolio. The court held that Shell was expected to implement "*significant best-efforts* . . . to remove or prevent the serious risks ensuing from the CO2 emissions generated by [the company and its customers], and to use its influence to limit any lasting consequences as much as possible."[27] That is, even in the most expansive readings of corporate human rights liability in other jurisdictions, courts have understood business responsibility as an effort defined by the Guiding Principles.

Nevsun's recognition of potential corporate liability flowing directly from customary international law creates uncertainty for the evolution of business and human rights. First, customary international law norms are more challenging to identify than convention or treaty rights because they depend on state practice. Second, translating "state practice" into the corporate sphere raises myriad unanswered questions on the exact scope of business responsibility. For instance, if the prohibition on slavery is a peremptory norm of customary international law, are its contours the same for private and public actors? Can a business be expected to enforce the prohibition outside its value chain? If so, what are legitimate private enforcement mechanisms under customary international law?

Third, it is unclear whether Justice Abella's reference to "different and stronger" remedies is meant to capture *restitutio in integrum* (total reparation) under international human rights law, which may extend far beyond damages: "[R]eparation can involve restitution, rehabilitation and measures of satisfaction, such as public apologies, public memorials, guarantees of non-repetition and changes in relevant laws and practices, as well as bring to justice the perpetrators of human

---

25 *Milieudefensie et al v Royal Dutch Shell Plc,* [2021] The Hague District Court [*Shell*]. English translation available online: https://climatecasechart.com/non-us-case/milieudefensie-et-al-v-royal-dutch-shell-plc/.

26 Above note 21, at GP 13(a).

27 *Shell,* above note 25 at paras 4.1.4–4.1.5 [emphasis added].

rights violations."[28] This array of options has largely been anathema to tort liability under the common law, which seeks restitution "in so far as money can do so."[29] The Guiding Principles recognize total reparation as the end goal of human rights remedy. Even they, however, condition expectations of business with reference to involvement in any harm and to the legitimate institutional constraints of private actors. While states have a duty to provide an "effective" remedy under international human rights law, businesses are expected to provide a "rights-compatible" remedy.[30] This need not be complete, as it integrates the institutional constraints of business as a private actor subject to law.[31]

These challenges and uncertainties make *Nevsun* an awkward addition to the business and human rights zeitgeist. Indeed, we would argue that the decision is better understood with reference to Justice Abella's equality jurisprudence. Rather than an evolution of tort law, *Nevsun* is a plea for a revolution in international law.

D. Applying Justice Abella's Substantive Equality Jurisprudence to *Nevsun*

Equality was Justice Abella's signature cause throughout her legal career. Her innovations in conceptualizing equality preceded her judicial career, but the core principles underlying her reasoning remained constant: a rejection of formalism and a focus on the rights-holder perspective. Justice Abella's *Report of the Royal Commission on Equality in Employment* added novel nuance and depth to the ideal of equality.[32] The Report firmly rejected the then-dominant concept of formal or procedural equality in favour of substantive equality, an ideal tailored to the context and lived experience of the most vulnerable: "[i]gnoring differences and refusing to accommodate them is a denial of equal access and opportunity. It is discrimination . . . This may mean treating some

28 *General Comment 31*, above note 14 at para 16. See also the *Basic Principles and Guidelines on the Right to a Remedy and Reparation for Victims of Violations of International Human Rights and Humanitarian Law*, E/CN.4/2000/62, Annex.

29 *Ratych v Bloomer*, [1990] SCJ No 37, [1990] 1 SCR 940 at 962 (SCC).

30 Yousuf Aftab & Audrey Mocle, *Business and Human Rights as Law: Towards Justiciability of Rights, Involvement, and Remedy* (Canada: LexisNexis, 2019) at 196–97.

31 *Ibid.*

32 Rosalie Silberman Abella, *Equality in Employment: A Royal Commission Report* (Ottawa: Minister of Supply and Services Canada, 1984) at 3 [Abella Report].

people differently by removing the obstacles to equality of opportunity they alone face for no demonstrably justifiable reason."[33]

The Abella Report had lasting impacts on Canadian public policy, legislation, and jurisprudence.[34] Its themes have run through Justice Abella's subsequent equality jurisprudence in *Quebec (AG) v A*,[35] *R v Kapp*,[36] *Rosenberg v Canada*,[37] *Ontario (Human Rights commission) v Mr A*,[38] and *Fraser v Canada (AG)*,[39] solidifying Canadian courts' commitment to a more expansive concept of equality, understood through the eyes of the most vulnerable. Beyond central equality precepts, her decisions have been shaped by a belief in the legitimacy of judicial engagement in "the definition of public policy"[40] — an imperative that demands a "unified purposive approach to rights claims"[41] rather than a "mechanical and sterile"[42] interpretive process.

Justice Abella emphasized the continued force of this moral imperative in her Supreme Court parting speech: "All of the social, political, and economic realignments that were happening around us meant that judges could no longer just be defenders of the status quo, we had to accept that justice was the application of law to life, not just the application of laws to facts."[43] This position echoes her earlier writing: "how well [equality] thrives will depend overwhelmingly on how skilfully its parameters are articulated by the lawyers and the judges in the justice system."[44]

---

33 *Ibid.*

34 Carol Agócs, "The Making of the Abella Report: Reflections on the Thirtieth Anniversary of the Report of the Royal Commission on Equality in Employment" in Carol Agócs, ed, *Employment Equity in Canada: The Legacy of the Abella Report* (Toronto: University of Toronto Press, 2014) 13 at 13.

35 *Quebec* (AG) v A, 2013 SCC 5, [2013] 1 SCR 61.

36 *R v Kapp*, 2008 SCC 41, [2008] 2 SCR 483.

37 *Rosenberg v Canada*, 1998 CanLII 3243 (ONCA), 158 DLR (4th) 664.

38 *Ontario (Human Rights Commission) v Mr A*, 38 CHRR 506, 195 DLR (4th) 405.

39 *Fraser v Canada*, 2020 SCC 28, [2020] 3 SCR 113 [*Fraser*].

40 Rosalie Silberman Abella, "Limitations on the Right to Equality Before the Law" in Armand de Mestral et al, eds, *The Limitation of Human Rights in Comparative Constitutional Law* (Cowansville: Yvon Blais Inc, 1986) 223 at 223 [Abella, "Limitations"].

41 *Toronto v Ontario*, 2021 SCC 34 at para 152 [*Toronto*].

42 *Fraser*, above note 39 at para 134.

43 Rosalie Silberman Abella, "The Honourable Rosalie Silberman Abella Bids Farewell to the Supreme Court" (webcast delivered at the Supreme Court of Canada 21 May 2021), online: www.scc-csc.ca/judges-juges/webcast-webdiffusion-farewell-aurevoir-rosalie-silberman-abella-eng.aspx at 10:47 [Abella Farewell].

44 Abella, "Limitations," above note 40 at 225.

Each of these elements inform her majority opinion in *Fraser*, which has been hailed as a landmark that "provides the Supreme Court's most helpful account of the law relating to indirect discrimination under s. 15."[45] The case concerned equal access to pensions for woman Royal Canadian Mounted Police officers. Justice Abella held that although the pension plan did not directly discriminate against woman officers, the broader employment context meant that women were adversely impacted by the policy in practice. Drawing on the perspective of the disadvantaged, Justice Abella noted that adverse effects discrimination is far more widespread than direct discrimination and "often poses a greater threat to the equality aspirations of disadvantaged groups."[46] Crucially, the decision stripped away any need to prove discriminatory intent by the legislature or causation between the policy and the discriminatory effect, focussing only on the impact on plaintiffs within their social context.

Nevsun is in keeping with the spirit of Justice Abella's substantive equality jurisprudence. In rejecting the parameters of conventional tort analyses, the majority opinion looked to an ideal beyond the horizon, one where international human rights law is freed from formalistic shackles to ensure that the most vulnerable can seek remedy for their suffering. Justice Abella's analysis was founded on the purpose of international human rights law and on realizing that purpose in practice: "[International human rights] norms were not meant to be theoretical aspirations or legal luxuries, but moral imperatives and legal necessities. Conduct that undermines the norms was to be identified and addressed."[47]

In line with her equality jurisprudence, Justice Abella sought to unearth the purpose of customary international law norms in the perspective of the rights-holder. Drawing on Hersch Lauterpacht's statement that "the individual human being . . . is the ultimate unit of all law,"[48] she found that the purpose of international law is no longer just to facilitate peaceful relations between states but primarily to protect the human rights of the individual. The focus on the rights-holder also explains Justice Abella's departure from existing tort law in favour of customary international law as a mechanism for corporate accountability. Her primary consideration was about which claim could best

45 Peter W. Hogg & Wade K. Wright, *Constitutional Law of Canada, 2021 Student Edition* (Toronto: Thomson Reuters, 2021) at 1497.

46 *Fraser*, above note 39 at para 35.

47 *Nevsun*, above note 2 at para 1.

48 *Ibid* at para 109.

address the harm experienced by the plaintiffs, as seen through their eyes. She quoted from Professor Graham Virgo to conclude that, "from the perspective of the victim . . . the fact that torture is characterised as a tort, such as battery, will matter — simply because characterising torture in this way does not necessarily reflect the seriousness of the conduct involved."[49]

This is also applicable to the remedy challenge inherent in private law: from the perspective of the plaintiffs — the right-holders — tort remedies may not be sufficient to address their injuries if the harm is an abridgment of a peremptory norm of international law. In suggesting that violations of customary international law require "different and stronger responses than typical tort claims,"[50] Justice Abella privileged the experience of the rights-holder over the formalism of existing law. It is a plea for judicial imagination grounded in the lived experience of the people that rights were conceived to protect.

The plea is perhaps more revolutionary than it first appears, for its core is a call to reimagine international human rights law by redefining what rights mean. A right is an enforceable claim that distributes power between parties.[51] Rights capture claims to act or not to act. Corresponding to these claims are obligations of others to act or not to act.[52] As David Lyons explains: "When *A*, in particular, holds a certain right *against B*, *A* is a *claimant* against *B*. . . . A claimant is thus one to whom the performance of a duty or obligation is *owed* — he is the one who holds the claim against the other and who is entitled to administer the claim as he chooses."[53] The form of rights is thus tripartite: rights-holder, interest, and duty-bearer. Understanding all three elements is essential to defining the right itself. This structure applies across the broad spectrum of rights, from contractual rights to constitutional and human rights.

Human rights are distinct from other rights in that they are intrinsic to all individuals, irrespective of the political regime to which they are actually subject: "For rights to be *human* rights, all humans everywhere in the world must possess them equally and only because of their status

49 *Ibid* at para 125.

50 *Ibid* at para 129.

51 Jonathan Wolff, *The Human Right to Health* (New York: WW Norton & Co, 2012) at 15.

52 Leif Wenar, "Rights" in Edward N. Zalta, ed, *The Stanford Encyclopedia of Philosophy* (Fall 2015 Edition), online: https://plato.stanford.edu/entries/rights/ [Wenar].

53 David Lyons, "Rights, Claimants, and Beneficiaries" in David Lyons, ed, *Rights* (Belmont: Wadsworth, 1979) at 60.

as human beings."[54] Such rights are conceived to redress power imbalances to protect and promote individual autonomy.[55] They are privileges, claims, powers, and immunities that help to protect people from political, legal, and social abuses;[56] protect certain conditions without which no person can lead a decent human life;[57] protect human agency and thus human agents against abuse, cruelty, oppression, degradation, and the like;[58] and protect important human interests against threats of state-sponsored neglect or oppression.[59]

Despite the claim that human rights are "inherent,"[60] internationally recognized human rights derive meaning from their enunciation in law. They do not exist in the hopes of putative rights-holders but in specific and recognized instruments of international law. Human rights under international law have traditionally been *state-centric* concepts, as "[t]heir fundamental purpose [is] to guarantee the freedoms of individuals against the state with its vast powers of detention, expropriation and censorship; to mitigate the imbalance between two unequal parties: the public authority and individual."[61]

The state focus of rights is also reflected in the *Canadian Charter of Rights and Freedoms*: "This Charter applies . . . to the Parliament and government of Canada . . . [and] to the legislature and government of each province."[62] Thus, the Supreme Court of Canada has held: "Where . . . private party 'A' sues private party 'B' relying on the common law and where no act of government is relied upon to support the action, the Charter will not

54 Lynn Hunt, *Inventing Human Rights: A History* (New York: WW Norton & Co, 2007) at 20.

55 Aharon Barak, "Constitutional Human Rights and Private Law" (1996) 3 *Review of Constitutional Studies* 218 at 244, online: https://digitalcommons.law.yale.edu/cgi/viewcontent.cgi?referer=&httpsredir=1&article=4699&context=fss_papers [Barak].

56 Wenar, *supra* note 52.

57 David Miller, Political Philosophy: A Very Short Introduction (Oxford: Oxford University Press, 2003) at 70.

58 Michael Ignatieff, *Human Rights as Politics and Idolatry* (Princeton: Princeton University Press, 2001) at ix.

59 Charles R. Beitz, *The Idea of Human Rights* (Oxford: Oxford University Press, 2009) at 11.

60 United Nations Human Rights Office of the High Commissioner, "What Are Human Rights?" online: https://www.ohchr.org/en/what-are-human-rights.

61 Yoav Dotan, "The 'Public', the 'Private', and the Legal Norm of Equality" (2005) 20:2 *Canadian Journal of Law and Society* 207 at 207.

62 *Canadian Charter of Rights and Freedoms*, s 32(1), Part I of the *Constitution Act, 1982*, being Schedule B to the Canada Act 1982 (UK), 1982, c 11.

apply."[63] That is, the duty-bearers of the most fundamental rights recognized in national and international law have long been understood to be public bodies, with the accompanying power and legitimate authority. The implication of this understanding is that the scope of rights-holders' legitimate claims presuppose a governmental duty-bearer.

Nevsun appears to consider this structural limitation from the perspective of rights-holders and deem it formal and technocratic: "the individual human being . . . is the ultimate unit of all law."[64] If this precept is true, and if the purpose of international human rights law is to protect individual dignity, then law's failure to provide an effective remedy for grave injury is the failure of law. Facing that abyss, it is incumbent on judges to apply a "unified purposive approach to rights claims"[65] to save justice from the law. This is the approach that Justice Abella deployed to save equality from its form. And she opened the door to that approach with her entreaty for courts to think "beyond tort claims" in search of "different and stronger" remedies for harms to peremptory norms of international law.

The ambition is as noble as the challenge is vast. It requires a reimagining of the content of international human rights with no duty-bearer or with an entirely new one — one without legitimate public authority to issue laws, investigate crimes, imprison offenders, or even issue commercial licenses. This is a possibly chimerical pursuit. In the words of Aharon Barak, former President of the Israeli Supreme Court, regarding constitutional rights:

> [T]he end result of application of constitutional provisions regarding human rights to relations between private parties is the infringement of human rights. If the prohibition on discrimination, for example, applies also to relations between private actors, does this mean that a testator is not entitled to discriminate between heirs, and a seller is not entitled to discriminate between buyers? . . . Will we say that everything that the government is not entitled to do, private parties are also not entitled to do? . . . many things that private parties are entitled to do (such as discriminate among heirs), the government is not entitled to do (to establish discrimination in legislation).[66]

---

63 *Retail, Wholesale and Department Store Union, Local 580 v Dolphin Delivery Ltd*, [1986] SCJ No 75, [1986] 2 SCR 573 at para 39 (S.C.C.). See also *Hill v Church of Scientology of Toronto*, [1995] SCJ No 64, [1995] 2 SCR 1130 at para 94 (SCC).

64 *Nevsun*, above note 2 at 109.

65 *Toronto*, above note 41 at para 152.

66 Barak, above note 55 at 232.

E. Conclusion

Justice Abella's decision in *Nevsun* suggests a possible fork in the evolution of business and human rights law. One path would reshape the understanding of the reasonable business, incrementally imposing greater human rights-related governance expectations, while continuing to operate within well-understood strictures of private law. The other path would have us reimagine customary international law to approximate the end served by international human rights *from the perspective of rights-holders*. It would have judges "accept that justice was the application of law to life, not just the application of laws to facts."[67] We have little doubt which path is more pragmatic. And yet Justice Abella has always dreamed for us.

67 Abella Farewell, above note 43 at 10:47.

16 Reflections on Justice Abella's Legacy in Immigration and Refugee Law

JAMIE CHAI YUN LIEW*

A. An Indelible Mark on Immigration Law

It is an honour to contribute to this collection of work reflecting on Justice Abella's legacy. As a child of immigrant parents, I found it inspiring to see the daughter of refugees sit on Canada's highest court of Canada. I remember being moved to tears when, flanked by students entering their first year at the University of Ottawa Faculty of Law Orientation, Justice Abella talked about the family members she lost in the Holocaust, how her parents were forcibly moved to labour and displaced person camps, and her Jewish identity. Rosalie Silberman Abella was born in a displaced persons camp in Stuttgart in 1946. After awaiting the bureaucratic immigration system to approve applications in Canada, Justice Abella and her family arrived as new immigrants in Canada in 1950.[1] At that orientation session, Justice Abella shared her family's migration story, their losses, and their survival. She talked about what motivated her to pursue a legal career. In her honest remarks, she not only moved the audience but motivated them in turn to seek the seemingly unattainable. As I will discuss in this chapter, Justice Abella's lived experience as a migrant has profoundly informed her judicial decision-making.

Beyond her presence at the Supreme Court, Justice Abella has left an indelible mark on immigration law. Of the 950 cases heard and 210 decisions Justice Abella authored at the Supreme Court, she was involved in

* Professor, Shirley Greenberg Chair for Women and the Legal Profession, University of Ottawa, Faculty of Law.

1 Sean Fine, "How Rosalie Abella's Personal History Shaped her Legal Legacy" *Globe and Mail* (26 June 2021), online: www.theglobeandmail.com/canada/article-how-rosalie-abellas-personal-history-shaped-her-legal-legacy/?cmpid=rss&utm_source=dlvr.it&utm_medium=twitter.

18 cases that included the word "immigration" in their indexing tags.[2] Of the eighteen cases, she authored five opinions.[3] These five cases will be discussed in this chapter.[4]

Abella has left an enduring and admirable legacy in the field of immigration law. Her decisions remind us that a purposive approach to interpreting law provides the framework by which we ensure that context matters and that compassion can and should inform decision-making.

B. Compassionate Purpose in Immigration Law

1. Hilewitz: *Opening the Door to Immigrant Disabled Children*

The 2005 case *Hilewitz v Canada (Minister of Citizenship and Immigration), De Jong v Canada (Minister of Citizenship and Immigration)* dealt with two principal applicants with families who applied to immigrate to Canada, at the time, under the "investor"[5] and "self-employed"[6] classes, respectively. The applicants all met the qualifications outlined in the then *Immigration Act*,[7] but they were found inadmissible to Canada on the grounds that they would pose "excessive demands" on social

2 I am grateful to the assistance of Stephen Bindman and Keenan Macneal for generating these numbers. The eighteen cases include: *Hilewitz v Canada (Minister of Citizenship and Immigration), De Jong v Canada (Minister of Citizenship and Immigration)*, 2005 SCC 57 [*Hilewitz*]; *Charkaoui v Canada (Citizenship and Immigration)*, 2008 SCC 38; *Charkaoui v Canada (Citizenship and Immigration)*, 2007 SCC 9; *Canada (Citizenship and Immigration) v Khosa*, 2009 SCC 12; *Németh v Canada (Justice)*, 2010 SCC 56; *Gavrila v Canada (Justice)*, 2010 SCC 57; *Canada (Attorney General) v Mavi*, 2011 SCC 30; *R v Pham*, 2013 SCC 15; *Agraira v Canada (Public Safety and Emergency Preparedness)*, 2013 SCC 36; *Ezokola v Canada (Citizenship and Immigration)*, 2013 SCC 40; *Canada (Citizenship and Immigration) v Harkat*, 2014 SCC 37; *Febles v Canada (Citizenship and Immigration)*, 2014 SCC 68; *B010 v Canada (Citizenship and Immigration)*, 2015 SCC 58; *R v Appulonappa*, 2015 SCC 59; *Kanthasamy v Canada (Citizenship and Immigration)*, 2015 SCC 61; *Tran v Canada (Public Safety and Emergency Preparedness)*, 2017 SCC 50; *R v Wong*, 2018 SCC 25; *Canada (Public Safety and Emergency Preparedness) v Chhina*, 2019 SCC 29.

3 *Hilewizt*, above note 2; *Harkat*, above note 2; *Febles*, above note 2; *Kanthasamy*, above note 2; *Chhina*, above note 2.

4 *Kanthasamy*, above note 2; *Chhina*, above note 2. I want to disclose that I was co-counsel for interveners in both *Kanthasamy* and *Chhina* at the Supreme Court, and my academic work was cited by Justice Abella in *Kanthasamy*.

5 *Hilewitz*, above note 2 at para 8.

6 *Ibid* at para 27.

7 *Immigration Act, RSC* 1985, c I-2. The decision took some time to reach the Supreme Court, given that the *Immigration and Refugee Protection Act*, SC 2001, c 27 [*IRPA*] replaced the *Immigration Act* in 2001.

services[8] because each family included a dependent child that was "intellectually disabled."[9] Both applicants provided evidence of their financial ability and willingness to contribute to the costs of the social services demanded of their dependents.[10] In both cases, immigration officers refused to take this into account.

In penning the majority opinion, Justice Abella found the refusal to consider the families' ability and willingness to assist financially to be unreasonable. She wrote, "It seems to me somewhat incongruous to interpret the legislation in such a way that the very assets that qualify investors and self-employed individuals for admission to Canada can simultaneously be ignored in determining the admissibility of their disabled children."[11] She considered the families' genuine ability and willingness to absorb some of the costs an important and relevant factor that must be considered in an assessment of whether or not a family would be pose "excessive demand" on social services. She pointed out, "The ban [on disabled people] was not absolute."[12]

Justice Abella provided much-needed guidance on how immigration applications that include disabled persons should be reviewed. She reminded decision-makers that the overall purpose of the legislation was not to unequivocally exclude disabled people through inadmissibility on health grounds but to consider all factors relevant to assessing the aim of the legislation, namely whether they would pose an "excessive demand." As Michael Battista and Jordan Battista write, Justice Abella's decision "drew attention to Canada's history of being overly restrictive in its immigration policies towards people with disabilities," and her reasons "acknowledge that these unjustified restrictions concealed prejudices about disability."[13]

Applicants and their lawyers now provide detailed information in their immigration applications about how their disabilities are to be assessed under the legislation. As scholars Robert Wilton, Stine Hansen, and Edward Hall note, "the space made for individualized assessment and contestation through *Hilewitz* is important in that it moves

---

8 See *Immigration Act*, above note 7, s 19(1)(a)(ii), which was replaced by s 38(1) of the *IRPA*, whereby a person is inadmissible if they will be reasonably expected to cause excessive demands on health or social services.

9 *Hilewitz*, above note 2 at paras 9 and 28.

10 *Ibid* at paras 16 and 30.

11 *Ibid* at para 40.

12 *Ibid* at para 42.

13 Michael Battista and Jordan Battista, "HIV and Medical Inadmissibility in Canadian Immigration Law" for the Canadian Bar Association, Immigration Law Conference (May 9–11, 2013), online: www.cba.org/CBA/cle/PDF/IMM13_paper_battista.pdf.

from a narrow and often generic focus on problems and costs at the time of application to a more contextual and longitudinal reading of the familial, social, and economic circumstances of individual applicants."[14] Despite this, they also point out that "there remains significant limitations to what can be accomplished in this legal space."[15] Ravi Malhotra adds, "While this is undoubtedly a victory, it should be noted that *Hilewitz* would only apply to the relatively privileged class of immigrants."[16]

While our immigration system continues to exclude disabled people, Justice Abella's approach in this decision has allowed applicants and lawyers to explain and educate decision-makers about why disabilities should not be seen as a burden and encourage them to consider how disabled people can contribute in a variety of ways to society and how including them could be managed. This is all due to Justice Abella's nuanced opinion, which discourages a default rejection of any application involving a disabled person.

2. *Febles: Accounting for Atonement in Refugee Protection*

Luis Alberto Hernandez Febles obtained refugee status in the United States after leaving Cuba.[17] While in the United States, he was convicted and served time in prison for two assaults with a weapon.[18] As a result, Febles's refugee status in the US was revoked and he came to Canada to claim refugee protection. The Immigration and Refugee Board (IRB) considered whether Febles was excluded from refugee protection as per Article 1F(b) of the *Refugee Convention*[19] on the grounds that he committed a serious non-political crime.[20] The IRB grappled with the scope of this exclusion — did it serve to exclude persons who were fugitives or did it also apply to persons who had served their sentences?[21] A major-

14 Robert Wilton, Stine Hansen & Edward Hall, "Disabled People, Medical Inadmissibility, and the Differential Politics of Immigration" (2017) 61:3 *Canadian Geographer* 389 at 407.

15 *Ibid.* See also Roy Hanes, "None Is Still Too Many: An Historical Exploration of Canadian Immigration Legislation as it Pertains to People with Disabilities" (2009) 37:1 *Developmental Disabilities Bulletin* 91.

16 Ravi Malhotra, "The Impact of the *Convention on the Rights of Persons with Disabilities* on Canadian Jurisprudence: The Case of *Leobrera v Canada*" (2017) 54 *Alberta Law Review* 637 at 643.

17 *Febles*, above note 2 at para 1.

18 *Ibid.*

19 *Convention Relating to the Status of Refugees*, UNTS vol 189 (28 July 1951) at 137.

20 At paras 2–3.

21 At para 4.

ity of the Supreme Court agreed with the IRB that Febles did not qualify for refugee protection because of the serious crimes he committed in the United States.[22] They held that Article 1F(b) was not confined to fugitives.[23]

Justice Abella penned a dissenting opinion that was supported by Justice Cromwell. She first pointed out, "In the wake of the mass persecution and displacement of persons during World War II, the international community responsively consolidated and entrenched international protection for refugees through the . . . *Refugee Convention*."[24] This introductory statement framed her dissenting opinion on the *raison d'etre* of this protection regime — a regime that was born out of the horrors her own family suffered and fled from.

Justice Abella used a purposive approach to interpreting the scope of the exclusion provision: signatories to the *Refugee Convention* did not want the integrity and the political viability of refugee protection compromised[25] by "individuals who would abuse the status of a refugee by avoiding accountability through prosecution or punishment for a serious crime outside the country of refuge."[26] Unlike the majority, however, Justice Abella took a compassionate approach to expiation and rehabilitation in evaluating whether Article 1F(b) should apply to an individual circumstance.[27] She pointed to the fact that Febles turned himself in after the commission of the crimes, served his sentences, admitted to having problems with alcohol, stopped drinking and completed an Alcoholic Anonymous course, was gainfully employed, and disclosed his criminal record to Canadian officials when he made his refugee claim.[28]

Justice Abella also noted, "The consequences of exclusion under Article 1F are significant," explaining that:

> If an individual becomes ineligible for the status of a 'refugee' on the basis of one of those exclusionary grounds, the humanitarian protections provided in the *Refugee Convention* are denied altogether, including the protection from *refoulement* under Article 33. An excluded individual is consequently at risk of being returned to face persecution in his or her

22 *Ibid.*
23 *Ibid* at para 22.
24 *Ibid* at para 71.
25 *Ibid* at para 73.
26 *Ibid* at para 101.
27 *Ibid* at para 74.
28 *Ibid* at paras 75–80.

> country of origin, barring the availability of any residual protection under domestic or international human rights law.[29]

She reasoned, "In light of the human rights purposes of the *Refugee Convention* and the dramatic consequences of exclusion from the status of a refugee, Article 1F requires a particularly cautious interpretation."[30]

Justice Abella applied a "'good faith' approach to interpretation required by the *Vienna Convention* and the *Refugee Convention*'s human rights purpose."[31] She held that individual circumstances reflecting "a sufficient degree of rehabilitation or expiation" should not exclude a person from refugee protection.[32]

Justice Abella's dissenting opinion invites a compassionate approach — one that militates against the turning people away from protection where they have demonstrated atonement for their crimes. Unfortunately, the predominant approach is one where atonement and remediation do not factor in. Molly Joeck writes:

> Disappointingly, the majority decision failed to clearly state the purpose underlying article 1F(b), embracing instead a vague and overbroad interpretation of the provision premised upon both deservingness and dangerousness — an interpretation that does not align with the broader scheme of the Refugee Convention and the debates that occurred during the drafting of the provision.[33]

James Billingsley agrees, stating that "[t]he majority judgement in *Febles* . . . creates a false dichotomy between a plain meaning interpretation of Article 1F(b), where the commission of a serious non-political crime excludes claimants *ab initio*, and a purposive interpretation of Article 1F(b), where exclusion is limited by implication to fugitives or currently dangerous criminals."[34] In my opinion, Justice Abella's humanitarian approach acknowledges that people evolve, change, can make amends. She advocated for a system where people should not

29 *Ibid* at para 87.

30 *Ibid* at para 92.

31 *Ibid* at para 131.

32 *Ibid* at para 132.

33 Molly Joeck, "Canadian Exclusion Jurisprudence post-*Febles* (2021) *International Journal of Refugee Law* 33:1 54 at 56.

34 James Billingsley, "No Second Chances: The Default Exclusion of Refugee Claimants on Grounds of Serious Criminality: A Case Comment on *Febles v Canada*" (2015) 20 *Appeal: Review of Current Law and Law Reform* 99 at 113.

forever be punished for mistakes, even if they are severe, in ways that may cost them their lives.

3. Kanthasamy: *Reinvigorating Humanitarian and Compassionate*

Perhaps the most important case that reflects Justice Abella's contribution to immigration law is *Kanthasamy*.[35] Jeyakannan Kanthasamy is a Tamil from northern Sri Lanka who fled after he was detained and beaten by the police and army.[36] His refugee claim was refused by the Immigration and Refugee Board.[37] Following this decision, Kanthasamy applied for permanent residence on humanitarian and compassionate (H&C) grounds.[38] At the time, he was seventeen years old.[39] The officer's rejection of this application was the subject of Justice Abella's 2015 decision at the Supreme Court.

Under subsection 25(1) of the *Immigration and Refugee Protection Act* (*IRPA*),[40] the Minister of Immigration, Refugees and Citizenship or their delegate has the discretion to grant permanent residence to a person even if they do not meet the ordinary requirements of the *IRPA* but where there are sufficient "humanitarian and compassionate considerations."[41] As Donald Galloway and I write, the H&C provision "is a discretionary device that introduces flexibility into immigration decision-making" and it "enhances the attainment of the objectives of the *IRPA* by allowing an immigration officer to weigh the reasons for admission instead of merely applying the rules."[42]

Prior to the 2015 decision in *Kanthasamy*, the rates of approval for inland H&C applications showed a diminishing trend: 56 percent in 2002,[43] 36 percent in 2011,[44] 27 percent in 2013, 49 percent in 2014.[45] The rates of approval alone don't tell us much, however, unless we consider

35 *Kanthasamy*, above note 2.

36 *Ibid* at paras 2 and 48.

37 *Ibid* at para 3.

38 *Ibid* at para 5.

39 *Ibid.*

40 *IRPA*, above note 7.

41 *Ibid.*

42 Jamie Chai Yun Liew and Donald Galloway, *Immigration Law* (Irwin Law, 2014) at 393.

43 Citizenship and Immigration Canada, DWS (FOSS) Finalized H&C Applications and Removals as of 29 June 2012 (requested by Andrea Asbil, 3 August 2012).

44 *Ibid.*

45 Citizenship and Immigration Canada, OPP-DART-2018-1397-H&C Decisions and removals (ATIP requested by Robin Seligman) [ATIP].

what role the H&C application plays in our legal system. The H&C application has at once been described as an "exceptional" or "special" measure,"[46] and yet its existence is used to justify Canada's adherence to the *Charter of Rights and Freedoms* in cases where persons claim their rights are infringed. To be clear, the existence of section 25(1) is seen as a safety valve to dampen any *Charter* rights infringements. For example, in the case of *Medovarski*, the Supreme Court saw H&C grounds as a means to "mitigate the finality" of the impugned provisions in the *IRPA* that took away the right to appeal an order of deportation.[47] This approach has been adopted in several cases.[48]

Kanthasamy challenged the problematic practice where immigration officers used restrictive language in operational instructions and guidelines as the legal test for subsection 25(1): "unusual, undeserved or disproportionate hardship."[49] In rejecting this test, Justice Abella, in her majority reasons, reminded decision-makers of the historical purpose of H&C relief in the *IRPA*.[50] She wrote, "as the legislative history suggests, the successive series of broadly worded 'humanitarian and compassionate' provisions in various immigration statutes had a common purpose, namely, to offer equitable relief in circumstances that 'would excite in a reasonable [person] in a civilized community a desire to relieve the misfortunes of another.'"[51] She found the words "unusual and undeserved or disproportionate hardship" to be descriptive rather than being "three new thresholds."[52] In focusing on the "equitable underlying purpose" of H&C applications, Justice Abella realigned the legal test towards a more compassionate stance.

46 For example, *Canada (Citizenship and Immigration) v Khosa*, 2009 SCC 12 [*Khosa*] at para 57. While in *Khosa* the court was referring to a different provision in the *IRPA*, the reference to using "humanitarian and compassionate" considerations and therefore its interpretation is the same. At the Federal Court, the H&C mechanism has been described as exceptional. For example: *Bhatia v Canada (Citizenship and Immigration)*, 2017 FC 1000; *Kaur v Canada (Citizenship and Immigration)*, 2017 FC 75; *Braud v Canada (Citizenship and Immigration)*, 2020 FC 132; *Zhang v Canada (Citizenship and Immigration)*, 2021 FC 328; *Ji v Canada (Citizenship and Immigration)*, 2019 FC 1219.

47 *Medovarski v Canada (Minister of Citizenship and Immigration)*, 2005 SCC 51 at para 11.

48 See, for example, *Toussaint v Canada (Citizenship and Immigration)*, 2011 FCA 146 at para 58; *Begum v Canada (Citizenship and Immigration)*, 2018 FCA 181 at para 24; *Moretto v Canada (Citizenship and Immigration)*, 2019 FCA 261 at para 65.

49 *Kanthasamy*, above note 2 at paras 6–7.

50 *Ibid* at paras 11–22.

51 *Ibid* at para 22.

52 *Ibid* at para 33.

Justice Abella also reminded decision-makers that taking the "best interests of the child" principle into account is a "highly contextual" exercise responsive to a multitude of factors including age, capacity, needs, and maturity.[53] She placed importance on considering mental health and psychological reports as proper evidence in that regard.[54]

In finding the immigration officer's decision in relation to Kanthasamy unreasonable, Justice Abella not only provided hope for Kanthasamy, but provided much needed guidance on the meaning of "humanitarian and compassionate," repositioning the legal analysis to equitable purposes and moving away from an improper restriction grounded in creeping language found outside the legislation.

The impact of this decision is not speculative, and I cannot help but notice how the decision echoes her lived experience as a migrant — a desire to have one's application treated with humanity and compassion. Rates of approvals of H&C applications increased following the release of the decision, with the H&C approval rates for inland applications at 63 percent for 2016, 60 percent for 2017, and 68 percent for 2018 as of the July 2018.[55] As Emily Chan and Jennifer Stone point out, "In many ways the SCC in *Kanthasamy* re-visits the seminal case of *Baker v Canada (Minister of Citizenship and Immigration)*, another decision about discretion in the immigration context, and it reaffirms that officers making H&C determinations must consider and weigh *all* relevant facts and factors before them without fettering their discretion."[56]

C. An Adherence to Purposive Approach in Interpreting Immigration Law

1. *Harkat: Protecting Informer Privilege*

Mohamed Harkat has a long and complicated history with our legal system and is known for being subject to the security certificate regime in the *IRPA*.[57] A 2014 Supreme Court decision involved questions around the constitutionality of the security certificate system as well as

53 *Ibid* at paras 34–41.

54 *Ibid* at para 49.

55 ATIP, above note 45.

56 Emily Chan and Jennifer Stone, "Where No Court Has Gone Before: Primacy and Centrality of the Best Interests of the Child Principle — Case Comment on *Kanthasamy v Canada*" (2016) 29:2 *Canadian Journal of Administrative Law & Practice* 219 at 221.

57 *Harkat*, above note 2 at para 11.

the right to access material and evidence provided by informants to the Canada Security Intelligence Service (CSIS).[58] Under this system, special advocates are appointed to protect the interests of a person subject to a security certificate in closed hearings with a designated judge. In this case, the special advocates sought to obtain disclosure of the identity of the human sources who provided information regarding Harkat to CSIS, as well as permission to interview and cross-examine them.[59] This request was denied by the designated judge, citing the common law police informer privilege.[60] A majority of the Supreme Court found the security scheme constitutional but disagreed that police informer privilege extends to CSIS human sources, given the different procedural safeguards in the criminal law system as compared to the security certificate process.[61] Dissenting in part, Justice Abella, again with Justice Cromwell, penned an opinion that agreed that the security certificate scheme was constitutional, but would have extended informer privilege to this process, citing the interests of the human sources.[62]

One can only speculate that Justice Abella and Justice Cromwell wrestled with the difficult balancing act in weighing the interests of sources to CSIS alongside the interests of persons subject to security certificates. They stated, for example: "given the intensity of the interests at stake in the security certificate context, we acknowledge that it would be appropriate to recognize a limited exception specifically crafted for the security certificate process which would address only disclosure to the special advocate, not to the subject of the proceedings."[63] Shortly after the decision, Parliament created a legislative privilege for CSIS human sources under section 18.1 of the *Canadian Security Intelligence Service Act*.[64] This was done despite views that the exclusion of special advocates and *amici curiae* from the circle of privilege was unnecessary.[65] Graham Hudson posits that it remains to be seen whether such a scheme will survive *Charter* scrutiny when balanced with its use in security certificate proceedings.[66] Kent Roach argues that this poses a wrench in

58 *Ibid* at para 3.
59 *Ibid* at paras 12–18.
60 *Ibid.*
61 *Ibid* at paras 110–12.
62 *Ibid* at para 113.
63 *Ibid* at para 137.
64 RSC 1985, c C-23.
65 John Norris, "Class Struggles: The New CISIS Human Source Privilege" (2017) 64:3–4 *Criminal Law Quarterly* 509 at 511.
66 Graham Hudson, "As Good as it Gets: Security, Asylum, and the Rule of Law after the Certificate Trilogy" (2016) 52:3 *Osgoode Hall LJ* 905 at 925.

the aim of combatting terrorism: "The new privilege silently privileges CSIS's ability to collect intelligence over the evidential and disclosure requirements of terrorism prosecutions" and "[t]his is a questionable choice of priorities and policy."[67]

2. *Chhina: Dissent on the Writ of Habeas Corpus*

Tusif Chhina obtained refugee protection in Canada and as a result was a permanent resident. His permanent resident status was vacated when he was found inadmissible.[68] As a result, a deportation order was issued against him.[69] After spending time in criminal custody, Chhina was in and out immigration detention, due in part to delays with the Canadian government obtaining travel documents from Pakistan to deport him.[70] Chhina filed a *habeas corpus* application arguing that his immigration detention was unlawful because it had become lengthy and indeterminate.[71] The judge hearing his application declined jurisdiction on the grounds that the *IRPA* has a comprehensive legislative framework governing detention and release.[72] The Court of Appeal reversed the decision and held that the chambers judge should have exercised his discretion to hear the application, reasoning that Chhina did not contest the determinations regarding his inadmissibility or deportation but the legality of his detention.[73] At issue before the Supreme Court was the scope and application of the *Peiroo* exception, namely: is an immigration detainee precluded from bringing an application for *habeas corpus* because of the statutory scheme for detention reviews in the *IRPA*?

A majority at the Supreme Court held that "provincial superior courts have inherent jurisdiction to hear *habeas corpus* applications,"[74] and that "[s]uch a court may only decline jurisdiction where the legislator has put in place 'a complete, comprehensive and expert statutory scheme which provides for a review at least as broad as that available by way of *habeas corpus* and no less advantageous.'"[75] There are only

67 Kent Roach, "The Problems with the New CSIS Human Source Privilege in Bill C-44" (2014) 61:4 *Criminal Law Quarterly* 451 at 455.

68 *Chhina*, above note 2 at para 8.

69 *Ibid*.

70 *Ibid* at para 9.

71 *Ibid* at para 10; at the time he submitted his *habeas corpus* application, he had spent thirteen months in detention.

72 *Ibid* at para 11.

73 *Ibid* at paras 12–13.

74 *Ibid* at para 17.

75 *Ibid* at para 18.

two instances where a provincial superior court may decline to hear a *habeas corpus* application: (a) where a prisoner seeks to attack the legality of their conviction or sentence; and (b) where a person is contesting a finding that there was no credible basis for their refugee claim and therefore no basis for a removal order issued against them.[76] The majority held that *habeas corpus* is not precluded in every detention arising in the immigration context,[77] and that the *IRPA* was "unable to effectively address the challenge raised by Mr. Chhina's application in a manner that is as broad and advantageous as *habeas corpus*,"[78] for three reasons. The first was that the Court found the detention review under the *IRPA* to be less advantageous than *habeas corpus* proceedings. The second was that the scope of judicial review in the Federal Court was narrower than that of *habeas corpus* in provincial superior courts. Finally, the court found *habeas corpus* as offering a timelier remedy than judicial review.[79]

In a lone dissent, Justice Abella held that the *Peiroo* exception applied and would have declined *habeas corpus* jurisdiction. She wrote that the *IRPA* "should be interpreted in a way that guarantees the fullest possible range of scrutiny for detention, including the conditions of detention" and that there was "nothing in the language of the *Act* that precludes such a comprehensive review."[80] She relied on the objectives of the *IRPA* to find that the "better approach is to continue to read the language of the *IRPA* in a manner that is as broad and advantageous as *habeas corpus*."[81]

This was the last case in which Justice Abella provided an opinion on immigration law, and it can be read as proposing an ideal approach to how immigration detention should function. True to her approach in previous cases, Justice Abella mined the purpose of the legislative scheme to advocate for an interpretation that provided *Charter*-adhering and fair reviews of detentions. In my view, however, her faith in the text of the *IRPA* and in those administering the legislative framework misses the mark. Her opinion would have foreclosed *habeas corpus* to those needing it the most.

Chhina was not just an isolated individual disappointed with the outcomes of his repeated immigration reviews. The majority pointed

76 *Ibid* at para 25.
77 *Ibid* at para 31.
78 *Ibid* at para 44.
79 *Ibid* at para 59.
80 *Ibid* at para 72.
81 *Ibid* at para 74.

to evidence of the lived experiences of several immigration detainees: "An external audit commissioned by the chair of the Immigration and Refugee Board offers a timely, and frankly unfortunate, picture of how the scheme is being administered for those in long-term detention. The 2018 audit highlights how, in practice, detainees do not receive the full benefit of the scheme."[82] Chhina's case symbolizes the long-suffering desperation and frustration detainees and their lawyers had with a legislative scheme that manifested in troubling detention review practices.[83] *Habeas corpus* was a measure of last resort, and it offered a new, fresh venue to plead relief. The problems with the implementation of the legislation were the reason detainees turned to this ancient writ.

What is curious is that Justice Abella stepped out on her own to provide a dissent. The evidence not only demonstrated a pattern of the failures of that system, but also how access to judicial review had no impact. Justice Abella seemingly applied blind faith to a system that had been documented to offer little relief for detainees. It is curious that she placed more weight on an ideal interpretation of a legislative regime over concerns about the legality of unlawful imprisonment in this exceptionalized administrative law space. Her decision obliges us to ask: how badly must an implementation of a scheme go before a court will intervene? How much deference should we give to a legislative scheme, especially when it impacts a person's liberty so profoundly?[84] The evidence of the external audit of the immigration detention review scheme was as damning as they come.[85] Sheila Wilderman writes:

> the majority took a hard look at the detention review regime in light of evidence of its functioning and saw an impenetrable, Kafkaesque bureaucracy inured to the seriousness of indefinite and/or otherwise illegal

---

82 *Ibid* at para 63.

83 I invite readers to look at the Audit to see the full range of problems, including the lack of procedural fairness and problematic evidentiary practices: Immigration and Refugee Board, "Report of the 2017/2018 External Audit" (Detention Review), online: https://irb.gc.ca/en/transparency/reviews-audit-evaluations/Pages/ID-external-audit-1718.aspx [Audit]. This report was in the record in *Chhina.*

84 This question is the subject of much debate. For example, Gerard Kennedy's response to Mark Mancini: Gerard Kennedy, "Deference to Administrators Must Be Legislated not Assumed" Advocates for the Rule of Law blog (22 May 2019), online: www.ruleoflaw.ca/deference-to-administrators-must-be-legislated-not-assumed/.

85 Audit, above note 83. To the IRB's credit, it conducted this review and has implemented changes as a result.

detention. Its answer was to open a *habeas corpus* escape hatch, previously sealed to immigration detainees in deference to legislative intent and administrative design.[86]

Paul Daly calls Justice Abella's opinion "clear-eyed," positing that she avoided creating a "procedural solution to a substantive problem" as the majority did.[87] With respect, *habeas corpus* is not simply a procedural mechanism but asks the important substantive question of whether the state is unlawfully interfering with a person's liberty — a legal question of such foundational importance that the inception of this writ can be traced to the Magna Carta.[88] As Siena Anstis, Joshua Blum, and Jared Will write:

> The effect of successful *habeas corpus* litigation in Canada could be the beginning of the end of the fiction of a 'separate but equal' detention scheme for non-citizens. By allowing non-citizens access to provincial superior courts, the immigration detention regime may no longer be able to operate in a state of exception, divorced from the principles of justice that apply to all other persons who face imprisonment in Canada.[89]

I admire Justice Abella's confidence in the administrative legal system. While my own preference would be to rid the immigration system of detention altogether, it remains, and I certainly hope that policy makers and those that implement law in our administrative state take Justice Abella's call for fairness to heart.

D. Conclusion: Justice Abella's Compassionate and Purposive Legacy

There is much to celebrate when it comes to looking at Justice Abella's legacy in immigration law. While I disagree with her dissent in the case of *Chhina*, I respect her steadfast commitment to a purposive

---

86 Sheila Wildeman, "Habeas Corpus Unbound" in Colleen Flood & Paul Daly, eds, *Administrative Law in Context*, 4th ed (Emond Publishing, 2021).

87 Paul Daly, "To Have the Point: *Canada (Public Safety and Emergency Preparedness) v Chhina*" Administrative Law Matters blog (5 June 2019), online: www.administrativelawmatters.com/blog/2019/06/05/to-have-the-point-canada-public-safety-and-emergency-preparedness-v-chhina-2019-scc-29/.

88 Wildeman, above note 86; William Duker, "The English Origins of the Writ of Habeas Corpus: A peculiar Path to Fame" (1978) 53:5 *NYU Law Review* 983.

89 Siena Anstis, Joshua Blum & Jared Will, "Separate but Unequal: Immigration Detention in Canada and the Great Writ of Liberty" (2017 63:1 *McGill Law Journal* 1 at 43.

interpretation of law, and ironically, I think her approach could be applied to the findings in the *Chhina* majority opinion. Overall, it is her purposive approach to interpreting legislation that I admire the most, since it has been used to remind decision-makers what the equitable, humanitarian, and compassionate aim of the immigration legal regime is. In doing so, she has demonstrated how a person's lived experience can inform a fairer and more just outcome. I congratulate Justice Abella on her retirement and hope future jurists are inspired to continue her work.

17 Les droits (de la personne) de l'enfant : regard sur les notions de vulnérabilité et d'égalité dans la jurisprudence de la juge Abella

MONA PARÉ*

Les droits de l'enfant ne font pas encore consensus. Bien que l'on dise que les enfants sont titulaires de droits, la nature et la dimension de ces droits font l'objet de désaccords. Ces droits sont rarement compris comme les droits et libertés garantis au niveau constitutionnel. Les droits de l'enfant sont souvent conçus plutôt comme des droits particuliers qui ne s'appliquent qu'aux enfants et que l'on trouve dans des instruments internationaux ou dans certaines lois. Au niveau interne, la prise de décisions dans l'intérêt de l'enfant en matière de garde ou d'adoption, les garanties procédurales particulières qu'ont les enfants dans le cadre de la justice pénale, ou encore leur droit à la protection face à la négligence et aux mauvais traitements, en sont des exemples.

Plutôt que des droits particuliers, ou encore comme un sous-ensemble des droits de la personne avec une application limitée, on devrait considérer les droits de l'enfant comme des droits de la personne exprimés d'une manière adaptée aux enfants[1]. L'honorable Rosalie Silberman Abella contribue à cette compréhension des droits de l'enfant dans sa jurisprudence, qui est conforme à la *Convention relative aux droits de l'enfant* (CDE) des Nations Unies[2]. La juge Abella a cité cette convention plus que tout autre juge de la Cour suprême du Canada (CSC). Lorsqu'elle fait usage du droit international, ses références lui permettent d'interpréter le droit interne de manière à

---

* Professeure titulaire, Directrice du Laboratoire de recherche interdisciplinaire sur les droits de l'enfant, Université d'Ottawa.

1 Voir Mona Paré, "Children's Rights Are Human Rights and Why Canadian Implementation Lags Behind", (2017) 4(1) *Canadian Journal of Children's Rights*, 24.

2 20 novembre 1989, RTNU vol, 1577.

assurer le respect de nos obligations internationales en matière des droits de la personne[3].

Cette contribution présente un examen sélectif de la jurisprudence de la CSC en matière des droits de l'enfant. Le choix des jugements a été fait en fonction des thèmes qui ont particulièrement marqué cette jurisprudence : la vulnérabilité inhérente à l'enfant et le double concept de non-discrimination et d'égalité comme notions clés en droits de la personne. Ces concepts permettent de mettre en évidence la nature unique des droits de l'enfant en tant que droits de la personne.

Divisée en deux parties, en reprenant chacune des notions, ce chapitre examinera l'application que la juge Abella en a faite pour avancer notre compréhension des droits de l'enfant, autant dans des jugements majoritaires que dissidents. Sans pouvoir en tirer de formule magique, certaines balises se dessinent qui mettent l'accent sur la situation particulière des enfants et le respect de leurs droits. À travers cette analyse, nous noterons également l'utilisation qui a été faite du droit international dans l'application des droits de l'enfant, sachant que les droits de l'enfant sont particulièrement bien protégés en droit international et qu'une interprétation de nos lois inspirée par les instruments internationaux ne peut que faire avancer les droits de l'enfant dans la société canadienne.

A. La vulnérabilité des enfants et ses effets sur la protection de leurs droits

La vulnérabilité inhérente à l'enfant est une notion qui permet de distinguer les enfants des adultes. C'est sous la plume de la juge Abella que la Cour suprême explore ce concept en détail et en fait un prisme à travers lequel interpréter et appliquer les droits de la personne lorsqu'on a affaire à des enfants.

1. *La vulnérabilité inhérente*

Dans *R. c. D.B.*, cette notion a permis à la CSC de reconnaitre un principe de justice fondamentale qui s'applique particulièrement aux enfants : la présomption de culpabilité moins élevée des adolescents[4]. L'affaire traitait de la constitutionnalité de deux séries d'articles de la

3 La CDE n'a pas été incorporée en droit interne, mais elle peut être utilisée pour l'interpréter : Baker *c.* Canada (Ministre de la Citoyenneté et de l'Immigration), [1999] 2 R.C.S. 817 [Baker].

4 R. *c.* D.B., [2008] 2 R.C.S. 3, 2008 CSC 25.

Loi sur le système de justice pénale pour les adolescents (LSJPA)[5]. La première prévoyait qu'un adolescent déclaré coupable d'une infraction désignée devait démontrer pourquoi il devrait être assujetti à une peine spécifique plutôt qu'à une peine applicable aux adultes. La deuxième prévoyait que ce serait également à l'adolescent dans cette situation de convaincre le tribunal qu'une ordonnance de non-publication devrait s'appliquer à son cas. La question se posait de savoir si le fardeau de la preuve qui incombait à l'adolescent selon la LSJPA était conforme à l'article 7 de la *Charte canadienne des droits et libertés*.

En s'appuyant sur les arrêts de la Cour d'appel de l'Ontario et celle du Québec, qui ont reconnu qu'il fallait prendre en compte la moins grande maturité des adolescents en examinant le fardeau de la preuve[6], la juge Abella affirme « qu'en raison de leur âge les adolescents sont plus vulnérables, moins matures et moins aptes à exercer un jugement moral. Cela leur donne droit à une présomption de culpabilité morale moins élevée »[7]. Elle applique les principes jurisprudentiels pour déterminer que la présomption de culpabilité morale moins élevée est bien un principe de justice fondamentale[8]. Après un examen de l'historique législatif elle affirme qu'il s'agit d'un principe juridique et que dans toutes les lois canadiennes portant sur ce sujet, on a « reconnu la responsabilité atténuée des adolescents et la vulnérabilité qui les caractérise »[9]. La juge Abella se réfère aussi à l'article 40 de la CDE prévoyant que les enfants accusés ou convaincus d'infraction à la loi pénale ont droit à un traitement qui tient compte de leur âge. Elle confirme qu'il existe un large consensus dans la société sur le fait que ce principe est essentiel au bon fonctionnement du système de justice étant donné que plusieurs sources jurisprudentielles et doctrinales se réfèrent à la responsabilité moindre des adolescents, à leur vulnérabilité et à leur manque de maturité. Ainsi, le renversement du fardeau de la preuve qui demande à l'adolescent de réfuter la présomption d'assujettissement à une peine applicable aux adultes l'empêche de bénéficier de la présomption de culpabilité morale moins élevée qui est fondée sur l'âge[10]. Le même rai-

5 LC 2002, c1.

6 R. *v.* D. B., 2006 CanLII 8871 (ON CA), Québec (Ministre de la Justice) *c.* Canada (Ministre de la Justice), 2003 CanLII 52182 (QC CA).

7 R. *c.* D.B, para. 41.

8 Voir R. *c.* MalmoLevine, [2003] 3 R.C.S. 571, 2003 CSC 74; Canadian Foundation for Children, Youth and the Law *c.* Canada (Procureur général), [2004] 1 R.C.S. 76, 2004 CSC 4 [Canadian Foundation].

9 R. *c.* D.B, para 48.

10 Traditionnellement, c'est au ministère public de démontrer qu'une peine plus sévère s'impose.

sonnement est appliqué aux dispositions portant sur la vie privée et exigeant de l'adolescent coupable d'une infraction désignée, même s'il a obtenu une peine spécifique, de prouver qu'il devrait pouvoir bénéficier de l'interdiction de publication. La Cour se fonde sur la jurisprudence, la doctrine et des instruments internationaux[11], pour démontrer l'importance de la vie privée pour les adolescents et le dommage causé par la stigmatisation et l'étiquetage. Elle note que la publication, ou son interdiction, fait partie de la peine et doit donc faire l'objet de la même présomption que le reste de la peine.

Ainsi, la vulnérabilité qui est inhérente aux adolescents justifie qu'on les traite différemment et qu'on reconnaisse leur responsabilité atténuée, résultant en une présomption de culpabilité moins élevée. C'est la première fois que l'on reconnait un principe de justice fondamentale qui permet d'adapter l'application de l'article 7 de la *Charte* aux enfants.

La notion de vulnérabilité se retrouve dans différents types de causes concernant des adolescents. Dans *A.B. c. Bragg Communications*, la juge Abella, rédigeant pour la majorité, réaffirme que la vulnérabilité est liée à l'âge[12]. En l'espèce, il s'agissait d'une adolescente de 15 ans qui avait été victime d'intimidation en ligne. Elle demandait de pouvoir procéder de manière anonyme pour demander une ordonnance obligeant le fournisseur de services Internet à divulguer l'identité de la personne ayant publié le contenu désobligeant la concernant. Il s'agissait de pondérer le principe de la publicité des débats judiciaires et la liberté de presse d'un côté et la protection de la vie privée et la protection des enfants contre la cyberintimidation de l'autre. Le jugement de la CSC renverse les décisions précédentes qui n'avaient pas permis à l'adolescente de procéder de manière anonyme parce qu'elle n'avait pas démontré l'existence d'un préjudice important justifiant cette demande. Selon la juge Abella, le risque de préjudice existe du fait de l'âge de l'adolescente. La vulnérabilité des enfants est inhérente, et la protection de la vie privée des enfants dans la législation canadienne et dans les accords internationaux est entièrement fondée sur l'âge et non sur le tempérament de l'enfant[13]. En se fiant à la jurisprudence et à la doctrine, elle reconnait les multiples conséquences préjudiciables que la cyberintimidation peut causer aux enfants. En outre, la juge Abella reconnait également que le refus de l'anonymat pourrait avoir un effet dommage-

---

11 *Ensemble de règles minima des Nations Unies concernant l'administration de la justice pour mineurs*, Doc NU A/RES/40/33, 1985 [Règles de Beijing].

12 A.B. *c.* Bragg Communications Inc., 2012 CSC 46, [2012] 2 R.C.S. 567 [A.B.].

13 Nous notons toutefois que la Cour ne cite pas l'article 16 de la CDE sur le droit de l'enfant à la vie privée.

able sur l'accès des enfants à la justice, car sans garantie d'anonymat, les jeunes victimes auront plus d'hésitation à engager des poursuites contre l'auteur de l'intimidation. Comme dans *D.B.*, elle reconnait le risque de stigmatisation qui est plus préjudiciable pour les enfants et cette vulnérabilité justifie de leur ôter un fardeau de preuve supplémentaire. Le caractère inhérent de la vulnérabilité de l'enfant ici permet donc une pondération des intérêts en faveur de l'enfant.

2. *La vulnérabilité face à la maturité*

L'arrêt suivant vient mettre certaines limites aux effets de la vulnérabilité inhérente aux enfants dans l'application des droits de l'enfant. L'affaire *A.C. c. Manitoba* est un arrêt phare en matière des droits de l'enfant, car il s'agit de la première fois que la CSC, sous la plume de la juge Abella, se penche sur la notion de l'intérêt supérieur de l'enfant (ISE) par rapport au respect de l'opinion de l'enfant[14], les deux étant des principes importants des droits de l'enfant[15]. Dans la pratique, l'ISE est souvent employé pour protéger l'enfant, en reconnaissant sa vulnérabilité. En l'espèce, la requérante, une adolescente Témoin de Jéhovah, et ses parents, font appel d'un arrêt qui confirme la licéité d'une décision prise à l'encontre des souhaits de la jeune fille. Celle-ci avait 14 ans et 10 mois au moment des faits, lorsqu'elle a été hospitalisée et a rédigé une directive médicale indiquant qu'elle refuserait toute transfusion sanguine. Après la détérioration de sa situation, le directeur des services à l'enfant et à la famille l'a appréhendée en vertu de la *Loi sur les services à l'enfant et à la famille*[16] du Manitoba et a demandé au tribunal de rendre une ordonnance pour l'administration de transfusions sanguines en application de l'article 25(8) de la loi, qui permet au tribunal d'autoriser les traitements qu'il juge être dans l'intérêt de l'enfant. Cette demande a été accordée et l'adolescente a dû subir le traitement. Cette dernière a contesté la légalité de l'ordonnance sur la base de la théorie de « mineur mature » en common law et des articles 2, 7 et 15 de la *Charte canadienne*[17].

---

14 A.C. *c.* Manitoba (Directeur des services à l'enfant et à la famille), 2009 CSC 30, [2009] 2 R.C.S. 181 [A.C.].

15 Le Comité des droits de l'enfant les considère comme des principes directeurs de la CDE : *Directives générales concernant la forme et le contenu des rapports initiaux que les États Parties doivent présenter conformément au paragraphe 1 a) de l'article 44 de la Convention*, Doc. N.U. CRC/C/5, 1991. .

16 CPLM, ch. C80.

17 Nous discuterons de l'analyse de la Cour sur la base de l'article 15 de la *Charte* dans la deuxième partie de ce chapitre.

Dans son analyse, la juge Abella accorde une grande place à l'interprétation de l'ISE, qui doit être « compatible avec les normes internationales, les développements récents en common law et la réalité de la protection de l'enfance et des enfants »[18]. Elle reconnait que l'ISE est intimement lié à la vulnérabilité de l'enfant : « Le critère de 'l'intérêt supérieur' de l'enfant a pour objet général d'indiquer aux tribunaux les considérations qui doivent les guider lorsqu'ils agissent au nom de personnes vulnérables »[19]. Toutefois, pour arriver à une interprétation de la loi qui soit conforme à la *Charte canadienne* et à d'autres normes, incluant la CDE[20], il faut tenir compte de la complexité de l'opposition entre l'autonomie grandissante de l'adolescent et la protection de l'enfant vulnérable. Le problème ne se pose pas au sujet de jeunes enfants ou de décisions à prendre lorsque la santé de l'adolescent n'est pas gravement menacée. C'est seulement dans les cas où un adolescent s'oppose à un traitement qui est considéré comme nécessaire pour sauver sa vie ou préserver sa santé qu'un examen rigoureux de la maturité de l'enfant s'impose. Cet examen doit permettre au tribunal de déterminer si les « volontés exprimées par l'enfant reflètent des choix véritables, durables et autonomes »[21]. Pour arriver à cette décision, différents facteurs doivent être examinés, incluant le type de traitement recommandé, la capacité intellectuelle de l'adolescent et l'impact de son entourage sur l'indépendance de sa décision[22]. La maturité aura alors un effet sur l'ISE. Selon la juge Abella, « [p]lus le tribunal est convaincu que l'enfant est capable de prendre lui-même des décisions de façon mature et indépendante, plus il accordera de poids à ses opinions dans l'exercice de son pouvoir discrétionnaire [. . .]. Dans certaines affaires, les tribunaux seront inévitablement tellement convaincus de la maturité de l'enfant que le principe du bienêtre et celui de l'autonomie ne seront plus distincts [. . .] »[23].

Le jugement tente ainsi d'établir un équilibre entre deux valeurs qui peuvent facilement s'opposer, mais qui sont toutes deux défendues dans la législation canadienne : « le droit fondamental de la personne de

18 A.C., para. 80.

19 *Ibid.*, para. 81. La juge Abella développe aussi la notion de l'ISE dans le domaine de l'immigration : Kanthasamy *c.* Canada (Citoyenneté et Immigration), 2015 CSC 61, [2015] 3 R.C.S. 909. Elle y fait notamment référence à l'arrêt *A.B.* en liant la protection des enfants à l'application de l'ISE (par. 36).

20 La juge Abella se réfère aux articles 5, 14 et 12 de la CDE : les capacités évolutives de l'enfant, l'exercice du droit à la liberté de religion et le droit de l'enfant d'exprimer son opinion.

21 A.C., para. 96.

22 *Ibid.*

23 A.C., para. 87.

prendre seule des décisions qui concernent son corps » et « la protection des enfants vulnérables »[24]. On peut la qualifier aussi de tension entre les principes de protection et de participation. C'est la première fois que la CSC tente de résoudre ce nœud qui occupe les chercheurs dans le domaine des droits de l'enfant[25]. Toutefois, bien que la juge Abella cherche à concilier le droit à l'autonomie des adolescents et l'intérêt de la société à protéger les enfants qui sont vulnérables[26], cette affaire laisse le lecteur sur sa faim. En l'espèce, l'adolescente avait été évaluée par des psychiatres et personne ne mettait en doute sa capacité de comprendre les raisons pour lesquelles le traitement était recommandé et les conséquences possibles d'un refus de transfusion. La juge Abella ne les mettait pas en doute non plus, mais ne s'est pas prononcée sur l'application des principes qu'elle a énoncés ici. Ce silence s'expliquerait par le fait qu'« aucun des tribunaux d'instance inférieure n'a évalué 'l'intérêt supérieur' d'A.C. eu égard à sa maturité » et donc la Cour suprême ne pouvait effectuer de contrôle judiciaire de décision « concernant la capacité d'A.C. de décider de façon indépendante et mature de refuser les transfusions de sang »[27]. De plus, la question est théorique au moment de la rédaction du jugement, vu qu'A.C. a plus de 16 ans[28]. Ainsi, la Cour a évité de se prononcer sur la question épineuse à savoir s'il est possible dans la pratique pour un adolescent de moins de 16 ans de refuser un traitement vital lorsqu'il n'y a aucun doute sur sa maturité. L'argument permettant de reconnaitre l'opinion de l'enfant comme étant dans son intérêt et d'écarter la vulnérabilité demeure donc entièrement théorique.

Nous retenons des jugements examinés que la notion de vulnérabilité est fondamentale dans l'application des droits aux enfants. La loi et la pratique doivent être évalués d'un œil critique pour s'assurer qu'ils

24 *Ibid.*, para. 30.

25 Voir par ex. Michael Freeman, "Whither Children: Protection, Participation, Autonomy", (1994) 22(3) *Manitoba Law Journal* 307; John Tobin, "Justifying Children's Rights", (2013) 21(3) *The International Journal of Children's Rights* 395; Samantha Brennan, "Children's choices or children's interests: Which do their rights protect?", dans David Archard & Colin MacLeod (dir.) *The Moral and Political Status of Children*, Oxford University Press, 2002, 53; Sarah Baldwin, "Choosing a Home: When Should Children Make Autonomous Choices about their Home Life?", (2013) 46 *Suffolk U.L. Rev.* 503; Claire Breen, "Difference or Discrimination? Exploring the Concepts Underpinning Children's Rights, Discrimination and the Need to Acknowledge Difference", dans Breen, *Age Discrimination and Children's Rights*, Brill, Nijhoff, 2006, 1.

26 A.C., para. 108.

27 *Ibid.*, para 120.

28 *Ibid.*

répondent à la situation particulière des enfants, caractérisée par leur vulnérabilité inhérente. La protection des enfants qui en découle doit être nuancée en prenant en compte les différences d'âge et de maturité entre les enfants, sans toutefois remettre en cause cette vulnérabilité qui est présente chez tous les enfants.

B. Égalité et non-discrimination

Après la vulnérabilité qui est clé pour les droits de l'enfant, l'examen de l'égalité et de la non-discrimination est intéressant en tant que principes primordiaux des droits de la personne qui ne sont pas spécifiquement liés aux droits de l'enfant. Avec l'examen de ces principes on observe un certain manque de cohérence dans l'analyse des droits de l'enfant, mais aussi des considérations prioritaires qui recoupent celles de la jurisprudence sur la vulnérabilité.

1. Discrimination et handicap

Les causes concernant l'égalité et la discrimination au sujet des enfants sont peu nombreuses dans la jurisprudence de la CSC. Nous nous intéresserons d'abord à des cas en lien avec le handicap comme motif interdit de discrimination.

L'arrêt *Moore c. Colombie-Britannique* concernait l'application de la législation provinciale britanno-colombienne en matière d'éducation et des droits de la personne à un enfant qui avait des besoins éducatifs particuliers[29]. L'enfant n'avait pas reçu les services éducatifs spécialisés dont il avait besoin pour pallier ses troubles d'apprentissage dans le cadre de l'éducation publique. La juge Abella, rédigeant pour la majorité, avait conclu qu'il s'agissait d'une violation du Code des droits de la personne de la Colombie-Britannique. Le district scolaire avait omis de répondre aux besoins de l'élève, alors qu'on en connaissait l'existence et qu'on reconnaissait le type remédiation dont il avait besoin. Le point essentiel du jugement était que l'élève devait pouvoir bénéficier des objectifs de la loi sur l'éducation (*School Act*)[30] sur un pied d'égalité avec tous les autres élèves. La juge Abella rejette l'argument de la Cour d'appel voulant que le groupe de comparaison applicable soit les élèves en situation de handicap. En effet, la loi sur l'éducation prévoyait que « tous les apprenants » devaient pouvoir « développer

29 Moore *c.* ColombieBritannique (Éducation), 2012 CSC 61, [2012] 3 R.C.S. 360 [Moore].
30 S.B.C. 1989, ch. 61.

leur potentiel » et « acquérir les connaissances, les habiletés et les attitudes nécessaires » pour contribuer à la société. Ainsi, dans les cas d'élèves avec des troubles d'apprentissage, des services adaptés « servent de rampe permettant de concrétiser l'engagement pris dans la loi envers *tous* les enfants en Colombie-Britannique, à savoir l'accès à l'éducation »[31]. Ce jugement a permis de reconnaitre la discrimination d'un élève sur la base de la déficience en allégeant le fardeau de la preuve du demandeur et reconnaissant le groupe de comparaison comme étant tous les autres élèves.

Toutefois, ce jugement a pu décevoir la communauté de familles à travers le pays qui luttent pour les droits d'éducation égaux de leurs enfants en situation de handicap[32]. En effet, la Cour a refusé d'accueillir le pourvoi pour ce qui est du caractère systémique de la discrimination, marquant un pas en arrière par rapport à son analyse précédente en la matière, comme le souligne Joëlle Pastora Sala dans cet ouvrage[33]. Il nous semble que la Cour n'a pas considéré que de nombreux parents et enfants doivent lutter pour des conditions adéquates en éducation et qu'il n'est pas réaliste de penser que chacun accèdera aux tribunaux en cas d'impossibilité d'obtenir les services auxquels ils ont droit. L'affaire *Moore* illustre bien la futilité de ces recours qui mettent des années à aboutir et ne bénéficient pas directement à l'élève en cause, puisque celui-ci est sorti du système scolaire avant la fin de la procédure judiciaire[34]. Bien que les cas de discrimination doivent être examinés au cas par cas, il est important de prendre en compte la dimension systémique de la discrimination, comme les questions d'égalité touchent souvent des groupes de personnes et pas seulement le demandeur en particulier. C'est donc aussi une question d'accès à la justice. Ce jugement est

31 Moore, para. 5.

32 Sur les difficultés, voir Marie-Eve Gagné, « Entre l'accommodement de la croyance religieuse et l'accommodement du handicap en milieu scolaire : les tribunaux devraient-ils adapter leur analyse ? » (2015) 4(3) Canadian Journal of Disability Studies 1; Mona Paré & Nathalie Bélanger, « La recherche de l'inclusion scolaire à travers les recours offerts aux familles : perspective comparative canadienne dans un contexte francophone minoritaire », (2014) 29(3) *Revue canadienne droit et société* 327.

33 Joëlle Pastora Sala, "Assessing Justice Abella's Contributions to the Law of Systemic Discrimination in Canada". Voir aussi Shelagh Day, "Moore: The Good News: Comment on Moore v. British Columbia (Education) (2012), 75 C.H.R.R. D/369, 2012 SCC 6" (2012-2013) 75 CHRR C/1; Joanna Birenbaum & Kelly Gallagher-Mackay, "From Equal Access to Individual Exit: The Invisibility of Systemic Discrimination in Moore" (2013) 10 JL & Equality 93.

34 Mona Paré, "Refining the Test for Discrimination in the Context of Special Education: Moore v British Columbia", (2013) 10 JL & Equality 71, p. 77 ss.

un exemple d'opportunité manquée de s'appuyer sur le droit international. Des références au droit international auraient été utiles, car autant la CDE que la *Convention relative aux droits des personnes handicapées* (CDPH) interdisent la discrimination envers les enfants handicapés[35], la CDPH étant particulièrement utile pour souligner le désavantage persistant vécu par les enfants handicapés et pour identifier les mesures à prendre afin d'améliorer leur place dans la société. Les travaux en lien avec cette convention montrent comment les enfants ayant des besoins éducatifs particuliers font partie des enfants handicapés qui ont historiquement souffert de discrimination dans l'accès à l'éducation[36].

Dans l'affaire *Ward c. Québec*, les juges Abella et Kasirer, rédigeant les motifs d'un jugement dissident avec l'accord des juges Karakatsanis et Martin, s'intéressent à l'intimidation envers un enfant handicapé[37]. Pour les juges dissidents, il s'agissait d'un cas d'application des articles 4 et 10 de la *Charte des droits et libertés de la personne* du Québec, avec une atteinte discriminatoire au droit à la dignité, à l'honneur et à la réputation qui consistait en des propos discriminatoires prononcés à répétition par un humoriste envers un jeune artiste handicapé, alors que celui-ci avait entre 10 et 13 ans. Ces propos diffusés en public et en ligne avaient causé à l'enfant beaucoup de détresse et de l'intimidation par ses pairs à l'école. Pour les juges majoritaires, les propos en question ne pouvaient être qualifiés de discriminatoires, puisqu'ils n'incitaient pas à la haine. Au contraire, les juges dissidents étaient d'avis que le discours haineux n'est pas la seule forme de discrimination. Ils ont rappelé que, selon l'arrêt *Canadian Foundation*, les recours en discrimination intentés par un enfant doivent incorporer le « point de vue subjectif de l'enfant, qui comportera souvent un sentiment d'impuissance ou de vulnérabilité »[38]. Ils ajoutent qu'« une jeune personne raisonnable qui se trouverait dans la situation de Jérémy Gabriel serait particulièrement vulnérable aux préjudices découlant de propos déshumanisants »[39]. Ils font le lien entre ce type d'atteinte au droit à la dignité et l'intimidation, qui est un problème touchant les personnes jeunes et vulnérables de manière

35 CDE art 2 et 23; CDPH (RTNU Vol 2515), art. 7.

36 Voir Comité des droits des personnes handicapées, *Observation générale no.4 sur le droit à l'éducation inclusive*, Doc. NU, CRPD/C/GC/4, 2016.

37 Ward *c.* Québec (Commission des droits de la personne et des droits de la jeunesse), 2021 CSC 43 [Ward].

38 Ward, para. 174.

39 *Ibid.*

disproportionnée[40]. Le jugement fait référence aux conséquences négatives de l'intimidation expliquées dans l'arrêt *A.B.* Les juges dissidents se penchent ensuite sur le handicap de Jérémy et, avec des instruments internationaux à l'appui, rappellent les droits des enfants handicapés et affirment que les propos de l'humoriste « ont joué sur des attitudes préjudiciables déshumanisantes à l'endroit des enfants handicapés »[41]. La CDE et la CDPH ont été adoptés pour le respect de la dignité des enfants et des personnes handicapées, alors que des propos tels que ceux dont il est question encouragent les « attitudes les plus répugnantes à propos de la place des enfants handicapés dans notre société »[42]. Les juges dissidents reconnaissent que l'appartenance de Jeremy à un groupe vulnérable et marginalisé à cause de son âge et de son handicap a une importance pour la décision. Comme le remarque Jamie Cameron, la protection de catégories de personnes particulièrement vulnérables est une des priorités de la juge Abella, comme c'est le cas dans *A.B.* et dans *Ward*[43]. Tel que nous l'avons souligné, cette reconnaissance de la particularité des enfants handicapés en tant que groupe défavorisé dans la société aurait été une approche bénéfique dans *Moore* également.

2. *Égalité et âge*

Il convient de noter d'emblée que l'on reconnait rarement l'âge comme un motif de discrimination lorsque l'on parle d'enfants[44]. L'article 15 de la *Charte canadienne* ne l'exclut pas, mais la preuve d'une distinction discriminatoire basée sur l'âge de l'enfant est rarement prouvée.

A.C. c. Manitoba permet d'examiner la légalité d'un traitement différent entre enfants de différents groupes d'âge. En effet, il s'agissait de déterminer si la loi manitobaine de protection de l'enfance enfreignait le droit à l'égalité des enfants de moins de 16 ans, qui auraient la capacité de prendre des décisions médicales les concernant, par rapport aux enfants de 16 ans et plus pour lesquels il existe une présomption de

40 *Ibid.*, para. 194.
41 *Ibid.*, para. 218.
42 *Ibid.*
43 Jamie Cameron, "Her Fundamentals: Justice Abella and s.2(b) of the *Charter.*"
44 Pour une discussion, voir Breen, *supra*, note 25 et Simon Flacks, "Is Childhood a 'disability'? Exploring the exclusion of children from age discrimination provisions in the Equality Act 2010" (2014) 26:4 *Child and Family Law Quarterly*, 421. Au Canada, les codes des droits de la personne de l'Alberta, de la Colombie-Britannique, de l'Ontario et de la Saskatchewan excluent les personnes de moins de 18 ou 19 ans de la protection contre la discrimination fondée sur l'âge.

capacité de prendre des décisions médicales. En effet, la loi prévoit que la Cour ne peut ordonner un traitement à un adolescent de 16 ans ou plus qui est capable de comprendre les renseignements en lien avec le traitement, ainsi que les conséquences possibles d'un refus[45]. Aucune restriction n'est prévue dans la loi concernant les adolescents de moins de 16 ans, qui peuvent se voir imposer un traitement considéré comme étant dans leur intérêt. L'analyse de la juge Abella dans cette affaire se distingue de celle de la Cour d'appel, car elle considère que la distinction entre les enfants de 16 ans et les plus jeunes est contraire à l'article 15 de la *Charte* si la loi ne permet pas de tenir compte de la maturité de l'adolescent visé et de « sa capacité d'exercer un jugement mature et indépendant »[46]. Il ressort de son analyse qu'il faut interpréter la loi comme permettant aux enfants de moins de 16 ans de prouver qu'ils ont la maturité nécessaire pour prendre une décision médicale de manière indépendante. Avec cette interprétation, la loi est conforme à la *Charte* et aussi à la CDE, qui inclut les notions de développement des capacités et de la maturité de l'enfant[47]. A contrario, la loi serait discriminatoire si on l'interprétait à la lettre, sans prendre en compte les différences de maturité entre adolescents. Le jugement met en lumière l'importance que l'on doit donner à l'opinion des enfants et à la maturité grandissante des adolescents, non seulement dans la détermination de l'ISE, mais aussi dans le respect du principe d'égalité.

Dans deux jugements portant sur la LSJPA, la juge Abella a pu se prononcer sur l'égalité entre adolescents et adultes dans l'application du droit criminel. Dans *R. c. K.J.M.*, la juge Abella a rédigé une décision dissidente avec le juge Brown et avec l'accord de la juge Martin[48]. En l'espèce, il s'agissait de l'application aux adolescents des délais maximaux applicables aux procès pour adultes établis dans l'arrêt *Jordan*[49]. Les juges majoritaires, sous la plume du juge Moldaver, avaient jugé que ces délais devaient s'appliquent aussi aux procès concernant les adolescents. Les juges dissidents ne contestent pas le fait que des délais maximaux s'imposent, mais ils sont d'avis que les délais n'étaient pas adaptés aux adolescents, car l'arrêt *Jordan* n'avait pas examiné leur situation particulière. Les juges Abella et Brown se prononcent pour

45 *Supra* note 16.
46 A.C., para. 21, 22.
47 La juge Abella fait référence aux articles 5 et 12 de la CDE : A.C., par. 93.
48 R. *c.* K.J.M., 2019 CSC 55.
49 R. *c.* Jordan, 2016 CSC 27, [2016] 1 R.C.S. 631. Cet arrêt fixe un maximum de 30 mois pour les affaires instruites par une cour supérieure et de 18 mois pour les affaires instruites devant une cour provinciale dans les procédures criminelles.

l'égalité substantielle en l'espèce: « l'octroi aux adolescents d'une *protection égale* à celle qu'obtiennent les adultes nécessite de leur accorder un *traitement différent* »[50]. Ils affirment que l'application des plafonds fixés dans l'arrêt *Jordan* aux adolescents se traduirait en une protection inférieure à celle octroyée aux adultes. En s'inspirant de la jurisprudence, ces juges soutiennent que le plafond pour les adolescents devrait être de 15 mois. Ils se fondent sur les objectifs de la création de la LSJPA qui étaient d'offrir des protections procédurales supplémentaires aux adolescents et de créer des procédures moins formelles et plus rapides[51] et qu'« [e]n raison de la plus grande vulnérabilité des adolescents ayant des démêlés avec la justice et de leur culpabilité morale moindre par rapport aux adultes, des protections procédurales supplémentaires — et solides — ont été intégrés dans ce système distinct »[52]. Ainsi, les principes de célérité et de diligence ont été codifiés dans la LSJPA en conformité avec les normes internationales et la jurisprudence canadienne[53]. Afin que les adolescents puissent bénéficier des mêmes protections que les adultes, il faut reconnaitre les effets qu'ont les délais des procédures sur eux et adapter les délais à leur situation, qui est caractérisée par leur vulnérabilité. Un examen de la jurisprudence montre qu'avec les délais de *Jordan* on tolérerait des délais plus longs que ce qu'on pratiquait auparavant.

Dans *R. c. C.P.*, le juge Wagner, rédigeant pour la majorité, et la juge Abella, rédigeant avec l'accord des juges Karakatsanis et Martin, mettent l'emphase sur des droits de l'enfant différents pour trancher une question d'égalité. En effet, une des questions à trancher par la CSC était celle de la constitutionnalité du par. 37(10) de la LSJPA[54], disposant que les adolescents déclarés coupables d'un acte criminel et dont la culpabilité a été confirmée par une cour d'appel n'ont pas de droit d'appel automatique à la CSC; la Cour suprême doit l'autoriser. Donc, les adolescents n'ont pas de droit égal aux adultes condamnés qui bénéficient d'un droit d'appel à la CSC en vertu de l'alinéa 691(1)a) du Code criminel, lorsqu'il y a une dissidence à la cour d'appel sur un point de droit, et de l'alinéa 691(2)b), lorsque la cour d'appel invalide un acquittement. Il s'agit ainsi d'une violation à première vue de l'article 15 de la *Charte canadienne*. La CSC adopte une approche fondée sur la distinction entre les adolescents et les adultes, notamment quant à l'effet différent de

50 R. *c.* K.J.M., para 165.
51 *Ibid.*, para. 136.
52 *Ibid.*, para. 143.
53 En se référant notamment à la CDE et aux Règles de Beijing, *supra*, note 11.
54 R. *c.* C.P., 2021 CSC 19.

l'écoulement de temps sur les adolescents et l'importance de la rapidité et de la diligence dans les procédures. Pour les juges majoritaires, la différence de traitement entre les adultes et les adolescents n'est pas discriminatoire et ne passe pas la deuxième étape du test pour prouver une violation à l'article 15 de la *Charte*. La juge Abella analyse la différence plutôt dans l'optique de l'accès à la justice et conclut à une violation de l'article 15.

Autant la célérité des procédures pénales que l'accès à la justice sont des droits de l'enfant. Il est intéressant de noter que dans cette cause, c'est la majorité qui cite la CDE pour rappeler l'importance de la rapidité des procédures pour les adolescents. Ce principe est en effet explicitement inclus dans la CDE à l'article 40(2)(b)(iii), alors que le principe de l'accès à la justice y est plus implicite et ressort des travaux du Comité des droits de l'enfant[55]. La juge Abella avait insisté sur l'importance de la célérité dans l'affaire *K.J.M.* au sujet du besoin d'adapter aux adolescents les délais maximaux des procédures découlant de l'arrêt *Jordan*. On peut donc se poser la question : où se trouve l'intérêt des enfants ? Faut-il privilégier l'accès à la justice avec des possibilités d'appel ou plutôt la célérité des procédures? Pour la juge Abella, la réponse est simple : « la rapidité, la réadaptation et la réinsertion sociale ne constituent pas des objectifs légitimes si le verdict de culpabilité sousjacent découle d'un procès inéquitable »[56]. Il faut donc donner les mêmes chances aux adolescents qu'aux adultes de corriger une erreur judiciaire.

Ce raisonnement démontre une volonté réelle de considérer les enfants comme de véritables détenteurs de droits. Cependant, le jugement de la juge Abella aurait bénéficié d'un développement de la notion d'égalité, notamment l'égalité réelle telle qu'appliquée dans *K.J.M.* Comment cette notion s'applique-t-elle en l'espèce? Comment explique-t-on ici le besoin de faire attention à la situation particulière des adolescents et leur vulnérabilité inhérente? Des références au droit international auraient aussi été utiles, d'autant plus que le jugement majoritaire s'y référait. D'aucuns pourraient déduire du silence inhabituel de la juge Abella que le droit international n'appuie pas ses motifs en l'espèce. Pourtant, il y eu des efforts considérables sur la scène internationale pour reconnaitre et définir l'accès des enfants à la justice[57].

---

55 Comité des droits de l'enfant, *Observation générale 12 : Le droit de l'enfant d'être entendu*, Doc NU CRC/C/GC/12, 2009.

56 R. *c.* C.P., para. 108.

57 Voir par ex. Conseil des droits de l'homme, « Accès des enfants à la justice », Rapport de la Haut-Commissaire des Nations Unies aux droits de l'homme, Doc. NU A/HRC/25/35, (2013); Conseil de l'Europe, *Lignes directrices du Comité*

Les décisions de la juge Abella en matière d'égalité et de non-discrimination démontrent l'importance qu'elle accorde aux enfants en tant que détenteurs de droits. Les violations doivent être corrigées et les situations examinées de leur point de vue pour appliquer le principe d'égalité, surtout lorsqu'on les compare aux adultes. Cependant, un cadre plus clair pour l'application de ces principes, en s'appuyant sur le droit international, aurait été fort utile pour le développement de la jurisprudence en droits de l'enfant.

C. Conclusion

La société canadienne est redevable à la juge Abella pour le développement des droits de l'enfant dans le contexte canadien. Les enfants ont souvent été les oubliés de la jurisprudence de la Cour suprême, incorporés surtout dans des causes concernant leurs parents. Les jugements de la juge Abella démontrent la multitude de situations dans lesquelles les enfants sont au premier plan et sa jurisprudence fait avancer la réflexion sur les droits de l'enfant dans différents domaines : justice pénale, vie privée, immigration, droits de la *Charte*, etc. Elle nous rappelle comment les enfants sont des sujets de droit qu'il faut considérer d'une manière respectueuse de leur dignité et reconnaissant leur vulnérabilité inhérente.

Souvent habile dans son utilisation du droit international, la juge Abella a su démontrer les liens entre les problèmes de droit canadien et le droit international[58], et particulièrement plusieurs articles de la CDE et non seulement l'article 3 sur l'ISE, qui domine la jurisprudence. Même au sujet de l'ISE, elle nous a poussés hors de notre zone de confort dans le domaine de la protection des enfants. L'ISE est lié à la vulnérabilité inhérente à l'enfant, mais cette vulnérabilité ne saurait justifier une attitude paternaliste envers les enfants. En effet, la vulnérabilité inhérente offre un outil important pour appliquer et adapter les droits de la personne aux enfants. Même les jugements concernant

---

des ministres du Conseil de l'Europe sur une justice adaptée aux enfants, 2010; Ursula Kilkelly, « Le droit de l'enfant d'accéder à la justice à l'échelon international : défi et possibilité », dans Mona Paré, Mariëlle Bruning, Thierry Moreau & Caroline Siffrein-Blanc (Dir.), *L'accès des enfants à la justice : bilan critique*, Dalloz, 2022, 121.

58 Elle se réfère à des instruments qui permettent de suivre l'interprétation faite des droits de l'enfant et du consensus qui se dessine sur la scène internationale en marge des traités. Voir la distinction entre les instruments internationaux contraignants et non-contraignants dans Québec (Procureure générale) *c.* 9147-0732 Québec inc., 2020 CSC 32.

l'égalité et la discrimination nous rappellent l'importance de la notion de vulnérabilité dans l'analyse juridique. Tous soulignent le besoin de protéger les enfants qui font face à des risques de préjudice plus importants, cette protection faisant avancer l'égalité et améliorant leur accès à la justice.

Finalement, nous soulignons un grand absent dans la jurisprudence examinée. L'affaire *Khadr*, jugée par la CSC en 2008, concernait un jeune de 15 ans[59]. Alors que dans les autres arrêts traitant d'adolescents on parle de leur vulnérabilité inhérente, la CSC n'a pas identifié Omar Khadr comme un enfant ou un adolescent et ne s'est pas référée à la CDE ou à son *Protocole facultatif concernant l'implication des enfants dans les conflits armés*. L'arrêt, rendu par « la Cour », est une occasion manquée de démontrer que les enfants ont des droits dans toutes les situations, même celles qui nous mettent mal à l'aise. La reconnaissance des droits de l'enfant comme droits de la personne gêne encore. Le fait que la majorité des jugements rédigés par la juge Abella qui concernent les droits à l'égalité et à la non-discrimination des enfants soient des jugements dissidents est révélateur de nos attitudes envers les enfants. Nous ne pouvons que souhaiter que d'autres juges reprennent le flambeau porté par la juge Abella pour aider à développer une approche envers les enfants qui soit respectueuse de leurs droits de la personne.

---

59 Canada (Justice) *c.* Khadr, [2008] 2 R.C.S. 125, 2008 CSC 28.

PART 5

The Future of Justice Abella's Jurisprudence

18 Dot-com Justice: The Progressive Bent in Justice Abella's Technology Jurisprudence

ANDREW BERNSTEIN AND AMANDA WOLCZANSKI*

A. Introduction

The "Progressive Era" from the 1890s to the 1920s was a period of enormous technological and social change. Inventions such as cars, radios, telephones, airplanes, and the assembly lines necessary to produce them created an economic engine that made North America ready for the twentieth century. However, it also resulted in mass urbanization and a variety of social problems that accompanied these new arrivals to industrial centres. This, in turn, generated a relatively new concept: the belief that governments and laws had a role to play in ameliorating those social problems. While progressives did not seek to stop technological change, they recognized the dangers it posed to the social order. As a result, they believed in regulating its excesses while trying to facilitate its benefits beyond the few fortunate enough to control these new means of production.[1]

---

* Andrew Bernstein is a Partner in the litigation group and one of the leaders of the appellate practice at Torys LLP. Amanda Wolczanski is an Associate at Torys LLP. This chapter was originally presented at the 2022 conference, *The Honourable Rosalie Silberman Abella: A Life of Firsts*. The passage of time has put a spotlight on many of the themes discussed, showing us once again Justice Abella's prescience.

1 See, for example, Steven J. Diner, *A Very Different Age: Americans of the Progressive Era* (Hill and Wang, 1998); John Whiteclay Chambers II, *The Tyranny of Change: America in the Progressive Era, 1890-1920* (Rutgers University Press, 2d ed, 2000); Maureen A. Flanagan, *America Reformed: Progressives and Progressivisms 1890s–1920s* (Oxford University Press, 2007) and the publicly available summary of and bibliography to the Progressive Era by the same author: Maureen A. Flanagan, "Progressives and Progressivism in an Era of Reform" *Oxford Research Encyclopedias* (5 August 2016), online: doi.org/10.1093/acrefore/9780199329175.013.84; Patrick C. File, *Bad News Travels Fast: The Telegraph, Libel, and Press Freedom in the Progressive Era* (University of Massachusetts Press, 2018); William J. Novak, "Institutional

Justice Rosalie Silberman Abella's law and technology jurisprudence, one hundred years later, fits remarkably well into the paradigm of the Progressive Era's reform-minded impulses. She recognized in the early twenty-first century that the internet was transforming our lives and that the law could not, and should not, inhibit that transformation. Some of her most forward-thinking opinions at the Supreme Court of Canada came from the world of internet defamation[2] and internet copyright,[3] and they reflected a staunch optimism about the winds of technological change. However, she retained a progressive's suspicion of influential private institutions, including the powerful companies that came to dominate the digital landscape.[4] As a result, this chapter posits that Justice Abella's decisions about technology constituted both a "progressive" and "progressivist" vision of Canadian law and society, as they reflected both an optimism about technological change as a means for social reform and a faith that law can be a tool for facilitating these ends.

This chapter proceeds in three parts. In Part B, we briefly set out how we understand progressivism within the modern law and technology paradigm. In Part C, we illustrate the progressive thread running through Justice Abella's technology jurisprudence by examining several of her technology decisions in two broad categories: those where she was a leader in facilitating technological change and those where she took a more interventionist approach to perceived threats from new technologies and the large companies that play an outsized role in making them available to Canadians. We focus our analysis on Supreme Court cases that touch on information technology and the internet. In Part D, we conclude by summarizing subsequent judicial treatment of two pre-eminent technology decisions from Part C where Justice Abella wrote for the majority of the Supreme Court: *Crookes v Newton* and *Google v Equustek Solutions Inc*. We show that these judgments had significant precedential value but that, in the reform-minded spirit of progressivism, they also left ample room for future technology cases to be decided on their particular facts.

Economics and the Progressive Movement for the Social Control of American Business" (Winter 2019) 93 *Business History Review* 665.

2 See *Crookes v Newton*, 2011 SCC 47 [*Crookes*]; *Haaretz.com v Goldhar*, 2018 SCC 28.

3 See Justice Abella's dissent in *Robertson v Thomson Corp*, 2006 SCC 43; and her reasons (at times for the majority, and at times in concurrence) in the four out of the five cases known as the copyright pentalogy: *ESA v SOCAN*, 2012 SCC 34; *Rogers v SOCAN*, 2012 SCC 35; *SOCAN v Bell*, 2012 SCC 36; *Alberta (Education) v Access Copyright*, 2012 SCC 37.

4 For example, see Justice Abella's concurrence in *Douez v Facebook, Inc*, 2017 SCC 33 and her majority reasons in *Uber Technologies Inc v Heller*, 2020 SCC 16 and *Google Inc v Equustek Solutions Inc*, 2017 SCC 34 [*Equustek*].

B. What We Mean by "Progressive"

It is foolish to pretend that the "progressivist" attitudes of what we now call the Progressive Era map directly onto contemporary social discourse on law and technology. Nor do we suggest that such alignment would be desirable. We live in a society that is very different (and far more socially egalitarian) than the Progressive Era.[5] But there is also what is, in our view, a familiar tension between the forces of technological change and the proper place of legal and regulatory intervention amidst that change today. The Progressive Era saw significant advances in transportation, energy production, and telecommunications that both solved problems and created new ones. In some ways, we are in the midst of a parallel renaissance.[6] Our increased dependence on the internet and information technology, the rise of artificial intelligence and automation, the proliferation of multinational corporations that enable access to those technologies such as Google, Meta, or Uber, and the digitization of everything from food delivery to currency have raised important questions about the place of law in our changing world.[7]

What makes someone progressive within the modern law and technology paradigm? In our view, a progressive outlook recognizes that

---

5 We also appreciate that while there are certain recognizable contours of "progressivism" and the Progressive Era, there were indeed many different types of "progressivisms" espoused during that time (not all of them consistent with modern progressive ideas or the notion of progress more generally). See, for example, Flanagan, *America Reformed*, above note 1, and Flanagan, "Progressives and Progressivism," above note 1, as well as Daniel T. Rodgers, "Capitalism and Politics in the Progressive Era and in Ours" (2014) 13:3 *Journal of the Gilded Age and Progress Era* 379.

6 See the discussion on the parallels between the Progressive Era and contemporary social and political discourse more generally in Harry J. Holzer, "Is Another Progressive Era Coming?" (10 November 2020), Brooking Institute (Commentary), online: www.brookings.edu/articles/is-another-progressive-era-coming/, discussing Robert D. Putnam and Shaylyn Romney Garrett, *The Upswing: How America Came Together a Century Ago and How We Can Do It Again* (Simon & Schuster, 2020).

7 The interface between modern information technology and law is the subject of a significant body of scholarship. For a selection of some more recent examples considering the regulation of new technologies, see Teresa Scassa, "Regulating AI in Canada: A Critical Look at the Proposed Artificial Intelligence and Data Act" (2023) 101:1 *Canada Bar Review* 1; Kristen Thomasen, "Safety in Artificial Intelligence & Robotics in Canada" (2023) 101:1 *Canada Bar Review* 61; Steve Calandrillo & Nolan Kobuke Anderson, "Terrified by Technology: How Systemic Bias Distorts U.S. Legal and Regulatory Responses to Emerging Technology" (2022) 2022:2 *University of Illinois Law Review* 597; Julie E. Cohen, "Internet Utopianism and the Practical Inevitability of Law" (2019–20) 18 *Duke Law and Technology Review* 85.

technology is a powerful force for social change. This was true in the Progressive Era as it is true now. Progressives of the early twentieth century generally looked optimistically on the improvements to their quality of life and the modernization of institutions promised by widespread advances in science and technology.[8] There is reason for modern-day progressives to maintain some of that optimism today. Over the past hundred years, technology has been a more reliable agent for social change than law. There are, for example, the obvious improvements to health and quality of life that have come through advancements in medicine, such as access to life-saving drugs, vaccines, and reproductive technologies.[9] These occurred at times despite the law's insistence to severely (and detrimentally) limit the public's ability to benefit from them.[10] And while it is presently in vogue to be skeptical about the positive impacts of information technology and the internet, the convenience and liberalizing

---

8 Particularly with respect to transportation, consumer goods, and the systemization of policy-making and government administration prompted by advancements in technology and the social sciences, see, for example, Chambers, above note 1 at 19–22, 61–64, and 124–27; Diner, above note 1 at 1–13, 102–24; Flanagan, *America Reformed*, above note 1, and Flanagan, "Progressives and Progressivism," above note 1; Herbert Hovenkamp, "The Mind and Heart of Progressive Legal Thought" (1995) 81:1 *Iowa Law Review* 149.

9 See, for example, "The Path that Ends AIDS: 2023 UNAIDS Global AIDS Update" Joint United Nations Programme on HIV/AIDS (2023), online: www.unaids.org/sites/default/files/media_asset/2023-unaids-global-aids-update_en.pdf; Till Bärnighausen, David E. Bloom, Elizabeth T. Cafiero-Fonseca & Jennifer Carroll O'Brien, "Valuing Vaccination" (2014) 111:34 *Proceedings of the National Academy of Sciences* 12313, online: doi.org/10.1073/pnas.1400475111; Xiao Chen, Hanwei Huang, Jiandong Ju, Ruoyan Sun & Jialiang Zhang "Impact of Vaccination on the COVID-19 Pandemic in U.S. States" *Scientific Reports* 12 (2022) 1554, online: doi.org/10.1038/s41598-022-05498-z; Martha J. Bailey & Jason M. Lindo, "Access and Use of Contraception and Its Effects on Women's Outcomes in the U.S." in L. Argys, S. Averett & S. Hoffman (eds), *Oxford Handbook of Women and the Economy* (Oxford: Oxford University Press, 2018); and NBER Working Paper 23465, online: www.nber.org/papers/w23465.

10 Consider, for example, the evolving situation with respect to access to abortion in the wake of *Dobbs v Jackson Women's Health Organization*, 597 US 215 (2022) and *Danco Laboratories, LLC, Applicant v Alliance for Hippocratic Medicine, et al*, 143 S.Ct. 1075 (Mem), (2023) in the United States: Sheila Kaplan, "After Two Conflicting Judicial Rulings, What's Next for Medication Abortions?" *Berkely Public Health Opinions* (13 April 2023), online: publichealth.berkeley.edu/news-media/opinion/whats-next-for-medication-abortions/(post-*Dobbs*, pre-*Danco*); and Robert Barnes & Ann E. Marimow, "Supreme Court Preserves Access to Key Abortion Drug as Appeal Proceeds" *The Washington Post* (21 April 2023), online: www.washingtonpost.com/politics/2023/04/21/mifepristone-abortion-pill-access-supreme-court/ (post-*Danco*).

effects of global connectivity and access to information are undeniable.[11] Democratizing access to information and communication technologies has tangible effects on individual autonomy and is positively correlated with economic indicators of well-being.[12] Access to the internet has also challenged government monopolies on information and spurred new thinking about how individuals can organize, interact with democracy and law, and communicate with political decision-makers.[13]

Of course, technology is not unambiguously good. Rapid unchecked technological change, often stimulated by private interests, is not necessarily conducive to building a just or more equal society. As alluded to above, you do not need to look far in the contemporary zeitgeist to find examples of this concern. Despite the promise and tangible benefits of information technology, anyone who has used a computer in the past decade will be unsurprised to learn that there is evidence to suggest that the expansion of social media has amplified political polarization and contributed to the spread of misinformation.[14] Recent discussion on the need for adequate regulation of artificial intelligence, and fear of the unequal and potentially dangerous consequences of autonomous technologies, also highlight underlying concerns about how technological development happens and who is in charge.[15] These issues would likely

11 See, for example, United Nations Human Rights Officer of the High Commissioner, "Disinformation and Freedom of Opinion and Expression: Report of the Special Rapporteur on the Promotion and Protection of the Right to Freedom of Opinion and Expression, Irene Khan" (13 April 2021), online: www.ohchr.org/en/documents/thematic-reports/ahrc4725-disinformation-and-freedom-opinion-and-expression-report.

12 See Kartik K. Ganju, Paul A. Pavlou & Rajiv D. Banker, "Does Information and Communication Technology Lead to the Well-Being of Nations? A Country-Level Empirical Investigation" *Management Information Systems Quarterly* (11 September 2015), online: ssrn.com/abstract=2659190; Irne Bertschek, Wolfgang Briglauer, Kai Hüschelrath, Benedikt Kauf, & Thomas Niebel, "The Economic Impacts of Broadband Internet: A Survey" (2015) 14:4 *Review of Network Economics* 201.

13 See Jane S. Schacter, "Digitally Democratizing Congress? Technology and Political Accountability" (2009) 89 *Boston University Law Review* 641; Tsvi Kahana & Rachel Stephenson, "The Promise of Democratic Constitutionalism: Women, Constitutional Dialogue, and the Internet" in Beverley Baines, Daphne Barak-Erez & Tsvi Kahana, eds, *Feminist Constitutionalism: Global Perspectives* (Cambridge University Press, 2012) 240.

14 See Nathaniel Persily & Joshua Tucker, *Social Media and Democracy: The State of Field, Prospects for Reform* (Cambridge: Cambridge University Press, 2020); Jonathan Haidt, "Why the Past 10 Years of American Life Have Been Uniquely Stupid" *The Atlantic* (11 April 2022), online: www.theatlantic.com/magazine/archive/2022/05/social-media-democracy-trust-babel/629369/.

15 See Kristen Thomasen, "Safety in Artificial Intelligence & Robotics in Canada" (2023) 101:1 *Canada Bar Review* 61; Cade Metz, "'The Godfather of A.I.' Leaves

seem familiar to an early twentieth century progressive, who would have been concerned with the growing power of railroad kings, shipbuilding trusts, and asphalt companies, rather than multinational technology companies. Understood in terms of the progressivist impulse to regulate excess, a progressive outlook posits that unchecked power over technological change, particularly in the hands of private actors, can and should be reined in.[16]

As will become clear throughout this chapter, we see a reform-minded impulse that mirrors such progressivist attitudes in Justice Abella's technology jurisprudence. The idea that she had a reform-minded impulse may, at first blush, be reminiscent of criticism she faced throughout her judicial career. She was no stranger to being called an "activist judge."[17] While we acknowledge that Justice Abella had a distinct point of view, we would disagree with the assertion that she was somehow radical, lacked principle, or was prone to becoming untethered from the law (connotations that tend to follow the "activist judge" label). Change, especially incremental change or "progress by precedent," is not foreign to the common law. Judges have the tools — albeit limited ones — to accommodate change: they meet each case equipped with facts, legal rules, legal principles, and legal precedents.[18] The question is how they choose to use them. We think that one way to make sense of Justice Abella's use of these tools in technology cases is through a progressivist

---

Google and Warns of Dangers Ahead," *The New York Times* (1 May 2023); Kevin Roose, "A.I. Poses 'Risk of Extinction,' Industry Leaders Warn," *The New York Times* (30 May 2023).

16 See Novak, above note 1; Chambers, above note 1 at 54–78 and 132–169; Diner, above note 1 at 30–49; Flanagan, *America Reformed*, above note 1, and Flanagan, "Progressives and Progressivism," above note 1.

17 See Bruce Pardy, "Bruce Pardy: Rosalie Abella Was Shameless in Making Up the Law and Mainstreaming Judicial Activism" *National Post* (18 June 2021), online: nationalpost.com/opinion/bruce-pardy-rosalie-abella-was-shameless-in-making-up-the-law-and-mainstreaming-judicial-activism; "Convenient Judges for Liberal aims" *Calgary Herald* (27 August 2004), reprinted in *Fraser Institute*, "Commentaries," online: www.fraserinstitute.org/article/convenient-judges-liberal-aims; Paul Wells, "Rosie Abella said she'd answer questions when she turned 75" *Maclean's* (15 June 2021), online: macleans.ca/news/rosie-abella-said-shed-answer-questions-when-she-turned-75/.

18 On the judicial toolbox more generally, see Robert J. Sharpe, *Good Judgment: Making Judicial Decisions* (University of Toronto Press, 2018). For a comment on how Justice Abella's decision-making fits within conceptions of the judicial role in the common law, see David Asper, "Robed Revolutionary? Not Quite" *National Post* (7 August 2004). See also Justice Abella's reflections on the judicial role in Rosalie Silberman Abella, "The Judicial Role in a Democratic State" (2000) 8:1–3 *Canada Watch* 8, online: robarts.info.yorku.ca/files/2012/03/cw_8_1-3.pdf.

lens. It is within this context that we turn to Justice Abella's technology jurisprudence.

C. Justice Abella's Technology Jurisprudence

Justice Abella's technology judgments demonstrate she was not intimidated by the challenges of technological innovation. But although her technology-related decisions were precedent-setting and, at times, controversial, her brand of progressivism closely mirrored wider public discourse about the promises and pitfalls of technological innovation. We see these themes emerge in Justice Abella's internet and information technology judgments, which span the breadth of defamation law, intellectual property law, constitutional law, and contract law. To illustrate our point, we examine several representative decisions in two groups: cases where Justice Abella tried to ensure that legal rules do not stifle technological progress, and cases where she recognized the threats technology could pose.

1. Ensuring Legal Rules Do Not Stifle Technological Progress

Justice Abella's forward-looking approach to existing legal rules was exemplified in her judgments on defamation and copyright, two areas that saw significant development during her tenure on the Supreme Court. In defamation law, the Court decided a number of cases throughout the 2000s that went some way towards bringing it into greater alignment with the right to freedom of expression under the *Charter*, [19] if (occasionally frustratingly) under the guise of *Charter* values.[20] At the same time that important changes to the law of defamation were happening on the Court, copyright law was experiencing its own renaissance. Beginning with its decision in *CCH Canadian Ltd v Law Society of Upper Canada*, the Supreme Court signaled a shift away from a view of copyright that focused exclusively on creators and towards a greater

19 See Iris Fischer and Adam Lazier, "Crookes v Newton: The Supreme Court of Canada Brings Libel Law into the Internet Age" (2012) 50:1 *Alberta Law Review* 205.

20 *Charter* values are generally understood as unwritten principles, such as liberty, equality, dignity, and freedom of expression, that derive their meaning from rights enshrined in the *Charter*. For further perspectives on *Charter* values, see Matthew Horner, "Charter Values: The Uncanny Valley of Canadian Constitutionalism" (2014) 67 *Supreme Court Law Review* (2d) 361 and Paul Daly, "The Doré Duty: Fundamental Rights in Public Administration" (7 June 2023) Ottawa Faculty of Law Working Paper 2023-11, online: SSRN ssrn.com/abstract=4472568.

emphasis on user rights.[21] Justice Abella played an important role in sustaining these tides of change by resisting the rigid application of legal rules in emerging technological contexts.

In *Crookes v Newton*, Justice Abella decided a very technical point: when you hyperlink to a story that contains defamatory content, you do not "publish" the defamatory words.[22] This new rule for hyperlinking was a departure from the common law rule, which captured a variety of conduct under the umbrella of "publication," including pointing to a sign espousing defamatory content or working a printing press even without knowledge of what is being printed.[23] To justify departing from the strict application of the publication rule, Justice Abella, writing for the majority, grounded her analysis in a contextual understanding of the internet and in the growing body of Supreme Court jurisprudence recognizing the delicate balance between reputational interests and free expression in defamation law. She recognized that hyperlinks play an important role in facilitating access to information online, observing that "[t]he Internet cannot, in short, provide access to information without hyperlinks. Limiting their usefulness by subjecting them to the traditional publication rule would have the effect of seriously restricting the flow of information and, as a result, freedom of expression. The potential 'chill' in how the internet functions could be devastating."[24] Given this context, Justice Abella reasoned that strict application of the publication rule "would be like trying to fit a square archaic peg into the hexagonal hole of modernity,"[25] which she (unsurprisingly) declined to do.

She continued to challenge the strict application of legal doctrine in concurring reasons in *Haaretz.com v Goldhar*, which considered the jurisdictional implications of internet defamation.[26] In this case, she proposed a new standard for determining jurisdiction and choice of law in a defamation suit.[27] The case concerned a defamation suit

---

21 See Myra J. Tawfik, "The Supreme Court of Canada and the Fair Dealing Trilogy: Elaborating a Doctrine of User Rights under Canadian Copyright Law" (2013) 51:1 *Alberta Law Review* 191.

22 *Crookes*, above note 2 at paras 27–42. In the interests of full disclosure, Andrew Bernstein was second chair counsel to the Canadian Civil Liberties Association in *Crookes*, and Justice Abella's judgment accepted the position advocated by the CCLA.

23 *Ibid* at para 18.

24 *Ibid* at para 36.

25 *Ibid* at para 36.

26 *Haaretz.com v Goldhar*, 2018 SCC 28 [*Haaretz*].

27 *Ibid* at paras 104–43.

brought by a Canadian businessman against an Israeli newspaper. The businessman alleged that an article about his ownership and management of an Israeli soccer team was defamatory. The article was not distributed in print form in Canada but was available over the internet. Traditionally, under Canadian law, a rebuttable presumption of jurisdiction could be established in a defamation suit based on the place of publication of the defamatory content (the location or *situs* of the tort).[28] Once jurisdiction was established, the place of publication would then again become relevant as one of several factors at the *forum non conveniens* stage, where choice of law could be determined on the basis of the place of publication as well.[29] The majority substantively affirmed this approach in *Haaretz*, finding that while Ontario had jurisdiction over the dispute because the defamatory content could be accessed there, the more appropriate forum was Israel.[30] But appreciating that a single download had the potential to give a plaintiff in Ontario an almost automatic entitlement to the jurisdiction of an Ontario court and application of Ontario law in future cases, Justice Abella proposed that the place of publication rule be replaced with an analysis of where the "most substantial harm" to the plaintiff's reputation occurred.[31] While acknowledging that the jurisdiction and choice of law analyses are distinct, she noted that it was worth considering whether the same approach should apply to both.[32] Specifically, she reasoned that because the essence of the harm in defamation is damage to reputation, a presumptive connecting factor determining jurisdiction ought to be rebuttable on the basis that the most harm to the plaintiff's reputation occurred elsewhere.[33] Once again, Justice Abella identified how the strict application of an existing legal rule was inconsistent with its overarching policy rationale in a new technological context, positing that the location most closely

---

28 *Ibid* at paras 35–45.

29 *Ibid* at paras 46–51.

30 *Ibid* at paras 35–98. Comparative convenience and expense for the parties and the witnesses, as well as fairness, favoured a trial in Israel at the *forum non conveniens* stage. In the majority's view, while the choice of law factor would still point to Ontario as the proper forum in the *forum non conveniens* analysis, it should be accorded little weight in cases where jurisdiction is established based on the *situs* of the tort, as it would inevitably point to the chosen forum on the question of applicable law.

31 *Ibid* at paras 106–113 and 120–31.

32 *Ibid* at para 120.

33 *Ibid* at para 129.

connected to the wrong was not necessarily any location where the defamatory content may be available.

In view of Justice Abella's emphasis on the principles and policy underlying legal rules, it is not surprising that she also emerged as a defender of technological neutrality in copyright law. The principle of technological neutrality is derived from section 3(1) of the *Copyright Act*, which defines copyright as the "sole right to produce or reproduce the work or any substantial part thereof *in any material form whatever*."[34] Technological neutrality posits that, absent parliamentary intent to the contrary, the *Copyright Act* should not be interpreted to favour or discriminate against any form of technology.[35] Justice Abella penned dissenting reasons on this issue in *Robertson v Thomson Corp*.[36] This case was about copyright ownership of freelance articles placed in an online database. The majority held that a newspaper publisher was entitled to reproduce the articles in electronic form on CD-ROMs but did not have the right to reproduce "decontextualized" versions of the articles in online databases.[37] The decontextualized versions did not contain the photos, artwork, or advertisements that were normally found in print versions of the newspaper, and in the majority's view, they were actually reproductions of the freelance author's original works, not the newspaper publisher's original works.[38] In the majority's view, technological neutrality operated to protect the rights of the freelance authors, regardless of the medium through which their work was reproduced.[39] Justice Abella took a different view of technological neutrality.[40] Writing in dissent, she reasoned that the act of republishing the articles in the database was akin to stacking print editions of the newspaper on a shelf, and was therefore an authorized form of

34 *Copyright Act*, RSC, 1985, c C-42, s 3(1) [emphasis added].

35 For example, see *Théberge v Galerie d'Art du Petit Champlain inc.*, 2002 SCC 34 at para 148 and more recently, *Society of Composers, Authors and Music Publishers of Canada v Entertainment Software Association*, 2022 SCC 30 at para 6.

36 *Robertson v Thomson Corp*, 2006 SCC 43 [*Robertson*]. In the interests of full disclosure, Andrew Bernstein was third chair junior counsel in *Robertson*, and his client (Thomson Corporation) advocated for the position that Justice Abella would have found for in dissent.

37 *Ibid* at paras 10 and 30–53.

38 *Ibid* at para 41.

39 *Ibid* at para 49.

40 See, for example, the discussion on the difference between Justice Abella's and the majority's reasons in *Robertson* on technological neutrality in Carys J. Craig, "(Pre) Serving the Purposes of Copyright Law" in *The Copyright Pentalogy: How the Supreme Court of Canada Shook the Foundations of Canadian Copyright Law*, 2013 CanLIIDocs 2.

reproduction by the newspaper publisher that could not be restrained by the freelance authors.[41] Any differences between the print and database versions of the articles were attributable to the particulars of the electronic "form" and could be justified by the application of technological neutrality.[42]

This functional approach to technological neutrality and copyright more generally would later resurface in Justice Abella's majority reasons in *ESA v SOCAN* [43] and *SOCAN v Bell,*[44] two cases in the Court's "copyright pentalogy."[45] In *ESA,* Justice Abella, writing joint majority reasons with Justice Moldaver, held that charging an additional "communication" tariff on downloads of videogames containing musical works violated the principle of technological neutrality.[46] Justices Abella and Moldaver reasoned that the act of downloading should not be treated any differently than picking up a physical copy of the game at a brick-and-mortar store.[47] In *Bell,* Abella had the opportunity to take an even more forthright stance on user rights. Writing for the full Court, she held that iTunes music previews were fair dealing for the purpose of research and private study under the *Copyright Act.*[48] The decision was an extension of the Court's existing fair dealing caselaw, primarily *CCH,* which laid the groundwork for a large and liberal interpretation of fair dealing for the purposes of research and private study under the *Act.*[49] In arriving at the conclusion that the music previews were fair dealing, Justice Abella observed that the result was ultimately consistent with the purpose of copyright in that context: encouraging the creation and dissemination of musical works by allowing consumers to sample limited previews of individual songs.[50]

---

41 *Robertson,* above note 36 at paras 86–90.

42 *Ibid* at paras 90, 98–100.

43 *ESA v SOCAN,* 2012 SCC 34 [*ESA*].

44 *SOCAN v Bell,* 2012 SCC 36 [*Bell*].

45 A collection of five decisions released concurrently in 2012: *ESA,* above note 43; *Bell,* above note 44; *Rogers v SOCAN,* 2012 SCC 35; *Re:Sound v Motion Picture Theatre Associations of Canada,* 2012 SCC 38; and *Alberta (Education) v Access Copyright,* 2012 SCC 37.

46 *ESA,* above note 43 at paras 2–5.

47 *Ibid* at para 5.

48 *Bell,* above note 44 at paras 17 and 49.

49 *Ibid* at paras 8–15.

50 *Ibid* at para 49.

2. Recognizing the Threats Technology May Pose

While Justice Abella was clearly willing to facilitate the development of the internet, her later jurisprudence reflects a progressivism that was also concerned about its excesses. As a result, in later judgments we see an emphasis on ameliorating the supposed threats that information technology may pose to civil liberties, fairness, and the rule of law (or as she has put it, the rule of justice),[51] when those threats arise in the context of perceived asymmetries between the parties.

The theme is well summarized in her dissent in *R v Jones*, a case about a text message production order under the *Criminal Code*.[52] Police obtained a production order against several mobile phone service providers. Only Telus, which happened to be the provider associated with a phone used by the defendant's co-accused, stored incoming and outgoing text messages for a period after the messages were sent.[53] The majority in *Jones* ordered that those text messages be produced.[54] But since it was Telus' unique storage practices and not any legitimate legal authority which deprived the defendant of privacy in their sent text messages, Justice Abella found that the order was an unjustified violation of *Charter* rights.[55] Commenting on the options available to law enforcement in the wake of jurisprudential gaps caused by new technologies, she reasoned: "It seems to me that the better judicial approach is one that encourages conduct on the part of the police that errs on the side of being protective of the rights of the public, rather than one that endorses *Charter* breaches in deference to the mechanics of new technologies."[56]

Justice Abella's proclivity for erring on the side of individual rights extended into the realm of private law, specifically in disputes between individuals and large technology companies. It may be no accident that this mid- to late-2010s turn in her jurisprudence coincided with public

51 Amanda Jerome, "'Rule of Justice' Needed as we Stand at Edge of 'Divisive' Future, Former Justice Abella Says" *Lawyer's Daily* (14 February 2022), online: www.law360.ca/ca/articles/1757296; Rosalie Silberman Abella, "The Arc of the Moral Universe Is Long, But . . ." (2019) 34:1 *Canadian Journal of Law and Society* 1; Andromache Karakatsanis & Sheila L. Martin, "The Joy of Judging with Justice Rosalie Silberman Abella," (2021) 105:3 *Judicature*, online: judicature.duke.edu/articles/the-joy-of-judging-with-justice-rosalie-silberman-abella/.

52 *R. v Jones*, 2017 SCC 60 [*Jones*].

53 *Ibid* at para 112.

54 *Ibid* at paras 56–81.

55 *Ibid* at paras 113–14.

56 *Ibid* at para 118.

concern about information technology amid the rising power of "Big Tech."[57] In *Douez v Facebook*,[58] for example, Justice Abella wrote concurring reasons, finding that a forum selection clause in favour of California in Facebook's user terms was unenforceable. Under the Court's existing precedents, there was a two-step test to determine whether a forum selection clause could stand: first, the party seeking to rely on the clause had to show that it was valid, clear, and enforceable as a matter of contract law; second, if the party seeking to rely on the clause succeeded, the challenging party was then required to show strong cause for not enforcing the clause despite its validity.[59] The majority held the clause was valid but unenforceable at the second step because of a number of factors, including inequality of bargaining power between the plaintiff (a consumer) and Facebook (a large technology company).[60] But Justice Abella took a tougher stance on the issue — she found the clause unenforceable as a matter of contract law at the first step.[61] While she relied on many of the same observations about inequality of bargaining power and fairness cited by the majority, she found these factors were sufficient to render the clause unenforceable on the basis that it was contrary to public policy and that it was unconscionable.[62]

This conception of the unconscionability doctrine would later reemerge in her joint majority reasons with Justice Malcolm Rowe in *Uber Technologies v Heller*.[63] Although there were precedents suggesting that more than just inequality of bargaining power and unfairness were needed to show unconscionability, including proof that the stronger party knowingly took advantage of the weaker party, Justice Abella disagreed with this characterization of unconscionability, based on her

57 See, for example Taylor Owen, "Big Tech's Net Loss: How Governments Can Turn Anger into Action" *The Globe and Mail* (28 December 2018), online: www.theglobeandmail.com/opinion/article-big-techs-net-loss-how-governments-can-turn-anger-into-action/; Clara Hendrickson & William A. Galston, "Big Tech Threats: Making Sense of the Backlash Against Online Platforms" *Brookings* (28 May 2019), online: www.brookings.edu/research/big-tech-threats-making-sense-of-the-backlash-against-online-platforms/.

58 *Douez v Facebook*, 2017 SCC 33 [*Douez*].

59 *Ibid* at paras 28–29.

60 *Ibid* at paras 45–76.

61 *Ibid* at para 94.

62 *Ibid* at paras 111–16.

63 *Uber Technologies v Heller*, 2020 SCC 16 at paras 79–99 [*Uber*]. In the interests of full disclosure, Torys LLP acted for Uber in this proceeding. The authors played no role in that case. Our characterization is an attempt to summarize the reasons for decision and is not based on any sort of "inside" information about the decision from our colleagues.

review of the caselaw and the principles animating the doctrine.[64] She observed that imposing a higher burden would effectively (and in her view, improperly) shield contracts of adhesion or standard form contracts from the reaches of the doctrine of unconscionability.[65] In doing so, she opened the door to more significant judicial intervention in standard form contracts.[66] Abella's reasons in *Douez* and *Uber* ultimately went one step further than merely pointing out a power imbalance. Much like *Jones*, they sought to limit the spaces in which technology and technology providers can be perceived as operating independently of Canadian judicial oversight.

The theme of closing perceived legal gaps caused by technological innovation reached international heights in Justice Abella's judgment in *Google Inc v Equustek Solutions Inc*.[67] Writing for the majority, she upheld a worldwide interlocutory injunction ordering Google, a non-party to the underlying lawsuit, to de-index websites selling certain trade-secret protected products. The injunction was the plaintiffs' last stop on a journey to shutting down the alleged wrongdoers, who had fled Canada and had become virtually untraceable. Noticeably absent from Justice Abella's judgment was any substantive discussion of Google's role as a facilitator of information akin to the discussion of hyperlinks in *Crookes*. In *Crookes*, Justice Abella framed hyperlinks as important facilitators of access to information.[68] But in *Equustek*, she got to where she wanted to go by framing Google as a facilitator of a harm.[69] She characterized the issues in *Equustek* narrowly and doubled down on the importance of law, holding that the case turned on "classic interlocutory injunction jurisprudence" and observing: "We have not, to date, accepted that freedom of expression requires the facilitation of the unlawful sale of goods."[70]

What happened to the Justice Abella who ardently defended free expression in defamation law or user rights in copyright? Respectfully, she seemed to have been replaced by a different jurist. In *Equustek*, Justice Abella avoided in-depth discussion about Google or its users'

64 *Ibid* at paras 79–86.

65 *Ibid* at paras 85–89.

66 See John D. McCamus, "The Supreme Court of Canada and the Development of a Canadian Common Law of Contract" (2022) 45:2 *Manitoba Law Journal* 7; Marcus Moore, "Controlling Fairness in Standard Form Contracts: What Can Courts Do, and What Should They Do?" (2022) 55:2 *UBC Law Review* 547.

67 Above note 4.

68 *Crookes*, above note 2 at paras 34–36.

69 *Equustek*, above note 4 at paras 35, 41–42, 48–49, and 53.

70 *Ibid* at paras 1 and 48.

interests in free expression by suggesting that legitimate interests in free expression were not engaged in the facts of the case. In exchange, she placed significantly more emphasis on the injustice to the plaintiffs caused by the continued sale of illegal merchandise online by ordering a global remedy for a global wrong.

D. Justice Abella's Progressive Legacy

Can Justice Abella's technology jurisprudence be reconciled with itself? We believe that it can, by appreciating that progressivism means both facilitating technological change and regulating its excesses. While (in our view) *Equustek* went too far, we recognize that the judicial impulse to protect the rule of law is not always easy to reconcile with the inherently limited tools courts have at their disposal. Moreover, a by-product of Justice Abella's considered and contextual approach to technological change is that it left the field open for future technology cases to be decided on their particular facts, where the equities may be different or where the underlying technological, social, or legal context has changed. Judicial treatment of two of Justice Abella's pre-eminent technology decisions, *Crookes* and *Equustek*, shows that this process is already underway.

Justice Abella's decision in *Crookes* was praised for laying the groundwork for a holistic understanding of defamation in the internet age, largely due to its emphasis on contextual understandings of free expression online.[71] But the result of that decision was not to suggest that sharing references to information online could never amount to defamation or other internet-based harms. Indeed, Justice Abella specifically warned against such an interpretation. Writing about the difference between "deep" and "shallow" hyperlinks, she observed that the continued evolution of the internet may give rise to hyperlinks, or similar sharing tools, with attributes that were not considered on the facts of *Crookes*, including those that do more than merely point users to the location of defamatory content. She reasoned that "[e]mbedded or automatic links, for example, may well prove to be of consequence in future cases, but these differences were not argued in this case or addressed in the courts below, and therefore need not be addressed here."[72]

---

71 See Iris Fischer & Adam Lazier, "Crookes v Newton: The Supreme Court of Canada Brings Libel Law into the Internet Age" (2012) 50:1 *Alberta Law Review* 205.

72 *Crookes*, above note 2 at para 43.

Courts have heeded that warning and continued to grapple with the extent to which sharing content online can give rise to liability for defamation or other wrongdoing. For instance, in *Baglow v Smith,* a case decided after *Crookes* but prior to *Equustek,* the Ontario Superior Court distinguished *Crookes* and held that the moderators and administrators of an anonymous message board had indeed "published" the allegedly defamatory content on the site.[73] It found that, unlike a hyperlink, the message board provided content directly to the public.[74] The court also concluded that the balance between reputational interests and free expression in contemporary defamation law favoured recognizing that the moderators and administrators of anonymous message boards could be held liable, as potential plaintiffs would otherwise have limited recourse against anonymous posters.[75] Courts have also considered whether and to what extent *Crookes* affects liability for copyright infringement when links to copyright-protected content are shared. In these cases, courts have been careful to draw distinctions between authorized and unauthorized sharing of links to copyright-protected works (with only the latter potentially amounting to copyright infringement) and between shallow links and deep links, the latter of which automatically display copyright-protected content. They have also considered the principles animating defamation law and copyright, particularly given that in the context of copyright, "wrongdoing lies not in the original work itself but in the very act of sharing access to it without the owner's authorization."[76]

Judicial treatment of *Equustek* has been even more varied. Unlike Justice Abella's decision in *Crookes,* which was largely met with acclaim for its forward-looking vision of the internet, *Equustek* has been more seriously criticized. Some alleged that the case was becoming a cautionary tale for online governance and overregulation,[77] while others saw it as inconsistent with the more considered view of the internet put forward in *Crookes.*[78] With the benefit of time, it is evident that *Equustek*

73 *Baglow v Smith,* 2015 ONSC 1175 [*Baglow*]. Note that the defendants were ultimately saved by the defence of fair comment.

74 *Ibid* at para 192.

75 *Ibid* at para 196.

76 *Proctorio, Incorporated v Linkletter,* 2022 BCSC 400 at paras 88–95, aff'd 2023 BCCA 160; See also *Warman v Fournier,* 2012 FC 803.

77 Michael Geist, "The Unintended *Equustek* Effect" *Center for International Governance Innovation Online,* online: www.cigionline.org/articles/unintended-equustek-effect/; Matthew Marinett, "The Race to the Bottom: Comity and Cooperation in Global Internet Takedown Orders" (2020) 53:2 *UBC Law Review* 463.

78 Robert Diab, "Search Engines and Global Takedown Orders: *Google v Equustek* and

has made it easier to justify injunctions and other far-reaching equitable remedies against internet service providers and platforms.[79] Yet *Equustek* did not turn out to be a watershed moment for judicial internet regulation.[80] Courts in other jurisdictions limited the effect of the order based on local laws.[81] And closer to home, Canadian courts have ultimately distinguished it based on Justice Abella's narrow framing of the issues in that case. For example, in *College of Optometrists of Ontario v Essilor Group*, a case about the regulation of online eyeglass sales across provincial borders, the Ontario Court of Appeal distinguished *Equustek* on the basis that it was a decision that, while acknowledging the new reality of online commerce, ultimately turned on existing injunction jurisprudence.[82] The Court of Appeal understood *Essilor* as a case fundamentally about the constitutional applicability of one province's laws to activities that occur in another. The Court declined to apply *Equustek*, or any other authority, to unnecessarily tighten its grip on online commerce.

There are also disagreements in the jurisprudence since *Equustek* about how law should deal with the realities of online commerce in other contexts, such as in criminal law. These disagreements show that the broader normative issues considered in *Equustek* (perhaps more than the judgment itself) are the centre of ongoing controversy and remain ripe for judicial interpretation. For example, in *British Columbia v Brecknell*, the British Columbia Court of Appeal held that a trial court had jurisdiction to issue a production order under the *Criminal Code* against Craigslist, a US company with only a virtual presence in the province.[83] The court relied in part on the trial judge's decision in *Equustek*, ultimately affirmed by the Supreme Court, which provided that once it was accepted that a court has *in personam* jurisdiction over a person (as evidenced by some presence in the province), the fact that an order may affect its activities in other jurisdictions is not a bar to issuing the order.[84] The Alberta Court of Appeal recently relied on *Brecknell* and *Equustek* to uphold a production order against Facebook on the same basis (an

---

the Future of Free Speech Online" (2019) 56:2 *Osgoode Hall Law Journal* 231.

79 See *Teksavvy Solutions Inc v Bell Media Inc*, 2021 FCA 100.

80 Barry Sookman, "The Unintended Equustek Effect: A Reply to Michael Geist," online: www.barrysookman.com/2019/04/02/the-unintended-equustek-effect-a-reply-to-michael-geist/.

81 *Google LLC v Equustek Solutions Inc*, 2017 WL 5000834 (ND Cal Nov 2, 2017).

82 *College of Optometrists of Ontario v Essilor Group Inc*, 2019 ONCA 265 at para 123.

83 *British Columbia v Brecknell*, 2018 BCCA 5 [*Brecknell*].

84 *Ibid* at para 51.

appeal to the Supreme Court was denied in this case).[85] But courts in other provinces have reached different conclusions. For instance, the Provincial Court of Newfoundland has expressly declined to follow the extension of *Equustek* in *Brecknell* on the basis that the authorization of the production order was contrary to Parliament's decision not to provide the relevant provision of the *Criminal Code* with extraterritorial effect.[86] This discrepancy has been noted by the Ontario Superior Court, which has acknowledged that there is a "real question" about whether Canadian courts have jurisdiction to compel the production of certain kinds of information in this manner.[87] In the end, these disagreements reflect the common law at work.

E. Conclusion

Justice Abella recognized both the dangers of law's conservative tendencies to the beneficial effects of new technology and the dangers of technology's potential disruptions to the rule of law and other important social institutions. We see this progressive bent throughout her internet and information technology jurisprudence. As courts explore the reaches of *Crookes*, *Equustek*, and her other decisions, we should expect that they will continue to grapple with the social, legal, and technological context bearing on the underlying issues that animated these disputes. While they may or may not decide these cases as Justice Abella would have, we suspect that, above all, she would want them to continue to carefully analyze these issues so that the law does its best to keep up with the rapid pace of twenty-first century technological change.

---

85 *R v Love*, 2022 ABCA 269, leave to appeal refused, 2023 CanLII 31586 (SCC). But see also *In the matter of an ex parte application for a production order in relation to data in the possession of Facebook, Inc*, 2020 NSPC 55, where the Nova Scotia Provincial Court declined to decide whether *Brecknell* was rightly decided on the basis that unlike Craigslist, Facebook had a physical presence in Canada through its offices in Ontario.

86 *In the Matter of an application to obtain a Production Order pursuant to section 487.014 of the Criminal Code of Canada, 2018*, 2018 CanLII 2369 (NLPC).

87 See *R v Strong*, 2020 ONSC 7528 at para 112(g).

19 Justice Abella: Staunch Defender of Privacy in the Digital Age

GERALD CHAN AND YADESHA SATHEASWARAN*

A. Introduction

Time and again over her judicial career, Justice Rosalie Silberman Abella harnessed the transformative power of the law to protect individual rights against changing social forces. An area in which her contributions are underrated — and the area this chapter focusses on — is the law of search and seizure.

Section 8 of the *Charter* guarantees everyone the right to be secure against unreasonable search and seizure. What section 8 once meant in the age of letters and land lines, however, is different than what it now means in the age of text messages and cell phones. Our law of search and seizure has adapted to new social and technological forces to ensure that the underlying value of privacy endures. This is thanks in no small part to Justice Abella.

Ever since her early days on the Court of Appeal for Ontario,[1] Justice Abella has been resolute in protecting individuals from state intrusions into private life. Her opinions — whether as part of the majority, plurality, in concurrence, or in dissent — consistently reinforced the need to keep police accountable under section 8. She not only took an expansive view of section 8's scope, but she also demonstrated a stronger willingness than her judicial colleagues to exclude evidence under section

* Gerald Chan is a partner at Stockwoods LLP where he practices criminal, constitutional, administrative, and select civil litigation. Yadesha Satheaswaran is an Assistant Crown Attorney with the West Toronto Crown's office. At the time of writing this paper, she worked as an associate at Stockwoods LLP.

1 See, for example, Justice Abella's dissenting opinion in *R v Edwards* (1994), 19 OR (3d) 239 [*Edwards*] and her opinion for the court in *R v Tessling* (2003), 63 OR (3d) 1 [*Tessling* (ONCA)].

24(2) where she found a rights violation.[2] In doing so, Justice Abella revealed a staunch unwillingness to allow police to exploit legal uncertainty and technological advancement to erode an individual's right to be left alone.

This chapter explores Justice Abella's contributions to privacy and the criminal law under section 8 of the *Charter.* We first provide an overview of the Supreme Court of Canada's development of search and seizure law from 2010 and onwards in light of digital technologies that made it easier for the police to collect information about our private lives. We then turn to Justice Abella's opinions in this area during her time at the Court of Appeal for Ontario and Supreme Court of Canada.

The theme that emerges from Justice Abella's section 8 jurisprudence is that she consistently and vigilantly stood guard to ensure that technological advances do not erode privacy. Rather than rigidly adhering to analog-era doctrines in a digital age, Justice Abella modified (and pushed her colleagues to modify) the rules of search and seizure to keep pace with the expanding powers of the state in light of new technologies.[3] In doing so, Justice Abella played a vital role in ensuring that section 8's promise of privacy protection endures.

B. Jurisprudential Context

Under the *Charter*, Canadians' right to privacy is protected by the section 8 right to be "secure against unreasonable search or seizure." State actors conduct a "search" when they invade an area in which we, as individuals, have a "reasonable expectation of privacy."[4] This can occur if state actors enter physical spaces, such as our homes ("territorial privacy"), inspect our bodies ("bodily privacy"), or obtain personal information which we wish to maintain control over ("informational privacy").[5] When an individual is involved in legal proceedings like a criminal prosecution and their reasonable expectation of privacy is violated, they have standing to challenge the violation as an unreasonable search or seizure under section 8 of the *Charter* and to request a remedy that excludes any unconstitutionally acquired evidence.

2 See, for example, her dissenting opinion in *R v Cole*, 2012 SCC 53, [2012] 3 SCR 34 [*Cole*] and *R v Saeed*, 2016 SCC 24, [2016] 1 SCR 518 [*Saeed*].

3 Justice Abella has taken a similar approach to technology in other areas of the law: see Andrew Bernstein & Amanda Wolczanski, "Dot-com Justice: Progress and Precedent in Justice Abella's Technology Jurisprudence" in this volume.

4 *R v Tessling*, 2004 SCC 67, [2004] 3 SCR 432 at para 18 [*Tessling* (SCC)].

5 *Ibid* at paras 22–24.

Since 2010, the Supreme Court of Canada has developed its section 8 *Charter* jurisprudence to address the novel privacy issues that have arisen from the increased use of technology by both individuals and state actors. In *R v Vu*, for example, the Supreme Court considered whether an ordinary warrant, issued for the search of a residence, permitted police to access and look through the contents of a suspect's computer.[6] Justice Cromwell, writing for a unanimous bench, concluded that it did not.[7] While a warrant allows police to search a place, including the receptacles within that place, Justice Cromwell noted that computers differed "markedly" from cupboards and filing cabinets. In particular:

> Computers potentially give police access to vast amounts of information that users cannot control, that they may not even be aware of or may have chosen to discard and which may not be, in any meaningful sense, located in the place of the search.[8]

Justice Cromwell observed that these "numerous and striking differences" between computers and traditional receptacles called for the distinctive treatment of the former under section 8.[9] He determined that police would have to obtain *specific* prior authorization to lawfully search a suspect's computer.[10]

One year later, the Supreme Court tackled another privacy issue in relation to computers: internet use. In *R v Spencer*, the police identified the Internet Protocol (IP) address of a computer that had accessed and stored child pornography. The police asked the internet service provider, without a warrant or production order, for the subscriber information associated with the IP address. This led them to the accused, who had put child pornography into an online computer folder that was accessible to other individuals using the same file-sharing program.[11]

Justice Cromwell again wrote a unanimous judgment for the bench. The central question was whether the accused had a reasonable expectation of privacy in his subscriber information. Justice Cromwell held that he did, and therefore the police's warrantless acquisition of his subscriber information was an unconstitutional search under section 8 of the *Charter*.[12]

6 *R v Vu*, 2013 SCC 60 at para 1.
7 *Ibid* at para 2.
8 *Ibid* at para 24.
9 *Ibid* at para 45.
10 *Ibid* at para 47.
11 *R v Spencer*, 2014 SCC 43, [2014] 2 SCR 212 at para 2.
12 *Ibid* at para 16.

Justice Cromwell cited the well-established "totality of circumstances" test; but he reformulated the various factors, which had been developed in the context of property searches,[13] into four broad categories so that the test could be applied equally to informational searches: (1) the subject-matter of the alleged search; (2) the accused's interest in the subject-matter; (3) the accused's subjective expectation of privacy in the subject-matter; and (4) the objective reasonableness of the accused's subjective expectation of privacy.[14] He focused on the first and third factors,[15] defining the subject-matter of the alleged search as not simply the name and address of the person in a contractual relationship with the internet service provider, but rather the identity of the subscriber whose proclivities and interests could be discerned from their internet use.[16] For Justice Cromwell, the police search raised concerns about "informational privacy" because the accused had revealed details about himself based on the belief that his online activities would remain anonymous.[17] This subjective belief, viewed objectively, was reasonable.[18] The police decision to pursue the subscriber information, without a warrant, was contrary to section 8 of the *Charter*.[19]

Vu and *Spencer*, along with *R v Morelli*,[20] *R v Cole*,[21] and *R v Fearon*,[22] clarified the law on when police can lawfully search our electronic devices and discover information about our online activities. However, until the 2017 case of *R v Marakah*,[23] the Supreme Court had not dealt with text messaging as a unique category of information as the target of a police search. *Marakah* raised the following question: if A sends a text message to B, and police subsequently discover that text message during a search of B's phone, have the police intruded upon A's reasonable expectation of privacy? Does an individual retain a privacy interest in a text communication sent to (and retrieved from) another's device? Chief Justice McLachlin (as she was then), on behalf of a majority, answered "yes."

---

13 *R v Edwards*, [1996] 1 SCR 128.
14 *Ibid* at paras 17–18.
15 *Ibid* at para 20.
16 *Ibid* at para 32.
17 *Ibid* at para 50.
18 *Ibid* at para 66.
19 *Ibid* at para 74.
20 2010 SCC 8, [2010] 1 SCR 253.
21 *Cole*, above note 2.
22 2014 SCC 77, [2014] 3 SCR 621.
23 2017 SCC 59, [2017] 2 SCR 608 [*Marakah*].

Chief Justice McLachlin characterized the subject-matter of the search not as the physical device, but as the electronic conversation between the accused and his accomplice.[24] The accused had a direct interest in the subject-matter of the search, since he was a participant in the electronic conversation and the author of various text messages introduced as evidence against him.[25] Further, the accused expected that the conversation would remain private.[26] His subjective expectation of privacy was objectively reasonable because the electronic conversation was a virtual "space" accessible only to the accused and his accomplice; the information shared in the conversation revealed details about the accused's personal lifestyle (his criminal activities); and the accused exercised control over the information he disclosed, and the manner in which he disclosed it.[27]

Marakah proved to be a massive step forward for the protection of Canadians' privacy rights in the digital era. The pivotal issue was how the subject-matter of the search should be characterized. If a majority of the Supreme Court had found the subject-matter of the police search to be the accomplice's physical device, then the notion of privacy would have been reduced to just the owner's interest in the device and its contents. The Court would have failed to appreciate that text messaging is a method of communication between two or more people, all of whom have an interest in safeguarding the information they send and receive. But that is not the route the Court took. Instead, it recognized that text messages function as a unique source of personal information, separate and distinct from the physical device on which they are located.

C. Justice Abella, Privacy Rights, and Section 8 of the *Charter*

In *Marakah*, Justice Abella formed part of the majority that found individuals to have a reasonable expectation of privacy over their text messages, even if the text messages were located on another's device. Justice Abella did not write the majority opinion, but her influence is readily apparent in the reasons of Chief Justice McLachlin.

Justice Abella's earlier work on section 8 of the *Charter* had emphasized the importance of context in identifying the nature of an individual's privacy right and the purpose of the state's alleged search. With respect to issues of informational privacy — especially those related to

24 *Ibid* at para 17.
25 *Ibid* at para 21.
26 *Ibid* at para 23.
27 *Ibid* at para 54.

the use of new technologies — she had repeatedly held that the crux of the courts' analysis should be the substance of what the state seeks to obtain from the individuals' private lives.[28] This sort of broad, contextual approach to section 8 of the *Charter* is precisely what the Chief Justice adopted in *Marakah* (and what Justice Cromwell adopted in *Spencer*). It is an approach that has enabled the courts to better protect the underlying value of privacy by constantly asking what the state is seeking to discover rather than focusing myopically on the way in which (or the technique with which) the state is seeking to discover it.

As early as 1994, Justice Abella made her mark on section 8 jurisprudence. The case, *R v Edwards*, involved an accused who was arrested after police performed a search of his girlfriend's apartment and discovered drugs.[29] The Court of Appeal had to consider whether the accused had a reasonable expectation of privacy in his girlfriend's apartment. Justice Abella, in dissent, found that he did. She observed that although the accused was not a tenant of the premises, he had been with his partner for three years and had been given the keys to her apartment. As a result, the accused had unrestricted access to the apartment and was entitled to use the space freely. For Justice Abella, the number of times the accused used the apartment was not determinative of whether he had a reasonable privacy interest in the space. Rather, the accused's privacy right attached to the apartment because of the broader context — he was in a long-term relationship with his partner and had her permission to use the apartment as he wished. The majority in the Court of Appeal did not agree with her, nor did the majority at the Supreme Court.[30] But their approach — which was to focus heavily on factors like possession and control of the place searched, as well as the ability to regulate access — has since been criticized as being unduly narrow and contrary to one of the foundational principles of section 8 jurisprudence: that the right "protects people, not places."[31] That principle is consistent with the broad, contextual approach that the Court adopted in cases like *Marakah*.

28 See, for example, *R v Jones*, 2017 SCC 60, [2017] 2 SCR 696 at para 106 [*Jones*].

29 *Edwards*, above note 1.

30 [1996] 1 SCR 128.

31 *Hunter v Southam*, [1984] 2 SCR 145 at para 159; Don Stuart, "The Unfortunate Dilution of Section 8 Protection: Some Teeth Remain" (1999) 25 *Queen's Law Journal* 65 at 70–71; see also Julia Lawn and Andrew Bernstein, "Primacy to Privacy? The Supreme Court and the Privacy Threshold in *Edwards*" (1997) 55:2 *University of Toronto Faculty of Law Review* 341 at 342–46 and Don Stuart, "Eight Plus Twenty Four Two Equals Zero" (1998) 13 *Criminal Reports* (5th) 50.

Nearly a decade later, while still at the Court of Appeal, Justice Abella wrote another significant section 8 opinion in the 2003 case of *R v Tessling*.[32] On behalf of a unanimous panel, she held that the police's use of a "Forward Looking Infra-Red" (FLIR) camera to take pictures of heat emanations from the accused's home amounted to a search under section 8 of the *Charter*. While the FLIR camera could not see past the walls of the home or detect the exact sources of heat production, Justice Abella noted that the sole purpose of this technology was to help police determine the nature of the activities inside the home. While police were mainly interested in the existence of a marijuana grow operation, the FLIR camera did not limit itself to detecting heat emanations coming only from a marijuana grow operation. Instead, its use could reveal details about a variety of heat-generating activities from within the home that were not otherwise observable by the naked eye or with enhanced aids. Justice Abella therefore concluded that the state's use of a FLIR camera was a search within the meaning of section 8 of the *Charter*. This conclusion was echoed by the United States Supreme Court in *Kyllo v United States*.[33]

Justice Abella's opinion, however, was overturned by the Supreme Court of Canada. Justice Binnie, on behalf of a unanimous bench, stressed that the use of FLIR technology in its current form did not constitute a search *of* the home, as Justice Abella claimed, but merely a search for information *about* the home.[34] In Justice Binnie's view, the crudity of the images created by the FLIR camera meant that police did not know exactly what type of activities took place inside the home.[35] The FLIR images could lead to a number of hypotheses, including the existence of a marijuana grow operation as one possibility.[36] Police had to possess additional evidence to obtain a warrant, search the accused's home, and confirm the grow operation.[37] Therefore, in Justice Binnie's view, the FLIR camera alone did not offer any insight into the accused's private life or affect his "dignity, integrity and autonomy."[38]

The conflict between Justices Abella and Binnie on this issue largely boils down to how the question should be characterized.[39] In Justice

32 *Tessling* (ONCA), above note 2.
33 121 S Ct 2038 (2001).
34 *Tessling* (SCC), above note 4 at para 27.
35 *Ibid* at para 36.
36 *Ibid* at para 53.
37 *Ibid* at para 36.
38 *Ibid* at para 63.
39 *Ibid* at para 63.

Binnie's view, the question was whether individuals have a reasonable expectation of privacy in the pattern of heat distribution on the external surfaces of their home. In Justice Abella's view, this characterization was "overly simplistic" because the surface emanations are "on their own, meaningless."[40] The question is what the state is seeking to find out about what's going on inside the home and what the surface emanations can reveal when combined with other information. The latter approach to characterizing the issue is closer to the method that the Supreme Court would eventually adopt in *Spencer*.[41] What mattered to Justice Abella in *Tessling* (and to Justice Cromwell in *Spencer*) was what the state was *really* after. Even if the police could not reveal the entire picture in one fell swoop, their conduct in uncovering part of the picture demanded constitutional oversight.

Justice Abella continued her robust approach to privacy when she got to the Supreme Court.[42] Among her most notable privacy and technology opinions was her plurality opinion in *R v TELUS Communications Co*.[43] Unlike most telecommunications service providers, Telus (at the time) routinely made copies of all the text messages its subscribers sent or received and briefly stored them in its database.[44] The question before the Supreme Court was statutory instead of constitutional: whether a general warrant, issued under section 487.01 of the *Criminal Code*, permitted police to request the daily production of text messages between two Telus subscribers for a two-week period in the near future.[45] Justice Abella, on behalf of the plurality, held that a general warrant was not enough. Instead, she found that the police search of the text messages was akin to a wiretap. Therefore, the heightened requirements of a "Part VI authorization" (often colloquially referred to as a "wiretap authorization") were required to protect the privacy interests at stake.[46]

40 *Tessling* (ONCA), above note 2 at para 66.

41 *Spencer*, above note 11 at paras 32–33. We maintain this point even though the *Spencer* judgment (in para 28) purported to rely on Justice Binnie's majority opinion in *Tessling* (SCC).

42 While not a technology case, Justice Abella's sole concurring opinion in *R v Patrick*, 2009 SCC 17, [2009] 1 SCR 579 is notable. She was the only judge on the Court to find that individuals retain a reasonable expectation of privacy over their garbage when left at the curbside for pick-up. As she wrote in the opening line of her opinion (at para 76), "What we inelegantly call 'garbage' may contain the most intensely personal and private information about ourselves."

43 2013 SCC 16, [2013] 2 SCR 3 [*Telus*].

44 *Ibid* at para 7.

45 *Ibid* at paras 8 and 15.

46 *Ibid* at para 45.

Telus pre-dated *Marakah* as the first Supreme Court case to examine privacy in text messaging, albeit from a statutory rather than constitutional perspective. Justice Abella characterized text messaging as an instantaneous form of communication, akin to a telephone conversation. The only difference, she found, was the transmission process. Justice Abella did not believe that the technical differences between text messaging and a telephone call should undermine the scope of protection afforded to the messages.[47] If police intercepted the text messages in the actual transmission stream, such as in the middle of a telephone call, then they would have required a "wiretap authorization." As she pointed out, the type of judicial authorization should not change just because Telus maintained a unique transmission infrastructure whereby it temporarily stored its subscribers' text messages.[48] Police were still "intercepting" the private communications, just in another form.[49] The best way to protect the informational privacy of Telus subscribers, she contended, was to mandate the police acquisition of a "wiretap authorization" for any search of prospective text messages with the service provider.

Although the issue in *Telus* concerned the statutory authority the police required to conduct a search rather than the threshold constitutional question of whether there was a search, Justice Abella's analysis reveals the primacy she placed on the value of privacy and the need to protect it against encroachment by changing technologies. By keeping her focus squarely on the purpose of privacy protection, she prevented herself from being distracted by the technological form of the information and, relatedly, the technological form of the police techniques used to target that information. Her plurality opinion was therefore critical in laying the foundation for the Supreme Court's subsequent opinion in *Marakah*.

In *Telus*, the police acquisition of text messages was *prospective* because the police were seeking to acquire future text messages going forward. In the subsequent case of *R v Jones* (which was a companion appeal to *Marakah*),[50] the police acquisition of text messages was *retrospective* because they sought access to historical text messages stored by the telecommunications provider. Again, Justice Abella adopted the more privacy-protective approach: she extended the logic in *Telus* to impose the same heightened requirement of a wiretap authorization

47 *Ibid* at para 5.
48 *Ibid* at para 40.
49 *Ibid* at para 39.
50 *Jones*, above note 28.

to a retrospective search of text messages. This time, however, she was alone.[51] Writing for the majority, Justice Côté found that while the accused had a reasonable expectation of privacy in his text messages,[52] the police did not need to obtain a Part VI wiretap authorization because that statutory regime applied only to prospective searches. Justice Côté held that the lower standard — that which applied to a production order (section 487.012 of the *Criminal Code*) — sufficed for retrospective searches of text messages.[53] Such searches did not involve an "intercept" that would trigger the wiretap regime because they did not involve the real-time acquisitions of private communications.[54]

Justice Abella strongly disputed Justice Côté's interpretation of "intercept."[55] Justice Abella noted the term should be construed broadly to uphold the purpose behind Part VI, which was to prevent the state from accessing private communications without lawful authorization and to protect the privacy interests of individuals.[56] To that end, she found that the interpretation of "intercept" should have turned on the substance, not the timing, of the text messages.[57] The only difference between a prospective search and a retrospective search, she contended, lay in the timing of when the police went to the court for judicial authorization. If the police went one day *before* the text messages are exchanged, that would be a prospective search. If the police went one day *after* the text messages are exchanged, that would be a retrospective search. In either case, however, the police could access the same (and often extensive amount of) electronic communications.[58] Therefore, Justice Abella held that a retrospective search of text messages was no less an intercept than a prospective search of text messages. The substance of the information sought — and therefore of the privacy interests affected — was the same. While the majority of the Court did not share this view, Justice Abella's reasoning was compelling. Like much of her earlier work on section 8, it was driven by a purposive approach to the values underlying the right to be secure against unreasonable search and seizure.

Justice Abella's work on section 8 of the *Charter*, whether as part of the majority or the dissent, was both innovative and foundational. She

51 *Ibid* at para 1.
52 *Ibid* at para 55.
53 *Ibid* at para 59.
54 *Ibid* at para 66.
55 *Ibid* at paras 99 and 104.
56 *Ibid* at para 105.
57 *Ibid* at para 113.
58 *Ibid* at para 106.

was bold and creative in her approach to legal interpretation, such as in her interpretation of "intercept" with respect to police acquisitions of text messages (a form of communication that did not exist when Part VI of the *Criminal Code* was enacted). At the same time, she refused to take her eye off the substance of what Part VI of the *Criminal Code* and section 8 of the *Charter* were originally intended to protect. Whether she was dealing with the contents of our private communications in *Telus* and *Jones*, or the private activities within our home in *Tessling* (or even another's home in *Edwards*), she demonstrated a steadfast commitment to protecting privacy, the value at the heart of search and seizure law. In this way, her jurisprudence in this area was both traditionalist and groundbreaking at the same time.

D. Justice Abella and Section 24 of the *Charter*

Justice Abella did not just limit her robust approach to defining the scope of the rights guaranteed by section 8. She also took a robust view of the remedy that should be granted in the event of a section 8 rights violation — even when she had to do so in sole dissent.[59]

The best example of Justice Abella's commitment to granting individuals a remedy for privacy violations was her dissenting opinion in *R v Cole*. There, the accused was charged and convicted of possessing child pornography after the police uncovered the material on his work computer.[60] The Court was unanimous in holding that an individual has a reasonable expectation of privacy in his *work* computer despite the fact that it may be owned by the individual's employer.[61] This was a landmark win for advocates of the right to privacy. It was not, however, a win for Cole, because the majority still declined to exclude the evidence. The majority found that the investigating officer "sincerely" believed his actions were *Charter*-compliant,[62] and that the law on privacy interests in work computers was still unsettled.[63] Further, the evidence was reliable and probative.[64] Therefore, the majority concluded that the exclusion of the evidence would have had a "marked negative

59 In *Saeed*, above note 2, for instance, Justice Abella wrote a sole dissenting opinion in which she would have excluded the evidence obtained by police through an unconstitutional penile swab (at paras 131–68).

60 *Cole*, above note 2 at paras 5–6.

61 *Ibid* at para 58.

62 *Ibid* at para 89.

63 *Ibid* at para 86.

64 *Ibid* at para 96.

impact on the truth-seeking function of the criminal trial process"[65] and held that the evidence should be admitted.[66]

By contrast, Justice Abella refused to excuse the unconstitutional behaviour of the officer on the basis of the legal uncertainty. She emphasized that the officer in question had several years of experience with his police force.[67] Although the law relating to the search of workplace computers may have been in flux, the law was settled that property rights did not dictate the reasonable expectation of privacy analysis.[68] Yet the officer based his decision not to get a warrant on the outdated belief that section 8 was all about property.[69] As a result, Justice Abella reasoned that any "good faith" on the part of the officer was compromised by his apparent indifference to longstanding section 8 principles.[70]

Justice Abella also showed a nuanced understanding of the technological context in assessing the second factor for exclusion of evidence under the test in *R v Grant*: the impact of the *Charter* breach on the accused.[71] While the majority relied on the diminished expectation of privacy in a person's *work* computer as weighing in favour of admission of the evidence, Justice Abella went beyond this general observation to look specifically at the personal information Mr. Cole had on his work laptop.[72] She appreciated that the line between work and personal use in computers is not a bright one — people use their work computers for personal reasons just as they use their personal computers for work reasons. That was true of Cole based on the evidence in the case. Therefore, Justice Abella found that the second factor — the impact on the accused — also weighed in favour of excluding the illicit images.[73]

On the third factor for the exclusion of evidence test under *Grant* — societal interest in an adjudication on the merits — Justice Abella reiterated that while the public has an interest in the prosecution of a serious offence, it also has an interest in the maintenance of a justice system above reproach, particularly where the penal stakes for an accused are

65 *Ibid* at para 97.
66 *Ibid* at para 98.
67 *Ibid* at para 110.
68 *Ibid* at para 114.
69 *Ibid* at paras 117–18.
70 *Ibid* at 123.
71 *R v Grant*, 2009 SCC 32, [2009] 2 SCR 353 at para 85.
72 *Ibid* at para 125.
73 *Ibid* at para 127.

high.[74] Balancing the three *Grant* factors, Justice Abella held that the evidence should have been excluded under section 24(2).[75]

In *Cole*, Justice Abella refused to accept the general assertions that so often go unexamined in section 24(2) analyses — namely, that legal uncertainty and diminished expectations of privacy in the workplace necessarily weigh against the remedy of exclusion. Instead, she dug into the record to probe the basis for the officer's decision not to get a warrant and the specific way the accused used his work device. Her rigorous dissenting opinion demonstrates both her general commitment to providing a remedy for a rights violation and her specific commitment to vindicating the right to be secure against unreasonable search and seizure.

E. Conclusion

Justice Abella's work on privacy has had a lasting impact on our law of search and seizure. At both the Court of Appeal for Ontario and the Supreme Court of Canada, Justice Abella pushed the law forward so that the fundamental value of privacy could keep pace with the rapid evolution and proliferation of technology and with the social realities of how we engaged with that technology. She was creative in her methods, but traditionalist in her fidelity to the original values that provisions like Part VI and section 8 of the *Charter* were enacted to protect. Moreover, she did not hesitate the hold the state accountable for privacy violations by granting the accused a remedy under section 24(2). Sometimes in the majority, sometimes in dissent, Justice Abella consistently stood guard as a staunch defender of the right to privacy. Her contributions in this area should be remembered as an important part of her legacy.

74 *Ibid* at para 134.
75 *Ibid* at para 135.

20 Pushing the Boundaries of International Law in Canada: The Legacy of Justice Rosalie Abella

SARA GHEBREMUSSE*

A. Introduction

Over her forty years as a judge, Justice Rosalie Silberman Abella's jurisprudence and other contributions have advanced principles of equality, justice, and human rights.[1] During her time on the Supreme Court of Canada, Justice Abella authored two notable decisions related to the adoption of international law that were influenced by her commitment to these principles. These related decisions — her dissent in *Kazemi Estate v Islamic Republic of Iran*[2] and her majority ruling in *Nevsun Resources Ltd v Araya*[3] — shaped her legacy on Canada's highest court. Though both decisions were contentious, they nonetheless pushed the

---

* Chair in Mining Law and Finance and Assistant Professor, University of Western Ontario Faculty of Law.

1 Some of Justice Abella's notable contributions include her 1984 report, *Equality in Employment: A Royal Commission Report*; her dissent in *R v NS*, 2012 SCC 72, where she held that the religious rights of a complainant who wears a niqab outweigh an accused's right to a fair trial, except in cases where the witness's face is directly relevant to the case; her majority ruling in *Moore v British Columbia (Education)*, 2012 SCC 61, where she found a school district discriminated against a student suffering from severe dyslexia by failing to accommodate him; her majority decision in *Kanthasamy v Canada (Citizenship and Immigration)*, 2015 SCC 61, where she expanded the consideration of humanitarian and compassionate relief under the *Immigration and Refugee Protection Act*, SC 2001, c 27 and allowed the appeal of a young Tamil man seeking refugee status in Canada after his application was denied; and her majority ruling in *Fraser v Canada (Attorney General)*, 2020 SCC 28, one of her last decisions before retiring, where she held that the unequal pension benefits of the Royal Canadian Mounted Police's job-sharing program, which mostly included women, disproportionately impacted its women members, violating their right to equality under section 15 of the *Charter of Rights and Freedoms*.

2 2014 SCC 62 [*Kazemi*].

3 2020 SCC 5 [*Nevsun*].

boundaries of the use and application of international human rights law in Canada. In *Nevsun*, Justice Abella finished what she began in *Kazemi*: she extended the protection of individual human rights under international law in Canada, while also creating more room for Canadian courts to be active contributors to the development of international law. This chapter considers how Justice Abella's potential international law legacy was formed in *Kazemi* and *Nevsun* before discussing the implications of the decisions and the potential they have to shape the future of Canadian law in this area.

B. Justice Abella's Key International Law Cases: *Kazemi* and *Nevsun*

Justice Abella's own engagement with international law at the Court prolifically unfolded in two seminal cases: *Kazemi* and *Nevsun*. While these two cases are unrelated in their content and applicable international law, the synergies between her dissent in *Kazemi* and majority ruling in *Nevsun* are integral to understanding her potential impact on future directions for international law and Canadian courts. In *Kazemi* and *Nevsun*, Justice Abella controversially deployed international law to supplant state-centrism in favour of individual human rights.[4] By doing so, she pushed the boundaries in which the Canadian judiciary has conventionally applied international law by bringing international law more into the fold of Canada's common law while also broadening Canadian courts' contributions to the interpretation of international law.[5]

On its own, Justice Abella's dissent in *Kazemi* was a stark contradistinction from Justice LeBel's majority ruling. Zahra Kazemi was a dual Canadian and Iranian citizen. She was a photojournalist who was working in Iran in 2003 when she was arrested and imprisoned after photographing protests outside a prison in Tehran. She was tortured, beaten, and sexually assaulted while in the custody of Iranian officials. She died from a brain injury sustained during her detention.[6] Three years later, Kazemi's son, Stephan Hashemi, instituted proceedings on behalf of himself and her estate against the Islamic Republic of Iran, its head of state, and two government officials.[7] Writing for the majority, Justice

---

4 H. Scott Fairley, "International Law Matures within the Canadian Legal System: *Araya et al v Nevsun Resources Ltd*" (2021) 99:1 *Canadian Bar Review* 193 at 194 [Fairley, "International Law Matures"].

5 Eva Monteiro, "Mining for Legal Luxuries: The Pitfalls and Potential of *Nevsun Resources Ltd v Araya*" (2020) 58 *Canadian Yearbook of International Law* 331 at 334.

6 *Kazemi*, above note 2 at paras 4–8.

7 *Ibid* at para 1.

LeBel considered whether relevant provisions of the *State Immunity Act*[8] immunized foreign officials from civil liability for torture. After examining the history and status of state immunity in international law, Justice LeBel concluded that the *SIA* provided a complete bar to civil claims against foreign states and officials. Despite the emergence of the prohibition against torture as a peremptory norm in international law, Justice LeBel held that customary international law had "not yet created an exception to state immunity from civil liability in cases of torture committed abroad."[9] For Justice LeBel, the *SIA* was a complete codification of Canadian law as it related to state immunity from civil proceedings. While he acknowledged academic arguments that the language of the *SIA* was not exhaustive and that the common law and developments in international law could inform its interpretation, Justice LeBel disagreed with this proposition and concluded that the *SIA* provided "an exhaustive list of exceptions to state immunity."[10] Thus, Justice LeBel found that the "common law, *jus cogens* norms or international law [could not] carve out additional exceptions to [state] immunity"[11] included in the *SIA*. For that to occur, Parliament would have to revise the legislation in accordance with emerging international norms.[12]

Read in conjunction with her majority decision in *Nevsun*, it becomes clear that Justice Abella took a principled approach to her use and interpretation of international law that acknowledged its evolving nuance and complexity.[13] In *Kazemi*, Justice Abella began her analysis by affirming that the prohibition against torture is a peremptory, or *jus cogens*, norm under international law, meaning that no state can derogate from such a norm. Moreover, the norm had also been codified in the *Convention Against Torture*, an international human rights instrument that,

---

8 RSC 1985, c S-18 [*SIA*].

9 *Kazemi*, above note 2 at para 153.

10 *Ibid* at para 55.

11 *Ibid* at para 56.

12 *Ibid*.

13 *Ibid* at para 175. Justice Abella similarly upheld the presumption of conformity in relation to international human rights law in *Divito v Canada (Public Safety and Emergency Preparedness)*, 2013 SCC 47. In *Divito*, a Canadian citizen was extradited to the United States, where he pleaded guilty to drug offences and was sentenced to serve seven and a half years in prison. Divito subsequently submitted a request to be transferred to Canada to serve the remainder of his sentence under the *International Transfer of Offenders Act*, SC 2004, c 21. His request was denied, which led him to seek judicial review of the decision based on his right to enter Canada as protected by section 6(1) of the *Charter*. Despite ultimately rejecting the appeal, Justice Abella interpreted the right to enter liberally based on international human rights law.

according to Justice Abella, did not create the prohibition but rather confirmed "its controversial and universal acceptance."[14] The treaty had also affirmed a victim's right to a remedy for torture. After identifying key norms in international human rights instruments that were crucial to her reasoning, Justice Abella went further and examined evolving state practice with respect to torture qualifying as official state practice, which would make the actions of the Iranian officials sued for Kazemi's death fall under the immunity afforded by the *SIA*.[15] The conundrum in international law between recognizing torture as an official state act giving rise to immunity and the prohibition against torture, along with providing redress to victims, led Justice Abella to conclude that "equivocal customary international law should not be interpreted so as to block access to a civil remedy for torture, which, at a *jus cogens* level, is unequivocally prohibited."[16]

As a statute that codified customary international law, Justice Abella held that any ambiguities in the *SIA* should be resolved with recourse to international law, not the legislature.[17] The uncertainty Justice Abella sought to clarify concerned whether immunity under the *SIA* extended to lower-level government officials or was limited to states. In her reasons, Justice Abella relied on customary international law to distinguish between the immunity *ratione personae* of high-ranking persons, including the head of state, versus the *ratione materiae* of former heads of state and lower-ranking government officials. Any immunity available to the latter group would only arise in instances where they were performing official acts "for or on behalf of the state."[18] Justice Abella drew further on evolving international legal norms to identify an additional gap in domestic law. She concluded that "the protection for and treatment of individuals as legal subjects" included "the recognition of a victim's right to redress for a violation of fundamental human rights."[19] In Justice Abella's view, this right was not grounded in domestic legislation extending remedy to victims of torture, but rather in "Canada's and Iran's obligations under international human rights law and the *jus cogens* prohibition against torture."[20] To support her conclusion, Justice Abella drew on extensive international legal

14 *Kazemi*, above note 2 at para 172.
15 *Ibid* at para 173.
16 *Ibid* at para 174.
17 *Ibid* at para 186.
18 *Ibid*.
19 *Ibid* at para 188.
20 *Ibid*.

sources, including jurisprudence of the International Court of Justice and the Inter-American Court of Human Rights, and on changing discourse in international law that acknowledged "victims' rights to reparations against individual perpetrators of international crimes."[21] By taking this view, Justice Abella did not limit the scope of her analysis to historical interstate restitution for violations of international law; rather, she expanded her perspective of international law to include the protection of individual rights, which have traditionally fallen under the purview of nation states.[22]

Justice Abella continued her embrace of international human rights law in her majority decision in *Nevsun*. As she did in *Kazemi*, Justice Abella drew the evolution of customary international law away from its traditional "state-centric template"[23] to support her reasons. Justice Abella's view of the case was outlined in the first paragraph of her ruling:

> This appeal involves the application of modern international human rights law, the phoenix that rose from the ashes of World War II and declared global war on human rights abuses. Its mandate was to prevent breaches of internationally accepted norms. Those norms were not meant to be theoretical aspirations or legal luxuries, but moral imperatives and legal necessities. Conduct that undermined the norms was to be identified and addressed.[24]

Nevsun brought the justiciability of transnational corporate human rights abuses to Canadian courts. Three Eritrean refugees — Gize Yebeyo Araya, Kesete Tekle Fshazion, and Mihretab Yemane Tekle — were indefinite conscripts in Eritrea's National Service Program (NSP) and were subjected to violent, cruel, inhuman, and degrading treatment while working at the Bisha mine, which was partly owned by Canadian mining company Nevsun Resources Ltd (Nevsun).[25] Conscripts were assigned to work at the mine through subcontractors Mereb Construction Company and Segen Construction Company, companies that were

---

21 *Ibid* at 194.

22 John H. Currie, *Public International Law*, 2nd ed (Toronto: Irwin Law, 2008) at 412–13.

23 *Nevsun*, above note 3 at para 106.

24 *Ibid* at para 1.

25 *Ibid* at para 3. Nevsun Resources was a publicly traded company incorporated in British Columbia. Through its subsidiaries, Nevsun Resources owned 60 percent of the Bisha mine, while the Eritrean government owned the remaining 40 percent (*ibid* at para 7).

owned and controlled by the Eritrean military and the People's Front for Democracy and Justice, Eritrea's only political party.[26] The three plaintiffs were assigned to work 10- or 11-hour shifts, six days a week, in gruelling conditions. After escaping Eritrea in the early 2010s, the plaintiffs launched a class action against Nevsun in 2014 on behalf of more than 1,000 former workers for breaches of domestic torts (including conversion, battery, and negligence) and for the novel breaches of customary international legal norms prohibiting forced labour, slavery, crimes against humanity, and cruel, inhuman, or degrading treatment.[27] The appeal concerned Nevsun's motion to strike the pleadings on the basis that the act of state doctrine prohibited Canadian courts from assessing the acts of a foreign government (in this instance, Eritrea's NSP) and that the claims based on breaches of customary international law had no reasonable prospect of success. In a 5–4 decision, the Supreme Court dismissed Nevsun's appeal.[28]

Justice Abella's assessment of the plaintiffs' novel claim regarding breaches of customary international law began with affirming Canada's approach to the adoption of thereof. She held that customary international law is automatically adopted into Canadian common law in the absence of conflicting legislation. While following Justice LeBel's conclusion in *R v Hape*, she also clarified that certain words in his judgment which appeared to muddy the state of Canadian law on this matter did not detract from the overall rule.[29] Thus, the customary international law norms the plaintiffs alleged Nevsun breached were Canadian law and "must be treated with the same respect as any other law."[30] Justice Abella reasoned further that the application of some of these norms was not restricted to interstate relations but could potentially extend to corporations. She stated that Nevsun's claim that it

26 *Ibid* at para 8.

27 *Ibid* at para 4.

28 The act of state doctrine forms part of the common law in England and Australia. It has not been a part of Canadian law (*ibid* at para 28). Seven of the nine judges upheld Canada's approach to the doctrine in *Nevsun*. This chapter does not discuss Justice Abella's reasons regarding the act of state doctrine, but rather focuses on her analysis of the parties' customary international law arguments.

29 *R v Hape*, 2007 SCC 26. Justice LeBel declared in *Hape* that "prohibitive rules of customary international law should be incorporated into domestic law in the absence of conflicting legislation" (para 39). Justice Abella confirmed that Justice LeBel's use of the word "prohibitive" did not create a separate category of customary international law but instead emphasized its mandatory nature (*Nevsun*, above note 3 at para 93).

30 *Nevsun*, above note 3 at para 95.

was immune from liability for breaches of customary international law because it was a corporation mischaracterized modern international law, which had evolved beyond its limited application to interstate relations due to the proliferation of international human rights law that viewed the individual and the protection of human rights as "an integral part of [its] legal domain."[31] While human rights may typically be enforceable against the state, Justice Abella took the view that these rights could also be violated by non-state actors, like corporations. She concluded that due to this evolution in international law, it was not "'plain and obvious' that corporations today enjoy a blanket exclusion under customary international law from direct liability for violations of 'obligatory, definable, and universal norms of international law', or indirect liability for their involvement in . . . 'complicity offenses.'"[32]

Moreover, Justice Abella also turned to international law to conclude that Canadian common law could develop remedies for breaches of adopted customary international law norms.[33] Specifically, she drew on international human rights instruments, including the *International Covenant on Civil and Political Rights* and General Comment No 31 of the UN Human Rights Committee,[34] to support her conclusion. She also acknowledged that access to remedy in the context of alleged human rights violations could be restricted by legislation expressly limiting its application within Canada. This was the case for the majority in *Kazemi,* which viewed the *SIA* as express legislation that prevented access to remedy against a state for a breach of the prohibition against torture. Justice Abella held that unlike in *Kazemi,* there was no law prohibiting the plaintiffs' claim in *Nevsun*. In fact, she pointed out that Canada had already adopted policies that respected an individual's right to bring claims against Canadian companies operating abroad.[35] For Justice Abella, the question of whether the plaintiffs' claim would lead to a finding that Nevsun had breached customary international law and

31 *Ibid* at para 107.

32 *Ibid* at para 113.

33 *Ibid* at para 171.

34 *General Comment No 31: The Nature of the General Legal Obligation Imposed on States Parties to the Covenant,* UN DOC CCPR/C/21/Rev1/Add13, 26 May 2004.

35 *Nevsun,* above note 3 at para 115. Justice Abella further noted that the Canadian government had also developed policies aimed at ensuring Canadian corporations operating abroad respected international human rights norms. She specifically referred to Global Affairs Canada's policy guidance *Doing Business the Canadian Way: A Strategy to Advance Corporate Social Responsibility in Canada's Extractive Sector Abroad.*

what remedies were appropriate were complex and should be considered at trial. Doing so would ensure that the common law continued to develop to meet new legal challenges that arise in our modern society.[36]

Like any court ruling, Justice Abella's decisions in *Kazemi* and *Nevsun* were lauded by some and critiqued by others. The polarizing response to both cases further highlights how each was pushing the boundaries of the application of international law in Canada. Her detractors found her reasons to be out of step with how international law had been historically applied in Canada. In *Kazemi*, Justice Abella gave more weight to Canada's international law obligations than to the constitutional role of Parliament, aligning domestic legislation with international law. Her generous reading of evolving customary international law domestically was considered to exceed limits that had been set by Parliament in the *SIA*. Similarly, in *Nevsun*, Justice Abella's assertion that corporations could be liable for violations of international human rights law did not align with the statutory landscape since there was no law that bound Canadian companies to breaches of customary international law. These critiques show the extent to which Justice Abella was willing to apply a generous reading to the application of international human rights despite more conservative precedents from the Court.[37] By doing so, Justice Abella created a legacy where the protection of individual human rights could serve as the standard to assess domestic Canadian law.

C. Justice Abella's Legacy: Future Directions for International Law in Canadian Courts

Justice Abella's use of international human rights law in *Kazemi* and *Nevsun* can potentially shape future directions for the use and application of international law by Canadian courts. Both cases demonstrate

36 *Ibid* at para 131, quoting Justice Wilson in *Hunt v Carey Canada Inc*, [1990] 2 SCR 959 at paras 990–91.

37 Jutta Brunnée and Stephen Toope described the Supreme Court's treatment of international law as a "hesitant embrace" in their 2002 article "A Hesitant Embrace: The Application of International Law by Canadian Courts" (2002) 40 *Canadian Yearbook of International Law* 3. Although Brunnée and Toope found that the Court was engaging with international law like never before in its history, they felt these cases affirmed the Court's conservative treatment of international law: it was "relevant and . . . persuasive, but not as determinative or . . . obligatory" (at 4 and 6). The phrase — though generated from Brunnée and Toope's assessment of cases from the 1990s and early 2000s — also captures the Court's approach in the succeeding years prior to Justice Abella's decisions in *Kazemi* and *Nevsun*.

her desire to see Canadian common law evolve in line with developments in international human rights law.

In *Kazemi* and *Nevsun*, Justice Abella demonstrated that not only is international law crucial to the development of Canadian law, but that human rights are a critical component of how international law can be used and applied by Canadian courts. As she stated in her opening paragraph in *Nevsun*, international human rights norms were not "theoretical aspirations or legal luxuries, but moral imperatives and necessities."[38] Justice Abella is not shy about her views on the importance and protection of international human rights. In past public remarks, she has described the relationship between human rights and justice as central to the modern international legal order since the end of World War II. However, in her opinion, the international community's commitment to human rights has diverged significantly from its peak immediately following the end of the war. Instead, international human rights have become rhetoric in her eyes that have "a dysfunctional relationship with justice."[39]

For Justice Abella, protecting human rights is a moral imperative that courts around the world, including in Canada, must uphold.[40] In her view, law is necessary to the advancement of justice. The global community has demonstrated the ability to create the necessary laws, legal systems, and institutions to protect international trade and commerce. Yet the same willingness and capacity to construct a world trading system with established norms and a dispute settlement body has not been replicated in the human rights field. Through her *Kazemi* and *Nevsun* decisions, Justice Abella demonstrated the importance of upholding international human rights law to protect individuals' access to justice and remedy domestically.

As Canadian courts potentially give more weight to the applicability of international human rights law in their interpretation of domestic laws, Justice Abella has shown that the Canadian judiciary can concurrently contribute to the interpretation of public international law. In *Nevsun*, Justice Abella described the important dialogue between

---

38 *Nevsun*, above note 3 at para 1.

39 Rosalie Silberman Abella, "The World is Not Unfolding as it Should: International Justice in Crisis," delivered at the Empire Club of Toronto (9 February 2011); and Rosalie Silberman, "The Arc of the Moral Universe is Long, But" keynote address of the Law and Society Association and Canadian Law and Society Association Annual Meeting (7 June 2018).

40 Rosalie Silberman Abella, "International Law and Human Rights: The Power and the Pity" (2010) *McGill Law Journal* 871 at 875.

Canadian courts and international law as "'international law not only [percolating] down from the international to the domestic sphere, but . . . also [bubbling] up.'"[41] Thus, actively implementing and advancing international law "allows Canadian courts to meaningfully contribute to the 'choir' of domestic court judgments around the world shaping the 'substance of international law.'"[42] This description captures the significance of her ruling. She notably recognized the important role the Canadian judiciary can play in advancing the interpretation of international law and customary international law, in particular. Unlike treaty law, customary international law is established by state action and states' belief in legally binding obligations.[43] Judicial actors around the world can thus contribute to the interpretation and advancement of customary international law by analyzing the development of these unwritten norms and opining on its status. In fact, the International Law Commission, a United Nations body of experts, has indicated that judicial decisions of national courts can constitute evidence of state practice or *opinio juris* in the formulation of customary international law.[44] This unique role judicial actors share is critical to shaping the global community's understanding of customary international law generally, and vital international human rights norms especially, in the absence of an accessible international court or tribunal.[45] Justice Abella carried out this role in *Kazemi* and *Nevsun*, demonstrating that the process of domestically implementing international law can also simultaneously advance global understandings of that law.

Perhaps Justice Abella's most noteworthy international law legacy will be her ruling in *Nevsun* opening the doors to the corporate liability for violations of international human rights. The outcome in *Nevsun* may have been different, if not for Justice Abella. From the first sentence, it is clear her reasons were profoundly shaped by her sense of justice and the purpose of international human rights law. Moreover, these beliefs meant she was willing to push the boundaries of the interpretation and application of international human rights law in Canada.

41 *Nevsun*, above note 3 at para 71.

42 *Ibid* at para 72.

43 *North Sea Continental Shelf Cases (Federal Republic of Germany v Denmark; Federal Republic of Germany v The Netherlands)*, [1969] ICJ Rep. 3.

44 ILC, *Identification of Customary International Law: The Role of Decisions of National Courts in the Case Law of International Courts and Tribunals of a Universal Character for the Purpose of the Determination of Customary International Law*, UNGA A/CN.4/691 (2016).

45 Karen Knop, "Here and There: International Law in Domestic Courts" (2000) 32:2 *NYU Journal of International Law and Politics* 501 at 516.

Justice Abella was unconvinced of the limits to the domestic application of customary international law that the defendants argued to dismiss the claim. Doing so, as she laid bare in her first paragraph, would hamper the moral imperativeness and legal necessity of modern international human rights law.[46]

Canadian courts are well positioned to contribute to developing international law concerning domestic liability and remedy for violations of international human rights arising from the activities of Canadian corporations abroad. The modern international business and human rights field lacks any substantive binding obligations, despite the existence of several international and domestic guidelines including the *United Nations Guiding Principles on Business and Human Rights*, the *OECD Guidelines for Multinational Enterprises on Responsible Business Conduct*, the ILO Tripartite Declaration, and Canada's *Responsible Business Conduct Abroad* strategy. In the absence of binding domestic and international obligations, litigation in Canadian courts has been used to advance corporate liability for human rights violations committed abroad. To date, this litigation has focused on such common law torts as negligence, battery, and assault.[47] *Nevsun* had been the first case to bring a claim based on violations of international law. While the precise nature of these claims must still be clarified, as the case did not proceed to a trial on the merits,[48] this nonetheless can be a significant development in Canadian and international law as the reach of Canadian corporations abroad continues to grow.[49]

46 *Nevsun*, above note 3 at para 1.

47 See, for example, *Choc v Hudbay Minerals Inc*, 2013 ONSC 1414, *Garcia v Tahoe Resources Inc*, 2017 BCCA 39, and *Das v George Weston Limited*, 2018 ONCA 1053.

48 Transnational tort cases typically face procedural hurdles raised by the defence before ever reaching trial. These challenges were overcome in *Nevsun* with Justice Abella's decision; however, the claim was settled out of court in October 2020 for an undisclosed amount (Julianne Hughes Jennett & Marjun Parcasio, "Corporate Civil Liability for Breaches of Customary International Law: Supreme Court of Canada Opens Door to Common Law Claims in *Nevsun v Araya*" *European Journal of International Law: Talk!* (blog) (29 March 2020), online: www.ejiltalk.org/corporate-civil-liability-for-breaches-of-customary-international-law-supreme-court-of-canada-opens-door-to-common-law-claims-in-nevsun-v-araya/; Yvette Brend, "Landmark settlement Is a Message to Canadian Companies Extracting Resources Overseas: Amnesty International" *CBC News* (23 October 2020), online: www.cbc.ca/news/canada/british-columbia/settlement-amnesty-scc-africa-mine-nevsun-1.5774910.

49 In November 2023, a claim was brought against Barrick Gold Corporation for alleged human rights violations committed at its North Mara Mine in Tanzania, including alleged violations of customary international law. If this case proceeds to

D. Conclusion

Canadian courts' engagement with international law necessitates weaving domestic law with international legal obligations. The Supreme Court of Canada has carried out this exercise by often taking a hesitant approach to international law in its past decisions. With her dissent in *Kazemi* and majority ruling in *Nevsun*, Justice Abella pushed the boundaries for the use and application of international law in Canadian courts and the role the courts can play in its development. Her expansive engagement with international law beyond the conservative approach that had characterized previous decisions of the Court offers three key lessons to future courts: 1) international human rights are a lens through which courts may contextualize the use and application of public international law in Canada; 2) the Canadian judiciary can become more active contributors to the interpretation of public international law through its domestic law-making; and 3), there is an opening for international human rights violations committed by Canadian corporations operating abroad to be addressed in Canadian courts. Justice Abella's use of international human rights law to advance the identification and protection of individual rights in *Kazemi* and *Nevsun* is a profound international law legacy that may shape future directions of Canadian courts in this area for years to come.

trial, it would be the first time corporate violations of customary international law would be litigated in a Canadian court.

21 Equality and the Judicial Role: Lessons from Singing in a Choir

ROSEMARY CAIRNS-WAY*

> Art was the unserious, self-indulgent path: law the hard-edged tool. . . . I am a constitutionalist because I want to make a revolution with law in my hand. I am an artist because I want to make a revolution with art in my hand. And after the revolution, I want both law and art in my hand.
>
> Mari Matsuda, "The Next Dada Utopian Visioning Peace Orchestra: Constitutional Theory and the Aspirational" (2017) 62:4 *McGill Law Journal* 1203 at 1707 and 1244

A. Introduction

I was delighted to be invited to address the legacy of Justice Rosalie Silberman Abella's vision of equality at the conference marking her retirement from the Supreme Court of Canada. I was also overwhelmed by the potentially enormous breadth of the topic. The panel format made a systematic doctrinal analysis of Justice Abella's equality jurisprudence out of the question. And it was obvious that doctrinal analysis was not the objective the conference organizers had for a penultimate panel in

* Professor, Faculty of Law, Common Law, University of Ottawa. This essay is dedicated to two extraordinarily gifted, personally inspiring, and dedicated professionals. The first is the conference honoree Justice Rosalie Abella. The second is my long-time choir conductor, Professor Laurence Ewashko. I have sung with Maestro Ewashko for almost thirty years. We have performed an eclectic mix of classical, contemporary, operatic, sacred, and popular music, singing for audiences numbering from a few dozen to a few thousand, in venues as diverse as a renovated barn, a Venetian church, Southam Hall at the National Arts Centre, and the Canada Day stage on Parliament Hill. Maestro Ewashko has taught me how to be a competent, considerate, and contributing member of choral ensembles large and small. These words are a small token of my gratitude.

advance of the closing one-on-one session with Justice Abella.[1] After some anxious reflection, I decided to shift my gaze away from the jurisprudence. Abandoning doctrine offered me the freedom to step outside legalistic constraints and reimagine how I might capture, in an interesting and perhaps unconventional way, this unique jurist.[2] I decided to immerse myself in Justice Abella's extensive extra-judicial oeuvre, particularly her public reflections on the role of the judge in a constitutional democracy.[3] What a joyful immersion it was! Justice Abella's writing and public speaking are a heart-affirming, thought-provoking antidote to an increasingly painful present. She offers a rejoinder to the "bombastic anti-intellectualism, sanctimonious incivility, unhealthy tolerance for intolerance, and cavalier indifference to equality"[4] that dominate much public discourse. Her words capture her personal and professional commitments to justice, human rights, mutual respect,

1 Justice Abella served on the Supreme Court of Canada from 2004 to 2021. A few of her most significant section 15 decisions include: *R v CP*, 2021 SCC 19; *Fraser v Canada (Attorney General)*, 2020 SCC 28; *Quebec (Attorney General) v A*, 2013 SCC 5, [2013] 1 SCR 61; *Withler v Canada (Attorney General)*, 2011 SCC 12, [2011] 1 SCR 396; *R v Kapp*, [2008] 2 SCR 483, 2008 SCC 41. Her majority decision in *Fraser*, arguably her capstone contribution to section 15 jurisprudence, was the first successful adverse effects claim based on the enumerated ground of sex and only the second section 15(1) claim won by women on the ground of sex in thirty-five years. The scholarship cited by the majority in *Fraser* offers an entry point into the vast literature on section 15. A comprehensive evaluation of the decision can be found in a journal issue devoted to it: *Constitutional Forum constitutionelle* (2021) 30:2, online: https://journals.library.ualberta.ca/constitutional_forum/index.php/constitutional_forum/issue/view/1955.

2 The fact that this was the last academic panel after lunch on Friday added an extra incentive to be refreshing. The panel was followed by an astonishing "Fireside Chat" between journalist Paul Wells and Justice Abella, who spoke from the hospital where she was with her husband Irving Abella.

3 See Rosalie Silberman Abella, "Judicial Independence, Democracy and Human Rights" (2019) 52:1 *Israel Law Review* 99; Rosalie Silberman Abella & Matthew Diller, "A Conversation with the Honorable Rosalie Silberman Abella and Dean Matthew Diller" (2018) 87:3 *Fordham Law Review* 843; Rosalie Silberman Abella, "Relating to Rights – A Judge's Perspective" (2004) 39:2 *International Society of Barristers Quarterly* 347; Rosalie Silberman Abella, "Judging in the 21st Century" (2002) 25:2 *Advocates' Quarterly* 131; Rosalie Silberman Abella, "The Judicial Role in a Democratic State" Keynote Address, 1999 Constitutional Cases Conference, Osgoode Hall Law School (April 2000), online: www.ontariocourts.ca/coa/about-the-court/archives/the-judicial-role-in-a-democratic-state/; Rosalie Silberman Abella, "Lawyers, Judges and Rights" (1998) 36:4 *Alberta Law Review* 990; Rosalie Silberman Abella, "Public Policy and the Judicial Role" (1989) 34:4 *McGill Law Journal* 1021.

4 Rosalie Silberman Abella, "The Rule of Justice: The Compassionate Application of Law to Life" The Coxford Lecture, Western University (9 February 2022) (Notes on file) [Coxford Lecture].

and personal engagement; in other words, her vision of what equality means and what it requires of the judge.

I think these extra-judicial contributions may be as significant a public legacy as her jurisprudence. Rosalie Jukier makes a similar point in her contribution to this collection, stating: "Justice Abella's impact cannot be fully understood with a focus solely on the substantive aspects of the decisions she rendered. Her overall judicial style must also be examined."[5] In my view, it is Justice Abella's understanding of equality that best explains her theory (and style) of judging, a theory and style grounded in listening to the voices that justice has failed to hear, deliberately ignored, or actively silenced. Her extra-judicial oeuvre testifies to her belief that judges occupy an important civic space, that they have obligations to the public they serve, and that those obligations include explaining what judges do and how and why they do it. They also reflect her view that judicial identity matters, that delivering justice is about more than simply applying the law, that open-mindedness is an essential judicial attribute, and that acknowledging perspective and experience enhances rather than detracts from the capacity to deliver impartial justice.

Quite simply, Justice Abella understands the important difference between an open mind and an empty one. I suspect that her willingness to describe the judicial role in this manner publicly was seen by many of her colleagues as unconventional (and perhaps inappropriate) early in her career.[6] Forty-five years later, in my view, her theory of judging dominates contemporary Canadian understandings of the judicial role at the highest institutional level.[7] Evidence of this can be found in the adoption of the *Ethical Principles for Judges* in 1998 — an institutional

5 Rosalie Jukier, "Justice Abella: Confronting the Authenticity-Professionalism Paradox," Chapter 5 in this volume at 92.

6 Justice John Sopinka famously addressed the question of accountability and judicial free speech in an address to the Canadian Bar Association in 1989. He revisited his remarks seven years later in John Sopinka, "Must a Judge be a Monk – Revisited," (1996) UNBLJ 167. For another contemporaneous analysis see Wayne MacKay, "Judicial Free Speech and Accountability: Should Judges Be Seen But Not Heard? (1993) 3 National J. of Constitutional Law 159.

7 Canadian Judicial Council, *Ethical Principles for Judges* (1998), online at https://cjc-ccm.ca/cmslib/general/news_pub_judicialconduct_Principles_en.pdf. The guide has since been updated, but the original edition was the work of a committee established in 1994 and was, according to the forward written by the Chair of the Canadian Judicial Council, Chief Justice Beverley McLachlin, intended "to ensure that judges and public alike are aware of the principles by which judges should be guided in their personal and professional lives." See infra at 369–370 for a discussion of the contemporaneous evolution of the CJC approach to judicial education.

response by the Canadian Judicial Council (CJC) to the increasingly public position judges occupied in a young constitutional democracy.[8] The first edition of the Principles established an aspirational frame of reference on judicial independence, integrity, respect, diligence, competence, equality, and impartiality. A revised and modernized version of the Ethical Principles was published in 2021. In a press release accompanying this publication, Chief Justice Richard Wagner, Chair of the Council, noted: "These revised principles explore new and emerging issues relevant to our modern times . . . to ensure that the values that underpin the role of judge continue to apply within an ever-changing societal context." The document offers the following context:

> Judges are expected to be alert to the history, experience and circumstances of Canada's Indigenous peoples, and to the diversity of cultures and communities that make up this country. In this spirit, the judiciary is now more actively involved with the wider public, both to enhance public confidence and to expand its own knowledge of the diversity of human experiences in Canada today.[9]

1. *Justice Abella and the Arts*

One of the most intriguing aspects of Justice Abella's public identity is her continuous intellectual and personal engagement with the arts.[10] Her extra-judicial writings are studded with references to literature, music, art, film, and theatre. Edith Wharton, Victor Hugo, Margaret Atwood, George Gershwin, Yasmina Reza, and Samuel Barber enrich,

---

8 Her impact is also obvious in how judicial education in Canada has evolved over her judicial career. See text infra at 370–371.

9 The revised and modernized version of the Ethical Principles was published in 2021 (https://cjc-ccm.ca/sites/default/files/documents/2021/CJC_20-301_Ethical-Principles_Bilingual%20FINAL.pdf) at 11. I acknowledge that these goals may be more aspirational than realized. But, there is no doubt, in my view, that they reflect the official and public understanding at the highest levels of the judiciary.

10 See Mary Liston, "Engaging Abella: Humanity, Imagination, and the Legal Profession," Chapter 6 in this collection. In her chapter, Professor Liston celebrates "the artistic and creative dimensions of Justice Rosalie Abella's career with an eye to reinforcing the importance of the humanities for" legal professionals (at 103). For a more visual sense of Abella's creative energy and a look at the exuberant décor of her judicial chambers, see Paul Wells, "A Rare Peek Into Justice Rosalie Abella's Office" *Maclean's* (15 June 2021), online: www.macleans.ca/society/a-rare-peek-into-justice-rosalie-abellas-office/.

complicate, and illustrate her ideas,[11] while her love of language is apparent in the lyricism and imagery of her public remarks. And her stint as a member of the Giller Prize jury, where she read ninety-eight novels while also sitting as a member of the Ontario Court of Appeal, is the stuff of (legal) legend.[12]

This deliberate and joyful engagement with the arts feels personal. I am a classically trained singer for whom law school was a second (but eventually satisfying) choice.[13] Although my youthful diva dreams were not realized (or realistic), I have continued to identify as a singer and musician. I have been both a semi-professional chorister[14] and a legal academic for more than thirty years. I am curious about how these two (of my multiple) identities[15] interact in how I understand,

11 These references are too numerous to recount. My personal favourite is the reference to the play "Art," by Yasmina Reza, which concludes Justice Abella's essay on "The Judicial Role in a Democratic State," above note 3. Briefly, the anecdote involves a large, over-priced, all-white painting with diagonal lines, a disagreement between long time friends, a blue felt pen, a skier in a woolly hat, and a reflection on shifting perspectives. For Justice Abella, the white canvas was a relatively new and indeterminate Charter of Rights. The disagreement and its resolution were metaphors for the need to be open, constructive, and willing to listen to different perspectives.

12 The year was 2003, and the winning novel was M.G. Vassanji, "The In-Between Life of Vikram Lall" (Toronto: Doubleday Canada, 2003).

13 Professor Mari Matsuda writes about her decision to abandon art for law as follows: "I walked away from art, and for forty years, carried regret. An art professor said I had talent, and I did nothing with it. This may happen to you: one day you might wake up and realize you are not going to live forever. . . . My possible talent lay in the graveyard of life's unfulfilled intentions, waiting for my body to expire and join it." Mari Matsuda, "The Next Dada Utopian Visioning Peace Orchestra: Constitutional Theory and the Aspirational" (2017) 62:4 *McGill Law Journal* 1203 at 1207. I do not share Professor Matsuda's apparent degree of regret. But I must admit that the contrast between the joy I experience during a musical performance and the tedium of administrative commitments (especially over Zoom) sometimes gives me pause.

14 By semi-professional I mean I get paid small amounts of money for enormous amounts of time and energy spent perfecting and then performing in a concert or opera.

15 See Rosalie Jukier, "Justice Abella: Confronting the Authenticity-Professionalism Paradox," Chapter 5 in this collection. Professor Jukier explores the connections between Justice Abella's identity as a Jewish woman and her dissenting decision in *Bruker v Marcovitz*, [2007] 3 SCR 607, 2007 SCC 54. Mary Liston, above note 10 at 120, writes: "Justice Abella's lived experience gives her a particular stance from which to view a legal system — multiperspectival."

study, imagine, and teach law.[16] Preparing my remarks for the conference opened a space for me to explore the resonances between equality, choral singing, and professional identity. In what follows, I consider the parallels between the theory and practice of choral singing and the theory and practice of equality-informed judging. Teaching has taught me that embracing different perspectives is both risky and transformative. A conference — and now a collection — that honour a career risk-taker seems like the perfect opportunity for embracing difference. For Rosalie Silberman Abella, risk-taking in the service of justice and equality was simply part of the job.

B. Equality

Equality is the intellectual and personal lynchpin that connects Justice Abella's remarkable life of firsts. Equality, theorized and explained, is threaded through much of her extra-judicial writing. The key components of her approach were identified early in her career. As the sole commissioner of the 1984 federal Royal Commission on Equality in Employment, Justice Abella grappled with the meaning of equality.[17] She concluded that "[s]ometimes equality means treating people the same, despite their differences, and sometimes it means treating them as equals by accommodating their differences."[18] This idea was constitutionalized by the Supreme Court of Canada in *Andrews*, its first decision on section 15,[19] and it remains central to all of Justice Abella's section 15 jurisprudence. In her view, equality is deeply contextual and requires "an understanding of what we are as a society."[20] It means

16 I sense the attention my identity as a musician attracts in my students. For some, it is simply an oddity. For others, it is a relief . . . a relief to realize that there may be a place in the legal system for their own, traditionally unorthodox backgrounds. I am increasingly aware (as is the profession) of the connections between mental health and "extra-law" involvement. For an interesting recent reflection on this issue, see Chief Justice George Strathy, "The Litigator and Mental Health" Court of Appeal of Ontario (5 May 2022), online: www.ontariocourts.ca/coa/about-the-court/publications-speeches/the-litigator-and-mental-health/.

17 Her description of this intellectual struggle appears in Abella & Diller, above note 3 at 852–53.

18 Rosalie Silberman Abella, *Equality in Employment: A Royal Commission Report* (Ottawa: Commission on Equality in Employment, 1984), online: https://publications.gc.ca/site/eng/471737/publication.html.

19 *Andrews v Law Society of British Columbia*, [1989] 1 SCR 143.

20 Rosalie Silberman Abella, "Equality, Human Rights, Women and the Justice System" (1994) *McGill Law Journal* 489 at 490.

acknowledging and accommodating difference, and it is intentionally remedial. Equality is a

> flexible, self-adjusting tool . . . both procedural as a social strategy and substantive as an objective. . . . [E]quality is realized in the reduction of inequality, and inequality is the existence of discrimination. . . . [S]ection 15 of the Charter is the guaranteed right of everyone to be free from discrimination.[21]

Justice Abella recognized very early the challenge of realizing this vision of equality through courts. In her keynote address at a 1986 conference addressing "The Socialization of Judges to Equality Issues,"[22] she said:

> Section 15 of the [*Charter*] is the most important legislative change in this generation. It is also the most complicated. Every single one of us has something to learn about equality and most of us have a great deal to learn. Unless the legal and judicial professions admit to their pedagogical need, we will be a profound disappointment to the public, most of whom . . . know far better than we the urgent need for an equality law.[23]

This is a remarkable passage. It names the complexity of interpreting and applying a constitutionalized equality guarantee. It recognizes the public interest in equality law and in how courts respond to inequality. It insists that judges rethink unexamined assumptions about impartiality and acknowledge their own inevitable partiality. It admits that all legal professionals, including judges, need to engage in sustained and self-critical learning about inequality and its manifestations. And it a remedial call to action.

---

21 *Ibid* at 492.

22 In Sheilah Martin & Kathleen Mahoney, eds, *Equality and Judicial Neutrality* (Toronto: Carswell, 1987). In the preface, the editors describe the conference as "[t]he first Canadian attempt to examine . . . the relationship between judicial neutrality and social equality" and note: "As the vast majority of Canadian judges are appointed from the privileged elite class of white, male, able-bodied persons, it is appropriate and inevitable that equality seekers question the judiciary's ability to be neutral on legal issues which challenge the disproportionate distribution of power and wealth to their class" (at iii).

23 Rosalie Silberman Abella, "The Dynamic Nature of Equality" *ibid* at 3.

C. Perspective, Impartiality, and the Judicial Role

Justice Abella's forty-five years on the bench closely track the profound changes to Canadian public law catalyzed by the inclusion of a substantive equality right in our *Charter of Rights*.[24] Constitutionalizing an equality guarantee undoubtedly contributed to the reimagining of the judicial role that occurred over this same period.[25] When the *Charter* was entrenched, the notion that impartiality required actively attending to equality, and that responding to inequality required hearing and learning about vulnerability, was deeply controversial.[26] Justice Abella, like many other committed jurists, played an important role in responding to that controversy with intellectual rigor and personal example.

Justice Abella regularly acknowledged what were, in her view, legitimate public concerns with the legal system and the judiciary. For her, accountability to the public required that judges "explain to the public what they do and why they do it."[27] Judges, while private people, "belonged to the public."[28] Public accountability meant that Justice Abella resisted the notion of a "hermetically sealed judiciary" and noted that "after forty-two years, . . . I cannot complain that I have not had a chance to say what I think matters related to being a judge."[29]

In addition to learning what judges do, Canadians have become increasingly attentive to who judges are, and, perhaps more importantly, who they aren't. In 1982, the public noticed and applauded the first woman appointed to the Supreme Court of Canada, Justice Bertha Wilson. In 2021, the public noticed and applauded when Justice Mahmud Jamal was the first racialized person to be appointed to the

---

24 *Canadian Charter of Rights and Freedoms*, Part I of the *Constitution Act, 1982*, being Schedule B to the Canada Act 1982 (UK), 1982, c. 11 [*Charter*].

25 Rosemary Cairns Way "Contradictory or Complementary? Reconciling Judicial Independence with Judicial Social Context Education" in Adam Dodek & Lorne Sossin, eds, *Judicial Independence in Context* (Toronto: Irwin Law, 2010) 220.

26 See, for example, Sheilah Martin & Kathleen Mahoney, above note 18 at iv. "The existence of non-neutral judicial behaviour conflicts with the common belief that judges are completely objective, disinterested and impartial in all cases. . . . Unquestioning acceptance of judicial neutrality limits the kinds and scope of questions that should be asked about judicial use of societally induced assumptions and untested beliefs." See also Allan Hutchinson, "Towards Judicial Accountability: Are the Excuses Getting Lamer?" (1996) 45 *University of New Brunswick Law Journal* 97.

27 Abella & Diller, above note 3 at 849.

28 *Ibid*. Mary Liston, above note 10 at 105, suggests that "in a constitutional democracy, the law is authored or authorized by the public and in a real sense *belongs* to the affected person individually when their issue is adjudicated."

29 Abella & Diller, above note 3 at 849.

Supreme Court. And in 2022, the public noticed and applauded the appointment of the first Indigenous member of the Supreme Court, Justice Michelle O'Bonsawin. In between, the public asked why these appointments were, in fact, remarkable. Why didn't the make-up of the judiciary reflect the make-up of Canadian society? Could Canadians expect that a bench that failed to reflect the diversity of Canadian society would nevertheless understand, interpret, and meaningfully apply the guarantee of equality?[30]

In 1997, the Canadian Judicial Council recognized the pedagogical need Justice Abella saw in 1986, with a national project of judicial education.[31] The mandate of the Social Context Education Project was to develop and deliver educational programming to assist judges in responding with impartiality and fairness to the needs of a rapidly changing society; in other words, to ensure equality in Canadian courtrooms.[32] Despite approval by the CJC, the Project was deeply controversial with members of the judiciary, who believed that it facilitated indoctrination inconsistent with judicial independence from "special interest groups."[33]

30 Sonia Lawrence's 2010 reflections on judicial diversity are one of the most powerful discussions of this issue. See Sonia Lawrence, "Reflections: On Judicial Diversity and Judicial Independence" in Dodek and Sossin, above note 25 at 193. See also Samreen Beg and Lorne Sossin, "Diversity, Transparency & Inclusion in Canada's Judiciary" in Graham Gee & Erika Rackley, eds, *Debating Judicial Appointments in an Age of Diversity* (Routledge, 2018).

31 For a description of the project, see Cairns Way, "Contradictory or Complementary?" above note 25. I was the first national academic coordinator.

32 Rosemary Cairns Way & Donna Martinson, "Judging Sexual Assault: The Shifting Landscape of Judicial Education in Canada" (2019) 97:2 *Canadian Bar Review* 1; Rosemary Cairns Way & Brettel Dawson, "Taking a Stand on Equality: Bertha Wilson and the Evolution of Judicial Education in Canada" in Kim Brooks, ed, *Justice Bertha Wilson: One Woman's Difference* (Vancouver: UBC Press, 2009) 278.

33 The question of who is a "special interest group" is fraught with political and ideological baggage. Often the terminology is used as a justification for both exclusion and trivialization. Those who were opposed to receiving information from special interest groups as part of continuing judicial education tended more often to characterize equality-deserving communities as representing special interests. Lawyers, legal academics, and other judges tended not to be labelled in that way. See the Honourable Justice Lynn Smith, "Contextual Judging" Paper delivered at the 2nd International Conference on the Training of the Judiciary (Ottawa: November 2004): "From an almost forbidden topic, raised in hushed voices as one tiptoed over eggshells and between landmines, in a territory explored only by a few brave pioneers, social context education has become the topic of [an international] symposium." For a sense of how much things have changed since then, see the announcement for the 10th Conference of the International Organization for Judicial

Not surprisingly, Justice Abella was an important player in the evolution of judicial education in the years leading up to the CJC resolution. She organized the first judicial seminar in which persons outside the legal profession were invited to participate. Resisting the practice of simply recreating educational "echo chambers," Justice Abella and others insisted that judicial independence is not threatened by listening to and learning from non-lawyers. In fact, judicial independence, the essential prerequisite to impartiality, is enhanced by ensuring that judges are exposed to unfamiliar or unacknowledged perspectives and experiences, especially from the vulnerable. In her view: "It does no good for the system to pretend that impartiality precludes openness to wider to points of view, nor is it fair to characterize the pleas of women or minorities for empathy as special-interest politics."[34]

Justice Abella also organized the first national conference for Canada's women judges held in November of 1995. In his welcoming remarks to the conference, Chief Justice Antonio Lamer, Chair of the CJC, described the meeting as historic.[35] He explained: "It is a historic first, and clearly most importantly, because it represents the largest gathering of women judges in this country's history."[36] The conference was the CJC's response to a specific recommendation of the Canadian Bar Association (CBA) Task Force on Gender Equality in the Legal Profession (chaired by Bertha Wilson).[37] This report was also influential in the authorization, two years later, of the Social Context Project. The Chief Justice specifically noted the direct connection between the conference objectives, the gender equality task force, and the promise of section 15

Training, which was held in Ottawa in the fall of 2022: https://iojt2022.nji-inm.ca/. The conference theme was "Effective Judicial Education: Understanding Vulnerable Populations."

34 Abella, "Equality, Human Rights," above note 20 at 498.

35 See Chief Justice Lamer, "Welcome Remarks" in the Conference Papers (on file). There were 126 federally appointed women judges at the time and apparently "many" of them were in attendance, alongside a number of provincially appointed women judges. Men judges were also in attendance as, according to the Chief Justice, the CJC "could not authorize the holding of a meeting to discuss matters of special interest to women." The conference was authorized as relating to "women and the law."

36 *Ibid.*

37 Canadian Bar Association Task Force on Gender Equality in the Legal Profession, *Touchstones for Change: Equality, Diversity and Accountability: The Report of the Canadian Bar Association Task Force on Gender Equality in the Legal Profession* (Ottawa: Canadian Bar Association, 1993).

of the Charter, a promise that he admitted "remain[ed] unfulfilled for many."[38]

Both of these educational initiatives were informed by Justice Abella's vision of equality and driven by her willingness (along with many others) to challenge the status quo. Both heralded a new era in judicial education in which the identity and perspective of speakers and attendees was seen as directly relevant to judging and especially relevant to the guarantee of equality.[39] Both conferences, and the authorization of a national program of social context education for judges, offer concrete evidence of the evolution of expectations about the judicial role and institutional public accountability.

D. Celebrating Justice Abella through Art: Equality and Choral Singing

The opening reception for the conference marking Justice Abella's retirement, held at the National Gallery of Canada, was intended to capture, in a non-traditional (and enjoyable) way, how Justice Abella's passion for the arts informed her vision of judging. I had the good fortune of helping to design the program for the reception. A selection of Canadian works of art was chosen to illustrate particular aspects of her career.[40] Planning the event involved many fascinating (and, frankly, fun) discussions about what pictures to select and what they could represent. These conversations reinforced the way open-minded engagement with different ways of seeing, hearing, and understanding the world is both enriching and humbling.

For my part, the most obvious work to include in our curated collection was Janet Cardiff's "Forty Part Motet," an audio installation reworking a sixteenth century choral work by Thomas Tallis, now

38 Lamer, above note 35.

39 Both conferences recognized that both federally and provincially appointed judges had a common pedagogical need related to equality. This mixing of court levels was virtually unheard of at the time.

40 A sub-committee worked on the reception. Colleen Baumann, partner at Goldblatt Partners LLP and former clerk to Justice Abella, and I prepared the materials distributed to attendees. A bilingual pamphlet directed attendees to nine works of art. A description of each work of art was accompanied by a commentary linking the work to Justice Abella. Staff at the National Gallery of Canada were tremendously helpful in suggesting works of art and in educating us about the work, what it represented, and the artist. Pamphlet on file with the author.

permanently installed inside the Rideau Chapel at the Gallery.[41] Cardiff made individual recordings of forty singers, playing each voice through its own corresponding speaker and placing the speakers, each separated by a few feet, around the chapel. The resulting "sound sculpture" allows listeners to "climb inside the music" by physically choosing to listen to an individual voice, or a group of voices, or the work in its entirety by moving within the chapel space. In other words, the piece embodies the positionality of personal experience.[42]

The way the work illustrates the connections between perspective, equality, and the judicial role is inescapable. Like judging, this piece requires intentional listening. It makes the interdependence between the individual and the group obvious. Each voice is an essential part of the whole. Hearing (and standing inside) these connections makes obvious what is risked by silencing even one voice, and what is gained by inclusion. The soundscape makes what and how we hear (and understand) concrete.

The fact that the sculpture is organized around a gorgeous, and haunting piece of choral music has special resonance for me. I have cultivated my own creative intelligence for the last three decades by singing in a choir. I bring the things I learn and experience in choir into my teaching and my scholarship, and I have no doubt that choral singing has nurtured my humanity, my relationships with students, and my scholarship.[43]

Accomplished choral singers see themselves as part of a larger process of making meaning through community building. Each voice depends on every other voice. Constant, committed, and attentive dialogue with other members of the community is essential. Choral singing, like judging, demands careful, intentional, listening. I can always hear myself, but I must step outside myself and listen to those around me, especially to those voicing different parts.[44] My listening is structured around music's organizing principles . . . melody, harmony,

41 For more information about the piece, see National Gallery of Canada, "Janet Cardiff: FortyPart Motet," online: www.gallery.ca/whats-on/exhibitions-and-galleries/janet-cardiff-forty-part-motet-2.

42 During choral rehearsals, choristers often achieve this shifting perspective by changing positions within the choir, that is by breaking with the tradition of standing with a group of singers singing the same part. Moving this way is sometimes disastrous, but more often exhilarating.

43 This idea is explored at length in Mary Liston, above note 10. See, in particular, her discussion of the legal professional as artist.

44 This capacity to step outside of subjectivity is central to legal theorist Jennifer Nedelsky's description of the "enlarged and embodied mentality" required for

timbre, and rhythm. It is my responsibility to make the most resonant and consonant sounds possible, in the context of the particular piece, while supporting every other chorister's effort to do the same. This often means restraining myself when I feel exuberant and being fearless when I might prefer to stay silent.[45] I need to hear and support vulnerability. (For choral singers, that usually means leaving more space for the tenors to shine.)[46] And I need to both respect and interrogate silence, realizing that music is being made (and stories are being voiced) by both silence and sound.

E. Conclusion

Connecting the themes of equality, singing, perspective, and judging has taken me beyond Justice Abella's words and encouraged me to revisit and appreciate again the scholarship of Mari Matsuda.[47] Over the years, her words have consistently struck a chord with me, and are central to my thinking about judging, equality, teaching, and learning.[48] Many readers will be familiar with her classic article urging the deliberate adoption of "multiple consciousness" as an analytic tool.[49] Matsuda writes:

> The multiple consciousness I urge lawyers to attain is not a random ability to see all points of view, but a deliberate choice to see the world from the standpoint of the oppressed. . . . We can choose to know the lives of others by reading, studying, listening and venturing into different places.[50]

---

judging. See Jennifer Nedelsky, "Embodied Diversity and the Challenges to Law" (1997) 42:1 *McGill Law Journal* 91.

45 Particularly the case when one part is responsible for a solo entrance. For those familiar with George Frederic Handel's "The Messiah," the soprano entrance in "For Unto Us a Child is Born" is an example. Listen to this performance by Toronto's Tafelmusik at Tafelmusik, "Handel Messiah, Chorus: For Unto us a Child Is Born" (24 August 2012), online: www.youtube.com/watch?v=Kn56_Fz6pKE.

46 This is an inside joke (which I could not resist).

47 It is also perhaps the first time I have written while listening to choral music (and occasionally singing along).

48 In particular, Mari Matsuda, "On Causation" 100 (2000) *Columbia Law Review* 2195 and Mari Matsuda, "Admit that the Waters Around You Have Grown: Change and Legal Education" (2014) 89 *Indiana Law Journal* 1381.

49 Mari Matsuda, "When the First Quail Calls: Multiple Consciousness as Jurisprudential Method" (1989) 11:7 *Women's Rights Law Reporter* 7.

50 *Ibid* at 9.

Justice Abella's engagement with art, literature, and music exemplifies that desire to explore, hear, and understand difference. It reflects her humanity as well as her multiple consciousness . . . both linked to her vision of equality. I conclude with her characteristically clear, empathetic, and frank assessment of the judicial role:

> Being fearlessly open to understanding how injustice sounds and feels to the vulnerable who come before judges is what judges are for. It is the compassionate application of law to life. Otherwise, what's the point?[51]

51 Coxford Lecture, above note 4.

PART 6

Speeches

22 Remarks

ALBIE SACHS*

The chair of this panel described Rosie's impact internationally as a "ripple effect." I'd say it was more like a "tsunami effect." In 1998, I was invited by the National Judicial Institute to speak at a conference in Halifax, Nova Scotia. It was to be about the future of law and the judiciary in the twenty-first century. Can you remember when the twenty-first century seemed so far away and so full of delight and promise . . . and maybe threat?

And I thought, yes, let me go. I hadn't been a judge for very long. I'd been appointed straight to the Constitutional Court of South Africa, never having been a judge. I hadn't learnt all the manner and style of being a good judge. So, let me go to Canada and maybe some Canadian gravitas will seep into me by magical osmosis.

The result? I met Claire L'Heureux-Dubé and Rosie Abella. I didn't get gravitas. But I got something much greater, much richer. I'm glad to be the first speaker at this lovely and meaningful event. It enables me to be a little bit irreverent, in the way that Claire and Rosie were irreverent. Irreverence — being yourself, being lively and funny, regardless of professional and other hierarchies — can be so enlarging, so embracing, so welcoming. It is different from wit, which can be sharp and can be cruel. What I got from Claire and Rosie was this tsunami, if you like, of enthusiasm, of fun, of provocation. If this was what Canadian judges were like, so be it, bring it on.

The background to their bearing down on me was the following. My presentation at the conference had dealt with what I called the difference between false dichotomies and real tensions. I don't remember exactly what I said, but I do recall emphasising the need to avoid binary

* Former Justice of the Constitutional Court of South Africa.

choices between objectivity and subjectivity, insiders and outsiders, passion and dispassion, and so on. The main thrust was not to see a total clash between rationality and dispassion, on the one hand, and passion and empathy, on the other, and not to believe that for the one to win, the other must die. I felt that this was a false binary and a very destructive one. If law is based only on rationality, on logic, on paradigms, and not on experience, on empathy, on feeling and history and emotion, it can be cruel, it can be heartless and be destructive of humanity. On the other hand, if it is all heart and emotion and bleeding-out in a way that is uncontrolled, without discipline, without logic, without thought, without respect for legal history, it can also be destructive.

And in making these points, I said thank you to feminist jurisprudence. It was the feminist movement that I paid tribute to. This movement was emerging strongly in Canada at the time of the conference. It seemed to me that half of the cheerful ebullience of Claire and Rosie came from the fact they belonged to a movement that was forceful in its thinking, aims, and strategy, but at the same time did not dictate to or control its members, but rather allowed people within its ranks to express themselves as they were, something that the movement was fighting for. Anyway, I used the word *feminist* from my heart in a positive and embracing way and at the end of my presentation was flattered to receive a decent round of applause.

Afterwards, I was mingling with people I didn't know, and I saw — I was going to say walking up towards me — no, they were barreling up on me, two women, arm in arm, laughing, chatting away to each other until they stop in front of me in joyful ambush and vivaciously introduce themselves: "Claire L'Heureux-Dubé" and "Rosie Silberman Abella." The conversation flowed nonstop. We walked up and down, we had a long chat. After some time, a man came on to the scene, and I see Rosie beckoning him to join us. As he enters our circle, she says to this man, a huge smile on her face: "Meet my fiancé!" The man she'd introducing me to as her fiancé is her husband Itchie, who is watching this remotely. I feel such love for both Rosie and Itchie, and for Claire, as I remember that particular moment.

When I say I got more than gravitas, let me put it this way: Rosie wasn't a person who followed her dreams. I'm told by somebody I trust very much on questions like these, a strong feminist, that most little girls grow up dreaming of becoming a princess. And I know from my own experience that most boys, from my generation at least, grew up dreaming of being strong and maybe killing people and rescuing princesses. So, in either case, if you followed your dreams, you would have ended up in a cul-de-sac of disappointment. I believe that what happened with

Rosie is that she, in fact, followed her life, and her dreams followed her. And to me that's the explanation of Rosie, the riveting pathbreaker.

Everything she did so young was because she insisted on her right as a person, as a human being, as a pregnant person, as a mother, to do what she was doing. This enabled her to identify with other people who were fighting for the right to be who they were, to express themselves in the way they wanted to do.

I mention Rosie and Claire together because I met them together, so dissimilar and yet such strong sisters and such wonderful colleagues. The impact that they had on me came not only from their unforgettable style and manner, their irreverential challenge to stultifying and overbearing formalism and egotism. It was also jurisprudential for us in South Africa. Justice Abella's name is known for the way she put substantive equality on the map. The theme of substantive equality resonated with us not simply because of the compelling argument in her famous report on equity in the workplace.[1] It resounded because the courage, vigour, and thoughtfulness of the Canadian women's movement gave it coherent energy and expressive power. Rosie's youthful and creative genius was to find just the right words in her report to revolutionize thinking about equality. With deft and eloquent phrasing, she shifted the lawmakers' gaze away from formalistic treatment of everybody in identical fashion towards looking at the ways in which rules and practices bear unfairly on certain disfavoured sections of society. And, encouraged by the growing acceptance of the principle of substantive equality in Canada, we managed to make it one of the two principal legs of equality jurisprudence in South Africa. It was particularly helpful to us that Canada, a country with a new Bill of Rights and a creative, forward-looking Supreme Court, was embracing and projecting substantive equality as a legal principle that was manifestly worthy and good and productive of greater fairness in society.

The second leg of our equality jurisprudence was also strongly influenced by my visit to Halifax and encounter with the reasoning of Claire L'Heureux-Dubé. I was entranced by listening to a talk by Professor Lynn Smith on how the Canadian Supreme Court justices were battling over how best to apply the principle of equality. I don't remember the numbers exactly, but as I recall, three judges supported formulation A, another three supported formulation B, while another two said they

1 Rosalie Silberman Abella, *Equality in Employment: A Royal Commission Report* (Ottawa: Commission on Equality in Employment, 1984), online: https://publications.gc.ca/site/eng/471737/publication.html.

preferred formulation C. There was one left, one who didn't agree with any of the formulations, and in fact didn't like the idea of definitional formulation at all. This was Claire L'Heureux-Dubé. In her view, the crucial test for unfair discrimination was whether the challenged measure or action impacted negatively on the dignity of people who belonged to particular communities that historically had been and continued to be subjected to disadvantage. Very simple, very clear. To me, this approach emerged from the feminist experience. Women had known as women what it was like to be treated as nitwits, frail creatures, whose destiny it was to support men in their activities.

The importance of substantive equality came from the fact that it wasn't based on the notion that men were intentionally going out of their way to be horrid to women. It wasn't derived from extending principles of criminal or civil liability for injuries intentionally or negligently inflicted. It came from the need for public law to deal with and counteract practices, customs, and legal rules that systemically diminished the worth and sense of self-worth of people belonging to affected communities. Yet, although triggered by the specific experience of women as women, the corrective and healing character of substantive equality could comfortably be extended to discrimination based on race, belief, sexual orientation, and other grounds of systemic oppression and disadvantage. So in a case that set the foundations of South African jurisprudence on equality, *Prinsloo v Van der Linde*,[2] we singled out Claire L'Heureux-Dubé's approach and imported it directly from Canada as a foundational element of our law. We've been criticized by some scholars for doing so, but I would say that the emphasis on human dignity being the touchstone of equality law has become so entrenched that it has now become axiomatic.

So in one breath I would, as a former South African Constitutional Court Judge, say, Thank you, Rosie, thank you, Claire, thank you all forward-looking lawyers in Canada.

I love the phrase Rosie the Riveter. I first heard it from one of the creatives on a programme we have in South Africa to tell the story of how we made our Constitution. She told me that the documentary that spurred her on to become a filmmaker was Rosie the Riveter. It reminded me of a poster put up in World War II in the United States to encourage the women to work when the menfolk were away fighting. Designed by Norman Rockwell, it showed a woman, not losing her

2 *Prinsloo v Van der Linde and Another* (CCT4/96) [1997] ZACC 5; 1997 (6) BCLR 759; 1997 (3) SA 1012 (18 April 1997).

femininity, but looking strong and thoughtful with a drill in her hand. Dignified and affirmative, it later became a poster of the women's emancipation movement. Our Rosie, if I may use that term, was and is a riveter. I might be wrong, but I don't think she's very good at handling a drill. Yet there is something fantastic about the way she handles her imagination, her thoughts, her tongue, and her word. I have seen this again and again in many different settings. Audiences are spellbound, inspired. Why, I wondered, is Rosie so riveting? Her language is rich, eloquent, and fluent. But the entrancement comes not from the fact that she produces amazing, extraordinary, fantastic ideas that nobody else could ever articulate. There's something inimitably Rosie-an at play. It's the superb and apparently spontaneous umbilical congruence of her mind and her heart and her feelings that make me starry-eyed. And I see that everyone else in the room is starry-eyed. I remember the glow of very sophisticated, post-graduate women at Yale University — you can't get more self-assured than that — open-mouthed and inspired as she addressed them. She, the judge on the highest court in Canada, looked and sounded so ordinary, so normal, so lovely, so nice, so thoughtful, so quick, so eloquent, so humane, and so funny. That's the person I would like to be. She is not a visitor from a judicial stratosphere, but an earthly being like me. Her language is so beautiful. And it's so beautiful in the way the law can be so beautiful. The heart, the mind, the imagination, the conscience, and the fun and richness of language all come together in one person, and that one person is Rosie Silberman Abella.

I'm thrilled to be participating in this particular occasion. I love it when I see you mention her name, and people smile. As I say my virtual goodbye and hi to Rosie and Itchie, I'm smiling.

Let me add a few words in conclusion concerning a question put to me on the role that International Law plays in our constitutional interpretation. Sitting on our court, I remember on at least two occasions saying, "South Africa itself was a creation of the international community denouncing apartheid, imposing sanctions to gradually go against apartheid. Our country was constituted with the support of international law." And so, when interpreting our Constitution, we must embody international law wholeheartedly. It was constitutive of the constitutional order that our people were longing for. It's not at all a case of feeling dragooned by all those people in the outside world telling us how we should behave, thinking they are smarter than us. The world outside, and universal principles of human dignity, played a fundamental role in bringing down apartheid and helping us to adopt a democratic constitution.

International law also played a crucial role when it came to the development of our law in relation to the treatment of refugees. Many of us have been refugees. I twice arrived as a refugee in England, first as a psychological wreck after solitary confinement in South Africa and then as a physical wreck after having been blown up by South African security agents in Mozambique, which had also granted me refugee status. Rosie was the daughter of a refugee who had to battle to be allowed to practise as a lawyer in Canada. I had the experience of sitting on the Constitutional Court in a case dealing with the rights of refugees. We couldn't see refugee law as being aimed simply at providing charity to refugees. We accepted that in a world where instead of protecting their citizens, states were humiliating and degrading them, it was the duty of all humanity to provide them both with safety and the elements of human protection they couldn't get from their own state. When it came to interpreting our very good refugee statute — not always well applied in practice — we had to bear in mind that we had been refugees and we had gotten succour from our neighbours, who had paid a very, very, very heavy price for doing so. The theme of human interdependence, particularly in an African context but in a global context as well, had to be an important interpretative guide to our constitutional responsibilities, not just a fleeting act of grace to be undertaken whenever so minded.

23 Writing Around the Rosie

BERNIE M. FARBER*

I must begin my remarks with an apology of sorts. This conference has been convened to honour Justice Rosalie Silberman Abella, an extraordinary jurist, an accomplished lawyer, and a remarkable human being. There is no shortage of people in the audience who can speak to her many accomplishments and breathe life into a resume that is a testimony to her passion for justice and equity.

With so many distinguished participants to write *about* Rosie Abella, I feel liberated to take a different approach, and write *around* her.

In a sense, the most marvellous thing about Rosalie Abella is that fate and good fortune conspired to preserve the lives of her parents, who welcomed her to the world in a displaced persons camp in Stuttgart, Germany after the end of the Second World War.

You needed to be lucky. My late father, Max, was the sole Jewish survivor of the town of Bocki. In 1942, the Nazis and their collaborators compressed the Jews into a small ghetto and later transported them to the *Treblinka* death camp. Included in the 700 who perished were Max's wife, children, and entire family. My father was lucky. Separated from his family, he found a loose board in the cattle car that carried the village to its death, and pried it free to make his escape. My father was lucky. He found a friend who hid him from the Nazis and their collaborators. He was lucky that he found a band of Russian partisans that welcomed Jews who were willing to fight. My father always said that to survive the Holocaust you needed a thousand miracles; that 999 were not enough.

* Many thanks to my wise colleague and friend, Len Rudner, whose valuable assistance and personal additions added immensely to this chapter.

Rosie's father, Jacob, survived *Theresienstadt* concentration camp. Of the 140,000 Jews who were sent there, 90,000 were sent to their deaths and more than 30,000 were murdered in the camp itself. Her mother, Fanny, survived *Buchenwald*, where more than 50,000 were murdered. They were fortunate. Millions were not. Rosie's older brother Julius was not.

But still more miracles were required. How can we, sitting comfortably in our homes, understand the trauma and guilt that the survivors experienced?

Lucky? Of course. But worthy? Well, that's a different matter. Why did one person survive and not the other? Why did they deserve to die? Why did I deserve to live? Questions that cannot be answered. Places of silence, where not only do words lose their meaning, but our tongues and lips cannot even give form to a sigh that of necessity remains formless.

My former Canadian Jewish Congress colleague Eric Vernon once told me about a remarkable novel by Nicole Krauss, *The History of Love*.[1] It tells of a boy and a girl in a small village in Poland growing up in the pre-war period and coming of age after the Nazi invasion. The boy, now grown, recalls that for her sixteenth birthday, he gave her an English dictionary, and together, they learned the words. Later, in the midst of unimaginable horror, she said to him, "When will you learn that there isn't a word for everything?"

Or, as Primo Levi observed in *Survival in Auschwitz*: "If the concentration camps had lasted longer a new, harsh language would have been born; and only this language could express what it means to toil the whole day in the wind, with the temperature below freezing, wearing only a shirt, underpants, cloth jacket and trousers, and in one's body nothing but weakness hunger and knowledge of the end drawing nearer."[2]

I mention this not as a digression but as a way of shining a light on what survivors felt after experiencing too long a time in the kingdom of death. Many suffered in silence, punishing their bodies from the inside, struggling to push down the darkness lest it devour them . . . Lest it devour their children.

The formation of Rosalie Silberman Abella required more than the survival of her parents and more than the happy occasion of her birth and more than their arrival in Canada. It even required more than her

1 Nicole Krauss, *The History of Love* (New York: W.W. Norton & Company, 2005).
2 Primo Levi, *Survival in Auschwitz* (New York: Touchstone Books, 1958).

graduation from law school and meteoric ascension to the bench. As we say during the Passover service, "Dayenu." None of these things would have been "enough."

It required that lessons be learned about the way that societies can disintegrate — unravelling from the margins — and the way that hatred can burn through all of the inhibitions and conventions and the polite posturing that we think make us civilized. It required hope. A belief that we could be better, that history neither had to repeat nor rhyme, that a better path could be found, one that placed a value on every human life and was founded on notions of the dignity and worth of every human being. These are lessons that survivors fought to extract from their agony.

When my father came to Canada to begin again, he met a woman, and they married and started a family. My mother told me that it took her five years to teach my father to smile again. I think I knew that something had happened to my father, but I didn't know what. It was not until I was twenty-two, at which point my mother, after being diagnosed with cancer, insisted he tell us, his children, the entire story. How I wish he had told me sooner so that maybe I could have carried some of that weight. How grateful I am that he spared me until I was old enough to begin to try to understand.

All praise and honour to the parents who protect their children and teach them the lessons but do not teach them to hate. All praise and honour to the parents who understand the power of memory and how it must be harnessed.

Memory. What a powerful thing it can be. A potion or a poison. Let's dwell here for a moment.

Jewish Scripture makes it clear that we carry our past with us. Like Jacob Marley, we sometimes drag it behind us. Or as the prologue to the movie *Magnolia* puts it, "just because you think you are done with your past doesn't mean it's done with you."[3]

Judaism has a complex relationship with the past and with memory. Confronted with the evil of the Holocaust, we say of Hitler, *Y'mach shemo v'zichro,* may his name and memory be erased. But how can it be truly erased when, confronted with the enormity of the Holocaust and the suffering of its victims, we say *Zachor!* which translates, with the force of a commandment, as *You Shall Remember!*

---

3 Paul Thomas Anderson, "Magnolia" Ghoulardi Film Company and JoAnne Sellar Productions, 1999.

It gets more complicated. One of the 613 commandments Jews are required to observe is that when a field is being harvested, the corners of the field should be left untouched so that they can be harvested by the poor. Some rabbis phrase this as a commandment to "remember to forget" — forget to harvest the corner of the field or forget to make sure that all the sheaves have been gathered up.

The contradictory messages do not admit an easy reconciliation. One can say, as Joep Leerssen does in *History and Memory in Modern Ireland*, that "the lesson to be drawn from past injustice is one of vigilance and assertiveness."[4] But that's easy to say and hard to do. *Never again* has enviable solidity but what does it mean in practical terms? How do we, in spite and because of our pasts — what we have done and what has been done to us — work to make the world a better place? If the much over-used notion of *Tikkun Olam* (repairing the world) is to retain any meaning, then we must seek to fulfil the words of the prophet Isaiah: *Learn to do good. Seek Justice. Correct what is cruel. Rule justice for orphans. Fight the widow's cause.*[5]

Seeking justice. Judging fairly. Remembering to remember but also remembering to forget. Great legal minds do not, like Venus, emerge from the sea, fully formed. Rather, like Athena, they are born from the foreheads of their fathers — from the place where memory resides — and garbed in armour, for it is not sufficient to be wise; one must also be ready to fight for what is right.

Another scriptural moment. The Torah instructs us "*Tzedek, Tzedek, Tirdof*,"[6] often translated as *Justice, justice shall you pursue*, with the repetition taken as a form of emphasis to show how important is the achievement of justice. I like that, but I prefer a different translation. Not justice, but *righteousness*. And with the change of a word comes a change of meaning, that we should pursue righteousness only through honest practice. The end cannot be justified by the means. But more than the scrupulous operation of retributive or distributive systems, justice must, in the words of Rabbi Steven Schwarzschild, be concerned with "the full enhancement of human and, above all, social life. . . . [I]t suffuses all human relations and social institutions."[7]

Rosie Silberman Abella was a judge who is Jewish. But more than that, she was a Jewish judge.

---

4 Joep Leerssen, *History and Memory in Modern Ireland* (New York: Cambridge University Press, 2001).

5 Isaiah 1:17.

6 Deuteronomy 16:20.

7 Steven Schwarzschild, "Justice" in *Encyclopedia Judaica*.

"I'm not just a judge," she said. "I want everyone to know that I was Jewish and my values system was shaped by being Jewish. Jewishness has been something I need people to know that defines me. The top line of my CV has *Jewish* . . . I could list 40 honorary degrees first, but I start with being a Jewish woman."

This conference is a fitting tribute to a woman born of immigrant parents who survived a conflagration and raised their children to embrace humanity, love, and kindness. Their eldest daughter born in the rubble of a nearly destroyed people rose to be a Justice of the Supreme Court of their adopted country, Canada.

In her final goodbye to the Supreme Court, Rosie characteristically, honoured her parents.

"I say to Canada on their behalf: Thank you. Thank you for giving them the life they dreamed of, and for giving me a life beyond their wildest dreams. I am so proud and lucky to be a Canadian."

Rosie's father died without seeing his daughter's graduation from law school, but I like to think that in a universe of infinite possibilities, the departed are aware of the honour that is bestowed on them through the merit of their children.

24 Rosie the Law Reformer: Viewing Public Policy Through Rosie-Coloured Glasses

DAVID LEPOFSKY*

A. Introduction

Alongside World War II's iconic Rosie the Riveter now proudly resides the similarly iconic Rosie the Reformer, who was eventually to become Justice Rosalie Silberman Abella, a widely revered member of the Supreme Court of Canada.

For decades, the legal establishment considered that the best qualification for a major judicial appointment was a successful career at one of Canada's biggest law firms. Similarly, all other lawyers' work performed outside the traditional job at a private firm was typically labelled "alternatives to private practice."

Therefore, the vast majority of judges when appointed to the bench brought with them a relatively narrow, though vital, portfolio of experience. They completed law school, were admitted to the bar, and practiced law. They had mastered key facets of legal analysis and legal writing.

Those with litigation practices brought to the bench their knowledge of the law of evidence, procedural intricacies, and courtroom practice and tactics. Some brought in-depth expertise in criminal or family law, but little exposure to any other facet of the law or of the human problems that can arrive in court.

That traditional paradigm does not include expertise in law reform/ public policy reform. For decades, law schools never taught this as a core

---

* David Lepofsky CM, O Ont, LLB (Osgoode Hall), LLM (Harvard), LLD (Hon; Queens University, University of Western Ontario, the Law Society of Ontario, and Brock University). I am a Visiting Research Professor of Disability Rights at the Faculty of Law at the University of Western Ontario. I am deeply indebted to my phenomenal research assistant Shirelle Cogan for her assistance with text editing and footnotes.

subject. Students were too often left to themselves to figure out how to analyze policy issues and formulate policy arguments.

The techniques of traditional legal analysis are quite different from law reform/policy reform analysis. Traditional legal analysis is the methodology applied to a dispute or fact situation, to try to evaluate what the law is on that issue, through an exposition of legislation, regulations and applicable caselaw and legal principles. In contrast, the methodology of law reform/policy reform explores how the law or public policy can or should be reformed. These two activities can implicitly or overtly overlap or converge when a court grapples with a dispute or issue where the law on point is unclear or ambiguous, and where the court can therefore engage in a degree of interstitial law-making.

There have been exceptional instances in which a person came to the bench after serving as a legislator. Even then, unless they had served as a cabinet minister, their direct participation in law reform while in politics could be limited. Policy decisions were often made elsewhere, deeper down in the public service.

But a thorough understanding of how to think through policy issues is an indispensable part of a judge's job, especially for appellate judges. The fiction that judges simply "interpret the law" in a sterile policy-free zone can rear its head when politicians and media are mired in a public frenzy over a new Supreme Court appointment, most notably in the United States. There, politicians' claims that "legislatures make laws and judges simply apply the law" denies well-known reality.

It is not only in the infrequent instances when a judge decides a major *Charter* case that policy analysis expertise is essential. It is also critical in the many other cases when a judge has a wide discretion to exercise. This includes discretion over how to interpret open-textured language in legislation or in governing caselaw. It arises when either legislation or caselaw explicitly requires the judge to adjudicate on what is "reasonable" or what a "reasonable person" would do. With alarming frequency, legislation and caselaw overtly duck important policy questions, delegating them to trial and appeal judges and to regulatory agencies that courts supervise.

The common law is the wellspring of so many rights and obligations that pervade our interactions with each other. Judicial decisions over what to include in the common law necessarily cry out for expertise in law reform/policy reform. Yet they are not preceded by input gathering processes like parliamentary hearings, nor enriched by cabinet options papers crafted by public service policy experts.

It is because law reform/policy analysis is central to the judge's role that modern judicial education programs increasingly include lectures by experts in diverse areas outside the law. We are systematically retrofitting our judiciary to train judges in important topics that they were not taught in law school, likely didn't encounter much if at all in their practice, and were not screened for before their judicial appointment.

B. The Making of Rosie the Policy Wiz

As with so much in Rosalie Silberman Abella's life story, her route to the judiciary approaches the unique. There is no doubt that some saw her appointment to the Ontario Court of Appeal and later to the Supreme Court of Canada as questionable. I would argue that she should instead be celebrated as a role model for senior judicial appointments.

Over a decade, from shortly after her appointment to the Family Court in Ontario until her joining the Ontario Court of Appeal, Justice Abella amassed an extraordinary curriculum vitae in law reform. In this, she was self-taught and self-driven. She developed this expertise in four overlapping phases.

In the first phase, from 1982 to 1983, while still an Ontario Family Court judge, Justice Abella conducted an inquiry into whether Ontario's legal profession was sufficiently meeting the legal needs of Ontarians with disabilities.[1] She was appointed to conduct this inquiry by another legal giant, Ontario's visionary Attorney General and future Chief Justice Roy McMurtry.

This first Abella Inquiry was low visibility, low profile, and low priority for both the government and the legal profession. Apart from her staff counsel, Abella was on her own to stick-handle her way through a novel issue about which the legal profession and academic community had devoted little if any attention.

Conducting this inquiry early in her law reform career, Abella drew on her natural instincts. They drove her to identify people who could help her think through the issue critically. She surrounded herself with those who she thought knew more than her on this topic, unremittingly grilling them for workable solutions. It was an incredible honour for me, an untested newcomer to the legal profession, to be included.

The second phase of Abella's schooling in law reform took place when she was appointed Chair of the Ontario Labour Relations Board

---

1 Rosalie Silberman Abella, *Access to Legal Services by the Disabled: Report of a Study* (Toronto, Ontario: Ministry of the Attorney General, 1983) [Access to Legal Services Report].

from 1984 to 1989. She was thrust into a highly specialized field brimming with life-long experts and entrenched, institutionally adverse labour and management interests. Her work and that of the Labour Board were always exposed to the possibility of very public external scrutiny by courts exercising their power of judicial review of administrative action.

Labour boards are expected to develop important labour relations public policy. Abella had an on-the-job crash course in a world of substantive law, sophisticated policy-based interest-balancing, and policy making. On day one, she had to be up and running as a credible leader on a tribunal staffed by people with years or decades of accumulated labour law expertise.

She plunged headfirst into this new job with zeal that is now legendary. Imagine how she felt on her first day, with other Labour Board members along with its regular union and management customers scrutinizing her every move to see if she was pro-labour, pro-management, or even up to the task. She could expect judges, hearing judicial review applications of the Labour Board, to ponder whether to show deference to her, if her expertise was being newly acquired on the job.

The third phase of the policy and law reform education of Justice Abella began in 1984, when the federal government appointed her to conduct the Royal Commission on Equality in Employment.[2] The problems in the workplace facing women and racialized minorities were well known in equality-seeking circles. However, finding an effective and publicly acceptable new solution to those problems had proven elusive.

For Indigenous employees and job-seekers and those with disabilities, their needs were then not even on the radar of policy-makers and industry leaders. "Affirmative action" had been the main American solution for racialized persons. But by the mid-1980s, it was plagued with a toxic level of controversy, especially in the United States, out of all proportion to its reality.

Here again, the Abella approach was to assemble people with diverse expertise and let them argue it out, while she listened and probed them with penetrating questions. As a young lawyer, I had the privilege of being invited to play a small part in that vibrant exchange.

---

2 Rosalie Silberman Abella, *Equality in Employment: A Royal Commission Report* (Ottawa: Commission on Equality in Employment, 1984), online: https://publications.gc.ca/site/eng/471737/publication.html.

Her investigation led her to invent the concept of employment equity.[3] She cleverly tailored it to circumnavigate affirmative action's actual or perceived shortcomings.

Justice Abella's vision of employment equity included employers systematically identifying and removing workplace barriers that impeded equality-seeking minorities from full participation in the workplace. Employers were also urged to take proactive steps to reach out to those equality-seeking minorities during job recruitment. Abella did not recommend any hiring quotas. Instead, she recommended that employers set carefully tailored hiring targets for those disadvantaged groups, to be hired consistent with the merit principle.

Her report generated employment equity legislation and grassroots action. In the early 1990s, The Ontario government adopted an accelerated employment equity program within the Ontario Public Service. This was later supplemented by Ontario's short-lived *Employment Equity Act*, enacted under then NDP Premier Bob Rae in 1993 and later repealed under Ontario Conservative Premier Mike Harris.[4] Parliament passed the *Employment Equity Act* in 1993.[5] On the other side of the planet, Aotearoa New Zealand's Parliament enacted its own *Employment Equity Act* in 1990, though it was repealed later in the same year.[6] Decades later, employment equity remains an influential principle, though it too has at times sadly attracted undeserved criticism that it contradicts hiring based on merit.

After that, Justice Abella reached the fourth phase, her three-year graduate school training in policy and law reform. In 1989, the Ontario government appointed her Chair of the Ontario Law Reform Commission.

When she arrived at this small, provincially funded think tank, it resided at the legal system's outer periphery. Prior to her arrival, it managed to produce a single large report on a single topic every three years. It was not a driving force for law reform, despite its high-quality work.

Then the enthusiastic Abella vortex arrived. She aimed to put the Law Reform Commission on the map by making it far more relevant to

3 See Government of Canada, "It Takes All of Us: Achieving Employment Equity through Transformation and Grace. Report of the *Employment Equity Act* Review Task Force" (18 December 2023), online: www.canada.ca/en/employment-social-development/corporate/portfolio/labour/programs/employment-equity/reports/act-review-task-force/introduction.html.

4 *Employment Equity Act*, 1993, SO 1993, c 35.

5 *Employment Equity Act*, SC 1995, c 44.

6 *Employment Equity Act* 1990 (1990 No 61).

the public. She refocused its work on cutting edge topics that governments were not taking the initiative to address.

Justice Abella rapidly accelerated the commission's output. She decided that instead of working on one massive report at a time, a larger number of smaller reports should explore a diversity of topics. The commission began producing upwards of five or six reports per year.

She wanted to connect the Law Reform Commission's work to the public's priorities. She assembled a community-based advisory group to give input on the topics the commission should investigate. She encouraged the commission to look beyond the sterility of the law itself and enriched its work by learning from other sources of public policy expertise.

As a result, the Law Reform Commission produced reports on such topics as drug testing in the workplace, AIDS testing in the earliest years of the epidemic, modernizing the treatment of child witnesses in court, evaluating damages for environmental harm, and the future of Ontario's outdated Film Review Board (previously called the Ontario Movie Censor Board), which could censor films before they were publicly shown.[7] No political party would have put any of these topics in an election platform or Throne Speech. Justice Abella put them on the public agenda, while expanding her understanding of how to decide what legal issues merit reform and how to reform them. This expertise is extraordinarily well-suited for a Supreme Court judge, particularly in choosing when to grant leave to appeal in a case by assessing which legal issues have national importance.

In an acknowledgement of all her accomplishments, Justice Abella was invited to moderate the 26 October 1988 televised leaders debate during that year's federal election campaign. To my memory, she is the only judge, and indeed the first non-journalist, ever to be invited to moderate a Canadian federal election leaders' debate. It was so fitting to choose Justice Abella, a wise, impartial, respected person with a keen insight into the law and public policy.

7 See the Ontario Law Reform Commission, "Report on Drug and Alcohol Testing in the Workplace" (1992) *Ontario Law Reform Commission* 147; Ontario Law Reform Commission, "Report on Testing for AIDS" (1992) *Ontario Law Reform Commission* 148; Ontario Law Reform Commission, "Report on Child Witnesses" (1991) *Ontario Law Reform Commission* 141; Ontario Law Reform Commission, "Report on Damages for Environmental Harm" (1990) *Ontario Law Reform Commission* 139; Ontario Law Reform Commission, "Report on the Powers of the Ontario Film Review Board" (1992) *Ontario Law Reform Commission* 174.

C. How Rosie the Reformer Helped Drive Forward Canada's Disability Rights Efforts

1. *Advancing Equality of Opportunity in the Workplace for People with Disabilities*

When enumerating Rosalie Silberman Abella's many extraordinary accomplishments, it is important to highlight her achievements for people with disabilities. People with disabilities have chronically suffered rates of unemployment that far exceed the rates for the general public. The Abella Report included people with disabilities among the designated equality-seeking groups who should be the focus of employment equity initiatives.[8] She found that people with disabilities should be included in programs that are designed to achieve equality in society.

Regrettably, we are still far from achieving Justice Abella's vision. Far too often, when employment equity efforts have been implemented, people with disabilities are left out entirely, or disability is given mere tokenism and lip service.

For example, in the early 1990s, the accelerated employment equity program in the Ontario Public Service commendably produced an increase in the representation of women and racialized persons in the Ontario Public Service. However, it saw a *decrease* in the representation of people with disabilities and Indigenous persons in that workplace, even though people with disabilities and Indigenous Peoples were enumerated as designated targets of that program.[9] I and other disability advocates condemned this as accelerated employment inequity.

This problem persists. Today, it is commendable that many corporations, school boards, colleges, universities, and government organizations have policies on Equity, Diversity, and Inclusion (EDI). Yet far too often, these EDI policies focus primarily, if not exclusively, on inequities facing racialized persons and Indigenous persons. Those measures are, of course, needed to redress unfair, deep-rooted inequities that those groups continue to face. But it is wrong and harmful for any EDI strategy to leave out or marginalize the barriers that people with disabilities continue to face. Disability advocates now increasingly call for this to be rectified, drawing on the core message of the Abella Report. They call

---

8 Above note 2 at ii, v, 19–20, and 38–46.

9 See M. David Lepofsky, "The Long, Arduous Road to Barrier-Free Ontario for People with Disabilities: The History of the Ontarians with Disabilities Act — The First Chapter" (2004) 15:2 *National Journal of Constitutional Law* 125 at 153.

for Equity, Diversity, and Inclusion to be expanded to include "accessibility." The acronym would expand from EDI to IDEA. This echoes the spirit of the Abella Report.

2. People with Disabilities Need Lawyers, Too!

In recent years, Canada's law schools have commendably expanded the curriculum delivered to law students on the law as it pertains to Canada's Indigenous Peoples. This has been in response to the report of Canada's 2015 Truth and Reconciliation Commission.[10] There have been similar commendable improvements in law school curriculum to better address issues relevant to racialized persons.

However, there have regrettably not yet been as many commensurate legal education reforms in response to comparable recommendations regarding law school curriculum on disability issues, which have been on legal educators' desks for four decades. The original source of those calls for reform was none other than Rosalie Silberman Abella. Most legal educators likely don't know that she first cut her law and policy reform teeth on the issue of expanding legal services for people with disabilities.

Justice Abella's ground-breaking 1983 report on Access to Legal Services by the Disabled found that Ontario's legal profession substantially underserved people with disabilities.[11] It concluded that the legal education system did not train law students in critical areas that are important to meet the legal needs of people with disabilities.

Four decades later, there has been some progress. However, it has been uneven from law school to law school, and far too little across Canada's legal education system. Serious disability barriers too often persist, impeding access to effective legal services for people with disabilities, which Abella called out four decades ago.

Where a law school does teach disability curriculum, it is likely only in a few optional courses (only sometimes offered), such as courses on disability rights, law and discrimination, or mental health and the law. Several Canadian law schools offer no comprehensive disability rights course at all. Some professors commendably choose to include certain content on disability issues or disability rights in a mainstream course. However, a law student can easily complete law school receiving little

10 Truth and Reconciliation Commission of Canada, "The Final Report of the Truth and Reconciliation Commission of Canada" (2015).

11 Access to Legal Services Report, above note 1.

disability curriculum beyond the "not criminally responsible by reason of mental disorder" defence.

Abella's 1983 report called for reforms to legal education and to the overall system of legal services to ensure that the legal needs of people with disabilities were not systemically underserved. While some of the terminology in her 1983 report is dated, the ideas, barriers, and recommendations are not.

I feel a special bond to this facet of Justice Abella's work. Since my retirement from thirty-three years as Crown counsel at Ontario's Ministry of the Attorney General at the end of 2015, I have served as a visiting part-time professor (first at Osgoode Hall Law School and now at the Faculty of Law at the University of Western Ontario), focusing on adding more disability content to the law school curriculum. I am implementing some of the forty-year-old Abella recommendations, delivering guest lectures on disability legal issues to law students in a wide range of courses. This has included lectures on disability issues in criminal law, administrative law, labour and employment law, family law, tort law, property law, constitutional law, intellectual property law, employment and labour law, legal ethics, and even municipal law.

In an attempt to fulfil Abella's vision, thirty years ago I authored a law journal article that made recommendations to law deans on how to implement the Access to Legal Services Report.[12] Twenty years ago, REACH Canada, a community legal education organization, undertook a study of what had been done by Canadian law schools to implement my 1991 article, which in turn was implementing the 1983 Abella Report.[13]

In January 2022, I delivered a detailed report to Osgoode offering recommendations for injecting disability topics into more than three dozen law school courses.[14] I transformed this report into a law journal article now published in the Windsor Yearbook on Access to Justice, entitled "People with Disabilities Need Lawyers Too! — A Ready-To-Use Plan for Law Schools to Educate Law Students to Effectively Serve the

12 See David Lepofsky, "Disabled Persons and Canadian Law Schools: The Right to the Equal Benefit of the Law School" (1991) 36:2 *McGill Law Journal* 636.

13 L. McChesney, *Promoting Disability Accommodation in Legal Education and Training: The Continuing Relevance of the 1990 Lepofsky Recommendations* (Reach, 2003).

14 David Lepofsky, *Educating Law Students to Serve the Legal Needs of Clients with Disabilities – A Practical Plan for Making Progress, A Report to Osgoode Hall Law School* (January 2002).

Legal Needs of Clients with Disabilities, as Well as Clients Without Disabilities."[15]

It is my hope and wish that the celebration of Justice Abella's career and legal legacy will include the belated comprehensive implementation of her 1983 report on expanding legal services for people with disabilities. May that report go from obscurity to the influential prominence it deserves.

D. Rosie the Mentor

Any exposition of Rosie the Reformer is incomplete without discussing Rosie the Mentor. For Justice Abella, making the world a better place is not only the stuff of abstract ideas, lofty principles, and legal doctrinal reform. It is ultimately all about people. She has touched the lives of so many, not only as a group but as distinct individuals, each of whose lives she has separately influenced for the better. Those individuals went on to play their own parts in law and policy reform.

Justice Abella assigned herself the role of lifelong mentor to so many. I am honoured to be among them. She did not do this because there was something in it for her, or out of some sense of charity or beneficence. She did not do this because her mentees asked for her mentorship. Most if not all of us would likely have been too terrified to ask.

She did this because that is who she is. She knew what it was like to be isolated, undervalued, and underestimated. She knew what it meant to stare down and overcome barriers. Even when we faced different barriers than those she had faced, she had a driving impulse to encourage, support and conspire to help us overcome them.

I can attest that Rosie's mentorship feels like the titanium bond between a single parent and their only child. It is amazing to encounter so many who attest to the same experience and bond, and impossible to comprehend how she managed it. The international union of Abella mentees will never be created, only because we have no way to find each other!

Part of the gift of Rosie's mentorship for me is that from the outset, she set an irreverent tone — one I would strive over time to emulate. I first met Rosie in 1983. I was twenty-seven and had just finished

15 David Lepofsky "People with Disabilities Need Lawyers Too! A Ready-To-Use Plan for Law Schools to Educate Law Students to Effectively Serve the Legal Needs of Clients with Disabilities as Well as Clients Without Disabilities" (2022) 38 *Windsor Yearbook of Access to Justice* 148.

graduate law studies at the Harvard Law School. I walked into a meeting room in Toronto along with a delegation from the CNIB to make a deputation to her inquiry into the sufficiency of legal services for people with disabilities. Nervous, I wanted to create an atmosphere of professional competence and confidence. I formally introduced our entourage to her. She responded:

> Your cousin Connie says you're wonderful!

So much for my setting a formal tone. Constance Glube, my distant cousin, was then a Nova Scotia Supreme Court justice.

After our deputation, Rosie came over to me, and straightened my coat's skewed collar:

> I want you to look good!

Days later, Rosie took me out to lunch to discuss her inquiry. In hindsight, I suspect she did so to coach me in my fledgling earliest years as a government lawyer. I was struggling to be accepted in my office and to be assigned challenging court work. I asked her about something, respectfully beginning my question with: "Your Honour . . ." She instantly cut me off with her signature audibly detectible ear-to-ear grin, quipping:

> What do you want from my honour?

For one's career path to criss-cross with Rosalie Silberman Abella is always a memorable honour. Some of my memories are packed with incredible irony. In the mid-1980s, the Canadian Bar Association organized a continuing legal education program at its downtown Toronto offices entitled *Two Perspectives on Equality*. It aimed to share disability and gender perspectives on equality. The speakers were Family Court Judge Abella, me, and Chaviva Hosek (president of the National Action Committee on the Status of Women and future provincial cabinet minister).

Our audience was a paltry handful of people. Down the hall was another Canadian Bar Association event with 200 attendees. That event was a wine-tasting. We saw once again how the road to equality was an uphill one.

My life again intersected with Rosie's in 1989 when the Supreme Court of Canada released its highly anticipated first decision interpreting section 15 of the Charter (equality rights). All eyes were on fax machines across Canada as the *Andrews v Law Society of British*

Columbia[16] decision was printing. I had served as co-counsel for Ontario as an intervener in the case.

The fax machine slowly printed the decision's headnote. The list of cited authorities crawled into view. Listed alphabetically, they included Abella, followed by Aristotle, and were later supplemented by a law journal article by me and my colleague Hart Schwartz.[17] Abella, Aristotle, and Lepofsky / Schwartz? I thought that Aristotle and Lepofsky / Schwartz should be proud to be in such amazing company.

After Justice Abella was appointed to the Ontario Court of Appeal and later to the Supreme Court, I faced a challenge, not unique to me. She had always called me David and I called her Rosie. It felt quite forced when I appeared before her in court and she addressed me as "Mr. Lepofsky." I had to call her Justice Abella, "Your Ladyship," or the demonstrably risky "Your Honour."

I felt driven to demonstrate my gratitude for her mentorship in rather unusual ways, typical of a friendship with Rosie. The first chance for this was the 1995 theft appeal to the Court of Appeal in *R v Thiffault*,[18] an unremarkable case. For the Crown, I was struggling to defend a strong defence appeal. Presiding were Justice Abella and two other judges, neither of whom was reputed to have a sense of humour.

The appeal considered whether the accused had the mens rea for his theft conviction. He didn't know it was stolen, he claimed. I was the blind Crown lawyer who got the joy of invoking the "wilful blindness" principle to justify his conviction. I concluded my uphill oral argument by pleading that whether or not the court overturned the conviction, could it please rename this wilful blindness doctrine! It wrongly equates blindness with being ignorant. I can still hear Rosie's resounding laughter, contrasted with her two judicial bench-mates' equally resounding silence.

Our paths crossed once again in court when the Supreme Court allowed me to intervene in an appeal on behalf of Ontario's Attorney General in *Cojacaru v BC Women's Hospital*.[19] The Court was considering whether or when a trial judgment should be overturned because the trial judge's reasons for judgment included too many passages that were taken verbatim from the winning party's factum. My mission was

---

16 *Andrews v Law Society of British Columbia*, [1989] 1 SCR 143, [1989] SCJ No 6 (QL).

17 See David Lepofsky and Hart Schwartz, "Constitutional Law – Charter of Rights and Freedoms – Section 15 – An Erroneous Approach to the Charter's Equality Guarantee: *R. v Ertel*," (1988) 67 *Canadian Bar Review* 115.

18 *R v Thiffault*, [1995] OJ No 196, 77 OAC 231.

19 *Cojocaru v British Columbia Women's Hospital and Health Centre*, 2013 SCC 30, [2013] 2 SCR 357.

to argue that this should not be a basis for ever reversing a judgment. A judgment should be assessed on whether it was substantively correct, not on the venue from which its prose originates.

Lawyers want judges to use wording from our factums. That is a measure of our success. If a judge is convinced that they cannot say it any better than did we, we have done our job well.

I decided to craft a written and oral argument that, unbeknownst to the bench, was in pure "Rosie-Speak," sounding as Rosie as possible, without being obvious. I wanted to sound more Rosie than Rosie, without her or her colleagues knowing this. Every adjective and adverb was unleashed as a piercing verbal elbow.

For example, I wrote this in my factum, intended as vintage Rosie:

> If this Court mandates appellate review on this ground, judges with heavy case loads will need to devote time to word-smithing to eliminate appellate fears of too much symmetry between reasons and the winning party's factum. Law clerks may be tasked to help sanitize the reasons' cosmetics. This catapults hollow formalism to a triumphant stature of ascendancy over substance.

I culminated my oral argument with a summation that was 100% undiluted Abella. I ended by telling the bench that this is such a good line, they should feel free to use it in their reasons!

Happily, the unanimous Supreme Court of Canada saw the case's merits our way for the most part. For me, the bad news was that, alas, the Supreme Court's reasons were not penned by Justice Abella!

E. Conclusion: The Unknown Rosie Achievement that Would Make Her Parents Even Prouder!

Rosie becomes justifiably emotional each time she publicly recounts how after her parents, Holocaust survivors, came to Canada, her father was not allowed to practice law here because of his foreign legal training. That his daughter became a member of Canada's highest court is of itself a breathtaking example of Canada's progress since then, including its increased capacity to let people succeed based on their abilities.

But there is a related Rosie "first" that goes beyond that show-stopping narrative. No one likely knew of it then or now.

In 2014, the Supreme Court heard *R v Jackson*,[20] a legally unremarkable murder conviction appeal with no lasting jurisprudential signifi-

20 *R v Jackson*, 2014 SCC 30, [2014] 1 SCR 672.

cance. Rosie likely and understandably would not remember it days after it was summarily decided from the bench.

The case's issues do not here matter. What was significant was who was on the bench that day. Because it was an as-of-right appeal, only five justices presided. Chief Justice McLachlin was not on that panel. Rosalie Silberman Abella, the senior judge on the panel, sat in the centre seat as the panel's president — functionally the Chief Justice for the day.

Sitting that day with Justice Abella were Justices Wagner, Karakatsanis, Rothstein, and Moldaver. For that hour, three of the five judges comprising the Supreme Court of Canada were Jews. The operational Chief Justice for that hour was Jewish. Canada, for that hour, had a majority Jewish Supreme Court of Canada with a Jewish president presiding. From the ashes of the Holocaust to such an event occurring seven decades later, with it not even seeming remarkable at the time,[21] is a testament to where we have come. We are indebted to Rosalie Silberman Abella for helping lead us there.

21 Adding to the force of this, Justice Rosalie Silberman Abella's late husband, Professor Irving Abella, of blessed memory, documented Canada's sorry record of systematically refusing to admit Jewish refugees during the Holocaust in Ian Abella and Harold Troper, *None is Too Many: Canada and the Jews of Europe 1933–1948* (Toronto: Lester & Orpen Dennys, 1983).

25 To Honour the Gatekeeper: A Beacon of Human Rights and Freedom

DORIT BEINISCH AND GONEN ILAN*

Justice is the application of law to life, *not just the application of laws to facts.*

Justice Rosalie Silberman Abella[1]

A. Introduction

Justice Rosalie Abella is a beacon of law and justice. It is our honour to take part in this book honouring a great judge and legal mind for her contributions to both Canadian and international jurisprudence through the years. Justice Abella's unique judicial attributes have made her a prominent figure in the legal world. In addition to her work in social and women's rights, Justice Abella is known for her unique humanitarian approach to the law. She has spoken about the importance of empathy and understanding in the judicial process and has worked to ensure that Canada's legal system is accessible to all. Finally, Justice Abella firmly believes that democracy depends on an independent judiciary. She has consistently spoken out against political interference in the judicial system and has worked to ensure that judges are free to make decisions based on the law and not on political pressure.

---

* Dorit Beinisch is Former Chief Justice of the Israeli Supreme Court (2006–2012). Gonen Ilan is a PhD Candidate at Bar-Ilan University (Israel). While writing this chapter, we were saddened to learn that Rosalie's husband, Professor Irving Abella, had passed away. Irving Abella (Itchie) specialized in the history of Jews in Canada, and his wisdom and knowledge were immense. Rosie and he shared a great and unique bond through their fifty-year journey as close partners, and we shall all miss him.

1 Quoted in Andromache Karakatsanis and Sheilah L. Martin, "The Joy of Judging with Justice Rosalie Silberman Abella" (2021) 105:3 *Judicature*, online: https://judicature.duke.edu/articles/the-joy-of-judging-with-justice-rosalie-silberman-abella/.

This short article comprises three sections. The first will examine Justice Abella's distinctive approach and her contributions to social and women's rights. The second section will explore Justice Abella's humanitarian judicial approach. The final section will explore her firm belief in the preservation of judicial independence as a means of safeguarding human rights and democratic principles.

B. Women's Rights and Social Rights

Justice Abella has dedicated her legal and judicial career to advocating for the rights of marginalized and disadvantaged communities. Her progressive and activist approach to the law is evident in her rulings, interpreting the law uniquely to promote and protect social justice. Justice Abella's roots and upbringing as a daughter to Holocaust survivors who came to Canada as refugees have instilled in her a deep commitment to social stability and social rights.

1. Women's Rights

Justice Abella exemplifies what it means to be a feminist advocate, both legally and personally. She has written several landmark decisions that have advanced women's rights in Canada. In addition to her legal work, Abella has also been an outspoken advocate for women's rights outside of the courtroom, speaking at events and writing articles on issues such as pay equity, work-life balance, and the importance of women's leadership. She has been a role model for many women, showing that it is possible to make a difference in the world by standing up for what you believe in. She has paved the way for a more just and equitable society, and she continues to inspire others to join the fight for gender equality.

In the landmark case of *Fraser v Attorney General of Canada,*[2] for instance, Justice Abella stated that:

> despite the sweep of legislative initiatives and the positive realignment of many social expectations, the long reach of entrenched assumptions about the role of women in a family continues to leave its mark on what happens in the workplace.[3]

2 2020 SCC 28 [*Fraser*]. For similar case involving the Supreme Court of Israel, see HCJ 1758/11 *Orit Goren v Home Center Ltd* (2012).

3 *Ibid* at para 1.

In 1997, the RCMP introduced a job-sharing program. The program primarily attracted women with young children. Individuals who participated in the job-share program were denied access to the pension program for full-time members of the Force. A group of women members who had job shared contended that this policy had a discriminatory impact on women contrary to section 15(1) of the *Charter*.[4] Their claim was unsuccessful at both the Federal Court and the Federal Court of Appeal.

A majority of the Supreme Court of Canada, led by Justice Abella, ruled that this arrangement had a disproportionate impact on women and perpetuated their historical disadvantage, in violation of section 15 of the *Charter*. The government, she wrote, had not provided a compelling reason for limiting pension credit for job-sharing members. The majority, thus, ruled that the appropriate remedy was a declaration of the breach of section 15(1) rights.[5]

The *Fraser* case provides but a glimpse into Abella's impact on protecting and promoting women's rights. It is not an exaggeration to say her *Report on Equality in Employment*,[6] which she wrote in the 1980s, is considered to be one of the most important works ever written regarding women's struggle for social and constitutional rights. In this *Report*, Abella, a young lawyer at the time, introduced the term and concept of "employment equity,"[7] highlighting how discrimination against women results from the routine practices of employers. Abella's analysis of systemic barriers was relied upon in the landmark 1989 case of *Andrews v Law Society of British Colombia*,[8] in which the Supreme Court of Canada concluded that it was discriminatory to prohibit non-Canadian citizens from practicing law.[9]

Abella's judicial rulings and *Report* have also inspired the Israeli High Court of Justice (HCJ). In the *Israel Women's Network v Government of Israel* case,[10] for instance, Justice Eliyahu Matza stated that:

---

4 s 7, Part 1 of the *Constitution Act*, 1982, being Schedule B to the *Canada Act 1982* (UK), 1982, c 11 [*Charter*].

5 *Fraser*, above note 2 at para 114.

6 Rosalie Silberman Abella, *Equality in Employment: A Royal Commission Report* (Ottawa: Commission on Equality in Employment, 1984), online: https://publications.gc.ca/site/eng/471737/publication.html [*Report*].

7 Carol Agócs, ed., *Employment Equity in Canada: The Legacy of the Abella Report* (Toronto: University of Toronto Press, 2014).

8 (1989) 1 SCR 143.

9 It is significant to note that the Abella *Report* recommendations were also adopted by other countries including New Zealand, South Africa, and Northern Ireland.

10 See HCJ 453/94 *Israel Women's Network v Government of Israel* (1994).

> It is merely that attitudes and assumptions from the past continue to exert their influence almost everywhere. Note that we are not dealing at all with discrimination based on a stated ideology but with social habits that have become entrenched and are fed by the existence of a kind of unconscious consensus — which prevails of course even among women themselves — that makes discrimination into a continuing social phenomenon.[11]

Justice Matza's ruling was influenced by Justice Abella's arguments regarding the prevalence of systemic discrimination against women, and the fact that discrimination against women isn't an "unusual phenomenon."[12]

2. Social Rights

Justice Abella's career has shaped numerous landmark changes to Canadian law, particularly for disadvantaged groups. She has been unwavering in her commitment to serving underrepresented individuals, recognizing that discrimination often stems from a lack of awareness and ignorance.

In various cases, Justice Abella has delivered progressive rulings and judicial statements promoting and developing the rights of the underprivileged.[13] This section highlights two of Abella's well known and significant rulings in this sphere: the *VIA Rail*[14] and *Ward*[15] cases.

In 2000, VIA Rail purchased 139 Renaissance rail cars but failed to ensure they were accessible for individuals with disabilities who use personal wheelchairs. The Council of Canadians with Disabilities (CCD) filed a complaint with the Canadian Transportation Agency, arguing that the Renaissance cars posed "an undue obstacle to the mobility of

11 *Ibid* at para 23.

12 *Ibid*.

13 See *Saskatchewan Federation of Labour v Saskatchewan*, 2015 SCC 4, where Justice Abella interpreted freedom of association to include the right to organize, the right to bargain collectively, and the right to strike. In that case, Justice Abella stated that the freedom of association is "a basic right derived from the right to human dignity." Her broad and progressive interpretation of the *Charter* is similar to a case where the Israeli Supreme Court dealt with an issue of social rights in HCJ 10662/04 *Salah Hasan v NII* 782 (2012), where the Court ruled that social rights are important as primary constitutional rights.

14 *Council of Canadians with Disabilities v VIA Rail Canada Inc*, 2007 SCC 15, [2007] 1 SCR 650.

15 *Ward v Quebec (Commission des droits de la personne et des droits de la jeunesse)* 2021 SCC 43.

persons with disabilities."[16] The Agency ordered VIA to modify several coach and service cars to accommodate personal wheelchairs. VIA appealed to the Federal Court of Appeal which referred the matter back to the Agency, while criticizing it for violating VIA's procedural fairness rights.

Justice Abella, delivering the majority opinion of the Supreme Court, upheld the Agency's decision, affirming that the Renaissance rail cars imposed undue obstacles on persons with disabilities. The Court ruled that VIA Rail failed to meet its duty to accommodate under the *Canada Transportation Act*, as it did not provide sufficient evidence to justify its claim of undue hardship in making the trains accessible. The ruling emphasized that the design of the Renaissance cars effectively deprived individuals using personal wheelchairs of independent mobility, contravening accessibility standards and established human rights principles. The Court reaffirmed that accessibility must be assessed within the broader legal framework of human rights and reasonable accommodation, rejecting VIA Rail's argument that its existing fleet or operational practices could compensate for the inaccessibility of the Renaissance cars.[17]

Fast-forward to 2021 to *Ward v Québec (Commission des droits de la personne et des droits de la jeunesse)*.[18] In that case, a professional comedian was accused of mocking a prominent young man (G) with a disability in his comedy shows and videos. G's parents filed a complaint with the Quebec Human Rights Tribunal which concluded that the comedian had interfered with G's right to dignity, establishing discrimination under the Quebec *Charter of Human Rights and Freedoms*.[19] The comedian's defence, based on his right to freedom of expression, was rejected, and he was ordered to pay damages to G. The Court of Appeal upheld the Tribunal's decision, except for one dissenting judge who did not find comedian's comments to be discriminatory.

A narrow majority of the Supreme Court ruled that the comedian's comments did not constitute discrimination under the *Quebec Charter*. The majority explained the legal framework that applies to a discrimination claim involving a public figure's right to dignity and a professional comedian's freedom of expression. The majority noted that a reasonable person would not view the comedian's comments as inciting others to

16 *Ibid* at para 14.
17 *Ibid* at para 109.
18 2021 SCC 43.
19 CQLR c C-12 [*Quebec Charter*].

detest or vilify the young person's humanity and that the comments did not exceed the limits of freedom of expression.[20]

Justice Abella, delivering the dissenting opinion, asserted that the legal question for the Court was "whether the child with disabilities lost protection from discrimination and the right to be free from public humiliation and bullying just because he was well known."[21] She explained that the comedian's jokes perpetuated harmful stereotypes and caused serious harm to the individual. The jokes were widely distributed and caused him to experience anguish and contemplate suicide. This violated his right to dignity, honour, and reputation, as protected by section 10 of the *Quebec Charter* which protects individuals from discriminatory speech that a reasonable person in the circumstances would refuse to tolerate.[22] Justice Abella also held that if the Court had applied the discrimination analysis, it would have determined that W's particular speech constituted discrimination in violation of the *Quebec Charter*. Finally, she concluded that the statements violated the child's right to dignity in violation of the *Quebec Charter*.[23]

C. Human Rights

Justice Abella is a prominent figure in the legal community, known for her unwavering commitment to upholding domestic legislation while adhering to universal standards. Her approach to human rights[24] has made significant contributions to the interpretation of international law. In her jurisprudence, Justice Abella emphasized the critical importance of safeguarding human rights both locally and globally. She advocated for restricting arbitrary state power, protecting against capricious decision-making, and ensuring that the law is a tool for procedural and substantive justice.

Rosalie Abella's life story has received international recognition. Her lifelong commitment to human rights is rooted in her unique upbringing and circumstances. Born in a displaced persons camp in Stuttgart, Germany, she and her family arrived in Canada as refugees in 1950. As a daughter of Holocaust survivors, Justice Abella remains steadfast in her commitment to the universal goal of preventing similar atrocities from happening again.

---

20 *Ward v Quebec (Commission des droits de la personne et des droits de la jeunesse)*, 2021 SCC 43 at para 83.

21 *Ibid* at para 10.

22 *Ibid* at para 12.

23 *Ibid* at para 36.

24 See *R v Turcotte*, 2005 SCC 50.

Her significant article "International Law and Human Rights: The Power and the Pity," exemplifies her dissatisfaction with the narrow approach to the term "rule of law," a universal principle we are commonly expected to give aspirational loyalty to and which is not solely a procedural concept but one with moral substance. Abella asserts that universal principles "should be unshackled from semantically ambiguous rhetoric"[25] and that such a narrow definition for them can erode the substance of democracy.

One example of this type of reasoning can be seen in Justice Abella's dissenting reasons in *Kazemi Estate v Islamic Republic of Iran*.[26]

Zahra Kazemi (K), a dual Canadian and Iranian citizen, was detained and tortured in Iran in 2003, leading to her death. Her son, Stephan Hashemi, initiated legal proceedings in Quebec, seeking compensation on behalf of his mother's estate and himself from the Islamic Republic of Iran and the officials implicated in the case. The defendants claimed state immunity. The Quebec Superior Court gave effect to a preliminary motion to dismiss the estate's claim on grounds of state immunity but refused to do so in respect of Hashemi's personal action. The Quebec Court Appeal dismissed the estate's appeal and allowed the appeal with respect to his claim. The case raised questions about the scope and constitutionality of the *State Immunity Act*,[27] the evolution of international law, and whether torture can constitute an official state act and benefit from immunity.

The primary issue before the Supreme Court of Canada was whether the *State Immunity Act* barred these claims for damages. Justice LeBel, delivering the majority opinion, dismissed the appeal, stating that "state immunity is not solely a rule of international law; it also reflects domestic choices made for policy reasons, particularly in matters of international relations."[28]

Justice Abella, in her dissenting opinion, argued that because the prohibition on torture is a *jus cogens* peremptory norm in international law,[29] it cannot be derogated from by any state. Also, she stated that Article 14 of *The Convention Against Torture and Other Cruel, Inhuman or Degrading Treatment or Punishment*[30] imposes an obligation on state parties to ensure

25 Rosalie Abella, "International Law and Human Rights: The Power and the Pity" (2010) 55:4 *McGill Law Journal* 871–882 at 877.

26 See *Kazemi Estate v Islamic Republic of Iran*, 2014 SCC 62 [*Kazemi*].

27 R.S.C. 1985, c. S-18 [*State Immunity Act*].

28 *Ibid* at para 45.

29 *Ibid* at para 172.

30 United Nations, *Convention Against Torture and Other Cruel, Inhuman or Degrading Treatment or Punishment* (adopted 10 December 1984, entered into force 26 June 1987) 1465 UNTS 85, art 14.

that victims of torture from their respective countries can obtain "redress and [have] an enforceable right to fair and adequate compensation."[31]

She also articulated, broadly interpreting the Convention, that the text does not indicate that the act of torture must occur within the territory of the state party for the obligation to be engaged. Therefore, in the face of the universal acceptance of the prohibition against torture, the Iranian officials' violation of human rights was not protected by the *State Immunity Act*, and, therefore, the lawsuit should proceed to trial.[32] She employed a non-purist interpretation of the *State Immunity Act*, stating that it was inapplicable to officials of a foreign state who engage in torture, "Equivocal customary international law should not be interpreted so as to block access to a civil remedy for torture."[33]

During her several visits to Israel, Justice Abella had the opportunity to witness the intricate interplay between international law and domestic legislation, which often presents challenges to established norms and values. Despite encountering these complexities, she expressed her profound appreciation for the country and its judicial system, particularly the Supreme Court's rulings in cases related to national security and terrorism. Her insightful observations regarding the legal complexities arising from the intersection of customary law, international conventions, and domestic mandates illustrate her deep understanding of the most problematic aspects of international and domestic legal relations.[34] Notably, the Supreme Court in Israel has been instrumental in safeguarding peremptory norms of public international law in several cases, particularly those involving the mandates of security authorities.[35]

1. *Constitutional and Administrative Interpretation*

Justice Abella often adopted a unique and creative interpretation of the text of Canada's constitution and *Charter*. She advocated for a broad rather than narrow interpretation of the legal text and administrative discretion, arguing that a purposive and holistic contextual approach

31 *Kazemi*, above note 26 at para 172.

32 *Ibid* at paras 229 and 231.

33 *Ibid* at para 175.

34 See, for example, para 203, citing the Israel Supreme Court in the *Eichmann* case; Supreme Court, 29 May 1962, regarding the concept that State-related motives are not the proper test for determining public State acts.

35 See HCJ 3799/02 *Adalah - The Legal Center for the Rights of the Arab Minority in Israel v IDF Central Commander* (2005) in the opinion of Justice D. Beinisch.

should be applied to allow *Charter* rights to adapt to changing realities.[36] However, in some cases, such as in *Quebec (Attorney General) v 9147-0732 Quebec inc.*,[37] Abella expressed her reluctance toward textualist judicial review. She stated that strict approaches to the interpretation of legal text could make Canadian constitutional law more insular. It, therefore, may not accurately reflect the evolving nature of the Canadian society and its values and potentially create a risk of eroding the fundamental values and principles upheld by the *Charter*.[38]

In *Quebec inc.*, a corporation was fined for carrying out construction work without a valid license in violation of the provincial *Building Act*.[39] The trial court imposed a mandatory minimum fine on the corporation, which unsuccessfully challenged the constitutionality of the fine under section 12 of the *Charter*, which prohibits cruel and unusual punishment. The Quebec Court of Appeal allowed the corporation's appeal, finding that corporations could face cruel treatment or punishment through severe fines. The dissenting judge ruled that section 12 does not apply to corporations.

In the Supreme Court of Canada, the Court confronted a basic question of constitutional interpretation: does section 12 of the *Charter* applies to corporations? Justices Brown and Rowe, delivering the majority opinion, ruled that section 12 does not protect corporations. While the entire Court concurred that "'cruel and unusual' denotes protection that only human beings can enjoy,"[40] the majority's approach differed fundamentally from Justice Abella's stance on the question of how the *Charter* should be interpreted. The majority criticized her concurring approach, which they said minimized the "primordial" significance of the constitutional text.[41] In undertaking a purposive interpretation of section 12, she explained, the Court should consider the language used, the historical origins of the concepts enshrined, and the *Charter*'s underlying principles and values.[42]

The majority also argued that Justice Abella gave too much prominence to international and comparative law in the interpretive process.[43]

---

36 *Quebec (Attorney General) v 9147-0732 Quebec inc*, 2020 SCC 32. p.430.

37 *Ibid.*

38 *Ibid* at 76–78. Also, see Aharon Barak, "A Judge on Judging: The Role of a Supreme Court in a Democracy" (2002) 116 *Harvard Law Review* 19 at p 83.

39 CQLR, c. B-1.1, s. 46.

40 *Ibid* at para 70–75.

41 *Ibid* at para 4.

42 *Ibid.*

43 See, for example, the majority opinion delivered by Justice Abella in *Saskatchewan Federation of Labour v Saskatchewan*, 2015 SCC 4 at para 73.

Specifically, she asserted that both binding and non-binding international and comparative law has always been indispensable to the interpretation of Canadian law[44] and particularly constitutional interpretation.[45] The narrowing of their importance by the majority, she argued, limited the Court's ability to consider them with discernment.

Another notable example of her approach can be found in *Loyola High School v Quebec*.[46] There, Justice Abella demonstrated her unique interpretation of administrative discretion.[47] In that case, the Supreme Court of Canada reviewed the Quebec Minister of Education's decision not to grant an independent Catholic school an exemption to the province's mandatory Ethics and Religious Culture (ERC) course. The legal question was whether, in exercising her discretion, the Minister proportionally balanced Loyola Catholic High School's religious freedom while still fulfilling the mandatory program's statutory objective of teaching different religions' fundamental traditions and symbols, given that the school proposed to offer an "equivalent" program which would have covered the same subject matter from a Catholic standpoint.

Justice Abella's reasoning relied on seeking the values ingrained in the constitutional right of freedom of religion and reflected the school's position. She explained that *Charter* values "underpin each right and give it its meaning."[48] On judicial review, the Court was required to "assess whether the decision is reasonable because it reflects a proportionate balance between the *Charter* protections at stake and the relevant statutory mandate."[49]

Applying this approach in *Loyola*, Justice Abella ruled that the school's equivalent program fulfilled the pluralistic elements of democracy in that it exposed its students to other religious perspectives. She concluded that the Minister's insistence on the school teaching Catholic doctrine from a neutral standpoint was unreasonable but that it was

44 *Ibid* at para 100.

45 See, for example, Ran Hirschl, "Going Global? Canada as Importer and Exporter of Constitutional Thought" in Richard Albert and David R. Cameron, eds., *Canada in the World: Comparative Perspectives on the Canadian Constitution* (Cambridge: University Printing House, 2018) at 305.

46 2015 SCC 12 [*Loyola*].

47 *Ibid*. Also, see Justice Abella's majority opinion in *Doré c. Barreau du Québec*, 2012 CSC 12, where she ruled that the proportionality exercise requires a decision-maker to balance the severity of the interference of the *Charter* protection with the statutory objectives.

48 *Ibid* at para 36.

49 *Ibid* at para 37.

reasonable for the school to be required to teach other religious traditions from a neutral standpoint.

D. Judicial Independence

In January 2023, Israel's Justice Minister Yariv Levin unveiled a series of "legal reforms" to transform the Israeli judicial and legal system. These changes would be the first in a series of planned reforms. Levin stated that the reforms would curtail the Supreme Court's authority to invalidate legislation passed by Israel's Knesset (Parliament), restrict the court's ability to review administrative actions, empower the executive and legislative branches in judicial appointments, and overhaul the process for appointing government legal advisors while reducing their legal power.

The proposed legal reforms haves attracted substantial criticism from opposition parties, as well as numerous voices within academia and the legal profession. Notably, both the current and former Chairs of the Israel Bar Association have expressed their opposition to the reforms. Additionally, the reforms have become the center of a growing protest movement, with hundreds of thousands of demonstrators participating in mass rallies across Israel, including Tel Aviv and Jerusalem. Protesters assert that the implementation of the changes would mark the downfall of liberal democracy in Israel. One aspect of the reforms has already been struck down by the Supreme Court.

Justice Abella contributed to a special discourse on the intricate legal and political turmoil unraveling in Israel, held in New York on April 18, 2023. She expressed her deep concern for the erosions taking place in constitutional democracies worldwide,[50] including the expansion of derogation clauses and demotion of the protection of human rights.[51] Abella also expressed her dislike of the abusive borrowing from constitutional reform provisions, such as the "override" clause in the *Charter*.[52]

She stated that comparative and international law should be an inspirational tool for different democratic regimes. However, it is essential not to employ abusive borrowing of constitutional reforms or provisions, thus displacing specific constitutional clauses, such as the "override" clause enshrined in section 33 of the *Charter.* Indeed, as discussed earlier, she believes that comparative and international law should serve as a source of inspiration for judicial rulings and specifically for democratic

---

50 See Samuel Issacharoff, *Democracy Unmoored* (Oxford: Oxford University Press, 2023).

51 See https://en.idi.org.il/articles/49057 (minutes 32–34).

52 *Charter*, s 3.

societies. But she argues it is critical to avoid misusing constitutional reforms or provisions by removing them from their intended, social and historical context, in particular when human rights are at stake.

These ideals expressed by Justice Abella trace back to her tenure as a justice of the Court of Appeal for Ontario. She delivered an important lecture at Queen's University, emphasizing the judiciary's crucial role in safeguarding democratic principles, protecting individual rights, and promoting broader participation in these rights.[53] Justice Abella is a strong advocate of judicial independence and plays a critical role in reviewing legislation, ensuring minimal and proportional infringements and curtailing of rights. She has, and constantly does, warn against anti-liberal tendencies such as populism and "bullying" of the judiciary, which pose severe threats to the fundamental principles of democracy.

Unfortunately, we live in a time when many democracies have lost their main characteristics, and politicians strive to narrow the power and authority of courts because of the claim that democracy means gaining a majority of the public's votes in elections.[54] Such voices, which support the majoritarian purist and narrow theory of democracy, are endangering the democratic regime by claiming that judges are not elected. These views are a serious threat to the independence of the courts.

E. Conclusion

Justice Abella is an advocate for the rights of marginalized communities and has worked tirelessly to ensure that everyone has access to justice. Her contributions to the Canadian legal system and to the liberal democratic judicial systems have been invaluable, and her legacy will continue to inspire future generations of lawyers and judges.

In addition to her legal work, Justice Abella is also a champion of diversity and inclusion. She has spoken out against discrimination and prejudice and has worked to create a more equitable and just society. Her leadership in this area has been recognized both nationally and internationally, and she continues to be a powerful force for change. Her unwavering commitment to justice, fairness, and equality serve as a model for all those who seek to make a positive impact in the world.

53 See Rosalie Abella, "The Judicial Role in a Democratic State" (2001) 26:2 *Queen's Law Journal* 573.

54 See Yaniv Roznai, "Who Will Save the Redhead? Towards and Anti-Bully Theory of Judicial Review and Protection of Democracy" (2020) 29:2 *William & Mary Bill of Rights Journal* 321; also see S. Levitsky & S. Daniel Zilblatt, *How Democracies Die* (New York: Crown, 2018).

Index

Abel, Albert, 30
Abella, Irving, 3, 29, 267
Abella, Rosalie Silberman
  advice to women on legal matters, 2
  appointment in Ontario Family Court, 3
  career plans, 2, 23
  as Chair of Ontario Labour Relations Board, 3, 16, 35, 72, 74
  as Chair of Ontario Law Reform Commission, 3, 19
  as Chair of Royal Commission on Equal in Employment, 193
  on collaboration and teamwork, 92
  copyright, defamation, contract, and civil procedure decisions, 18
  definition of equality and discrimination, 38–39
  early childhood and family, 2, 15, 24–28, 283
  engagement with arts, 364–366
  extra-judicial contributions, 37, 71, 362–364, 366
  as a Family Court judge, 36
  first female Jewish judge, 36
  impact of International Teach-In, 29
  impartiality and fairness, 368–371
  important appointments, 3, 16, 19, 35–37, 72
  influence of Hugo's *Les Misérables*, 26
  intellectual interests, 33
  judicial persona and philosophy, 24, 72–73, 127
  lecture on legal professionalism, 73
  legal career, 34–40, 132–140
  legal education, 29–34
  memory of an early injustice, 27
  as Ontario Human Rights Commissioner, 35
  personal qualities, 259–260
  publications, 37
  university education and experiences, 15–16, 26, 28–34
  views on feminism and advocacy, 39–40
  vision of equality, 18, 361–367
  work in labour relations, 39
Abella method, 41–45, 53
Abella Report (*Report of the Commission on Equality in*

Employment), 38, 41–42, 48–53, 58–62, 68, 91, 218, 276–277
creation of employment equity program, 58–59
description of systemic discrimination, 58–59
substantive equality, 58
Aboriginal law and rights, 203–214
AB v Bragg Communications, 163
Adams, Eric, 2, 121
administrative law and administrative justice, 71–73, 71*fn*3
Canadian administrative law, 123–127
Charter values, 81–82
distinction between courts and tribunals, 74–77
due process, 75
importance of deference, 73, 79–80
judicial review, 78–79
Labour Board's obligation, 75
legitimacy and value of administrative decision-makers, 78
potential of, 83–85
procedural fairness, 75
relationship between courts and administrative decision-makers, 76–77, 82
responsibilities of public decision-makers, 72–73
role of specialists or expertise, 80–81
Agócs, Carol, 38
Agricultural Employee Protection Act (AEPA), 224
Alberta *Public Service Act*, 222
Alberta v Hutterian Brethren of Wilson Colony, 103, 106–107, 147
Amsterdam, Anthony, 116
Andrews v Law Society of British Columbia, 39
authenticity-professionalism paradox, 16, 88–89, 98–101
Avrich, Barry, 88

Back to Schools Act, 251, 253, 255
Baglow v Smith, 332
Baker v Canada (Minister of Citizenship and Immigration), 291
Barak, Aharon, 281
bargaining power, 218–221, 225–226, 228, 329
Battista, Jordan, 285
Battista, Michael, 285
Beinisch, Dorit, 19
Bell Canada v Canada (Attorney General), 126, 126*fn*95
Bill of Rights, 379
Blueberry River First Nation's (BRFN) treaty right, 211–212
Board of Inquiry of Nova Scotia (the Board), 63–65
Bolton, Sharon, 219
Borrows, John, 203–204
Brown, Russell, 135
Brown, Wendy, 175
Bruker decision, 93–94, 97–98, 101, 114*fn*48
Bruker v Marcovitz, 4, 89, 106, 172, 181–182
Bruner, Jerome, 116
Buber, Martin, 173

Cahn, Sammy, 39
Canada's child welfare funding formulas, 66
Canada Security Intelligence Service (CSIS), 292
Canada's property laws and land tenure systems, 203

Canada's *Responsible Business Conduct Abroad* strategy, 359
Canada (Director of Investigation and Research) v Southam Inc, 80
Canada (Minister of Citizenship and Immigration) v Vavilov, 72, 76, 79, 84, 123–124, 126–127, 139
Canadian Aboriginal law, 203–205, 213–214
  access to justice, 212–213
  Crown's fiduciary obligation to Indigenous peoples, 205–209, 212–213
  duty to consult and accommodate, 208–210
  property law and ownership, 206
  protection of Blueberry River First Nation's (BRFN) way of life, 211
  for treaty infringements, 206, 210–212
  Tsartlip First Nation's (TFN) treaty rights, 210–211
Canadian administrative law, 123–127
Canadian Bill of Rights, 33
Canadian Charter of Rights and Freedoms (the *Charter*), 3–4, 39, 45, 261, 280, 290
  section 2(d), 217
  section 8, 335–345
  section 15, 230–232, 247, 253–254
  section 24, 345–347
Canadian citizenship, 123
Canadian common law, 266, 270–271, 354–355, 357
  civil liability of corporations, 272
Canadian Courts, international law in, 356–359
Canadian legal education, 30–32
Canadian National Railway's operations and procedures, 59
Canadian public law, 263–266
  civil remedy in domestic law for corporate violations, 265–266
  doctrine of "adoption," 265*fn*25
Canadian Security Intelligence Service Act, 292
Canadian Supreme Court justices, 379
Caring Society v Canada, 58, 65–70
case histories, 118–119
Charron, Louise, 101
Chaudhury, Shantona, 93, 96, 99
children
  human rights, 299–314
  vulnerability of, 300–306
City of Toronto v Ontario, 148
Civil Right Act of 1964, 254
Cole, R v, 345, 347
collective action, 217
collective bargaining, 221–225
Confederation of Tomorrow Conference, 1967, 33
Constitutional Court, 382
Constitutional Court of South Africa, 377
Constitutional Law, 32–33, 33*fn*36
Continental Life Insurance Company, 26
Convention Against Torture, 351
Cooper decision, 105
Côté, Suzanne, 133, 135, 137
Council of Canadians with Disabilities v VIA Rail Canada Inc, 139
courts and tribunals, distinction between, 74–77
  due process, 75
  mutuality between, 76
  procedural fairness, 75
  processes, 75–76

Criminal Code, 328, 333–334, 342, 344–345
Cromwell, Thomas, 137
Crookes v Newton, 324, 330–332
Crown-Indigenous relationships in Canada, 204
CUPE, Local 963 v New Brunswick Liquor Corporation, 79
CUPE v Ontario (Ministry of Labour), 244, 247–248, 252

Daniels v Canada, 205, 207
Darwin, Charles, 108
DB v R, 4
De Jong v Canada (Minister of Citizenship and Immigration), 284
Delgamuukw v British Columbia, 208
Denis v Côté, 161, 167
Deschamps, Marie, 101
Dickens, Charles, 120
Dickson, Brian, 109, 127, 217
  dissent in *Alberta Reference*, 221–223
dignity at work, 218–221
Disability Rights Coalition v Nova Scotia (Attorney General), 62–63
discrimination and disability, 306–309
distributive systems, 386
Divito v Canada (Public Safety and Emergency Preparedness), 261
Divorce Act, 1968, 35
domestic courts, 260–261
Doré v Barreau du Québec, 4, 13–14, 72, 81, 148
Douez v Facebook, 329
Drybones, R v, 33
Dunsmuir v New Brunswick, 76
Dyzenhaus, David, 105

Edwards, R v, 340
ellison, Ralph, 122
employment equality jurisprudence, 229–232
employment equity, 39, 43–44
Employment Equity Act, 393
employment law jurisprudence, 225–228
enlarged and embodied mentality, 115
equality and equity jurisprudence, 185–186, 361–363, 366–367
  age and, 309–313
  in bargaining process, 223
  claims of positive rights, 187*fn*7
  in employment, 193–194, 218
  equality of condition, 190
  formal or procedural equality, 276
  individualized accommodations, 193–198
  levelling up or levelling down, 196–198
  liberty *vs*, 199, 199*fn*43
  nondiscrimination and, 306–313
  of pay, 229–230
  remedying inequalities, 195–198, 201
  resistance to remedial efforts, 198–200
  right to counsel, 187
  same treatment, 188, 190, 192
  in schooling, 191–192
  seeking equal protection, 192
  substantive equality, 189
  as vigilance and continual efforts, 200–201
equality in Canada, 45
Equality in Employment Report, 232
Ethical Principles for Judges, 363–364
eunomia, 111
Evans v Teamsters Local Union No 31, 218, 226
Expenditure Restraint Act, 223

extra-judicial writings and speeches, 71

false claims of neutrality, 15
Farber, Bernie, 18
Febles v Canada (Citizenship and Immigration), 262
feminist movement, 378
Fish, Morris, 135
France, Anatole, 187
Fraser v Canada (AG), 3, 12, 52–53, 57, 62, 218, 252, 277
freedom of association, 221–222, 224–225
freedom of expression, 149–150, 156–160, 165
freedom of press, 159–163
Friedland, Martin, 28, 30
Fuller, Lon, 109

Garfield, Howard, 34
gender roles and stereotypes, 200
gig workers, 218
Gilmour, Julie Frances, 26
Ginsburg, Ruth Bader, 200
Girard, Philip, 23
Google Inc v Equustek Solutions Inc., 330–334
Grant, R v, 346
Griggs v. Duke Power Co., 46

Habeas corpus jurisdiction, 293–296
Hall, Edward, 285
Halwani, Sana, 95
Hansen, Stine, 285
Hape, R v, 354
Health Services and Support-Facilities Subsector Bargaining Association v British Columbia, 222, 225
Hilewitz v Canada (Minister of Citizenship and Immigration), 284–286
History and Memory in Modern Ireland, 386
The History of Love, 384
humanities dimensions of legal profession, 16, 103–104, 260
  embodied and empathetic cognition, 117–118
  empathy, 115–120
  equality and fairness, 111
  impartiality, 115–116
  for learning and teaching law, 127–128
  mindfulness/mindful reasoning, 116–117
  morality of aspiration, 110
  morality of duty, 110
  needs of vulnerable persons and communities, 107
  religious freedom, 106–108, 106*fn*12–13, 107*fn*15–17, 111–113
  self-sufficiency, 112
human rights, 261–262
  of child, 299–314
  complaints, 63
  corporate liability for violations abroad, 264–266
  corporate responsibility, 272–273, 275
  distinction between public and private, 274
  under international law, 3, 18, 260, 263–265, 271–272, 275–276, 278–282, 350–351, 353, 355–360
  positive and negative obligations of states, 274
  standard of care, 275
  transnational corporate, 353

Iacobucci, Frank, 30
Ignatieff, Michael, 28
Ilan, Gonen, 19

ILO Tripartite Declaration, 359
immigration and refugee law, 283
  admissibility of disabled people, 285–286
  "best interests of the child" principle, 291
  Chhina decision, 293–296
  compassionate approach, 284–291
  Febles decision, 286–289
  financial ability and willingness to assist financially, 285
  Harkat decision, 291–293
  Kanthasamy decision, 289–291
  protecting informer privilege, 291–293
  purposive approach, 291–296
  Refugee Convention, 288
  refugee protection, 286–289
  Vienna Convention, 288
  writ of *habeas corpus*, 293–296
immigration detention, 293–296
indirect/adverse effect discrimination, 46, 51–52
infringement of treaty rights, 206, 210–212
inherent vulnerability, 300–303
International Covenant on Civil and Political Rights, 355
international law, 260–261
  in Canadian Courts, 356–359
  corporate liability for violations abroad, 264–266
  customary, 352–355
  good faith approach, 262
  human rights obligations of corporations, 272
  immunity under, 264
  influence in Canadian public law, 263–266
  interpretation of, 261–263
  private right of action against corporations under, 271–272
  protection of human dignity, 261–262
  and South Africa, 381–382
  spousal equality, 263
  Ukraine genocide case, 262–263

Jamal, Mahmud, 93
Jewish refugees, 25
Jewish Scripture, 385
Joeck, Molly, 288
Johnson, Mark, 116
Jordan's Principle, 66–67, 66*fn*61, 68
Journalistic Sources Protection Act (JSPA), 161
judges' personal characteristics and commitments, 1
judicial approach of Abella, 5–7
  case law analysis, 16
  Charter protections, 13
  decision-making, 13–15
  employment jurisprudence, 17. *See also* employment equality jurisprudence
  engagement with international law, 349–360
  equality, 16
  feminist commitments, 6–7
  freedom of religion jurisprudence, 16. *See also* religious freedom
  humanitarian considerations, 16. *See also* humanities dimensions of legal profession
  human rights, 13, 18. *See also* human rights
  indirect discrimination cases, 9, 12, 60, 278
  judicial reasoning, 12–15

judicial review, 13, 76, 78–80, 84, 107*fn*17, 208–209, 294–295, 351*fn*13
jus cogens prohibition against torture, 352
labour law jurisprudence, 11. *See also* labour law jurisprudence
power, hierarchy, and vulnerability, 11–12
progressive legacy, 322, 331–334
relevance of lived experience and contexts, 7–11
technology decisions, 18. *See also* technology jurisprudence
judicial education, 363*fn*7, 369, 369*fn*33, 370–371
judicial impartiality, 93–94
judicial non-transparency, 114
judicial role, 40, 99, 363, 368–372, 374
Jukier, Rosalie, 4–5
Justice Beyond Orwell, 104
JV Kelly Law, 35

Kafka, Franz, 108
Kahkewistahaw First Nation v Taypotat, 98
Kapp, R v, 277
Karakatsanis, Andromache, 90–92, 133, 137
Kazemi Estate v Islamic Republic of Iran, 264, 349–360
Abella's dissent in, 350–351
King, Thomas, 127
Kiobel v Royal Dutch Shell, 266, 266*fn*29
Krauss, Nicole, 384
Kyllo v United States, 341

labour law jurisprudence, 221–225
Lakoff, George, 116
Lamer, Antonio, 370
Langille, Brian, 229
Laskin, Bora, 30
Law Reform Commission, 394
Law Society of British Columbia v Trinity Western University, 147
Leerssen, Joep, 386
legal career of Abella, 34–40, 132–140
avoidance of legal jargon, 142–144
cases heard by year, 132
cinnamon words, 141–143
decisions, 138–139
least used words, 146
most used words, 145
quantitative insights into writing style, topics and ideas, 140–144
rate of dissent, 134–136
rate of opinion writing, 136–139
at Supreme Court of Canada, 133
unique words used, 139–140, 139*fn*13
legal fictions, 203–204
legal pluralism, 32, 37, 121
legal professional
as artist, 104–109
as craftsperson, 109–114
as embodied and empathetic thinker, 115–120
as instruments, 104–105
as narrator and storyteller, 120–123
legal rules, 379
legal storytelling, 121–122
legal writing, 120
L'Heureux-Dubé, Calire, 5, 91, 105, 127
licence as a "privilege" *vs* licence as a "right," 122
Liston, Mary, 14, 91–92

Local 579 v Bradco Construction Ltd., 80
Loyola High School v Quebec (AG), 107

MacDonald, Flora, 39
Macdonald, Ronald St. John, 30, 33–34, 87
MacLean v Nova Scotia, 58
Malhab v Diffusion Metromedia, 163, 166
Malhotra, Ravi, 286
Manitoba Métis Federation decision, 207
Marakah, R v, 338–340, 343
Marley, Jacob, 385
McGhee, Heather, 199–200
McGill University, 87–88, 100
McLachlin, Beverley, 91, 101, 105, 108, 137, 148, 160
McMurtry, Roy, 35, 94, 391
Meredith v Canada (Attorney General), 222–223
Mikisew Cree v Canada, 205, 208, 211
Milieudefensie et al v Royal Dutch Shell PLC, 275
Milner, James, 30, 32
mindfulness, 116
Moldaver, Michael, 137
Moore decision, 57, 60–65
The Morality of Law, 109–110
Morris, R v, 205, 210
Mounted Police Association of Ontario v Canada (Attorney General) (MPAO), 222
Mouvement laïque québécoise v Saguenay (City), 107
Mulroney, Brian, 38
Multani v Commission scolaire Marguerite-Bourgeoys, 106

National Action Committee on the Status of Women, 2, 35
National Corn Growers Assn. v Canada (Import Tribunal), 80
National Judicial Institute, 377
National Post, R v, 160
Nazi atrocities, 25
Nazi invasion, 384
Nedelsky, Jennifer, 115
Nevsun decision, 4
Nevsun Resources Ltd v Araya, 264–265, 269–272, 349–360
  Abella's majority decision, 270–271, 351
  application of substantive equality jurisprudence, 276–281
  business and human rights perspective, 272–276
  distinction between parent company and its subsidiary, 273
  issue of remedy, 271–272
  majority's reasoning, 272
  minority opinions in, 273
Newfoundland and Labrador Nurses' Union v Newfoundland and Labrador (Treasury Board), 72
Newfoundland and Labrador v Uashaunnuat, 205–206
Newfoundland and Labrador (Attorney General) v Uashaunnuat, 212–213
Nicolaides, Aliki, 173
NL v Uashaunnuat, 206
NS, R v, 107, 147
Nussbaum, 120–121

O'Bonsawin, Michelle, 369
O'Connor, Day, 92
OECD Guidelines for Multinational Enterprises on Responsible Business Conduct, 359
Oliver, Mary, 127
Ontario Court of Appeal, 391
Ontario Labour Relations Board, 391

Ontario Movie Censor Board, 394
Ontario Study on Access to Legal Services by the Disabled, 37
Ontario (Attorney General) v Fraser, 217
Ontario (Human Rights commission) v Mr A, 277
Orwell's *1984*, 235
Osgoode Hall Law School, 31

Paikin, Steve, 88
parliamentary sovereignty, 209
Philip, Roth, 40
Poetic Justice, 115
Pope, Elizabeth M., 173
Posner, Richard, 120
Priestley, Diana, 31
privacy protection, 335–336
- Abella's opinion, 339–345
- difference between prospective search and retrospective search, 343–344
- informational privacy, 339–340
- interpretation of "intercept," 344
- in property searches, 338
- reasonable expectation of privacy, 340
- in relation to computers, 337–338
- remedy for privacy violations, 345–347
- under section 8 of *Charter*, 336–345
- in text communication, 338–339, 342–344
- against unreasonable search or seizure, 336–337
- use of FLIR technology, 341–342

"progressive" and "progressivist" vision of Canadian law and society, 317–318
Progressive Era, 317–323
proportionality balancing, 151–156, 162
public accountability, 368, 371
Punishment Gap, 96–98

Quebec *Charter of Human Rights and Freedoms*, 164
Quebec's *Pay Equity Act*, 230
Québec v A, 98
Quebec (AG) v A, 277
Quebec (Attorney General) v Alliance du personnel professionnel et technique de la santé et des services sociaux, 218, 229–230
Quebec (Attorney General) v 9147-0732 Québec inc, 261

racial disparities, 191, 194
Rae, Bob, 28
Rankin, David, 93
rational emotions, 121
refugee law, 382
religious freedom, 16, 106–108, 106*fn*12–13, 107*fn*15–17, 111–113, 147
religious freedom jurisprudence
- constitutional right, 179
- cross-cultural communication, 172–175
- *Hutterites* case, 108, 111–113, 117, 172, 175–178
- *Loyola* case, 180–181
- religious remarriage, 182–183
- respect, 175–178
- sense of self-awareness, 174–175, 178–181
- translation of religious legal norms, 181–183
- value of tolerance, 178

Report of the Commission on Equality in Employment (Abella Report), 38, 41–42, 48–53, 58–62, 68, 91, 218, 276–277
retributive systems, 386

"ripple effect," 377
Risk, Dick, 32
Risk, John, 34
Risk, R.C.B., 30
Roncarelli, Frank, 122
Roncarelli v Duplessis, 122
Rosenberg v Canada, 277
Rothstein, Linda, 95–96
Rowe, Malcom, 137
Royal Commission on Equality in Employment, 37, 45, 392, 366
Royal Commission on the Status of Women, 33
RS v PR, 263
Ruggie, John, 272

Sachs, Albie, 5, 18, 100–101
Sacks, Oliver, 118
same-sex marriage bill, constitutionality of, 94
Sandomierski, David, 32
Saskatchewan Federation of Labour decision, 4, 11
Saskatchewan Federation of Labour v Saskatchewan, 147, 217, 262
Scanlan, Thomas, 185
Second World War, 383
section 2(b) jurisprudence, 147–151
  civil liberties, 149, 149*fn*12, 150–151
  dissenting opinion's framework of values, 163–166
  freedom of expression, 149–150, 156–160, 165
  freedom of press, 159–163
  imprimatur, 166–167
  Lessard framework, 162
  opinions, 168–169
  proportionality balancing, 151–156, 162
section 35 of *Constitution Act, 1982,* 203
  access to justice, 212–213
  Crown's fiduciary obligation to Indigenous peoples, 205–209, 212–213
  Daniels v Canada judgment, 205, 207
  duty to consult and accommodate, 208–210
  infringement of treaty rights, 206, 210–212
  Mikisew Cree decision, 205, 208, 211
  principle of reconciliation, 204
  recognition of positive duties, 206–208
section 91(24) of *Constitution Act, 1867,* 207
Silberman family
  Fanny, 25–26
  Jacob, 25–26, 34
  memory of an early injustice, 27
  reaching Canada, 26
  Rosalie, 26
  Toni, 26
Social Context Education Project, 369
Sound of Music, 24
speaking rationality to power (SRTP), 235–237, 254–256
  duty of fair representation, 253–254
  duty to exercise power for rational reasons, 254
  "even if," 244–247, 251
  Greenberg v Meffert, 241–243
  guarantee of equality, 251–255
  idea of legal equality, 255
  in private law, 241–243
  Roncarelli v Duplessis, 237–242, 248–251
  Smith & Rhuland Ltd v Nova Scotia, 240–241

"why" at common law, 243–247, 251
speaking truth to power (STTP), 236–237, 247, 252–253
Spencer, R v, 337
spending disparities, 191
Steel, Freda, 92, 94–96
Steele v Louisville and Nashville Railway, 253–255
student movement in Toronto, 29
substantive equality jurisprudence, 276–281
Supreme Court, 390
Supreme Court of Canada, 389, 391
Survival in Auschwitz, 384
Swan, Angela, 30
Symes decision, 90
systemic discrimination, 42, 44, 46–49, 193
Abella's influence on, 57–62
adverse effects of, 63–64, 68
Caring Society decisions, 65–70
CN decision, 59–60
description of, 58–59
determining, 63–65, 67
on First Nations children and families, 65–69
guidance to avoid approaching, 63–64
guiding principles for dealing, 65–69
misunderstandings about, 62–65
Moore v British Columbia (Education) decision, 57, 60–65, 69
prima facie discrimination test, 60–61
systemic remedies for, 67–68

technological changes, 321–322
technology jurisprudence, 317–318
Abella's technology judgments, 323–331
legal rules, 323–327
Progressive Era, 319–323
recognition of threats, 328–331
TELUS Communications Co., R v, 342–344
Tessling, R v, 341
"totality of circumstances" test, 338
traditional legal analysis, 390
Trial Lawyers Association of British Columbia v British Columbia (Attorney General), 213
Trudeau, Pierre, 37, 45
Tsartlip First Nation's (TFN) treaty rights, 210–211
"tsunami effect," 377
two-step *Charter* analysis, 13

Uber Technologies Inc v Heller, 218, 227–228, 329
UN Guiding Principles on Business and Human Rights (Guiding Principles), 272–276
United Brotherhood of Carpenters and Joiners of Americ, 80
United Nations Guiding Principles on Business and Human Rights, 359
United Nations Human Rights Committeee, 272

Vedanta Resources PLC v Lungowe, 266, 266*fn*28
Vedanta Resources v Lungowe, 273
Vu, R v, 337

Waddams, Stephen, 30
Wagne, Richard, 137
Ward v Quebec, 139, 148, 163–166
West, Robin, 120
Westen, Peter, 197
West Virginia v Environmental Protection Agency, 126, 126*fn*96
Whatcott decision, 165

White, Emily Kidd, 178
White, James Boyd, 105–106, 121
"Why" at common law, 243–247
Wildlife Act, 210
Wilson, Bertha, 109, 127
Wilson v Atomic Energy of Canada Ltd, 72, 218, 227
Wilton, Robert, 285
Without Precedent: The Supreme Life of Rosalie Abella, 88
women
  challenges for women jurists, 96
  point of view and participation in law, 89–94
  rights of, 4
  tangible and intangible challenges in legal profession, 89, 94–98
women judges, 92
worker vulnerability, 217–221, 225
  discrimination on vulnerable woman workers, 231
  income inequality and, 220
  power imbalance and, 218–220
  structural inequalities in employment relationships, 224
workplace equality jurisprudence, 220–221
  collective bargaining, 221–225
  conditions of freedom and dignity, 218–222, 225
  employment equality jurisprudence, 229–232
  employment law jurisprudence, 225–228
  freedom of association, 221–222, 224–225
  ILO's 1998 *Declaration of Fundamental Principles and Rights at Work*, 219
  labour law jurisprudence, 221–225
  section 2(d) *Charter* jurisprudence, 221, 224–225
World War II, 380, 389

Yahey v British Columbia, 211
Yale University, 381
Youth Criminal Justice Act, 4
Yukon Francophone School Board case of 2015, 93

zero-sum game, 199–200